SOLO AND DUET

including

The Honeysuckle and the Bee

and

Water-Music

by

Sir John Squire

THE REPRINT SOCIETY
LONDON

PUBLISHED BY THE REPRINT SOCIETY LTD. 1943
BY ARRANGEMENT WITH WILLIAM HEINEMANN LTD.

PRINTED IN GREAT BRITAIN AT THE WINDMILL PRESS
KINGSWOOD, SURREY

The Honeysuckle and the Bee

To
ALICE WARRENDER
This prelude to a more chronological
set of recollections

CONTENTS

FIRST DAY

"Well, why don't you?" said she.

I had just remarked that the way I should really like to take a holiday would be by going through the South and West of England on a horse. I had, I said, when young, done a very great deal of walking in those parts. I had regularly walked home from Cambridge to Devonshire, and, later on, I had done several long walks with nothing in my pocket except what I picked up by cutting people's grass or holding horses' heads. Then, after the war, for year after year, I had escaped the urban pressure in a car and investigated inns and churches and just rung up anybody I knew within driving distance for a bed for one night. But cars, I said, go too fast, and have to be driven, and tempt one to go too far. And, on foot, I said, one sometimes gets impatient with dull country, and annoyed because one cannot see over the hedges. "A horse," I said, "would be the ideal thing; a horse at a walking pace with just an occasional trot."

"Well, why don't you?" said she.

"All sorts of reasons," I replied. "For one thing I don't suppose that nowadays you could get a horse put up in this country. When I was young every country pub had 'Good Accommodation for Man and Beast' written up on it. The sign might well still stand as half the motorists are beasts, but they don't expect horses now and they'd be staggered if one presented them with one. The modern innkeeper probably doesn't even know what horses eat."

"Nonsense," said she, "they'd probably be able to give your horse a shake-down somewhere and you could always get provender from a neighbouring farmer."

"Perhaps you're right," said I, "but the drawback is that I haven't got a horse."

"Can't you buy one?" she exclaimed impatiently.

"That's precisely what I can't do," I said, "because I can't afford it."

"Then," she rejoined with the logic of her sex, "why don't you take a holiday on foot, write a book about it, and buy a

I

horse with the proceeds?"

"And then," I continued, "take a holiday on the horse, write a book about it and buy a Rolls-Royce with the proceeds. And then take a holiday in the Rolls, write a book and buy a steam-yacht (which I've always wanted) with the proceeds and then . . ."

I was interrupted.

"Don't dodge," said she. "It would do you all the good in the world to go off on foot again. As a matter of fact, I don't believe you could."

That is the way one is made to do things. "Can't I?" thought I. But what I said was: "I daresay a little solitude would do me good, and I shall start off on Monday." That is precisely what I did.

But first I had to decide where to go. And then I thought: "Why not walk home to Devon as you used to do?" And then, my mind wavering over that varied country, which seemed in youth so illimitable, thinking of Dartmoor, Exmoor, the Tavy valley, Bideford Bridge, the grey moorland churches, the rich fabrics of Ottery and Cullompton, I thought suddenly of my old school, Blundells, within four miles of that last. It would be empty and I would go there for an hour or two, wander about, and recover the past.

It was three years since I had felt that nostalgia and made that resolution: and then I did not keep it. The feeling came to me in a strange place and an indirect way.

Far from the stage, at the back of the circle, I stared across the vast arena of Drury Lane at the shifting scenes of Mr. Coward's *Cavalcade,* taking an infantile pleasure in the skilful reproduction of a railway station in a fog, the departure of a steamer, and other spectacles which one can see any day without paying even entertainment tax. The connecting thread of story may have been a "bald and unconvincing narrative," but nothing ever stayed long enough to become tedious, and it was exciting never to know what was coming next—a storm, an earthquake, a fire, Queen Victoria reviewing the troops, General Booth addressing his followers in the Albert Hall, W. G. Grace, huge and bearded with a shrivelled red-and-yellow M.C.C. cap, marching to the wicket at Lord's, or a vast assembly of Liberals singing that ineffable "Land Song." There wasn't room for these: there was so much else. But one was swept through a pageant of the last thirty-two years.

And one made, like everybody else, all the appropriate comments. Included amongst these was: "How clever of this very clever young man to recover the atmosphere of the South African War which ended when he was in the cradle; fancy his knowing all about 'Dolly Gray' and the C.I.V.s and the legend of the old Queen whose presence covered the Empire like a canopy!" And then—for I was fifteen when it started and eighteen when it ended—I remembered the South African War myself, recovering things in my mind which I had no idea were there. And one thing that came back was a tune not found amongst those resurrected by Mr. Coward.

It was 1902, all those years ago, and in the summer term; the war dwindling to an end, in spite of all the efforts of that surprising guerillist De Wet, and peace in sight. Peace was more than in sight for me; it was present: I was swathed and bathed in it, as I have never been since I emerged into a struggling world. I was in the upper sixth—peaceful even there, as I had just become what was then a rare bird, namely a History Specialist, had bid a lifelong farewell to Trigonometry, Conics, Dynamics, Statics, Hydrostatics and the whole of that mathematical harem with which I can hardly now believe I was ever involved, and was allowed to sit by myself at the back of the Classical Sixth Form Room, nobody even guessing that propped up against my pile of works by Dicey, Bryce, Bagehot, Seeley, Cunningham and the like, all full of quotations from Aristotle and wool-prices under Edward III, were rather lighter compositions by Haggard or Merriman. I had, as I shared a study with the Head of the House, more fags than anyone was officially allowed or I knew what to do with. I was privileged to avoid cricket—which I enjoyed, though bad at it, but enjoyed exercising a privilege more. Plenty of friends, an easy-going temperament, not a worry in the world. Cambridge and more *dolce far niente* ahead, then perhaps the Indian Civil Service—which to school-boys of that time did not mean service, danger, heat, tiffin, polo, or anything in the world but that pension of £1,000 a year on early retirement, which all our elders dinned into our ears as a sublime inducement. Had I gone I should be taking it now, minus a ten-per-cent cut; and a lot it would be worth . . . !

Yes, it was a lovely summer afternoon; a sky of unbroken purity, a light wavering breeze, and a row of great trees flinging patches of blue shadow on the long quiet red sandstone wall of School and School House, and the square tower, with its flag, its clock, and its empty niche for the founder's statue, which his shade has been expecting for over three hundred years. There was nobody about: they were all playing games in the field beyond the buildings, and not even the click of ball on bat could be heard. Hours before or hours afterwards, the drive and the road behind would have been full of hurrying boys carrying books or implements of play. Now there was no one.

A fag had brought me a rug; another a deck-chair, should I prefer the seated posture; one or other of them had also brought my book. There I lay in flannels and a red, black and white blazer, propped on my right elbow, the daisied, tree-shadowed lawn all round. What the book was I do not remember. It was not that summer but the next—my last—that I went through the six green volumes of the old Aldine Spenser in such beautiful weather and places that I can never think of Una or Britomart without also thinking of a field of golden charlock, mounting larks, and a deserted canal covered with lilies.

"A gentil knighte was pricking o're a plaine——"

I seldom open Spenser now; but if I do, that scene comes back. A field at the end of a grass-grown, blind-alley lane; a gate on the right; a push at the gate; and then subsidence into that mustard-yellow field, and the company of Spenser's crooning stanzas, heroes, villains, injured ladies and beasts, even the most boring of the stories lovely because of the music, and no thought taken of the allegories about Queen Elizabeth, Lord

Essex and so on which I have heard about since.

It wasn't Spenser that sunny afternoon. It may have been *Erewhon,* of which there was an early (perhaps a first) edition in the school library; it may have been *Moby Dick, Typee* or *Omoo,* which were all also there. Whatever it was I laid it down, whilst the small gusts of June breeze brought the melting strains of the town brass-band to my ear:

> "You are my honey, honeysuckle,
> I am the bee——"

The words meant nothing; but at that distance there was a bee-like murmur about the tune, and a plangency—an augury of life which one had not yet encountered, and a summary (though one did not know it and felt it but vaguely) of all the regret of later years for early years, in a fifth and a third. Then, the tune carried me into some vague infinite; but now it carries me back to scenes then concrete and commonplace, but now irrecoverable and poignant. . . .

As I walked out of London, knapsack on back, and the temperature over eighty degrees, I recovered something of my youth. I had last walked up Putney Hill in 1907. It was just before lunch-time; a toothbrush was my only luggage; I left London with one and threepence in my pocket; I ate bread and oranges; I mistook the way from Guildford in the dark and went to Alton by way of Godalming, instead of over the Hog's Back; and I then went to Salisbury through Romsey instead of through Stockbridge. It made the journey not much less than a hundred miles, and I was in Salisbury twenty-eight hours after I started, having snatched half-hours of sleep under gorse-bushes and in woods. But as for Putney, going up that hill, and having passed the very unimposing portals of "The Pines," I was thinking of Algernon Charles Swinburne.

It was a legend amongst my generation that Theodore Watts-Dunton kept him strictly under control (having rescued him from the brandy-bottle) but allowed him to take a morning walk to an inn on Putney Common where the landlord had

A*

strict injunctions to allow him one bottle of beer and no more. Contemporaries of mine at Cambridge had timorously ventured into the inn and observed the poet, whom no one dared, and no decent person wished, to accost, and returned to the university to report that the legend was true. As I went up the hill my brain was singing with:

"When the hounds of spring are on winter's traces"

and

"With lisp of leaves and ripple of rain,"

and I was wondering whether I should have the hardihood to go into the "Green Man" and peer sideways at the little old man who in his flamboyant youth had written those lines. It wasn't necessary. For in the middle of Putney Hill I met him, coming back from his modest morning potation.

He was almost a dwarf, almost a gnome, very short, with a huge bald forehead, a shapeless black hat perched thereon, a smooth face, an attenuated grey-red beard, long neck, champagne-bottle shoulders and tiny feet, and an old rusty overcoat. Just as I approached him he stopped to give pennies and a pat on the back to two little urchins who were playing with a hoop. This was the roaring Republican who had made England shiver with his denunciations of throne, hearth and altar. I had an impulse to stop and speak, and then a better impulse not to stop and speak; after I had passed the benevolent little thing I couldn't help turning round. He was still there, still talking to the children. He was probably late for lunch, in which event I feel sure that Watts-Dunton sternly reproved him.

Yes, but that was nearly thirty years ago. George Meredith also was alive then, and him also I had seen, sitting on Edward Clodd's balcony at Aldeburgh, a rug over his knees and a pile of yellow French novels on the table at his side. There hadn't been a war then. It was only two terms since I had first met Rupert Brooke, "young Apollo golden-haired" in a Cambridge street—he was a freshman and his serenity and beauty made,

even at the first casual encounter, such an impression on me as
I never received from any other man. King Edward was on
the throne, Campbell-Bannerman was Prime Minister, Asquith
was a coming man, we had a Two-Power Standard on the seas,
and, for me, I was taking a brief and inexpensive holiday from
a Plymouth daily paper, now extinct, which was staffed by
very good fellows who were supposed, in some mysterious
way, to be training me for a writing career. Long, long ago.
But Putney has not changed, and as I passed "The Pines"
everything came back and I half expected to see Swinburne
rambling down the hill again. But, stop: weren't there horse-
buses then, and wasn't there a white one that went to Putney,
now gathered to its fathers with the "Monster," the "Angel,"
and all the rest of them? I suppose so; but they seemed so
ordinary then that one didn't notice them.

So, remembering rather regretfully that I had not accepted
an invitation to "The Pines" from Watts-Dunton in 1913, I
got to the Heath and turned right along what, in that earlier
year, had been a pleasant quiet road, shaded by birch and ash,
with glimpses of ponds through the trees, and an occasional
dray, carriage or trap driving along it, but is now the Portsmouth Road, with its swarming Kingston By-Pass, no place at
all for a foot-passenger. Being of an equable temper, I did not
fret because of the stream of eager drivers rushing towards me,
or the perpetual hooting behind me of people exasperated at
the continued existence of mere legs and feet: I merely thought:
"I shall get out of this soon; anyhow, one doesn't get covered
with dust as one used." So on I trudged; my forehead was
streaming with sweat but I was glad that I was disappearing
for a time, that neither letters nor telephone messages would
reach me, that I could start when I liked and stop when I
liked, that time, rain and shine meant nothing to me, that I
could converse or be silent with whomsoever I met, and that
no one could interfere, or would even know, whether I slept
under a hedge or (again, freely, under a real or a false name—
which last I didn't!) in a hotel. I had recovered, thought I,
my youth.

But not altogether, thought I, a little later. After I had

passed Coombe and the Equitation School which heralds the Kingston By-Pass, I saw a policeman, and the sight reminded me of the difficulties of recovering the past completely. A series of pictures passed through my mind evoked by memories drawn from walks a generation ago.

For instance: When I was at Cambridge I made a habit of walking home to Devonshire, usually through Oxford, where I picked up Francis Burrows, of Lincoln, who had been at school with me—the Oxford term ending a little later than ours. The beginning of the journey was always the same—Madingley Hill, with about the only view of Cambridge which shows town and towers in the Oxford manner, St. Neot's with its bridge, Bedford with its countless swarms of boys and girls bicycling home from school to the colonels' wives who bore them, Wolverton, Stony Stratford, Newport Pagnell, Buckingham and Bicester. It was a pleasant route, though unexciting. One passed over a bridge, which went over a railway bridge, which went over a canal; one passed, also, a signpost pointing to Olney, whose spire could be seen in the distance, but I never followed the road to it. Except for the few small towns little can have changed since Cowper (who, even in his age, had to lament some change) wrote:

> The poplars are felled, farewell to the shade,
> And the whispering sound of the cool colonnade.

There was no traffic, the country was undulating and modestly wooded, and passers-by were few. Here and there one would encounter an old pedlar squatting under the hedge rearranging the cheap jewellery and reels of cotton, ribbons and scissors which the innocent cottagers' wives of that day welcomed as Zulus welcome glass beads. Here and there one might stop for a pipe and a talk with a vagrant, usually a moustached veteran of the South African and Frontier Wars, confessedly restless. And, in the heat of the day, there was always an inn at a road's angle, elm-shaded and with wooden benches in front, where a waggoner's horses slumbrously drooped their heads while their driver quenched his thirst.

George Morland would not have been uncomfortable there and then. He certainly would not like it now on any road approaching the "Major" category—cars, motor-bicycles, motor-vans, advertisements and above all a law, which Morland would never have understood, enjoining men to take their beer at certain hours of the day and not at certain others. Bread and cheese and beer at five past two is no longer in the country obtainable or legal; and we have to console ourselves by reflecting that at least we do not have dictators who take away our liberties.

I have not travelled that road for thirty years; I will not say that I never shall again, for I am not one of those who take a pleasure in losing as many things as they possibly can. I may even find again the beechwood into which I escaped from the sultriness of a summer afternoon, and where I took out a pencil and a little black notebook, which I still have, and began a verse, expecting, in the warm hush, the presence of Pan, fauns and nymphs, and finding only silence, smooth trunks, great curlings of leaves and shadows dappling the undergrowth, which was quite good enough. Once again I may see a distant train leaving astern a level row of white puffs, seemingly motionless behind a thin row of tall poplars. And once again I may find a pair of old stone gates and wonder what lies behind the curving avenue. Whether I do or not, at least the road, in the end, bends into Oxford, and, ultimately to the Oxford of the colleges.

There did I always stay for a night, playing billiards, which to the Oxford undergraduates of that day was (I believe) in taverns a prohibited game. At Cambridge the game was played everywhere. Saloons were numerous, and one could openly enter for a trophy called the University Cue in order to be beaten by a little Chinaman. And from Oxford, term after term, we sallied forth, resolved always to take a new route to the west, as far as we were able.

Once we started rather late, intending to walk all night and find, in the morning, not bed and breakfast, but breakfast and bed. We climbed out of the town, remembering what snatches of Matthew Arnold we could, and it was midnight and moonlight before we reached Faringdon, now adorned by one of the newest and one of the tallest of Folly Towers, Lord Berners'.

Our clothing—tweed coats and grey flannel trousers—was much what might be expected of walking youths to-day: the *laudator temporis acti* was quite wrong who, the other day, grumbled in the Press that thirty years ago undergraduates all wore smart lounge suits like the gentlemen they then were but, alas, no longer are. But we had on our heads soft felt slouch hats of a somewhat Colonial type; and that was a day when nobody wore soft hats, and to go out without a hat at all was to invite jeers and following from infants everywhere and lumps of coal from the miners of Radstock. These hats were suspicious in themselves; so was walking at night; so was walking in step. We had passed most of the way up the dark street, not a dog barking, not an owl hooting, no other sound expected, and the last bedroom light just being extinguished in the "Star Inn," when suddenly a shadow loomed out of a doorway and a bull's-eye lantern was flashed in our eyes. "Where are you off to?" asked a deep and surly voice. "Swindon," we replied. "You come along o' me," said the policeman, "you're deserters."

Had we not been so astonished at first and then amused, we might have reflected, made a bolt for it, and had some fun in the dark woods with the county constabulary, which an innocent person, in such circumstances, is perfectly entitled to do. But unreadiness, and perhaps a latent (however deeply latent) sense of law and order, and perhaps curiosity as to what would happen, made us accompany the constable like lambs. He took us into a room, catechized us at length, and ultimately let us go on, very charily. We arrived at Swindon footsore, cold and stiff at six and did manage to get beds in a wretched little lodging-house. We were asked if we minded lodgers having just got out of them. We were too tired to mind anything—even the discovery, half a minute later, that our predecessors between the sheets must have been firemen or greasers who slept in their clothes.

That was one experience with the police which, pausing for a rest on the Portsmouth road, I thought would probably not be repeated. I remembered another. In the year 1907 I walked from Devonshire to London in ragged clothes and with a horrible beard—breaking the journey for a night or two at Balliol where I temporally lapsed into such civilization as the place has to offer. I started with about eighteenpence, occasionally slept in woods, haystacks (it is unpleasant to have a rat biting one's nose when one is asleep) and casual wards, and now and then replenishing my purse with sixpences earned by holding horses' heads or cutting people's grass. One night, about the time of the closing of inns, after a whole day of rain had rained itself out, I crawled into a hamlet somewhere west of Frome. I saw a lighted doorway, obviously that of a public-house, with a bareheaded man standing at the top of the steps against the light and a group of persons below saying good night to each other and to him: "Goo'night, Bill," "Goo'night, Ern," and all the traditional, ritual, rigmarole. "A bed at last," thought I, and modestly approached. For I had over two shillings.

"Can you give me a bed for the night?"

"No; full up."

"I don't care what it is, as long as it some sort of shake-down?"

"Full up; better try the next place."

"But anything will do. I've got money, look! Even a lie down in a barn or shed."

At this point I observed that the departing drinkers, mostly hobbledehoys of twenty in the so-called "jolly" stage, were clustering all round me and nudging me; and then, before I could say more, either by way of menace or appeal *ad misericordiam,* a policeman, greeted on all hands with: " 'Ere, look at 'im, Sam," barged through the muster and towered over me, asking what this was. All were silent; *"Conticuere omnes,"* as Virgil remarks at the beginning of the second book of his *Æneid*—which, for some reason, at school, I was made to learn before the fourth and sixth books, never coming to the first book at all until, in later life, I thought I might as well learn a little Latin. "I was asking the landlord for a bed for the night," I explained. The policeman, a big hog-faced man, shot his face forward at mine, and glared in a manner meant to be terrifying to me and comic to his friends. "We've seen your sort here before," he said; and looked around to the rustics for applause, and got it in a sort of blend of cheer and hoot. "But," I protested, remembering some sort of second-hand, word-of-mouth information, "there is a law that every landlord is bound to give anybody who comes some sort of bed, and food too, if he can pay for it." "'Ark at 'im," observed the august embodiment of the law; and, in the wan lamplight in the middle of that world of dark dampness, the flushed faces of his comrades assumed an uglier look while, with a suspicion of bared teeth, they let forth gusts of wolfish laughter. The policeman, born leader of men, now assumed the air of a dictator implacably condemning a helpless suppliant.

"You better move on," he said. "You ain't goin' to sleep nowhere in this parish. They'll look after the likes o' you along the road."

I prepared, though soaked and fatigued, to plod again my far from homeward way. Just as, with difficulty, I had elbowed my way out of the little crowd, the constable's coarse voice was again uplifted behind me. "Boys," he shouted, "wot price that for a German spy!" This, as the Americans were later to put it, was "a new one on me," but even with Thermopylæ in mind, I could think of no practical way out except trudging on, pretending to take no notice. Trudge on I did. They followed me some distance along the muddy road, hooting and cat-calling; I went on, not turning my head, and the clamour gradually died away as they faded off to their homes and warmth. A mile or so out, the sky having cleared of clouds and an arch of cold stars come out, I rested under a hedge, a dripping elm above me, lit a pipe and endeavoured to become indignant. I failed. Nothing with the element of the comic in it could ever make me indignant, nor anything in life, I think, except cold-blooded cruelty to the helpless. Also I remembered some other policemen I had met that selfsame day. One, in the morning, a large kind man, who had looked compassionately at my ragged waterproof, passed the time of day and asked me what I was. I pitched, in the usual way, the usual yarn about being a "clurk" pronounced to rhyme with the work of which I was in search, and I had had to take his offered sixpence, because it would have been beastly (and discouraging to him) to admit that I was a hoax. And then, somewhere on the Taunton–Langport road, just about noon, I had been trudging along in such rain as I had never encountered before. Pillars and flung splashes of it came down; my hat dripped, my hair was soaked, my eye-brows poured water on to my spectacles, rain ran in runnels down my neck, front and back, my chest was wet, my mackintosh was heavy with flood, my boots were full of water, and the road at which I patiently stared was a muddy lake with clayey islands in it. I splashed along, empty of all thought, when suddenly I heard trotting behind me and a trap suddenly stopped at my side. Two men in shiny waterproofs were in it, and the driver offered me a lift which I jumped at. They then resumed their conversation as though I (very down at heels, be it remembered) did not exist, and very peculiar and touching it was. For they were plain-clothes men in pursuit of an absconding thief and they did not want to catch him, because they knew him and were sorry for him.

He had been embezzling his employer's money, and had just disappeared with a last lump of it. He was, I learnt by overhearing from the back, a decent quiet citizen, and his temptation had been great, as he had an extravagant wife about whom the policemen used blunt words. Their instructions were to "comb" all the inns of the district, as it was believed that the fugitive would wish to drown his sorrows in drink. Their technique was simple and effective. They rolled up to the front door of an inn with a great clatter and loud talk and took so long descending and entering that there was plenty of time for their quarry to get out of the back door. Somebody would arrest him sometime, but they didn't want it to be themselves; they had played snooker with the poor fellow. Ultimately we stopped at a rather imposing tavern. The two men got down, so did I, and I was just going to leave them with humble and hearty thanks, when the senior one, remarking that I was wet and probably hungry and could do with a bit of lunch, suggested that I should hold their horse's head while they were eating and then go in and have whatever I liked, which would be charged to them. Pelting as it was, and whetted though my appetite was by a rumour of roast beef, I declined the hospitality as I knew I was a fraud, held the horse's head for half an hour in the rain and felt myself entitled to the sixpence (which got me bread and cheese) which they ultimately gave me. . . .

And—for it took much less time to remember (although I was frequently distracted by the pace of the cars or the oddity of their occupants) than it does now to write—as I lit a second cigarette before resuming my pack and my journey I thought of one more encounter with the Force which was likelier to happen to a young man than to a sedate citizen of my present age.

In the Summer Term of 1905 a man I knew in Sidney Sussex became (*a*) enamoured of a young woman; (*b*) determined to see as much of her as possible; and (*c*) bitten by the theatre. He therefore conceived the notion of forming a theatrical company which should tour East Anglia during the Long Vacation, the high motive being provided by his determination to give all his profits to the East Anglian hospitals. The girl, who later became his wife, arranged to come under the protection of an aunt; a number of undergraduates produced a sufficiency of sisters and friends, a professional leading lady was brought along by a Clare man who could talk about a lot of actors and actresses by their Christian names, halls were booked in three shires, and a week after term ended we assembled at Bury St. Edmunds for rehearsals.

The excursion lasted several weeks. The plays we did were chosen because they were out of copyright. *East Lynne* was discussed, and, much to my regret, turned down; but we had *The School for Scandal,* a comedy of the eighteenth century by Planché, full of marquises and minuets, called *The Follies of a Night,* Taylor's *Still Waters Run Deep,* and for pastoral purposes (for we knew several archdeacons with nice gardens) a work in very dull blank verse called *King Réné's Daughter.* Little of these last three can I now recall. In *Still Waters* the villainous captain who tried to make the tempted wife elope with him lured her with the prospects of "the orange groves of Seville"; and the lady, when saved, said to her strong, stern husband: "Tell me of my faults, John, and I will try to correct them." In *King Réné's Daughter* I was allotted the part of a venerable Arab physician named Ibn Yahya, who droned interminable sage speeches through a long white beard in front of the archidiaconal rhododendrons and laurels, while rows of garden-party ladies sat on chairs and waited patiently for their tea. We made no profits for the hospitals. Here and there, as at Felixstowe, where there must have been a shortage of pierrots that year, we played to packed, and easily pleased audiences, but in some of the town halls of the Suffolk backwoods we used anxiously to peep through the curtains in the hope that enough people would arrive to pay for the rent of the hall; while once, at Bury I think, we acted in a vast old semi-derelict theatre to a few dimly descried and scattered pilgrims who might have been left over, with the decorations and the cobwebs, from the last visit of Mr. and Mrs. Vincent Crummles. We learned what it was to stand about on junction platforms on Sunday, and also what theatrical lodgings were like. These last had to be booked in advance, and our advance agent used to go ahead of us to make these and other arrangements and get bills out, usually rejoining us at night. His name I need not mention here: he is now an imposing country clergyman; and he had concocted for himself the remarkable alias of Eli Maggott, which appeared on the programmes, and must have astonished the landladies when he left his cards on them.

There came a day when he thought he would like a rest, and I was asked to deputize for him; I was to go to Felixstowe, do our business and then return to, I think, Mildenhall. When I had finished at Felixstowe I thought to myself that I would like a walk, so I decided to walk through the night and get to Mildenhall at least for lunch next day. I was not ideally equipped for all weathers; I had no hat, no kind of overcoat or mackintosh, and instead of the customary stout brogues, my feet were adorned by a pair of dancing pumps of the old bow-ribboned type. However, it didn't look like rain, and, after some beer and sandwiches off I started.

About twelve midnight, the sky being dark, a cool breeze blowing, and the streets deserted, I reached without adventure the middle of Ipswich when, under a street lamp, I was brought to a stop by a policeman.

"Where are you going?"

"Mildenhall."

"What are you going to do there?"

"I'm in a theatrical company which is acting there, and I'm walking all night."

"You have no visible means of support."

My pocket was full of silver. I pulled out a handful of it and showed it to him. "I'm afraid you're wrong there," I said politely. He was a resourceful man, and I admit that his next remark aroused my admiration.

"Where did you get that money from?" he asked, in a suspicious growl. My explanation that it was my own appeared to satisfy him; he let me go and I marched on and out of the town.

I had walked, I suppose, for half an hour and was on a dusty road between hedges, thinking about anything in the world except policemen, when I heard a bicycle bell behind me. I turned round and before I knew where I was I was lit by three lamps on three bicycles besides which three police-men were standing, one of them being my original interro-gator. It was evident that he had shrunk from tackling so dangerous a customer as myself alone, and gone back to the station with his alarming report to secure reinforcements. "You'd better come back with us," said the senior member, a man with a heavy Kitchener moustache. I expostulated, protested, spoke of charges and legal rights, all to no avail; my depression became worse when I was made to mount the step of one of the bicycles and take hold of a policeman's shoulder, for the sharp step almost cut my foot in half through my thin sole and it was with great difficulty that I kept myself from groaning. However, we got to the station and went into the comparative glare of the office. Nobody of importance seemed to be in charge. My name and alleged occupation and habitat (there were sneering smiles and references to "a pretty sort of stoodent" when I mentioned my college) were taken down; and I was then informed that I should be looked after in the morning. An officer took a key and walked down a little passage to open a cell, while another pointed at a pile of mattresses standing endways up against a wall and told me one of them was mine. I stood and stared in my inexperience, when he exclaimed: "Well, do you think I'm going to carry it in for you?" I took the hint, shouldered the heavy thing, carried it to the cell, laid it on the bed, and was then locked in. "Oh well," I thought, as I curled myself up on it, "it's quite warm and this is as amusing a way of spending a night as any, but I must say I'm glad I'm not a poor homeless man whom nobody knows." I had shut my eyes and had almost forgotten where I was when I heard a loud and continuous crackling in the straw of the mattress underneath me. I sat up sharply. "Mice?" I wondered, and then the revolting truth dawned on me. I had never seen or heard bed-bugs before; but these could be nothing else and there must be scores of them. Feeling slightly sick I got up, beat on the door and called out. Probably they were used to such noises there; at all events nobody took the slightest notice; and there was only one thing for it—I must stand in the corner until morning brought release.

I did; I daresay for five hours; until a turnkey came (the huge insects were by then visible on the floor) and led me along to the little office where a benevolent-looking chieftain was now sitting with a large book open in front of him. It did not take long to convince this sensible being that a mistake had been made. He became almost effusively kind and ordered me a mug of hot cocoa and some slabs of bread and butter which I consumed in his presence. I shook hands, went out, and sat by the parapet of a bridge glad of the fresh air.

When I got to Mildenhall, by train, most of my friends merely guffawed; the single serious one, a person very strong on the liberties of the subject and the insolences of "a little brief authority," was passionately keen that I should kick up the devil of a row about wrongful arrest, sue for damages, and have the Ipswich Police Force turned upside down. I simply couldn't, partly because I was too indolent, partly because I loathed rows, and partly because I was afraid I might get that jackass of a constable the sack.

"I don't believe I shall walk a whole night on this trip," I meditated on the Portsmouth road, "and I don't believe they'd arrest me if I did, and I am sure I could not persuade anybody I was an out-of-work clerk who wanted sixpence for grass-cutting. Here am I, comfortably clad, with a knapsack on my back, and enough money to get me to Devonshire. Even granted that I could still bleat my woes in a Cockney accent without giving myself away by either self-consciousness or grins, how could I, without going into an impossible conceal-ment, grow a shaggy beard? Where should I acquire the right kind of clothes? Could I now, with the price of a bed on me, sleep in a damp wood with pheasants flopping about? And what on earth should I do with my pack and my money, how should I explain my sound garments, all with my name on them, if I really did try to see again the inside of a Casual Ward?" I realized now that I had been silly when I had airily toyed with the idea of sampling a few modern Casual Wards with a view to comparing them with those of a generation ago; I hadn't at all foreseen all the arrangements that would have to be made, nor why I should even have to get two new pairs of spectacles, for they certainly wouldn't swallow my yarn at a "Spike" if I turned up in tortoiseshell rims, let alone the obvious golfing shoes. "Another time, perhaps," I sighed, wondering whether the bread was still so hard at that place in Wiltshire, or the porridge so thin in the Ward at Isleworth.

Isleworth Workhouse. I haven't seen it since I slept there; I didn't even remember to ask if I might revisit it, as it were semi-officially, when I was a Parliamentary candidate for the neighbouring constituency of Brentford and Chiswick. Was there still, I wondered, a forlorn hedge leading to it in which the more experienced vagrants hid their pennies before going in for the night? Did an official still stand over one in one's bath with a fearsome brush, like a witch's broom, in case one needed a little extra scrubbing? Were the wire mattresses still so near the skin, and still framed on such stout lines that they left red diamond patterns on one's flesh?

All these thoughts and many others passed through my mind as, walking mechanically, feeling singularly free, and not taking too much notice of surroundings with which I was very familiar, I passed through Cobham, up the hill under the iron bridge, and then past the woods and along that undulating piece of pretty common which skirts the Horticultural Gardens at Wisley. It was late afternoon, the sun very hot, there was not much traffic, and I thought I would sit down again. I went a few yards in, took off my pack, and sat down under a bush. I had barely lit a cigarette when I noticed in front of me a man who obviously knew a great deal more about Casual Wards than I did. He was holding an unlit stump of a cigarette, and asked me in a gentle voice for a match. I asked him to join me in a cigarette; he took one, sat down beside me, and looked ruminatively towards the horizon. As he sat down I noticed that his big toes were out of his boots and both were encrusted with blood.

His face startled me with a resemblance. It was weak and delicate, but the straight, sensitive features, the nose thin and just faintly tilted, the soft, pointed, prematurely-white beard, and blue eyes, might all have been those of George Meredith— and, oddly, he was also a Welshman. He looked ill, and he was in thin rags, but he was obviously eager to talk, and it was pathetic to notice his rapid changes from enthusiasm to the hopelessness of a man who calmly contemplates opening an arterial vein.

With the fluency of his race he soon gave me all the personal particulars about himself, showing his army papers. He was a native of Cardiff, forty, unmarried, a mason by trade and had had no work since the Welsh depression set in. He was now, as is the wont of these lost wanderers, on the way to some quite unlikely and unpromising place (he had probably heard of it from some other tramp), as it might be Lincoln or Grimsby. He had no hope really; and when, in his soft tenor voice with its Welsh accent, he spoke of suicide it was rather in meditation than in menace. He made no attempt to beg, or to move my compassion by whining; he just soliloquized on, occasionally turning his wistful eyes to me as I prompted him with questions.

He came to a pause and then, as though he were speaking of some place which he had known long ago, he asked me directly: "Do you know Cardiff?"

I said I had been there.

"Do you know Cathays Park?" he went on.

I said I did.

"Aren't those buildings grand?" he exclaimed.

I did my best to do justice to those imposing classic piles which house the National Library, the County Council and various other institutions, certainly the most ambitious piece of modern planning in this country, and, as I disclosed an acquaintance both with the buildings and with the names of their architects, colour came into his cheeks and his eyes flashed. "I am," he said, in one of the most surprising sentences I have ever heard on human lips, "a citizen of no mean City." His toes were out of his boots, and they were bleeding on the highway.

Then, somehow, his whole æsthetic soul poured out. He had only had the most elementary education. But when he was young he had been working on a chapel, and a dissenting minister had fallen into conversation with him about building and had lent him a book. He had forgotten the name of it (I suspected Ruskin), but one loan had led to others. He talked of Shakespeare and of the eminent (he had never seen any of them but seemed almost to persuade himself that he had) who had acted in the plays; he repeated scraps of Keats which he said he had found quoted in old newspapers; he went into something like a paroxysm over Shelley's *Skylark* which I think was the only work of Shelley's which he had encountered; and then he surprised me once more, all innocent that anybody thought of these authors as being on rather different planes, by remarking, in awe-struck tones, on the greatness of Marie Corelli.

I am glad I had self-possession enough to prevent surprise

from appearing in my face or qualification in my voice. I could see, as he developed his theme, what it was that had appealed to him in the works of the female Swan of Avon; she had, like all best-sellers of her kind, so great a belief in the nonsense that she wrote, that it was burningly vivid to those who were able to accept it. Wit my Welshman had none, nor scholarship, nor sense of likelihood, but he was emotional and imaginative and would take colour and passion where he found them; and I was glad indeed, when I had racked my brains for reminiscences of *The Sorrows of Satan,* to find that I could share with him the not quite Miltonic splendours which he innocently supposed that the mysterious and fortunate few, who had the key to the world's libraries, ranked with *Hamlet* and *The Midsummer Night's Dream.* Any knowledge wider than his own I hope I concealed; and he was egoistic enough, certainly unfortunate enough, not to show the slightest curiosity as to my occupation or the source of the acquaintance, which I shared with him, with the mighty creations of Keats and Miss Corelli.

The conversation began to run dry, he to repeat himself, and the sun to sink towards the westward hill; I rose to part, and so did he. He took what I was able to give him with a womanly smile, shook hands and went slowly, his head bowed, towards London, much too much of a gentleman to be effusive in his thanks, and much too reflective to suppose that a day or two's food and shelter would solve his problem. As I mounted the rise and went down that pretty drop to the pine-fringed lake (so like pictures of British Columbia) in front of the "Hut Hotel" at Wisley (where they used to have a collection of albino birds, from swallow to snipe, in the bar but have now removed them for smart tea-room furniture) I was wondering what accident or design could ever set straight such a wasted life as his.

I could not see him, in whatever industrial recovery, fitting in (had he ever really fitted?) with the modern machine; he would have dreamed on a scaffolding, dropped his trowel through the air, been sacked by the foreman for mooning, done his work badly or not at all because his heart and mind were in Paradise, Utopia, Elsinore, Auburn, Betelgeuse and all the other far kingdoms of dream whose names he did not know but whose qualities were of the substance of his daily life. Vision had probably been his only vice; but it was not possible to think of him working as one of a gang or even doing a solitary job competently. I could just imagine him in the affectionate and humorous care of a mediæval monastery which was able to view indulgently the ineffective efforts of lay-brother Llewellyn in the garden, and willing occasionally to delight his innocent childish eye with bright pictures in an illuminated manuscript.

For there is a variety of types on the road. To the ordinary citizens there are just tramps and "a strange man at the door, mum," but those silent figures who, in ones or twos, at intervals pass along the great main roads are of all kinds as well as of all ages. Some are fresh from employment and will soon get employment; sturdy sailors, for instance, walking because they have no fares—I remember one such who, when helped, said he would like my address (I did not give it) so that later he could send me something "as it might be a parrot." There are the semi-criminals who scowl and mutter; there are the young men genuinely in search of work; there are those who (like many modern parlourmaids) prefer temporary work, with intervals of ease and plenty of change; and there are various kinds of "unemployable."

Some are like my friend who looked like George Meredith; not made to cope with modern regulated life. But there are many, and no reform and no charity is going to change them, who simply don't like it, who prefer a gipsyish existence and are strong and cunning enough to lead it.

> We be soldiers three
> Lately come from the Low Countrie
> With never a penny of mony. . . .

That old song comes from King James's time, and there are plenty of them on the roads still, some with pensions, who contrive to exist without too much hardship, with the help of sturdy begging, rabbit-snaring, pheasant-knocking, vegetable stealing and the workhouses, leading the life of perpetual motion without which they would pine. They know, by virtue of the secret signs they chalk on gate and fence, where they can at least get a kettle of hot water to make their tea, a gift which is seldom unaccompanied by food or money. One such, long ago, kept me entertained half a night, and I wish I could remember all he told me, but I was sleepy and warm.

I was walking late one moonlight night and had gone some miles past Totnes, when I went into a wood to rest. To my astonishment I saw the gleam of a fire through the trees; and, on approaching it, I saw a little old man crouched over it, cooking something. He looked not only harmless but attractive as, hearing the crackle of my feet on twigs, he looked up; he wore a bowler hat, had a beard, and was very wrinkled round the eyes. "Thought you was a keeper," he explained as I came near; though I must say the thought didn't seem to have alarmed him very much; he probably knew he could charm even a keeper.

He was cooking a red herring on a toasting-fork; he had a second with him, and a hunk of bread, and he asked me to share his meal, which I was glad to do; and as he chattered away about his roving, his merry gnome-like face firelit against a background of dark boughs and moon-silvered glade, I could almost believe I had met Pan in some modern disguise, a Pan who had marched with Roberts to Kandahar and knew every road, wood and common in Southern England, and every stratagem for obtaining creature comforts that any gipsy knew. He was full of jokes and chuckled freely at them, but the food and the fire prevented me from talking with much intelligence. In the end he rolled up in his old coat and I lay down on the other side of the fire and went to sleep instantly. When I woke at dawn, a little chilly, I expected to find him gone; or, rather, did not believe he had ever been there. But there he was, still lively as a cricket. He invited me, a little surprised that I actually had a fixed determination to go in another direction, to join him on his westward way; when we parted I thought: "There, unless he gets ill, which he doesn't look like doing, is a happy man."

None such did I meet on this first day; mostly they were a melancholy brotherhood and a dull. There were not, either on this day or on the others, as many as usual; perhaps, since it was August, as many of them as were willing to do casual work had found employment with the harvest. In any event dark was approaching, and when I reached Ripley, I felt I must push on, and resisted the temptation to enter either that noble inn "The Talbot" or the little old "Anchor" which went from father to son all the generations from the Armada to just the other day. The seven miles from Ripley to Guildford is dull going, even when not infested by cars coming from behind, and I was not sorry when I got to Guildford. It was a temptation to stop there for the night. But Godalming had been my objective; unlike Mr. Belloc, when he marched on Rome, I had not made a vow not to use "any wheeled thing," nor indeed any vow at all; and though I had had quite enough walking and the pack had become a burden to the flesh, I went on. I caught a train to Godalming. When I got there, I had suddenly got so stiff in the evening air that I hired a taxi to take me the few hundred yards to the hotel.

It was almost ten. I had once been known there and I had no doubt about a bed, as the swarm of Charterhouse parents would not be there in the holidays. The bed arranged, I asked after my old friend the landlord, and was told: "Oh, Mr. —— he isn't here any longer." So sad it is to leave such gaps between visits. But, happily, cold beef was there, and the bed was there, and very soon, glad that I hadn't hard ground under me or the wind on the heath whistling round my ears, I was snug in the bed. I just managed to turn the light out, and fell into dreamless sleep.

SECOND DAY

It has long been known that it is one thing to intend to do something and another thing to do it.

Nobody could have been more firmly resolved than I to make an early start next morning, and I had asked for tea at seven. Unfortunately, after I had been waked I fell at once asleep again, and when I got downstairs at half-past nine the landlady, as one knowing the worthlessness of men's promises, remarked: "I thought you said you were going to be out of the house at eight." Still, she didn't seem to mind, and when I had refreshed myself with a kipper I set out with kind farewells.

As I stepped out into that ancient street, every gable-end and Lipton's window of which had been for years familiar to me, I caught sight, at the far end where roads meet, of a small hexagonal plastered building set in the middle of the road. A sudden idea struck me and made me pause on the pavement. "Here am I," I thought, "exploring my native land; I ought to be sight-seeing; I haven't seen a sight yet; why not see one?"

There was that venerable pile, the Godalming museum. For years I had passed it daily, noting the grave letters MUSEUM above the portal; for years I had resolved to investigate it; and never once had I remembered my firm intention and passionate curiosity when I had had time to go in. "I will go in now," I determined, "even if it means getting a key from the verger's cottage, or whatever it is." With elated heart I strode on past the butcher's, the baker's, the draper's and the ironmonger's, until I reached the hexagon; and, having tried five sides in vain for a door, found one on the sixth. There, as is everywhere too visual on public institutions, was a board explaining that the Museum could only be seen at certain hours on certain days, none of which this particular day was. Baffled and bitter I muttered to myself: "It was bad enough, earlier in the year, to go to Cairo without seeing the Sphinx and to Constantinople without seeing the Golden Horn—but at Stamboul there was rain and mist, and in Egypt I did engage to lecture on litera-ture and was kept busy answering questions by brown majors in red fezzes about D. H. Lawrence and James Joyce. But to visit Godalming once more without seeing the Museum—well, it's disgustingly unfair." I'm quite sure I shall never know what is inside it now. There may be most interesting flint arrow-heads and some of those little serrated things with which early man cut off the ears of his corn. There may be some broken pots. There may be a Cromwellian pike, or some little yellow snakes, going woolly in bottles of spirit; or some dried and tattooed Maori heads, or some Polynesian paddles, or perhaps even the local stocks and ducking-stool, relics of a darker day. "Of course," my thoughts ran perspicaciously on, "the place is pretty small, and there couldn't be any really large things here, like those skeletons of whales at South Kensington, for instance." And then I remembered that even size could sometimes be dealt with by ingenuity.

Long ago I had to turn an ancient printing works into offices, and one of the things I rejoiced in was that, when partitions had gone, there was a top attic for me as big as a chapel, full of light, whitewash and oak supports. I wanted a picture rail and asked a builder and decorator in to discuss it with me.

One morning he came. His name was Mr. Porter. He was huge, fat, red-faced, heavy-moustached, rolling and lumpish in his gait, and his bowler hat was not removed, even when he was in his shirt-sleeves. He was obviously not one of those ruthless business men whose delight it is to plunge *in medias res,* without a little preliminary human intercourse to break the ice. He took out a pipe, sat down and told me that I had a nice little place there, mentioned horse-racing, described his preferences in the way of liquor, and then, by an easy transition through foreign drinks, got to his travels.

He had been, he said, a sailor and a great traveller. There were few parts of the world that he had not seen, though I must admit he gave some, to me, novel pieces of information— as, for example, that the inhabitants of Japan were Mohammedans. Ultimately I said to him: "And I suppose you have been to South America?" "There for years. Know it inside aht," he replied in his rich Cockney accent. "Have you seen the Amazon?" I asked, thirsting for more enlightenment. "Why, yes; been right up it," he observed. Then taking his pipe from his mouth and using it as an aid to gesture, he volunteered all I needed in the way of butterflies, alligators, and macaws, until at last we came to boa-constrictors.

Here he became eloquent. Boa-constrictors, he said, were the most remarkable things in creation; for they were faithful beyond human hope or aspiration. They wedded for life; they always went about in pairs; and, if one partner to a boa-constrictor union was shot the other invariably returned to the forest and died of grief. After something approaching a sermon on this supreme example of Nobility among Reptiles, he concluded with an emphatic bang on the table with the flat of his hand and these striking words: "Boa-constrictors: True-Blue, I calls them!"

I assumed, as best I could, an air of serious assent and sympathy; and then, when I thought the theme exhausted, he leant forward earnestly and said: "Would you like a boa-constrictor skin?"

"Rather!" I said, suppressing a lament over the deceased snake's disconsolate mate.

"Well, I've got a very nice one at home," he proceeded; "I like you, mister, and it's yours. I should think," he reflected, turning sideways, "it would just about go on that there long wall. It's a big one; but I *think* it'll do."

Rising, he drew a foot-rule from his waistcoat pocket, rolled to the wall (which was some thirty feet long) and solemnly began to measure it from one end to the other. Coming at last to the near corner he uttered a regretful: "Tut-tut!"

"What's the matter?" I enquired.

"Just won't go," he complained; but then he cheered up, ran his rule for a few feet along the next wall, and said: "It's all right, we can just turn the 'ead a few feet round the corner."

The serpent never arrived; but though never seen it is still to memory dear. Much have I travelled in the realms of gold, some things done and many, alas, left undone, but at least this may be written in my epitaph: "He had his walls measured for a boa-constrictor."

Wistfully I turned away; I will go, I thought, into the "White Hart" for consolation; it's only just opposite, that most ancient inn in the town, curving beautifully at the corner with its simple gables, its oak, its plaster, its overhanging storeys, and above all that lovely old sign, the meek hart lying with his feet underneath and a golden collar round his neck; a hart like that in the Wilton Diptych in the National Gallery that was the badge of poor, melancholy, perverted, self-pitying Richard II, a hart that might have made friends with St. Hubert himself. I began to cross the road. There was the building. The sign had gone, the ground-floor had been turned into shops, though not one of them was yet adorned with that maddeningly monotonous red-and-gold Woolworth fascia which, in the end, without respect to local architecture, old or new, Tudor or Tartar, will be seen in every great or small town from Lake Erie to Lhassa. "In the end," I say: but the end is not yet. . . .

Depressed, and meditating once more on the imbecilities of our licensing system, I passed along the road, with a garage on my left, and a glimpse of lake through the old cottages and the new cinema site on my right. Once more I was astounded at my country, and at the brewers, and at the Tory Party. It was a Conservative Government which introduced a Licensing Act which arranged that "redundant" licences should be abolished; that brewers (and why on earth should they own inns and tie them to their own brand of beer, good or bad, paint out the old signs and scrawl the names of their ales—one is called "Shrimp"—across the old fronts?) should surrender an old licence if they wanted a new one, and that benches of "Licensing Justices" (usually and deliberately packed by the most revolting type of whining, nonconformist teetotallers ever conceived of by the author of *Hudibras*) should have the power of deciding what should be shut, what should be open and when—people who regard a harmless village club as rather worse than a brothel, and immeasurably worse than a factory. "The people have the power of altering things," reply the blind worshippers of what is a nominally democratic system. "The people" is but a phrase; "the people" in France or Italy would make short shrift of anyone who attempted to take away their wine in return for giving them votes, i.e., the choice between one caucus nominee and another, each frightened of offending some small minority of cranks whose blinkered minds, on one issue alone, may swing an election one way or another, incidentally and in the mad manner of the Gadarene swine, flinging the country into ruinous war, or disgraceful peace, or the loss of Empire or any other minor matter simply because

they cannot bear the idea of not interfering with their neighbours' personal habits. They have not dared to go to the
lengths that they and their insane female accomplices went in
America. Try England with Prohibition and it will go back
to Chaucer, Shakespeare, Dr. Johnson and Cobbett as it did in
1914 and during the General Strike, throwing off its back all
the England-hating Welsh from Henry VIII and Thomas
Cromwell to Oliver Cromwell (*né* Williams) and the rest.
But take away from the ordinary Englishman only some of
his liberties, remove his landmarks only in part, and, good-
tempered and patient as he is, he will merely assemble where
and when he is allowed to assemble, lament the passing of the
"Old Ship" or the "Burlington" at Chiswick (which dated
from Agincourt, was frequented by Thames ferrymen and had
probably never seen a man drunk in our day), complain that
the new pubs are not what the old ones were, that they are
more crowded, that managers from the north are not the same
as landlords from one's own locality, and that it is abominable
to have to drink quickly at ten o'clock, but that "they're all the
same, the —— politicians"—and they stand it and console
themselves with memories of horses and cricket, characters
long dead and campaigns long over.

So the "White Hart" has gone. "The 'Saracen's Head' looks
down the lane where we shall never drink wine again." That
was Chesterton, in *The Flying Inn,* of which Flecker, dying,
wrote to me saying that he thought it was the grandest of
modern fictions.

From one point of view alone, of course, he was talking; he
was regarding, not construction or dramatization, but opinion
and power of writing. As I walked, in the heat, along that un-
interesting road from Godalming to Milford, redeemed, in one
marsh patch, by the pool, near the road to Compton and the
relics of G. F. Watts, in which the cows, in summer, stand up
to their knees, placidly in the placid water, I wondered about
the urbanization of our recent literature, the loss of religion, of
passion, of humour, of historical sense, and of style. I remembered that, when I was young, those of us who were constantly
aware of the mystery of life, who cared for continuity, who

B

had no illusions about automatic progress, who did not necessarily believe that to-morrow would be better than to-day or that to-day was necessarily better than yesterday, used to curl our lips at Mr. Bernard Shaw and Mr. H. G. Wells, the oracles of that time, both of whom, we held, might have been men-of-letters leaving permanent legacies behind them had they not chosen rather to produce cheap-jack systems in journalistic language. What we would have thought could we have foreseen the present day I do not know: a day which lacks even idols with feet of clay, a day of painters mincingly fencing with technique, of musicians who make cacophonous noises or linger tediously in dark forests of echoes, of versifiers who attempt to astound by fanatical or cynical opinions or lack of melody. We shouldn't have believed it could happen; and perhaps it wouldn't have happened if it hadn't been for the war which blew to pieces a whole generation which had just learnt to reconcile faith with fact, song with reality, and left its children too weak and bewildered to face an age, after all no wickeder than previous ages though its machines may be more terrible than theirs, in which all the easy optimisms from Rousseau's onwards have been thrown into the dust-bin after the philosophies, theologies and ethics that those replaced.

"Lord, how hot is it!" The sweat was pouring down my brows and leaking over my spectacles; well, it was only a mile or two to Milford, and then I should get into the open country. I passed the "cottage" where Theodore Byard used to live, after he had lost his singing voice in the war (a place with a miniature, but real, park, elms and grass and cattle, which, on so small a scale, I have only seen elsewhere in Lincolnshire), bought a whiting (skinned and tailed, and put in a newspaper wrapping) at a fish-shop, and began the pleasant climb up through Witley Common, which showed no trace of the thousands of Canadians who camped there during the war, but was covered with St. John's Wort, the last top buds of willow-herb, and the grey-lilac fluff of thistles. The view spread and spread as I mounted, and indignation swelled in my breast against the superior persons who imagine that Surrey is all villa-dom, sand, golf-courses, gas-works and

Woking; for, south of the Guildford–Dorking line nothing could be more beautiful and varied, and here for miles to right and left of me, were open primitive commons without a house visible.

Nearing the top I blushed. I had killed there—well at any rate not a fox, but a game bird out of season. Once, on a fine August morning, I had been chasing townwards alone in a car when I saw coming towards me on the left a covey of seven partridges. Primitive man arose in me; I thought nothing of licences or Game Laws; instinct merely yelled at me: "Can you hit one of them with the windscreen?" I accelerated to about sixty. It was nicely timed, though I cannot honestly swear that, in the really orthodox way, I picked the outside bird. But at any rate one came down.

I stopped. I didn't know what to do about it. What was the good of a single partridge to a household like mine; how preposterous it would be, since I was to be in town for the night, to "park" it either with a garage-proprietor or a club-porter, either of whom might have looked strangely at me for being in possession of partridges, or even a partridge, before September 1st? The *Deus ex machina* appeared in the shape of a smart, military-looking A.A. Scout with a motor-bicycle and side-car. He saluted. I saluted. "I've knocked down a bird there," I said; "perhaps you might like it." He walked to the spot indicated and brandished his trophy. I saluted; he saluted; then I skimmed on my way. . . .

Just over the top of the hill there was a sandy track to my left; I felt like a change from the high-road so I took it, though I knew where it would lead me. Through the heather I went, drinking in an occasional waft of breeze, avoiding beetles and hole-drilling bees under my feet, enjoying the colour of the gorse, the heath and bell-heather, pausing now and then to look at the wide stretches of moorland and the blue hills far away, once putting up a night-jar which may have had a very late brood, until the path led downwards to a mingling of trees and common and I was passing the Hammer Ponds. Small lakes with that name are not uncommon in Surrey and Sussex; once they were used for the southern, wood-smelting, ironworks; now they are the haunt of trout and wild duck and at peace, and ravens may yet build their nests in the slag-heaps of Staffordshire. To the right again and, after ten minutes, I found myself near the primitive cricket-ground of Thursley village. It is not so eminent in the annals of Surrey county cricket as the neighbouring ground of Tilford, where Silver Billy Beldham played, and the Cæsars, and where the local publican umpire once gave an opponent "out" with the verdict: "Out, the damned teetotaller!"; but the game is played there with much amusement and not too many appurtenances.

The pavilion was shut; the roller was idle; the vast land-scape all around was deserted; the struggle with the wicket and heather and gorse around the out-field was still, evidently, not perfect; though it had made some ground since the days when I used to be afraid of putting the late Reginald Berkeley on there for fear he should kill somebody who was gallantly fighting the losing battle of British agriculture. I sat on a bench and thought of the village. Down the hill and up the hill in the trees to the left was the Dye House, where old Mr. Gough, the squarson, used to live, a man who deserved Jack Russell's epitaph of a great Christian and a great sportsman. When I first knew him he was already eighty and blind, but he could sit in a chair downstairs. When I last saw him he was bedridden, had a shawl over his head, and was consoled by that marvellous modern invention the wireless, over which he sometimes heard the voices of people whom he had met. First and last he was as young, simple, sweet, good and universal as any man I ever knew; and he looked, with his clean, full, Victorian features and white side-whiskers, like one of those steel engravings of deceased and venerable landlords, with reproduced signatures beneath, which still adorn the walls of country hotels, in proportion as they are farther from London. (There is one of Mr. Garth in a humble ale-house on the Reading road, whose description of the Garth Hunt was passed on to me long ago as: "Fust come the gentlemen from Sandhurst, then the gentlemen from the Staff College, then the gentlemen from Aldershot, then the fox, then the hounds, and, last of all, poor bloody old Garth!") Mr. Gough had been an

Oxford rowing man and a county cricketer in his day; and very old and blind had caught salmon on his fishing in Norway, being told where to cast by his wife. He knew all about birds, and was ardent in the shooting of some and the preservation of others; he upheld the local Bench for fining his keeper for shooting a Montagu Harrier, and, of course, paid the fine himself. Much of our conversation concerned such subjects as that, but some of it ran like this:

G: So you knew Sir Alfred Bateman, did you? He was a goodish cricketer. He was secretary to Lord Palmerston. But I suppose Palmerston was before your time?

S: I'm afraid he was.

G: I thought so; enterprising fellow. Did you know W.G.?

S: No, I wish I had; but I once saw him play.

G: Most amusing fellow. I doubt if we shall see anyone like him again! Did you know Alfred Lyttelton?

S: No. Of course I've often seen him and heard him speak; but I only wish I *had* known him.

G: But I am sure you know E. V. Lucas?

S: (On firm ground at last.) Yes, very well.

G: Most excellent fellow, and very kind. He's been down here to see me before now.

And who wouldn't have done so, who had any sense? He knew Squire Osbaldeston's riding weight, very likely saw Sayers and Heenan fight, and seemed the joint descendant of John Nyren, White of Selborne, the Vicar of Wakefield and Colonel Newcome.

Once, and once only, I recalled, as I sat on that bench on that hill-top cricket ground, did I send a man to him with an introduction, and that was shortly before he died—or "passed away," for never was there man to whom that euphemism was more suitable—one felt that even Death could do him no violence or distort that gentle smile which blindness had only made the kinder.

We had talked once, in his study, full of faded old sporting books, and I (who do not smoke cigars and seldom drink sherry) smoking one of his cigars and drinking a glass of his sherry, about that elusive bird, the Dartford Warbler. Somebody had recently told me that it was disappearing from its old nesting-places and could now be only rarely, and with difficulty, stalked by bird-watchers and photographers. I, haunted by the sad ghosts of bittern and bustard, large copper butterfly, all gone, and swallow-tail and fritillary flower, almost gone, had accepted the statement gloomily: after all, an age of limited-liability companies, jerry-builders, and egg-collectors (all of which, or whom, have much the same mentality) would, in time, destroy or deface everything in nature that one loved. "I hope not," said Mr. Gough, his blind eyes gleaming, his hand rearranging his shawl; "I believe the bird is actually increasing in numbers. There are always several pairs nesting in the garden here, and if you care to go up to Thursley Common and watch 'em, you're bound to find 'em."

I neither watched nor found, but some time later I had lunch in London with a rare visitant, not a bird but a man, who had come up from Somerset to renew his annual disgust with the Great Metropolis, and do some tiresome family business. He was—I may add, happily, still is—a great ornithologist, and knew the notes, habits, and habitats of all sorts of rare birds which I only knew from pictures or repute. There was hardly a recorded British bird which he had not watched (always excluding things like the Baltimore Oriole which come so seldom that clergymen hardly ever had a chance of shooting them even in the palmy days of the Reverend Mr. Morris) but he said: "The odd thing is that I have never seen a Dartford Warbler; they don't come our way."

What a chance! I have had few real triumphs in my life; very often I feel a fool in the presence of other people's superior knowledge; they say: "My dear fellow, I'm very sorry, but you don't happen to have been there and I have"—and collapse and silence are inevitable. There was, and I feel fortified as it comes to mind, a moment during Armistice week when, though it was but for a moment, the spirit of Alexander, Cæsar, Napoleon, and Cardinal Mezzofanti blew through me, and I

stood on the top of the world—which, naturally, recalls Cortes.
During the war, with many other rejects and indispensables, I
paraded Buckingham Palace gardens at night, guarding with
great loyalty, no gallantry, and a considerable risk of pneu-
monia, His Majesty against whatever dangers might threaten
him. "Ours not to reason why," we couldn't have been much
protection against bombs, and other dangers seemed nil.
Hundreds of men, including Sir J. Smith, K.C.B., and Sir T.
Jones, K.C.B. (they were mostly Civil Servants in my squad,
and mainly Educational), sergeants and corporals in the force,
turned out night after night, year after year, crunching through
snow or yearning to the Harvest Moon, relieving each other
every two hours or so with challenges, salutes and flashings of
torches, the relieved proceeding to the King's Stables for cocoa,
biscuits and bridge. Wiser men might perhaps have insisted
on our going to sleep instead; but we were proud of our job,
and when, late in the war, we heard that another company
had arrested a drunken Australian soldier for throwing the
hat of another drunken Australian soldier over the Royal and
Imperial wall, and actually got him fined a shilling, we felt
proud of our Corps (H.Q.C.D.) and very envious of the other
company which had bagged the villain. For ourselves we consoled ourselves with Education. Past Grecian portico, grove
and lake we tramped; flashed lights when we met, and then
for a minute or two, communing strictly against orders, in rain
or frosty moonshine listening for the sergeant's grim approach
(the sergeant having been either at school or college with most
of us), we eagerly exchanged information about Secondary
Schools, and Schools for the Feeble-minded, with explanatory
discussions concerning the connection between left-handedness
and stammering.

Came a time, after all these ardours, when, at the eleventh
hour of the eleventh day of the eleventh month (which all
sounded like something out of the Book of Revelation, which,
indeed, it proved to be), and we were suddenly told that we
must parade the streets of the West End for a week—in pairs,
of course, for policemen should not, in times of popular turbulence, go about alone.

On Armistice evening I found myself separated from my companion, and endeavoured, with no great ardour and less success, to prevent a large number of lithe and powerful Australians, with attendant maidens, from pulling a captured German gun along the Mall and up St. James's—at the top of which they left it (me in charge), having discovered that Highgate, which they had originally announced as their destination, was a long way off and (in Christina Rossetti's words) "uphill all the way." Little harm had I seen that evening done; a bonfire made under Landseer's Lions, and a number of soldiers and girls dancing, the soldiers because they themselves were not going to be killed and the girls because the soldiers were not going to be killed—and, when I read the Press next morning, I wondered whether the stories about Mafeking night (also the outcome of a poetic and popular relief and release) had been as mendacious as those about the excesses of Armistice night.

However, some other night that week, when the cheering had subsided and the streets were again dark and solitary at midnight, I was walking along Pall Mall, arm-in-arm with another constable, not a member of my own squad, but one whom I had known long since and lost awhile. He was a dear and simple soul; a barrister, full of the milk of human kindness; I need scarcely add that he did not practise. We had just reached, on our eighth or ninth circuit, the sooty portal of the Reform Club, when a man appeared from nowhere and began gesticulating and emitting strange, inhuman moans. My companion started: he thought it was a lunatic and hurriedly glanced at me as who should say: "Oughtn't we to arrest him?" Happily the deaf-and-dumb finger language came at once to my mind. It was only a lost and dumb Frenchman trying to find his way to Victoria, and by dint of various motions indicating "straight on," "second right," and "bear right," I told him what he wanted to know, and was rewarded by a lifting of the hat, a bow, and as grateful a smile as ever Frenchman gave Englishman.

That was all quite ordinary; but when, under the lamp, I turned to my companion, I saw a face irradiated, as Joan's may have been when she was listening to her "Voices." He had no idea what was up; and, when I explained that I had been talking deaf-and-dumb language to a deaf-and-dumb Frenchman, he was awestruck. That night he spoke no more; and if he lives to-day he probably thinks that I could readily respond in Amharic or Hittite or the cryptic semaphoring of the tictac men to whomsoever might accost me.

That is, of course, harking back; I was talking about Dartford Warblers. The point is, that my ornithologist friend looked almost as astounded when I said: "Well, if you want to see Dartford Warblers, you've only to come down to me and I can show you any number any day of the week." "Do you really mean that, Squire?" he asked, in that solemn way that truly earnest observers here. "Of course I do," I protested; "come down to-morrow if you like. I'll book you a room at the local pub for two nights and put you on to a man who can tell you exactly where they are to be found." "Right!" he said.

I did. He went to Mr. Gough. He went to the Common. Through his glasses he watched several pairs all day; and I, also with glasses, have been there time and time again and never seen a thing except rabbits and snakes.

That is probably the fate of countless country-lovers who endeavour to make valuable and exciting notes about wild life like White, or characters, customs and seasons like Miss Mitford; the diaries are kept, and turn out to be, in the worst sense of the word, common-place books. Sitting on that Thursley bench and thinking of when I lived within three miles of the place, I remembered how one day I had come back to my house and garden after a day's reading for a publisher; the books perused had included no fewer than three country diaries, written by women, and of so outrageous a banality that even had I recorded my own rural observations they could not have been so devoid of interest. Alone, after dinner, over my fire, I tried, not without sympathy, to envisage the type of person who could be so eager to keep country diaries and so ignorant as not to know what would have a chance of being published. So I began to write a story; I called it *The New House* and it ran something like this:

"When Elvira Hobbs retired to the country, her husband having just pulled off a coup and bought an old house with five acres on the Surrey-Hampshire borders, her first thought was naturally to get a proper, honest, polite, reasonably cheap, reasonably reasonable, and quite permanent staff of servants. Her next was to get 'settled in,' all the furniture nicely placed, everything working properly, contacts with a few neighbours established, the local churches tested, and her husband's trains more or less regulated. But after all that had been fixed, and a reliable nurse engaged for the children, her third thought was that, now she had achieved the summit of her desires and won a beautiful house and garden in real well-wooded country, she would keep a Nature Diary, with a view, primarily, to her own education and delight, but, secondarily, to publication. When I say 'publication,' I am not suggesting that she had illusions about vast and immortal fame: she was too practical to think of such things. But, after all, the world was full, nowadays, of women no cleverer than she, earning good livings by their pens, with novels and miscellaneous literature, so why on earth should not she also, who was intelligent, well-read, and observant, supplement her own income? However humble the increment, it would always come in useful for hats, bulbs, shrubs and, with luck, motor cars.

"She had read 'White of Selborne' in her youth: she had received him as a Prize for an Essay on 'How I would Like to Spend my Holidays,' in which she had openly aspired after cows and cowslips. There, surely, was a good enough model! There was no question but that Nature's Year aroused more interest nowadays than ever; even the popular papers had an inch a day about it. The letters, and still more the Points from Letters, in *The Times,* were even more powerful proof: one could scarcely open that or any other respectable periodical without seeing an article on how to plant ranunculi, or a picture of a kestrel on her nest or a cat suckling a young weasel. Punctual as the arrival of the swallows were the letters about their arrival, and the earliest primrose never missed its chronicler. Moreover, it was perfectly evident that anybody who really took the trouble, with the help of a good pair of field-glasses, to watch birds for an hour a morning, and do a field and hedgerow prowl for an hour an afternoon, simply could not fail to record things seldom, if ever, or at least so early, seen in his own or even in any other neighbourhood. There was plenty of time. She was well staffed; there was a good little shopping town not far away; Roger was in the City every weekday except Saturday, when they would play golf or tennis; and there was no reason why she shouldn't do a book, unique in its way, about the wild life on her own five acres, supplemented by occasional observations drawn from woods and commons immediately adjoining."

Thus far and rather like that, did I get with my introduction; whether or not I made her tell her husband of her intention I do not remember. If I was in a cruel, cynical mood, I must obviously have made her tell him, and make him so rude about it, that she, poor misunderstood girl, would keep her diary secretly. If I was in a sentimental mood, perhaps I made her begin with secrecy, but only with a view to giving him, understanding lover, a delicious surprise at, say Christmas. All I remember is that I did get to specimens of the diary.

There, for a time, I was stuck. All I could remember of the real manuscripts I had read was sentences like, "Still raining to-day," and "The postman has just gone by; still no letter from M." I knew if I started inventing a procession of flowers and birds I should not merely slip into forgetfully entering the appearance of the starwort as an autumn phenomenon, but put down all sorts of book-knowledge which these diarists, being truthful observers, do not drag in. So I thought I would, in order most realistically to fill in the quotational gap in my story, make a few daily observations myself in the few minutes I could spare: that way I would at least get the facts right.

I did. I do so wish I had kept it: it might have comforted

many earnest students of Nature. I can only remember the
kind of thing it was, and that kind of thing was this kind of
thing:

Sept. 8. "How this place swarms with robins," I said
yesterday while the gardener forked up bunches of pink-and-
white King Edwards and shook them free of clods. A robin
perched, immobile and dignified, on a neighbouring potato,
presented his profile, not even bothering to notice us. "Yes,"
replied the gardener, "but it is them chaffinches that is the
greatest pests."
The point of view: all birds are pests. But this morning, a
grey-green morning with the grass pale with the relics of
rain, I half agreed with him. The chaffinches here are what
the sparrows were in my London garden; so great a multitude that there scarcely seems room for other birds. Without
cessation, in all directions, their white feathers conspicuous,
they criss-cross the garden, in shoals, in chasing pairs, or
singly, the orchard their chief resort. Sparrows here are few.
A robin came for the crumbs below my study window, and
I watched the gymnastics of a blue-tit hanging upside down
picking for insects in an apple-tree near the toolshed. Over
the hedge of the paddock two young men and a keeper
trudged the stubble for partridges: I heard, later, constant
guns but saw no coveys. Three nights ago there were two
pheasants in the garden: there are, of course, blackbirds
scuttling low through the bushes with replete chuckles as
one approaches. After tea John and I found a worm semi-
swimming in a semi-puddle. A little water assisted him; he
moved like a swimming snake. A great deal did not; he
sank and feebly writhed. A creature who can move in either
direction indifferently one scarcely pities.

Sept. 9. After breakfast still cold, wet, windy. A starling
perched on the top of the fir tree by the N.E. corner of the
tennis-court, damp and alone, whilst a chaffinch huddled on
a lower branch. The starling cheeped feebly; I could hear
the noise plainly only when I watched his beak opening

through the glasses. Finally, he gave several vast quick yawns which opened his thin beak to a right-angle and flew away. Several flights of starlings passed over, and flocks of chaffinches flew briefly in the sky over the tree-tops. There is a rookery somewhere near; as I walked down the oak hedge a vast confused cawing began in the middle distance.

Late at night driving up the lane I saw a stoat slink across the road right under my headlights. It is an odd instinct that makes these things go forward from hedge to hedge, instead of staying where they are and reversing. . . .

Thus, I recall, at any rate at about that daily length, did I begin; but I couldn't stay the distance as my heroine would have done, and I proceeded more in this wise:

Sept. 10. Morning on the lawn wet and grey. Thrush, blackbird, sparrow.

Sept. 14. Sunny morning heavy dew. Saw a blackbird at my crumbs. So far only blackbirds and sparrows and a robin seen there, the last the only one to remain under my eyes not minding.

Sept 15. On the tennis lawn, first a female dishwasher, then a male; then both together. The male, spick and span, black cowl and bib, white face, striped wings. Walked, then ran, stopped, flirted, walked, ran, took quick turn. Stopped by post and preened himself, nuzzling under wings. Female appeared and he ran all over the lawn two yards behind her, moving and stopping. Robin on net, robin on ground, brilliant in sunshine.

Sept. 28. Ten days since I last saw swallows. This morning, damp and grey; many starlings. A cluster in the top of the tall pine. The trees, after two months of frequent rain, still mostly green; but the birches have thinned and browned, and are draped now in fine spare veils of lace.

So I might have proceeded. But one morning, after some more variations on the now familiar starling and robin themes,

I saw a nuthatch on the lawn, and, after a moment's delight, I quailed. It wasn't that I shouldn't be able to leave the nuthatch out of my heroine's diary; anyhow she would probably not have known what it was and thought it some robin or chaffinch of unusual colour and shape. But I felt enthusiasm swelling in my bosom. I had never noticed a nuthatch in the garden. Who could say what mightn't turn up next, especially in the spring, if I really began watching properly, and not merely putting in a few minutes a day for facetious purposes? I was faced with a precipice below me. Once let me get that nuthatch entered and I should be well on the slippery slope that leads to the bird-watcher's camera, the botanist's box, and (Heavens!) perhaps a whole year's diary and a book, increasingly mendacious as the need for variety of flora and fauna became more evident, entitled "My Five Acres."

"In that book I wrote no more that day," as Dante would have said. Nor on any other day; I was resolved that, henceforth, should all the bluebreasts and hoopoes in creation swarm around me, I should never make written note of them. I comforted myself with the reflection that even if I had supplied our Elvira Hobbs with a sufficiency of specimen diary I should never have been able to finish her story off very effectively. For it would have been rather lame, although like the truth, to have had her completed diary rejected by all the publishers' readers in London, including myself, and then either put away in a drawer to be forgotten or else published at the expense of her kind husband. And to have her irate, unkind husband murder her when he found she was becoming "one of those writing women" would have been too sensational for my habitual manner of treatment; though it would have given the magazine illustrator the chance which he usually demands of a prone form, a stern man in a dinner-jacket, and a revolver with smoke still spiring upwards past the napery, the glasses, and the decanter of port.

*   *   *   *   *

(But I was still on the bench at the Thursley Cricket Ground.) It was almost too hot to move, but very pleasant up there with the commons below, ridge after ridge of hills fading behind them and, in the other direction, the red roofs of the village outskirts. It would have been pleasant to stay there, or to tread again the old street of cottages and climb to churchyard and church and Rapley's farm which has King John walls in it. The church has newly discovered Saxon windows with the original wooden frames in them; it has also a magnificent lot of oak supporting roof and tower. And in the churchyard by the wall, above the steep declivity, there is a tombstone bearing the inscription "John Freeman, Poet" —for there lies there, within sight of Crooksbury Beacon and in the heart of the country of Cobbett, whom he loved, one of the strongest, most delicate, most profound, and most neglected of poets of our time. But I had set myself a long journey that day; I wanted to get as near Winchester as I could; I should have to stop for lunch; and it was already half-past eleven. So I rose, and marched off to rejoin the main road, which climbs for three miles or so until it reaches Hindhead, the Punchbowl, and the monument of the murdered sailor, What with the sun and the pack on my back, I certainly did not run; but neither did I stop, even at that gap in the hedge on the left, opposite the strange pyramidal hill, from which you, as it were from a balloon, can see to the north Godalming, Guildford and the great promontory of Blackdown, and to the west, far below, what seem to be solid miles of round tree-tops, and then the whole weald, and then what must be the faint hills of Kent eighty miles away. I did pause a second just under the gibbet and looked into the deep bowl to the west, searching in vain for a little stream over which, in 1920, my horse had jumped, and a path leading upward and south-ward from it. For that horse, when we came to a fork, shied at a goat tethered between two tracks, tried to go one way when I wanted to go another, and hurtled me a complete somersault in the air to fall half stunned on the heather. People came out of the haze to catch him and to carry me. I was next aware of a couch in a refined cottage with two sweet, if donnish, ladies bending over me with a half-tumblerful of brandy. Restored, I was next aware of their bookshelves above me and caught sight of the labels of the Collected Poems of two tame poets then most fashionable, though now superseded by others dull in another way. More restoratives, I remember, were needed; and then I went my way, remounted on my sorry (I hope sorry) steed, and never could find the cottage again to renew my thanks.

But past the gibbet I went, past the car-parks and garages, past the tea-shop which so oddly calls itself The (or is it Ye?) Punchbowle Inn, and then, since I was thirsty, into the Huts where, as I meditated over my glass of beer, I overheard a conversation which showed that the memories of the Jubilee were still locally warm, and which ended (so far as I was concerned, for I had to go) with the sentence: "Well, what I say is, if the Germans 'ave a man like 'Itler, it's just as well we 'ave a man like King George."

I bought some bread and cheese and an apple—it was after half-past twelve—and thought I would get into the country again before eating my lunch. For Hindhead, in spite of its noble position and the magnificent country all round, is not itself country, but a little blot of urbanization, and I am not sure about Haslemere. As I walked out of it along that straight road that swoops to Liphook, flanked by anomalous conifers, civic paths and even, for some distance, street lamps which might have been imported from Wimbledon, I remembered Hindhead twenty-five years ago.

It was very much then what it is now: a vast brick hotel over the Punchbowl, a number of villas in their own grounds, a few old cottages, a new church, and an untidy cross-roads now, at week-ends and on Bank Holidays, repellently busy. It suffered from early development; were it started now it would not be so towny, the likely limits of its growth would be limited and its finest prospects might be entirely saved. But somebody about 1890, as it might be a medical friend of Grant Allen, on account of its height, its sand, and its pine-laden breezes, recommended it as a health-resort, and it very soon had its residential hotels and its roads of ugly villas prosperously squatting behind their laurels and their firs.

It had, from the first, a formidably intellectual atmosphere.

Dons settled there in retirement, or during their vacations,
architects who had known William Morris, cultivated rentiers
who had been disciples of Ruskin, Members of Parliament
who adored Sir Edward Grey in spite of his Imperialism and
detested Mr. Joseph Chamberlain, candidates with polo-collars
and red ties who were acquainted with Keir Hardie, authors of
text-books on law and economics who took a correct interest
in spinets and the Dolmetsch family, professors of Greek who
drank no wine and supporters of the proletariat who had
never tasted beer, and were resolved, if they could, to deprive
the proletariat of it. I hope my memory does not betray me
when I say that most of the villas contained grand pianos,
portraits of Wagner and Beethoven, the works of Mill, Morley,
Mr. Bernard Shaw and the young Galsworthy, that there were
reproductions of the pre-Raphaelites on the stairs of all the
houses, and that all the gentle grey ladies had been at Girton
or Newnham, wore their hair flat and parted in the middle,
and were friends of Mrs. Fawcett and Mrs. Garrett Anderson.
More water and barley-water were drunk to the acre than in
any other parish in England, and the conversation at dinner
mildly seethed with such subjects as the Progressive Drama,
Garden Cities, Proportional Representation, Co-Partnership
and Women's Suffrage.

It was this last matter that first brought me to stay there
for any length of time, two or three years before the war—
though I had often spent week-ends at Wheelside with
Aneurin Williams from 1910 onwards. A charming elderly
couple of reformers had heard that I was an ardent young
advocate of the Female Vote, and they wrote and asked me
to come and stay for a week and help with a speaking campaign in favour of the Cause. I did not quite know what it
involved: all I knew about the Division politically was that the
people of Liphook (Lippuk) had a reputation for electoral
ferocity unparalleled outside the denser quarters of Liverpool
and Belfast. Nor did I feel my qualifications very strong. It
was true that I had once marched in a procession, miles long,
which went to Hyde Park to listen to Miss Pankhurst and
dozens of other orators: and I could remember little of that

except two young men with weak beards who, fire in their pale eyes, walked beside me, and the iron sardonic face of Sir Henry Craik as he contemplated the slow cortège from the window of the Athenæum smoking-room. It was true also that, against my convictions and common sense, I had been induced to spend the night of the 1911 census in a hall on the Kingsway site, the militant pioneers believing that the Government would be baffled and enraged if those who were not allowed to vote refused to be counted; and all I remembered of that was a silly, jolly party, and the image of a celebrated art-critic swarming up an iron pillar in order to drape the rafters with the purple, green and white colours of the W.S.P.U. However, I went, made several speeches a day, mostly out of doors, and have ever since had great sympathy for the promoters of new causes in rural districts.

Certainly no speaker could have had less trouble. As I was not a member of the unenfranchised sex the audiences could scarcely hurl at me what was reputed to be their stock remark: "Go home and mind the baby!" The audiences I got could hardly have been roused to interrupt anybody unless he had first insulted them, and, except in the larger places, the audiences hardly existed. In the daytime the car would stop outside a village inn, and for an hour I would address two gaping yokels and one puzzled woman with all my appeals to reason and sympathy, and statistics about factory legislation in Norway, Finland, Tasmania, or whatever the places were in which women, at that time, already possessed the vote. In the evenings a school, dimly lit by gas and rather draughty, would hear me addressing a chairman, a water-bottle, four well-known supporters and a sprinkling of the dumb curious on the back seats.

As I left Hindhead behind me I reflected grimly that there was at least one experience of my life that was not likely to be repeated. But then, I felt, in a manner, sad that that should be so: for almost all those devoted and kind, if rarified, people who I then knew there are now dead. And two of them, in especial, I shall always regret, the Aneurin Williamses.

I had met them first through their son (they were distantly

connected with my wife's family) who was then an undergraduate at King's, and is now well known as an author and
bibliographer. The wife, a gracious, tall, and beautiful woman,
humorous, widely cultivated, and a good pianist, died before
her husband, and he continued alone what had always been
a life of pure philanthropy. Somebody once said that all
politicians, unless they are mere villains, want to make everybody happy; the trouble is that we all differ as to how to do
it. I am sure that Mr. Williams's Utopia would have been a
little too tame for me and mine a little too highly coloured
and disorderly for him; but I never more reverenced than in
him the workings of a clean and fearless conscience in a crystal
vase. His inherited means he regarded as a public trust; in and
out of Parliament, in accordance with the general fluxes in the
fortunes of Liberals of his quiet and industrious type, he never
showed the slightest trace of personal ambition, merely serving
the causes of political and economic reconstruction as he saw
them. Nobody ever, I am sure, started a Garden City without his taking shares; he was a lifelong "worker for Peace"
and belonged to a type of idealistic agnostic family common
in his day and rare in ours. I never think of his quiet, serious,
round, ruddy, grey-moustached face without remembering his
tolerance and kindness to those whose opinions he hated. He
was wounded to the heart if one attacked Proportional Representation, and incapable of ever conceiving that there could
be reasonable arguments against it: opinions as to what
"works" best could never compete with his geometrical library-
made theories; yet, unlike many of his kind, he did not think
anybody who was opposed to him the devil incarnate, though
he perhaps suspected they might not be wholly serious.

All that came back to me as I put distance between myself
and the churchyard where I saw him buried years ago. But,
sitting under a hedge, and eating my bread and cheese, I
remembered a thing which, curiously, I had long forgotten
and which has been forgotten by most people. The men at
the Hindhead inn had been talking about Abyssinia; and,
though it was two months before the Mussolini crisis really
arrived, one of them had mentioned, with no air of intimate

knowledge or profound respect, "that there League of Nations."

It was at Hindhead that the League of Nations, so described, was invented. In, I think, December 1914, Aneurin Williams wrote in the *Contemporary Review* an article demanding much such a Society of Nations as now exists, and I think that he was the first to use the term "League" for it. He certainly founded the "League of Nations Society" shortly afterwards (I was an original member, though even then I did not believe in the "one nation one vote" theory, Haiti being equal to England—which has partly led to the Abyssinian crash— or to anything but a gradual building up from Western Europe and, if possible, America). That was before the days of the League of Nations Union, the Society's child; and by the time all the Archbishops and Party leaders had come in, Aneurin Williams had lapsed into comparative obscurity. He was a saint all the same.

*   *   *   *   *

"Well," thought I, as I resumed, in the hot afternoon sunshine, the road to Petersfield, "men have died and their dreams have survived them, and though every leaf on every bough seems to whisper 'Abyssinia,' though the world may be rocking to another calamity, though the ground elsewhere may be shaking to the tramp of armed men and the great halls echoing to the thunders of dictators, though half the world dreads and half the world threatens, and the air may rain bombs on us at any moment, the Thirty Years' War was worse in its way, but it didn't make Grotius or Puffendorf lose heart." The sky was blue, the world around was quiet in the sun, willow-herb took light and shade in the woodland clearings, heather trembled on the open hill-sides, the dogs slept on doorsteps in the few villages, the old signs of the "Half Moon" and the "Flying Bull" hung quietly outside the closed inns, and it seemed preposterous, in such surroundings and with my own heart at peace, that the lines of Chesterton should come back to me:

"Earth will grow worse ere men redeem it,
And wars more evil ere all wars cease."

At Petersfield I turned right, along that narrow, hilly, rustic road to Winchester which is so much quieter and prettier than the main road through Alton. I was but a mile or two past Petersfield, and going slowly up a hill through high thick woods, when I heard a rustle to my left, and there, staring me in the face, poised ready to disappear in a flash, was a thing I had never seen, alive, so close before. It was a fox, his mask lifted straight at me, his glowing amber eyes with their pin-point pupils glaring at me like a mixture of searchlight and gimlet. For several seconds we stared at each other, fear, cunning and courage in his heart, a sudden foolish desire to make friends in mine, to pat him and say "Good fox!" He was there; then, in an instant, he had slunk out of sight to resume his far from vegetarian career. "Blood on his pads," I thought, "and blood on my hands, and that of all our race, not least those members of it who refuse to face facts, and pretend that all the world is the same, and assume that if some of us behave like sheep the rest will stop being wolves." The usual tangle of thoughts followed, as I plodded on noticing neither the landscape nor the passing cars—the heresy of thinking man not a separate thing from animals—was nationalism worth it— how far is climate irresistible—is peace worth mongrelism of race—can it be secured otherwise—how far was the Frenchman of 1789 right when he said that the Prussian was a born soldier and war was to him a national industry—and memories of Germany in 1914, the subtle propaganda about Russia, the vulgarity of Berlin, the ugliness of the Reichstag members, the German professor who lent me £20 to get home with and was repaid in time—August 4th—the four years' dreary massacre— and Mr. Bonar Law welcoming the first Russian revolution with:

"Bliss was it in that dawn to be alive,
But to be young was very heaven!"

which led me once again to that solitary habit of brooding over the revolutions of history, pre-history and the early slime,

Winwood Reade's haunting and horrible *Martyrdom of Man* and the problem of the existence of Evil—which is the end of all such thoughts and leaves a man stranded unless he has the help of a Church without or the finger of God within, and must burden him at times whatever his faith and his charity.

Sharply I pulled myself together: "You're getting tired," I muttered to myself, "that's what's wrong with you. You came here to get away from your thoughts, not to indulge in morbid broodings. Stop this squirrel-in-a-cage business. Use the Free Will in which you so firmly believe and think of something else."

It was all like a voice speaking aloud inside me. It even tried to make jokes. "Think about cricket, for instance! You ought to be able to think of it easily enough, considering that that bowler broke your right forefinger on Saturday; it's bound up and aching, and you won't be able to use or move it for a month. Probably," went on my genial comforter, "it will be crooked and useless for the rest of your life, and you'll always have to do up buttons and laces with your left hand." I *was* getting tired, and no memories of greensward, stricken fields, luncheon tents, deck-chairs under elms, blazers, champagne cup, summer frocks and victories off the last ball of the last over would come; had I been able to think of cricket at all it would only have been about dropped catches and wet afternoons in cold pavilions. "The sun is sinking through the trees," the voice went on, "and the sky is untarnished pearl. 'Look on the West,' as Housman says." "He doesn't," I grumbled back, "he says 'Look *not* on the West.'" "Have it your own way," replied the voice, "if you don't want to be cheered up, you needn't."

So I went on not thinking at all, except that blisters seemed to be forming on the balls of my big toes, that my back was aching, that my knees were not so taut as they had been, and that I should like to lie down—though I dared not—for fear of increasing stiffness and a bedless night in the dark. Chin down, mechanically, I went on, until, surprisingly, I came suddenly on the cross-roads and an inn. "A bed at last," I thought; "I've done thirty miles and I've earned it." I went in and asked. They were very kind, but they were full up. I ordered a drink. "Probably," they said, "if you turn left, you'll be able to get a bed at the 'Dog and Pheasant,' a couple of miles on." It was nine o'clock and the light late. Time, and the braggadocio of a townish-looking young man who boasted to his experienced elders of his triumphs with poultry farming and market gardening, drove me rapidly out in the faint hope of a bus.

I asked the pleasant A.A. man about buses, but all he could suggest was that if I walked on some passing driver might offer me a lift. I said good night and doggedly, if slowly, walked on in the fading twilight, a little chilled by weariness, and occcasionally counting my steps up to a hundred in order to pass the time. Darker and darker it grew, and nothing passed but fast cars going the wrong way, but it seemed more like an hour than half an hour before I found myself in front of the "Dog."

Yellow light streamed from the open doorway, and a cheerful noise of pre-closing hour's conversation. "Thank God I may get a bed at last," I thought, stepped through the door, and, before I had got any farther saw advancing towards me, tankard in hand, the beaming round face and burly figure of my old friend Aubrey Robinson. Out shot his free hand: "What will you have?" he demanded, heartily.

For a moment I forgot thirst, bed, fatigue, knapsack and blisters in utter astonishment at his sang-froid. I knew he lived in Hampshire now, but not where; he could not have had the slightest notion that I was within a hundred miles; we had not met since the last Newbury Races; it flashed through my mind that this was the sort of man who, without preliminary curiosity, would have addressed a returning Rip Van Winkle with "I say, old fellow, I can tell you where you can get your beard trimmed."

"What will you have?" he asked, with the air of a man whose next proceedings would be to introduce me to his friends and suggest a game of darts. "An armchair, if there is one," I groaned. "Oh, that's easy," he assured me, and pushed me through to a little back-parlour, where I discarded my gear and fell back into aching comfort. "I say, Fred!" he called; and got what we wanted. "Where are you sleeping to-night?" was his next enquiry.

"Here, if I can. I'm walking."

"So it seems. Why not have a bed at my place?"

"I'd love one if it isn't too far to walk."

"Just round the corner, and I've got the car here. I can only offer you some cold bacon."

"The two things I want," I said, glowing with gratitude, "apart from a deep chair and a bed."

"Indeed yes," thought I, as I crept into a car whose antiquity even darkness could not conceal. I was rather cold but very stiff, and warmth would soon unbend me. As for cold bacon, call it that or pickled pork, what better food is there at any time of the day, preferably with potatoes, fried or boiled, and tomatoes, with English Cheddar, butter, bread and more tomatoes to follow? I have not eaten rats, mice, snakes, or elephant's feet or any of the fauna of Africa; the humble best I can do in the exotic way is horse-meat, sea-weed, sharks' fins, bird's-nest soup, frogs' legs (eaten on the *Olympic* after she had called at Cherbourg for passengers, mails, frogs and snails), reindeer (eaten at Upsala and in Helsingfors), terrapin soup and raw canvasback duck (eaten in Baltimore), tinned Canadian salmon (eaten in Samaria), and hot roast kangaroo, with pineapple chunks and their syrup, which, in 1910, made me very sick at a small Rotterdam hotel. Nightingales' tongues in aspic; peacocks, swans and bustards went out before my time. Of things not so exotic, but mostly expensive there are many familiar and, at moments of delicacy or connoisseurship, excellent: as truffles, *pâté-en-croûte,* caviare, asparagus, stuffed olives, sole *volt-au-vent,* sole *délice,* sole (or, for that matter, fresh mackerel or herring) bonne femme, haddock Sovrani, cold grouse, cold partridge, cold quails, cheese soufflé, mushrooms, and ten thousand other viands. But also there are stuffed roast veal, porterhouse steaks, boiled salt beef with dumplings, carrots, mashed turnips and potatoes in their jackets and white sauce, duck and green peas, goose. . . . I came suddenly out of this dizzy reverie about food, induced by heat and hunger, as the car jolted through a gateless gateway, up a rutted drive and came to a stop in front of a creeper-draped Elizabethan porch, the door in which opened at once. "Here we are," said Aubrey, "get out if you can manage it."

I got out amid the barking of many dogs from barns in the background. My things were taken from me. I was led upstairs and shown my bedroom and the bathroom. I came down into the sitting-room, was dumped into a deep arm-chair, and was informed that Sally would have supper ready in ten minutes. Aubrey went off to help with the preparations while I lit a cigarette and looked around me.

All his old treasures were there; the worn comfortable furniture, the prints of the ancient race-horses being proudly exhibited by dukes, marquises, trainers and jockeys long dead, and the strange litter of books. The desk behind my left shoulder was piled with papers and in a little table book-rack I could see the *Oxford Book of English Verse* and diverse works on food and gardening, and two deep in the shelves was the odd assortment he had had in his other house of Shelley and Pierce Egan, Verlaine and *The Sporting Magazine*, Baudelaire, Coventry Patmore, Beckford, Pitcher, Nimrod, the Druid and Ruff's *Guide to the Turf,* with hundreds more. Thinking what an agreeable dinner-party might be selected from Aubrey's heroes, I pulled out the *Life of John Porter,* but had read only a few pages when he appeared, beaming and rubbing his hands, to say that supper was ready and did I mind having it in the kitchen? Far from it.

The meal I need not describe; conversation, until it was finished, was at a discount. When we had done we retired again to the sitting-room study, drew two arm-chairs to the fire-place and, with a bottle of claret between us, began to inform each other of what we had been doing since we last met. The meal and the warmth ought to have made me sleepy, but they had the opposite effect, and I was soon being in-structed, as often before, concerning the descendants of Eclipse and Herod, the stable of the Duke of Cumberland, Hermit's Year, Lord Hastings and Mr. Chaplin, Ormonde, Sceptre, as well as a whole world of bygone rascality on the part of owners, jockeys, bookies and punters. How glad we both were that all this crookedness had existed in order that it should leave funny stories behind it! It is a strange thing that men who would not dream of frequenting the society of a known sharper would be miserable if they were told that the whole type of low race-train frequenters was to be obliterated to-morrow; they would feel rather as though one were told that Dickens's novels were henceforth to be published only in expurgated editions with all the bad, coarse, grubby, dissipated and grotesque people left out. scores of anecdotes I heard, and many dignoses of the breed, build, pace, staying powers, virtues and foibles of living race-horses. We had reached a sentimental union on Brown Jack and both stopped to look into the fire-place to recover glimpses of the glorious finishes of Donoghue on that lovable old animal, when my eyes wandered to the mantelpiece. "Good Lord," I said, "it's two o'clock."

"What of that?" he exclaimed, with a look of real bewilderment on his face. Then awaking to the astounding truth, he shook his head, shot out his hand to the bottle, filled two glasses and observed: "Nonsense, the night is still young." "It's no good, old thing," I said, "I'm longing for bed. I simply must go up in five minutes."

His normal disapproval of non-stayers showed in his face. "My God!" he said. "I'd love to talk a whole night another time," I went on apologetically, "but I've got to cover some ground to-morrow."

He rose and went to a side-table to light two candles. "It all seems very silly to me," he murmured, "why on earth can't you lie in bed in the morning, and then run over to Alresford to see George in the afternoon, and then come back and stay the night?"

"Duty, my lad," I said, and followed him up the steep staircase and parted after he had once more seen that everything was all right. The bedroom was vast, and the largest four-poster I have ever seen lived up to it: canopy, dark thin mahogany posts, blue head and corner curtains and valences, and room enough in it for four. I was in bed in half a minute, and for a minute more luxuriated in the softness and peace, the

dim reflection of yellow light on frames and glass, thought of
Lady Macbeth's candle, and then blew the light out. Momentarily I was aware that the moon was up, and that shadows of
diamond panes and leaves from the casement were silhouetted
on the wall to my left. Then a great billow of sleep came over
me and I did not even dream.

THIRD DAY

I was half-awake, and blinking to the brilliant sunshine,
puzzled by the unfamiliar room and beginning to reconstruct
the evening before with a view to discovering where I was,
when there was a knock at the door and full enlightenment
came. It was Aubrey, cheerful and well-soaped, wearing a very
florid red silk dressing-gown and carrying an equally florid
blue one which he dropped on the bed. I said I would like
some tea, and he called down the stairs: "Sally, our visitor
would like some tea," and at once and imperturbably resumed
where he had left off with: "Well, now, of course you're staying over to-night, and will run over and see George this afternoon."

"I really *can't*, Aubrey," I said.

"Of course you will," he repeated, with friendly contempt.
"Would you like breakfast in bed?"

"Certainly not," I replied hardily. "I'll stuff some paper in
my shoes, soap my blisters, and get on to Winchester as soon
as I've had breakfast. You don't seem to understand I'm
on a walking tour."

"Well, you can walk to-morrow, can't you!" he ejaculated.
"Would you like some eggs or will you carry on with the cold
bacon?"

"Cold bacon for me."

"Well, sing out when you're nearly ready and we'll make
the coffee."

When I got down he was ready with another opening.

"You'd much better take a day off to-day," he said. "We can
see George this afternoon, and it's just occurred to me you'd

be sure to like to run over and see the 'Tichborne Arms' this morning."

"Let's talk about it after breakfast," I said, as I helped myself to coffee, quietly resolved on no account whatever to change my decision to cover a decent distance that day. The last temptation, though, I must admit, was a real one, for the little inn at Tichborne meant a great deal to me.

Suppose, about 1906, a man now in his twenties were suddenly to encounter, in a remote Kentish huddle of cottages, with an ancient church and an ancestral park, a shy inn, thatched, dormered, covered with roses, benches in a little garden in front of it, a great heraldic signboard hanging over it, and written on the lintel: "Frank Woolley, licensed to sell wines, spirits, beer and tobacco." His impression would be much the same as that which was made upon men of my generation in the post-war years when they visited the exquisite and secluded village of Tichborne and found Maurice Read in charge both of the inn and of the cricket ground. One of the most polished bats—he was also a wily bowler—who ever played for Surrey, he played for England both here and in Australia, but retired early, in the 'nineties, when Sir Joseph Tichborne offered him the job of looking after his private ground. There, for more than thirty years, he was a kind of secondary king of the place and, after his old master died, a perfect host both on and off the field. The inn was a minor interest, though, in his quiet way, he loved seeing natives and visitors foregathering in bar and courtyard for beer and laughter in the evenings after matches were over. The ground was his passion; in the early morning and at twilight, whenever he could, he would steal up to it looking for the least blemish in wicket and outfield. And, to the last, he himself played in his peaceful corner, against local sides and men on holiday, a straight bat to the end and, in his late sixties, a beautiful judge of a run and a wary fielder.

On cricketing days and others I had often talked to him, in company and alone. The last time I had seen him was in Winchester Hospital, a few days before he died of a wasting internal disease. There he lay, tired, faintly smiling, uncom-

plaining. His face—he had a high head, candid blue eyes, a
thin aquiline nose, hollow cheeks, fair-grey drooping moustache
and brief cropped side-whiskers—a more humane version of
the late Lord Lansdowne—was like parchment stretched over
bone, and his hands, all knuckles and cords, drooped weakly
over the coverlet. An English side was in Australia; he knew
every man's form and abilities. "Incidents" had occurred; he
remembered tours of forty years before, and said that they
would always occur because of differences in national character.

A nurse brought some minced chicken. He ate a little, then
lay back again. He looked the great gentleman he was; there
was still in his face the old beauty, modesty, intelligence,
dignity, nothing of collapse except extreme leanness; and
smiles came into his eyes (for he had never been one, even in
health, to laugh aloud except very quietly) as he recalled games
long over, and the lusty figures of the past—the bravery of
Richardson, the pace of Spofforth, the cunning of "W.G.," and
the sheer impudence of E. M. Grace, "the Coroner" who, he
said, used to insist on a waiter bringing out a large whisky-
and-soda as he reached each fifty, and who had once marched
out on the field and stayed there in a county match when his
name, because he was out of form, had been left out of the
XI. We parted at last; he was still talking of "next season"
and playing again. . . .

Breakfast over, we went outside to see the dogs, fowls, geese,
ducks, turkeys, beans, vegetable marrows, and jungle-surrounded
barns, and I picked up the thread again. "I must go on,
Aubrey," I protested. "I'd like to see Tichborne again; but
I'd rather do so when there's a match on, and as for George,
you can give him my regards. I shan't go fast to-day and I'm
still pretty stiff, so I'd better start at once."

"Well, look here," he offered, "I'll tell you what I'll do.
You'll hardly get to Stockbridge to-day, let alone Salisbury.
So you'd better let me run you into Winchester, and you can
go on from there. It's quite all right; I've got some shopping
to do."

The flesh was weak, and the spirit was only too willing. I gave way, collected my traps, said good-bye to Sally and the nearest of the hounds, and we rattled off. From the heights above Winchester, near that strange great hollow, the Punch-bowl, which has lynchet-like ridges running round the top, and a floor which might have once been the floor of a lake, we halted. We thought we could see the sea, and the far hills wrapped in heat-haze were the hills of the Isle of Wight. We went on, ran down the narrow steep hill, and were presently in that wide piazza which has the giant be-sworded statue of King Alfred at the hither end, and, dominating it on the south, that Town Hall which is a disgrace to a Cathedral City. Aubrey parked his car, induced me to "wait a moment," while he bought some tobacco, cigarettes, beer and fish, and then came out, started the car again and said: "We will now go to a little pub I know, just on the edge of the town."

"What on earth for?" I asked, adjusting my knapsack.

"Jump in," he said, "and I'll tell you. You see," he continued, as the car started off, "the beer's good there, and the buses to Stockbridge stop just outside."

"What in the world are the Stockbridge buses to me?"

"We'll talk about that when we get there. You'll like this little place. A very amusing crowd of people there."

I resigned myself. After all, I hadn't taken a holiday in order to argue with my friends, and it was once more getting too hot and dazzling bright to argue with anybody. A few serpentine turns and we were in a restful-looking inn at the foot of a semi-rural hill.

"Good morning, good morning, good morning," called Aubrey to the landlord and various men who waved back to him; and then to me: "What will you have?" I was introduced to the landlord, who, in the intervals of serving and wiping glasses, produced several pithy apophthegms about Muzzle-ini, Mr. Lloyd George and the Life of Earl Haig. Aubrey, with an apology, had marched over to a far corner to talk to two horsy-looking friends. Left alone I fell into converse with two other men, weather-beaten, middle-aged, clean-shaven and clad in plus-fours; had I been thinking in the parlance of Mr. Wodehouse's Mr. Mulliner, I should have described them as Two Double Scotches. "So you're walking, are you?" said one, who must have heard Aubrey's introduction of me to the jockey-like little landlord. "I went a long walk once."

"When was that?" asked the other, sceptically.

"During the war," was the answer, "when I was convalesing. I walked all one bloody hot afternoon just like to-day's going to be. And when I got to Malvern about six, half-dead, covered with dust, throat like an oven and tongue hanging out, I knocked at a pub door and asked them if they were open yet? D'you know what they said?"

"No," we both remarked.

"My God, I shall never forget it. They said they'd been open all the bloody day. My God, I *was* fed up. They didn't have those regulations down there until long after the other parts of England."

"They didn't in Somerset either," said his friend.

"Didn't they?"

"No, I was down there on leave. I remember I climbed Keynsham Church tower."

"Did you?"

"Yes; you can see Weston-super-Mare from there."

"What the hell would anybody want to do that for?"

To that there was no answer. The check seemed to remind them that they had business elsewhere, and with a last swallow and a "Good-bye, Walter," to the landlord, they hurried out.

I was alone again; but when Aubrey, deeply engaged, glanced in my direction to see if I were happy, I made a sign of reassurance, for I was already overhearing a conversation between two elderly, heavily moustached men, in working clothes, and one veteran in shabby mufti, who were clasping glass pints on a bench against the wall on my other side.

They appeared to be talking about horses.

"Give me Park 'Ero," said one.

" 'E's all right," agreed the second, "but Solidity'll beat 'im any time."

"Excelsior's every bit as good as Solidity. 'E's a good 'un, 'e be," wheezed the old man, "but I puts my money on Ailsa Craig."

"Ay," said the other two in unison, "that be a good 'un, that be."

I was puzzled. It wasn't so much that I didn't know the names of any of the horses; Ailsa Craig sounded very much like the name of a Grand National winner—though I couldn't recollect the year and, anyhow, the flat-racing season was still on. There might be a local meeting, and I might not know the names of any horses running at local meetings, such as those of Newton Abbot, Wincanton, or almost any cathedral town. What beat me is that there should be a local meeting on and that Aubrey should not have tried to persuade, and indeed have persuaded, me to go to it.

"Newnham Park," I heard in a husky voice; then, "What about White Lisbon?"

They all sounded likely nags to me; though, like the ancient, I couldn't help fancying Ailsa Craig, a winner's name if ever there was one. "Just as Colombo's was," I reflected, then remembered that Colombo didn't win.

I was just wondering whether to sound the landlord about a flutter, when Aubrey, shouting for another drink, rejoined me. "Sorry, old man," he said, "I've been trying to sell old Bob a pig."

"Don't mention it," I replied, "I've been having a grand time. I say, is there any racing on to-day?"

"Not that I know of," was his answer, "unless there's something at Catterick, or Carlisle, or Ayr, or one of those damned places up north that I never touch."

"Well," I said, putting my hand on his sleeve, "just listen to those men over there."

We listened. Another man, tall, lean, clad in cap, keeper's coat and leggings, had joined them and was being temporarily called in as arbiter. "What do you think, Sid?" they asked him.

"If you want to know what I think," he replied with a shrug and lifted eyebrows, "I don't think there's anything to beat Giant Lemon Rocker . . ." (I shrank at this unorthodox name for horse, mare, colt, filly or gelding.) "James's Keepings, or Sutton's Improved Reading."

I couldn't adjust. I turned to Aubrey and stammered: "What on earth are they talking about?"

Aubrey's face had gone red. His tankard flourished in the air. His eyes closed, his mouth opened, and chuckles worthy of Sir Toby Belch rose from the depths of his throat. With bursts of chuckling coming between every word, he managed to say: "Dear old soul, they're not talking about horses, they're talking about onions." He summoned all within sight to a drink to my health. I was greatly embarrassed, but I hope that I carried it off.

I had had enough of this place, and wanted to get on. "What about that bus you mentioned?" I enquired.

"There isn't another bus for two hours, and if you wait for that you'll have to spend the last hour waiting outside on the gravel," replied Aubrey, commiseratingly.

"But you said there was a bus!" I reminded him, angrily.

"So there was," he said. "Didn't you hear it come up and go away half an hour ago? Didn't you see those two chaps in plus-fours rush out to catch it? As usual, I suppose, you were deep in conversation."

It was one o'clock. My whole programme for the day had been spoilt. There, on the floor in the corner, was my knapsack, but there, outside, was the car. "Look here," he said, "you'd much better come back to the farm to lunch. I've got some fish on board, and, if you really must, you can walk back to Winchester in the cool of the evening and sleep at the 'God Begot.'"

Through my head there ran some rhymes which I had written long ago and never printed, and which had a refrain beginning "Sheep as a Lamb, Sheep as a Lamb." "No more friends on this journey, I sincerely hope," was my next reflection; but aloud I said: "All right, Aubrey, it won't make much difference, so long as I get to Devon on the day I said I would. And it is hot, I admit, and I am still stiff."

A complacency of foreknowledge shone across his face. "Of

c

course," he cooed, "I knew you'd come back. It's all rot you
were talking about having to go on. I knew it was all the
time; we can get back for lunch at three. The worst of you
men who've got tangled up in engagements . . ."

But by this time we were out and mounting the car, my
knapsack going into the dickey with the beer and fish. "There
in no time," said Aubrey resolutely; we whizzed off, skimmed
round corners, mounted hills, skirted woods, and quite
definitely were.

Sally was on the doorstep as soon as the car reached it,
while the dogs yelped and bayed all round. "Mr. Aubrey said
you'd be sure to be back, sir," she said, welcoming me in the
most humiliating manner.

I very nearly went away, sulkily. In other words, I didn't.

This time it was fillet of sole, fried potatoes, and Double
Gloucester; then coffee and brandy in the sitting-room. "I
say," I said suddenly, "I really must get back into Winchester
to-night. Do you mind if I go and lie down just for two
hours; I'm still pretty tired."

"Certainly not," said Aubrey. "I'll wake you at six, and
then we can go over and see George."

I mumbled: "Yes, splendid," though there was nobody in
the world whom I wanted to see less than George, who, anyhow, I reflected with bitterness, was only a fat facetious
farmer, and I went upstairs, took off coat and shoes, put the
eiderdown over me, and relapsed into a dream of racing
horses with onions' heads and glaring lobsters' eyes on stalks,
all heading for my hapless self.

When I awoke, the full daylight was still streaming through
the windows. I rose, rinsed my face, and descended the stairs.
Aubrey was deep in an armchair with a bottle of beer beside
him, several books open on a table at his other hand, and an
exercise book on his knee. His head was down and he was
industriously writing. I felt like retiring, he looked so busy;
but, hearing me, he flung everything down, exclaimed: "Only
filling up the time with a few more notes on my *History of
the Thoroughbred,*" and added: "Well, if you're ready; supper
isn't till eight and I hope you won't mind cold bacon again,

and we might as well go and look them up at the 'Hare and Hounds.' "

I forgot, at any rate I did not mind forgetting, my resolution to proceed to Winchester that night. "But," I rejoined, "I thought you said we were going over to see George?"

"What, didn't I tell you?" he asked, surprised. "I thought I'd told you George has been off all day buying beasts near Basingstoke, and he won't be back till late."

There was no point in arguing, though such deceitfulness deserved rebuke. Once more the car was started and o'er moor and torrent, we reached the "Hare and Hounds." As we entered it loud voices, very late in the day, were discussing Larwood, Jardine, and the leg-theory; to my surprise, in the middle of the group, I saw the Gargantuan form of George, complete with his old school tie, vast expanse of yellow suit, and little eyes sunk deep in his pig-like face.

"Well, well, well!" gurgled George, extending a hand to each of us.

"Thought you were up around Basingstoke, George," said Aubrey.

"Beasts too dear, everything's too dear," said George. "I just came away. What'll you have?"

A confidential sermon on farming followed, from which I could only deduce that everything was at once too dear and too cheap; but we soon got back to cricket, and harmony with "dear old Maurice Read." Two hours flashed by in a general din, when Aubrey, who had been doing a circuit of the bar, came up cheerfully and said: "Look here, if you aren't hungry, I am." I was, and said so.

Shadows gathering, we drove back once more to the cold bacon. Something had changed Aubrey's mood. The silence in which he ate his meal was not the silence of appetite but the silence of worry. I felt uneasy; his brows were knitted, he ate, as it were, vindictively, and he looked as though he had something on his mind. When we settled down in the sitting-room he was uncharacteristically offhand when Sally brought in the coffee, saying: "Just put it down there and bring us in a bottle of claret and two glasses." "Good night, sir," said Sally, with unusual reserve, as she set the last things down. "Good night," he replied abstractedly, with his chin upon his hands and his eyes staring forwards and downwards. In the lamplight the sporting prints looked down on him compassionately; the old furniture was undisturbed.

I watched him with an unaccustomed scrutiny. That usually jolly and care-free face had become suddenly sombre and brooding.

He threw away a cigarette impatiently, and lit another. Then he turned to me and, speaking in a slow incisive voice, said: "Do you suppose that any of those chaps we saw to-day ever *think?*"

"I don't know," I replied. "I expect they do, when they're in trouble or in the silent watches of the night. I expect that everybody does who isn't a mere animal. You can't very well suffer without wondering why, or meditate alone without wondering where you came from."

"I've been worrying about it lately," said he, whom I had always supposed to concern himself only about cricket, beer, the crops, the garden, racing, and the utterly damnable eating-up of England by speculative builders, taxation, and the urban mind.

"About what?" I asked.

"About Truth," said he, "about what it's all about."

There flashed through my mind an old *Punch* dialogue: "What abart it?"—"Well, what abart what?"—"Well, what abart what you said abart me?" I checked myself, on grounds of tact and consideration, from repeating it, as flippancy, at the moment, would have been no balm for him. Nor did I remind him of the happiness of his diurnal pursuits; for he was aware of that, and trying, if not to escape from it, to relate it in some manner to the unhappiness of others, to the Universe, and to the ultimate mysteries of Death, Evil, and that wavering thing, the Categorical Imperative, which is (or was) a Prussian name for Duty and Conscience. Had it been earlier in the day and he in another mood I might have fetched his Bible (probably kept between Pitcher and Mrs. Earle) and read to him from the seventeenth chapter of the Gospel according to St. John. But I was his guest, I had to consort to his mood, I had (if possible) to cheer him up. I remembered that both St. Augustine and Cardinal Newman had had their doubts and guessed that St. Ignatius had had his, and I felt that, as his faith was waning with the night, the best thing I could do would be to sympathize with his scepticism and put the jolliest face possible upon that state of mind which was habitual to Pyrrho and the late Lord Balfour, and, probably, to the late Pontius Pilate. "Did I ever," I asked him, lighting a preparatory cigarette, pouring out another glass, and wishing there were a log to kick into a blazing fire, "tell you about that night I spent in Venice?"

"I suppose you mean you talked to a Catholic priest?" he replied, with the sullenness of the man who has been on the verge of Catholicism all his life.

"Nothing of the sort," I remarked, soothingly, "it's only that I had a dream and I don't know whether it was a dream."

"That sounds pretty good nonsense," he retorted, already resuming some semblance of his normal hearty, combative self.

"Not at all," I proceeded. "Did you ever hear of Chuang Tzu?" There was a long pause.

"No; I suppose he was a Chinese philosopher?"

"An easy guess, and quite correct. He lived some thousands of years ago. It is reported of him that when the Emperor (it was about the time when the earliest fine pots were made, which fetch so much in Boston) sent emissaries to ask him to be viceroy of a province, he replied that he was too busy watching a frog dive into a lily-pond. But there is also extant a story about him saying that he had dreamt he was a butterfly and that, for the rest of his life, he would not know whether he was a man dreaming that he was a butterfly or a butterfly dreaming that he was a man."

"Tight, I expect," said Aubrey surprisingly, with his usual gurgling laugh.

"Not at all," said I; "he knew a lot more about it than most of our modern philosophers, let alone all the business men to whom you object. But am I to go on with my story?"

"Carry on," said Aubrey, encouragingly, and emerging so far from his gloom as to fill his glass to the brim, "what was it?"

"You seem to have forgotten rather rapidly. But it doesn't matter: I will go on. I will tell you what happened to me in Venice."

"Leave out anything you don't want to tell," he interrupted, with some coarseness. I was tempted to reply rather hotly, but remembered that I was playing the game of distracting him, and merely remarked: "Now, are you going to listen?"

"Of course I am, old boy," he responded. "Carry on."

"Well," I went on mollified, "you can hear about my meeting with Truth, which I don't know whether it was a dream or not." Aubrey murmured something about grammar, but I went on, taking no notice.

"It had been," I said, adopting that artificial crooning voice which is usual with English people who think they are using poetical words, "a perfect evening after a long train journey. Dinner over the Lagoon, with the Maritime Customs House and Santa Maria della Salute, ornate but dignified, peacefully reposing across the end of the Grand Canal; an hour on the balcony, watching the pearl-grey of the far waters and sea-green of the near ones flushed red by the sunset and then dwindling into darkness, crossed by rippling plates of gold; then good night, early to bed, comfortable sheets, and a pink-shaded light on the little bedside table.

" 'I can't go to sleep yet,' I thought. 'Venice is much too lovely and I want to lie and think about it.' "

"Quite right," observed Aubrey, sipping his claret with his eyes closed, "but, I say, old boy, are you reading this?"

"No, I'm not! You can't expect me to talk about Venice in your Kempton Park slang, can you?"

"I didn't mean any offence. But there are rather a lot of adjectives, aren't there?"

"Venice is built of adjectives; am I to go on, or am I not?"

"Why, certainly, I am getting interested."

"Well, prove it by keeping your mouth shut. Now listen! Besides that, the motor-boats were still roaring up and down the waters. Not quite so good as the Bucentaur from which a thousand years of Doges married the Republic with golden rings. What should I read, I thought? I was in pyjamas and much too comfortable to dress again and wander downstairs to search the hotel library for a Wodehouse I had often read before or a Tauchnitz Elinor Glyn. I had a small attaché case with me as well as my large trunk; I remembered cramming papers into it as I left the train. So I reluctantly got out of bed, fetched the case, detached (with difficulty) the lock, undid two straps and unveiled the contents.

"There were two evening papers, bought at twelve o'clock on Tuesday morning, dated at five o'clock on Tuesday evening and definitely the worse for wear on Wednesday night. There was an *Illustrated London News*. I had read it through: coloured pictures of the latest-discovered head-dresses of Queens of Ur and the latest-found pots from Peru. Odds and ends also there were; but, at the bottom of the pile, there was *Truth*."

"Good God, Jack!" exclaimed Aubrey. "You don't mean you still take up *Truth*?"

"I don't see how that can concern you," I said. "I remember it longer than you can! My mother must have introduced it to my infant notice at about the same time as she tried to make me understand whist, solo-whist, euchre, nap, the poetry of Longfellow and Scott, and Racine. Being young (and I expect you to remember this, too), I did not relate the cover to the contents. On the cover was the figure which you can still see there; inside, after the accounts of royal movements, Admiralty improvements, Indian army promotions and questions about the law, there were paragraphs (and occasionally leaders) about crooked company-promoters, money-lenders, reverend bogus-charity swindlers, which fascinated me then and fascinate me still. But I never troubled, as a child, to relate the cover of *Truth* to truth itself. I was content to think of her as a goddess, virtuous and impeccable.

"So, in my room at Venice, with night outside and that

august circle of pink palaces ringed round the many-islanded lagoon, I picked up *Truth*. I did not look once more at the inside—I simply looked at the cover."

"I will say that about *Truth*," remarked my conservative friend, "that they do stick to their old cover instead of always changing it like all those other damned papers."

"You are quite right. And there my attention dwelt. Truth was represented (in the tradition of Florence Nightingale but with much less than her ferocity) as a yearning, aspiring feminist. She had a severe, though decent, face; her hair was parted in the middle; her dress was Greek (or rather, Grecian) and fell in respectable folds over her bosom and limbs Over her head, with her left hand, she held a Roman lamp. Serene, austere, severe. I looked at her from my pillow and I thought: 'Can this figure, which I have known from my childhood, and which has cast such a spell over me, really be Truth?' In my youth I thought she was; and I didn't try to reconcile her to the money-lenders. Truth was one thing and this life was another; the Synthesis need not be made. In my bed, in Venice, trying to be honest I looked at her again."

"Now you know, Aubrey, I hate to use words like 'schoolmarm.' It simply isn't English. But that woman. One can just hear her, as the head-mistress of the Athens High School, saying to her pupils: 'Well, of course, girls, hockey isn't everything, but I do hope we shall beat the Old Palladians on Saturday, and I expect every girl in the school to turn up and cheer. In spite of what all the moderns say, there is really something about loyalty. I think I hear Diana in the back row, tittering; as I do not believe in punishment I shall inflict no punishment, but I hope Diana will remember this rebuke.' Contemplating that figure I heard all this and more. My thoughts drifted far away from the sage-green covers of *Truth*. I don't know where I went—I was thinking only about truth, and the stars, and God.

"Now a strange thing happened, Aubrey. I suddenly sat up: in the bed where I had been before. There was a kind of whirling in the air. The lights went round, and then they settled down. Rather puzzled, I re-settled myself as the disturbance subsided and my glance fell on the cover of *Truth,* still in my hand. Then I looked across at a dim little picture on the opposite wall which I suspected to be 'A Village in Surrey.' Vaguely from somewhere on the right I heard a tremolo voice, like a voice in dreams. It said: 'Oh yes! and——?'

"I started, leapt, turned. 'Oh my God—what's that?' came instantaneously through my mind, with thoughts of demons, ghosts, and fetches. As I turned the voice said mockingly: 'Sorry you've been troubled!' Simultaneously I was troubled even more. For there stood between me and the door a tall slim young woman, of perhaps twenty-eight, as cool as a cucumber and with every reason for her coolness. Her hair was red—neither purple-red nor yellow-red—but even at that I could not have taken my oath as to whether it was dyed or not. She had pointed cheeks, a pointed chin, a long neck, small pointed breasts, pointed shoulders, pointed hips; her eyebrows were raised, her eyelids lowered, her nostrils tinged with disdain. Her chin was strongly-cloven, her eyes cold and hard. 'I'm glad you've noticed me at last,' she said. 'You see, I'm Truth.' "

"I believe I've met that girl in Fitzroy Street," said Aubrey reminiscently; "let me fill your glass. Carry on; I want to know what's going to happen next. I know what would happen if it were Anatole France all right."

"Well, it isn't!" I said, "and so do I. All right. Yes, that will do. Well, I suppose I shall have to remind you again that I was in a room in Venice and had been tucking myself into bed and I was going to sleep in two minutes and it was infernally unfair that an unexpected visitor should consider herself expected. 'Look here,' I said, 'I don't want to be rude to a lady—but what in the devil are you doing here?'

"Against the remoter wall she displayed herself in all her downy and disdainful glory, and then she came to the side of the bed and glowered over me. That red head leant over me; those eyes leered; those flexible lips conjured me; and then Truth leapt into the bed."

Aubrey started to speak.

c*

"Look here," I said, half rising, "if you interrupt again I shall go upstairs——"

"I'm so sorry," he replied apologetically, "I swear I won't say another word until you've finished. Just carry on." Mollified, I proceeded.

"It was an extremely uncomfortable situation. But one must accommodate oneself to everything that turns up, and I tried to accommodate myself to this. 'I say,' I said, 'I do hope you're warm enough; wouldn't you like—er—a rug——?' She wriggled and snuggled and her crimson hair spread in twists over the pillow. 'Please don't bother,' said she, 'don't you see, I spend most of my life naked, and a great deal of it up to my neck in water——' and here she shuddered—'and it's a lovely change for me to be in a comfortable bed.' She appeared to forget me altogether and stared at the ceiling, as though neither I nor anything else (except all things) existed. This went on for five minutes or so. Then I began to reflect that, after all, it was my room and my bed, and I was entitled to go to sleep untroubled. The clock was ticking; the gondolas, now rare, splashed by; I was going to the ancient cathedral of Torcello in the morning; why on earth should I be kept awake by a total stranger who had invaded my room, not even explaining who she was or why she had come?

"It took me a long time to make up my mind. But I couldn't go to sleep with that compromising creature there; after all, she might be seen by a maid, and then where should I be? Ruthlessly, and in spite of her probably bogus snores, I nudged her in the ribs. She appeared to wake, though I don't believe she had ever been asleep, passed her fingers over her eyes, turned toward me, gazing dreamily, and said: 'Sorry, what is it?'

" 'Look here,' I said, 'you say you are Truth, and I daresay you are, but I don't see why you shouldn't observe the ordinary courtesies and decencies of life.' Sleepily she replied: 'Oh yeah!'

"The Americanism stung me. I had always thought that Truth would talk English, or (at the worst) French. What on earth have I got mixed up with, thought I, and how can I get rid of this perfectly awful woman? But at that moment, in spite of her affectation of an American accent, she was looking rather gentle and charming. I thought: 'Damn it all, tiresome as she is, she isn't so bad. Can't I give her something she'd like?' I thought of fruit—there was some in the room, ripe pears and apples. I touched her sleepy head: 'Would you like an apple?' I said.

"She sat up at once. I reached out for an apple from the table.

" 'I should jolly well think so,' she replied, taking it, 'considering (at any rate, according to one story) that if it hadn't been for apples nobody would have bothered about me at all.'

" 'Oh, don't say that,' said I impetuously. 'People couldn't have overlooked a person like you for long.' 'Nonsense,' she replied, taking a great bite out of the apple.

"She closed her eyes and munched it contentedly. A distant chugging from the direction of the Lido reminded me of the outside world and the oddity of the situation. There was I, propped on my elbow, contemplating the pretty face of a completely strange young woman with a half-eaten apple in her hand and an expression of utter insouciance on her face. Insouciance! thought I, it almost amounts to impudence! And then I realised that the red of her lips was paint, and that her old-gold complexion was not entirely innocent of powder. How could Truth thus lie? I reflected. Minutes passed, she resting immobile in the silence and the rosy light.

"Suddenly her eyes opened, her eyebrows lifted, she pouted and shot a mocking glance at me. 'You don't seem to have much to say to a girl,' she remarked; 'I must have been mistaken when I thought you liked me.' I deserved it, I knew. 'Oh,' I said, 'I'm frightfully sorry, how dreadfully rude of me! I was thinking about you, really. Would you think it insolent of me if I asked you an absolutely straight question, as man to man?'

" 'As man to what?' she asked with quiet disdain. I felt myself flush, as so often, with anger. 'I do wish you wouldn't pick one up so! You know quite well what I mean.'

" 'All right, don't be annoyed,' she returned; 'what was it you wanted to know?' 'Well, just this—and I don't care if you get in a rage with me or not: how can you be Truth when you use make-up?'

" 'Oh, is that all?' she replied. 'That's quite easy. It's just to show that you mustn't judge by appearances. Have you ever read Bradley's *Appearance and Reality?*"

"I admitted that I had, but that youth had been my excuse. But I discovered early, I added, that I wasn't meant for philosophy. 'Nor are the philosophers,' she replied. 'Look, I ask you, at the complications of that Bradley. Can you really think I'm as dull and confused as all that? As a matter of fact, I'm a simple girl, I am.'

"I felt indignant and sympathetic towards all the philosophers who, for thousands of years, had adored their imaginary pictures of this minx, and spent their whole lives looking for her. Ungrateful creature, thought I; even if she *is* a goddess she doesn't deserve to be one. My cynicism expressed itself. 'Can I offer you a cigarette?' I asked, reaching out for one from the table on my left. 'Other girls may—I don't,' she remarked contemptuously. Checked and chilled I removed my proffered hand and smoke. 'Oh, for God's sake don't take me literally,' she snapped. 'Of course I'll have one.'

"Patient as ever I returned the cigarette and painstakingly lit it. She puffed. 'Now look here——' she began. 'Yes?' said I. 'Damn you and your yesses,' she snarled. 'Are you listening?' 'Of course I'm listening,' I replied, 'and in any case, since you weren't asked to come in here, and are robbing me of my sleep, you might at least keep a civil tongue in your head.' This seemed to soften her; I got the impression that she rather liked people to stand up to her.

" 'Don't get angry,' she observed, in a quite mild tone. 'It's only my way. Haven't you heard I'm stranger than fiction? Besides,' she added, completely bewildering me, 'it all helps to create atmosphere, doesn't it?' Unable to think of any other answer I naturally, and humbly, replied: 'Oh yes, of course. Yes.' 'Now you're being sensible,' she said. And then flinging the cigarette on the floor, and sitting up with an exposed torso (which embarrassed neither of us, as we were thinking of the things of the mind), 'I'm absolutely sick of lying in this prone position. I want to talk to you, my lad.' 'All right; lovely!' said I. 'You mayn't think it so lovely after all,' she remarked; 'I might as well come straight to the point.' 'Please do,' said I, in the emphatic accents which a man uses when he is utterly at a loss as to how to be pleasant to a pretty but puzzling woman.

"She sat upright in the bed. I, happily covered by my pyjama-coat, sat up too, wondering what on earth was going to come next. She stared straight in front of her as though she were gazing through the opposite wall, dressing-table mirror, country-side views and all. 'Are you prepared,' she enquired, 'for me to talk to you quite seriously?' 'Why on earth not?' I asked impatiently. 'All right,' she went on, 'don't get hot and bothered! But it appears to me you attach too much importance to all those silly philosophers . . . give me another cigarette.'

"I gave her another cigarette, lighted it, dimly apprehended the humming of a motor-boat far out on the lagoon, and then stuck up for myself. 'I don't know,' I said, 'why you should single me out as one who stands up for the philosophers. In point of fact there are a great many people who stand up for them much more than I do. But, since you force me to say something, I don't think they're too bad. After all, even if they never really understood you, they did love you and try to understand.' 'Love—my foot!' said she inelegantly, 'they didn't care two hoots about me—they only loved their own silly ideas!' 'That's very unfair!' I replied. 'Dash it all, think of Plato who dedicated his whole life to you!'

" 'Oh yes, Life and Works,' she interrupted, with a worse sneer than any she had worn before, 'Plato, potato. Ideas and all that. Do you really suppose that I'd reveal myself to a man who gave rise to an adjective like "platonic"?'

" 'Please, please, please!' I observed, 'don't get excited. I only want a quiet talk—I simply want to get at the truth.'

" 'Well, aren't I the Truth?' she observed. 'Of course, my dear, I know you are,' I answered, 'but I want you to be fair to the people who have spent their lives loving and looking for you, instead of seeming to keep something up your sleeve.' 'I don't care tuppence for the lot of them,' she retorted; 'besides, I've never had a sleeve, so how can I keep anything up it?' She lay down and snuggled under the bed-clothes.

"Furious, and resolved not to be baffled, I grabbed her round the waist, sat her up, and said: 'Sleep if you want to, you can sleep in five minutes, but you're jolly well not going to until you've answered a few questions I want to ask *you*. . . .' She rose and looked at me almost flirtatiously. 'Very well, sir,' said she, in the accents of a subservient chambermaid.

" 'Well,' said I, 'I know it's late and I know you're tired, and I don't want to be discourteous. But anyhow, I didn't ask you to come here—you've been a damned nuisance, and I think I'm entitled——' A tremulous smile went over her lids and lips, her head now again resting on the pillow. 'Remember the Old School tie!' she whispered. 'I could wring your neck!' I exclaimed, exasperated.

" 'Everybody would like to wring Truth's neck,' she replied. 'But somehow, nobody ever succeeds in doing it. She always will prevail, you know.' I wanted to, but as I looked at her I knew I simply couldn't. 'Yes,' I said, 'I quite agree. Nothing would please me better than wringing your neck, but I can't do it, and that's that. You are being too annoying for words. You might at least answer the few simple questions I want to ask you.' She wriggled sleepily on the pillow, momentarily unveiled a pair of far from sleepy eyes, shut them again and said: 'All right. I didn't say I wouldn't answer them, did I?' Lord, these women! I thought, but after all, especially in the presence of Truth, one must face facts as one finds them. So I put it to her.

" 'Now listen!' I said, 'I don't care whether you go or stay, but you've got to admit that you've been grossly unfair to those poor old gentlemen who've done their best for you.' 'High bald domes and long white beards!' came the murmur from the pillow. 'You've ridiculed Plato——' I insisted. 'Oh, *go* on,' she said, 'just go on like all the other silly men who fall in love with illusions. If you want to know, I couldn't stand Plato at any price. He was simply a dreamer.' 'Well,' said I, 'at least you can't say that about Aristotle.' She shook her head on the pillow. 'Oh, for God's sake,' she muttered, 'don't talk to me about Aristotle. He was almost as bad as Bacon.'

" 'Surely both of them cared about Truth?' I queried. She flung herself up and cried: 'They didn't! They didn't! They didn't! They didn't care for me one little bit; they only cared about facts, for all their beastly brains.' She collapsed back on the pillow and sobbed and sobbed. 'All you do,' she lamented, 'is to pity all those silly old men and you don't think at all about what I've suffered at their hands. You men are all the same!' It's difficult enough, as every grown man knows, to console and comfort even a woman with whom one is intimately acquainted, but think of consoling a *déesse incomprise*, a refractory female whom one has never met before, and a border-line goddess at that. There was still the throbbing of a motor-boat on the lagoon; I looked at the still face and the recumbent form and I simply didn't know what to say. My problem was resolved by the lady. She peeped over her arm. "I wonder, dearie,' she said in a cajoling manner, 'that you didn't mention Schopenhauer.'

" 'Well,' I said, stumblingly, 'I don't much like him myself, and I think he must have been dyspeptic, but I do think he cared for you and that you ought to honour him.' She sprang up until she was almost out of the bed, her face contorted, her mouth working, her eyes as red as a ferret's. 'What!' she yelled, 'that horrible German beast? Why, he was a woman-hater!' Soothingly, her voice changed; in an enchantress's manner she said: 'Do *you* think I'm ugly?'

"I leant over her, as languorously she lay, and saw her face change from beauty to beauty; now that of a proud Egyptian queen, now that of a mysterious sibyl, now that of the soul of knowledge, now that of the soul of love, now that of a demure young virgin, innocent and wistful, early Florentine. In that one face, in that one minute, I saw all earthly and unearthly beauties.

" 'How,' thought I, 'could I ever have doubted this woman? Why should such a brute as myself have been vouchsafed such a vision?'

"She opened her eyes.

" 'Well,' said she, 'did you like it?'

"I couldn't answer.

" 'Anyhow,' she continued, 'do *you* think I'm ugly?'

" 'Goodness, goodness no!' I exclaimed, 'you're the loveliest thing that ever I saw in my life!'

" 'That's just where you're mistaken,' she remarked, very slowly and solemnly; and facing me square, squeezing up her eyes, projecting her lower jaw, and thrusting out her tongue between teeth that suddenly seemed to have grown like fangs: 'I can look like this, my boy, and don't you forget it! Oh no, it's no good thinking of hitting me. Even if you tried to, you couldn't hit *me!*'

" 'I wasn't even thinking of hitting you,' I grumbled.

" 'Don't lie!' she said. 'You can't take Truth in by lies, you know.'

" 'I wasn't lying!' I said.

" 'Don't lie again,' said she, looking as cunning as Satan. Then she turned her face into an image of The Soul's Awakening.

" 'I'm not lying!' I almost shouted; 'I'm only trying to understand you. You come in here and rob me of my sleep and I do my damnedest to find out what you want and I honestly think if you'd stay long enough and explain it I might be able to produce it, and it's horribly unfair of you to be evasive and elusive. I also think it's unfair of you to be so abusive about those unfortunate philosophers who only tried to do their best for you.'

"She leapt out of the bed.

" 'If anybody ever catches *me*,' she said disdainfully, "it will be a poet!'

"I moved to spring after her.

" 'Why shouldn't it be me?' I cried.

" 'Stay where you are!' she cried imperatively, stretching herself to her full naked height. I stayed where I was, as though shackled by iron.

" 'Sorry old thing!' she said, 'I've got to get back to my well!'

"Of course, she had the last word. Raising both arms and crooking both elbows she snapped the thumbs and fingers of both hands. There was a kind of whirling in the air, the lights swam, and when they settled down again she was gone.

"But there I was, in the bedroom of a Venetian hotel, with the water lapping against the sides of the moored gondolas and one solitary motor-boat humming far off in the distance. My hand automatically stretched out. It caught a paper; I lifted it up and gazed again at the effigy on the cover—that erect, virtuous, innocuous, sexless, lamp-bearing personality—so straight, so incapable of humour, beauty, wit or cruelty.

" 'You call yourself Truth,' I murmured, 'but little do you know what Truth really is!' "

*   *   *   *   *

It is all very well. But would you believe it? Just when I had finished telling Aubrey the story about my dream (if dream it was) I put out a hand in gesticulation, heard a dim crash, sprang up, listened for footsteps with a palpitating heart, switched on the bed-head light and saw the floor strewn with books, fruit, plate, knife and broken glass, and realized that I had never told Aubrey the story at all, that I had dreamt I had told him about my dream (if it was a dream), that I had gone to bed and that I had no dialogue with him at all! All the comments he had made; all my impatient retorts (not here recorded) about Anatole France's easy play with easy erudition, references to Tanagra statuettes and the philosophic fragments of Hypodermos of Syringa, were the mere smoke of slumber.

Happily it hadn't been a nightmare; I hadn't been falling over cliffs, fighting goblins who came together when hewn to pieces, or taking ten giant crocodiles on at once; so I re-arranged my pillows, turned out the light, curled up, and did not wake again until——

FOURTH DAY

ONCE more the sunshine was streaming through the window, and Aubrey was standing there in a florid silk red dressing-gown, carrying an equally florid blue one for me.

"Look here, Aubrey," I said, "I can't tell you how I've enjoyed my stay here. When I set out I thought I might see somebody in Kent and somebody in Wiltshire; but it was ever so much nicer seeing you."

"All right," said he, "but you must have breakfast before you go; what about a little cold bacon?"

Cold bacon it was, with the kind of chopped-up potatoes that I knew in Devonshire when I was a boy. Gorged, I remarked: "Old thing, it's extraordinary nice being here, but I simply must get on, for I have promised to be in Devonshire by a certain date."

"All right," he commented sulkily, "if you must go, you must go. I expect you will go farther and fare worse; but have it your own way."

He looked rather pathetic. It might be months before anybody who knew his primary language turned up again: he had his farm, his books, his Sally, and his neighbours, but all the winter might pass before he met another man who had heard of Baudelaire and Verlaine, let alone translating them at school. I was sorry for him (just as I was envious of him —he the Settled, I the Visitor, on and over the land we both loved) but I really had to remember that I was a householder with a programme, a father with a family, and an author with a contract.

So I set my upper lip and, to the epilogue of an orchestra of barking dogs, left him for the second time.

I went out of the village. I remembered, as I went, a poem which I had written when I was young, all about a man walking out of a village to the rainy hills, remembering the old gaffers and grannies, the blacksmith's shop, the old oak with the immemorial seat under it and the dogs asleep on the door-steps in the middle of the day. That poem I never published, for I knew it was false; I preferred *Cranford* and Miss Mitford, and thought that the dogs were sensible to lie on the doorsteps in the idle of the day. But now I was forsaking all the comfort which was open to me to go off into the . . .

But of course I wasn't going "off into the . . ."

The world is getting gradually (I think it is the word) "taped." Young men wander, with cameras, through Chinese Turkestan and the Gran Chaco, and come back rather bored, to talk deprecatingly at cocktail parties about places concerning which Sir John Mandeville mightily lied, and of which all Othello knew was that there were people there who ate strange flesh, and others whose heads grew beneath their shoulders—whom we now knew not to have existed, whatever may have been the truth in Othello's time. All I was doing, never having heard the Abyssinian bird sing at that season of the year or been tempted to shoot an albatross, was to set out on a walk, well furnished with clothes and money, in the easiest climate and country in the world, and able to stop when I liked and where I liked.

Stop I did; on the top of a hill which surveyed fields (which looked good partridge-fields) and woods, which seemed to offer, provided the keepers and beaters got the birds up properly, good pheasant shooting. On that summit I rested, at about twelve-thirty, and took out of my pocket a hunk of bread and the last (if, indeed, it was the last) of Aubrey's cold bacon.

* * * * *

Seated alone, with a world of downland and sky around me, I found myself thinking of shooting. It was August, and already in Scotland the annual campaign had begun; men were standing in butts, all their senses keyed up to animal intensity, and for months now the whole island would ring with shots.

Suddenly remembering, I took from my pocket some tattered scraps of paper which I had intermittently carried about with me for years whenever there seemed a chance of leisure for concentration and completion, and which I had deliberately brought with me this time. On a sparkling November morning, starting early across the uplands for a day's pheasant shooting, I had felt exalted by the freshness of the earth, stopped the car, and written down lines whose meaning was perhaps more implicit than explicit:

> Could something stir in the lines
> Of the dark pines,
> And the pale ponds,
> And the fronds
> Of the bracken that browns
> On the downs:
> Could a word come down from the sky
> So blue, so pure, and so high.

And that night I sat alone, in front of a fire, in my study and meditated on the day and the poetry of it.

At luncheon in a hut over a tree-girt lake, we had been talking, as shooting men sometimes do talk, about the pros and cons of the pursuit, reassuring ourselves with the usual commonplaces about pheasants dying as comfortably as farmyard fowls and the absurdity of meat-eating reformers attacking "blood sports." Somebody had said that, though he did occasionally like to let off his gun, he believed that the chief joy he found in a day's shooting was got between drives—all the wild life that was not shot and the lovely seclusion of preserves. Reflecting on all this alone I remembered many ecstatic moments I had had when shooting, twilights by duck-ponds, mornings on Scotch mountains, woodlands in mist, the glimpse of a wild deer in a Sussex thicket, the gorgeous feathers of a pheasant half-buried in deep snow, with drops of its blood looking like dry crimson dust on the soft whiteness. I was soon in a complex of memories and bewilderments, at one moment trying to recover a precise scene or train of thought and emotion, and at another wandering off in contemplation of the lives and deaths of birds and men; and then my mind harked back to the lines I had written in the morning and I thought they might be the opening of a poem on all the aspects of shooting and the vistas which it opens up, and in a heat of imagination I wrote, very rapidly, several disjointed passages which I thought might fit later into some shapely frame as yet undesigned.

There was a passage about watching a single high partridge coming over a hedge like a black star in the sky, and how, in its swift mounting approach it looks so intent and almost vindictive, like a bolt from the sling of an enemy, and how, the moment one goes to pick it up behind one, it seems so frail and harmless:

Here, alas!
Here it is on the grass.
Here dead did it fall;
And now lies so pathetic and small,
Weary small head, soft feathers, a little bird,
Such as long ago heard,
Standing eager and trustful arow,
(Heads up, being little) the happy miraculous words,
The voice of the tender St. Francis, so patient and slow
As he spoke to the birds:
As he told the small birds that brothers, though simple,
    they were,
And the Lord had a thought for the fate of each bird of
    the air;
Though three farthings each worth
It was known to the Lord as the greatest and proudest
    on earth. . . .
And he, 'neath the sky,
So vasty and frore,
Though a gown and a rope and a cowl and a halo he
    wore
Knew no more of the wherefore and why
Than the stupidest bird of them all.

He told them also (I thought) that men, like birds, were timid and feared for their children and fluttered in senseless alarm—and I remembered a place where all these thoughts had flashed through my head, simultaneously (for one's thoughts have no regard for consistency and decency) with the old jingle about Frederick, Prince of Wales:

> Here lies Fred.
> Who was alive and is dead,
> There's no more to be said.

I went to pick the bird up; everything was as it was a few seconds before when it was alive and flying. There was an orchard of apple trees behind, a few brave clinging leaves and ruddy globes of fruit. Beyond the trees was a farm, and a child calling to another; up the hillside a plough was jingling; a car moaned by; but the bird was dead and nothing could bring it to life; and another bird, though it knew nothing of death or destiny, would be cold without a mate. And I consoled myself with common-sense reflections about the universality of death, and the mercifulness of this as compared with what birds have to face from Nature—frost, shortage of berries or water, the murderous nips of stoat and rat and fox—and I recalled how often that partridge, in unnecessary fright, had flown as fast before, because of passing cars or labourers, and how it had never known it was alive, or even for a moment that it was seeing the sun for the last time.

All that, seasons ago, I had written down. And I had tried to recover in verse the whole thrill of expectation in a ride curving through copses—alone in the world with a gun, the other guns hidden somewhere, young bare trees all around, twigs and fallen leaves on the dry grass, a pale sky and silence everywhere. There is a long wait, and then a rustle, and then silence again. There is a distant cry, a distant shot, and then silence again; and then there is a loud rattle of leaves in front and an old cock patters up, pauses, starts again, stares, then hurries on stirring leaves as he goes. Another rustle and a rabbit goes back; a jay crooks away; a grey squirrel meets its end; and then tap-tap, tap-tap, far right and far left and in front, comes the slow, relentless advance of the beaters, and rustling becomes multitudinous, and sly phantoms can be descried darting about in the depths of the wood, the cunninger, stealthier, quicker, and some scuttle forward and run sideways, and come back because of the tapping and stop on the flank, and the beaters grow louder and louder, and at last there is nothing for it but to take wing and soar, and then amid halloes and fusillades they break out in swarms. . . .

For the hundredth time I looked at these fragments of paper high on that Hampshire down, and I knew at last that I should never finish them and why. What I had thought of was the sort of comprehensive poem that could really only be written in the mood and manner of the eighteenth century—the more intense moments would never "connect up." What *is* the good of keeping all these pieces of paper and backs of old envelopes with the pencil gradually rubbing off? Why be encumbered with what will never come to anything? With a pang I tore up some hundreds of lines, of which I now remember but few, and, out of respect for the Anti-Litter Campaign put them down a rabbit-hole. So if the really solid shooting poem is ever to be composed somebody else will have to do it.

As I went on my way I felt for a moment very much relieved. Why, when one is dead certain one will never finish a piece of work, does one waste time and trouble continually taking it up again in a sort of preposterous hope that by some miracle it will have shed its defects or even expanded, as though manuscripts could mature in storage, like wine, or sprout like seed potatoes? "Anyhow," I comforted myself, "what does it matter? there is a date to the durability even of the Venus di Milo, and I don't suppose this would have been that." Then I remembered the parable of the talents and the dying man who murmured: "So much to do, so little done," and then, for the ten thousandth time said, "down, devil, down" to hesitation and fruitless internal debate.

"Are you really going back to that rabbit-hole?"

"No."

"Well, forget all about it then, and remember, 'Would that he had blotted a thousand . . .'"

There was no wind. The great downs swelled away on both sides under a pure sky. I swung on and down to Winchester. There I thought of having one more look at Sir Herbert

Baker's beautiful (in spite of its difficult lettering) War Memorial Cloister: it seems a pity that we should have to owe such things as that and Giles Scott's grand chapel at Charterhouse to the deaths of the young. But I did not go. I went through Winchester without stopping, wondering if they were really going to scar Saint Catherine's Hill with a by-pass or some such road, a white weal. "Ten to one on," I thought; and wondered once more what maladies they were which made us destroy recklessly the beauty we have inherited, making long rural streets instead of villages, allow people to erect the vast majority of our buildings without employing an architect, and appoint more and more professors of Town Planning whilst doing less and less Town Planning and even destroying squares, terraces and crescents which were built by our ancestors who had never heard of Town Planning but merely did it. I searched my mind for examples in the past of villainies as bad as our own. After all there was that prime instance of Sir Christopher Wren who planned an entirely new London after the Fire, but the parsimonious and unimaginative tradesmen insisted on having the whole thing run up on precisely the same old lines, much to the detriment of modern traffic and of the eyesight of people in City offices. And think of the amount of destruction of our mediæval glories under Henry VIII, Edward VI, Cromwell, and by all the vandals of the eighteenth century! But the worst of it is that what they put up in the place of the old was not bad, and that even Nash himself, though no great architect with his stucco falsities, did plan and did put up harmonious things. It remained for the nineteenth century to discover architectural ugliness and for the twentieth to scatter it all over the place as from a pepper-pot and to spread it in straight lines beyond the urban centres with increasing rapidity. Think of the Great West Road ten years ago and now! It was virgin country with orchards; it might have been a string of pretty villages; it is now a jerry-builder's wilderness. Think of the even-newer Watford By-Pass, full of Baronial Halls and Cosy Palaces with new graves for peace and beauty being dug daily! Spirits of Adam Smith, Peel, Arkwright and Hargreaves behold your work! Spirit of Pugin, never come back to revisit these glimpses but keep company in the shades with Ruskin, Morris and the strong men before Agamemnon! But spirit of the Reverend Mr. Malthus, return to smile sardonically at the generations which have followed you and pullulate in these many-millioned towns without outlet!

I walked on, down a long tree-bordered hill, with the great dark branches of the trees motionless and a powder of golden sunlight coming between them in shafts as in an eighteenth-century landscape. It is still a peaceful road, with little to offend the eye; most of the westward traffic goes through Romsey.

The side-roads off it would be more peaceful still, and there is this compensation for great main roads (if not for the unholy messes that are made along them while officialdom turns its back and prosecutes people for selling chocolates five minutes after hours), that they do canalize motor-traffic, most of the drivers preferring to dash as fast and as far as possible. In a way main roads may be regarded as main drains for motorists; a man who chooses his roads carefully, whether walking or driving, may go as quietly as ever he did.

At five o'clock I was at Stockbridge, an unspoilt little place with a pleasant hotel which has a round portico, and a garden at the back, and is the headquarters of an ancient fishing club which fishes the Test. Had it been a little later I might have gone in and met, perhaps, over a tankard somebody who would have told me something about the season's fishing. I have never dropped fly, or for that matter (has anyone ever?) worm in that stream, as sacred in the eyes of some of my friends as ever was the Tiber to the ancient Romans. The Grosvenor is, as it were, the Capitol of the Test, and I should have had my small contribution to the talk, for years ago it was in the Test that I had seen the largest trout that—never having been to New Zealand, where they swell enormously like the red deer—I had ever seen in my life. It was at Long Parish, up by Whitchurch, when Guy Dawnay had it; a comfortable old house with a long stretch of the Test running through water meadows. As we walked along it in the afternoon the surface was covered with mallard, teal and moorhens, but I had no eyes for them, as wherever one looked into the clear stream there were monstrous fish, slowly waving their tails, which seem in recollection like dark torpedoes, and to have numbered hundreds. But that perhaps is the way of fish in recollection. What is certain is that that property (a revolting word—there are people who would call Windsor Castle a fine property) has seen things as remarkable as mammoth trout. It was in front of the drawing-room windows that a cuckoo settled on the hair of the owner's small daughter and laid an egg, a photograph of the strange event appearing later in *Country Life!* It was also the scene, a hundred years ago, of the last (as of many a previous) exploit of Colonel Peter Hawker who may have been, and by his own statement must have been, the greatest gameshot of all time, though he may not have accumulated the 600,000 odd head of the late Lord Ripon. He lived for shooting and his diaries are the raciest reading; he records with such complacency the way in which he would go out alone, with man and dog, and get thirty woodcock, snipe or partridges with as many shots. The trouble was he would shoot anything: the celebrated anecdote about the late Sir William Eden might well have been applied to him.

I remember when I was young a not very literate habitual burglar came to me for assistance and advice. He wanted a new leaf and a job. I asked him what steps he had already taken to obtain one, and he said he had applied to the then Home Secretary, Mr. Herbert Gladstone, for a job as a hangman. "What did you say to him?" I asked. "I sent 'im," said he, "a nice piece o' rope I'd made and told 'im that 'e could bring any man 'e liked to me, and I'd 'ang 'im." The letter, I daresay, was passed from basket to basket for comment; at any rate Charlie L. did not get the office. Peter Hawker, a man of similar scope, was on his death-bed. A bird perched on his window-sill. The window was open. The colonel asked weakly for his gun, which was always by his bedside. He raised it and fired. The bird fell. He had made his last kill. It was an owl.

I passed a road on the left leading to the Wallops—Nether Wallop, Middle Wallop and Over Wallop—and remembered that when I had first heard of them I had been sad that one of the new public schools had not been founded there. "Nether Wallop *v.* Birchington," at Lord's, should certainly have drawn the crowds. But, in point of fact, the Wallops are older than the verb they suggest. It was Sir John Wallop, of Wallop, who in the thirteenth century so smote the French at sea that he endowed the language with a new word like Captain Boycott, Mr. Hansom, Mr. Macadam, Mr. Macintosh and others. I was sorry I had not time for the Wallops; strung along their little stream they make as pretty and secluded a walk as any in these parts, though the incidental architectural beauties hardly compare with those of the hamlets which lie along the valley of the Coln in the Cotswolds. On the left past Lobscombe Corner there was a hill where part of a wood had been felled and was now in evening sunshine solid red with willow-herb which delights in clearings of all sorts. Then a mile or two more brought me to the Pheasant, south of which are the Winterslows, frequented by Hazlitt. Much as one may regret the way in which many brewers take down old inn-signs and replace them by unnecessary advertisements of, or unconscious warnings against, their own beer, and much as one applauds those who continue the old habit, I confess that the sign of this particular Pheasant seems to me rather too large. And thus was I meditating when I realised that the hour was late, that I was tired and very hungry, and that there was a bus coming up behind me.

Somebody else got out with her bundle; I got in with mine; and in a quarter of an hour I was in Salisbury. A few minutes more brought me to a hotel which Aubrey had mentioned to me as being much more suitable to me than the ancient hostelry which I had always used in the town and which he said (though he admitted he had never seen it) must be full of copper warming-pans, Americans, and the ghost of William Pitt. When I saw the Victorian pile he had sent me to I wondered at his taste; but I was tired, the place was no doubt comfortable to every sense except that of the eye, I took a room, sent my things to it, washed, had a latish dinner of soup, fried plaice and cheese, and then walked into the lounge, sat down and rang for coffee.

I looked around. There were several wicker chairs, three Scotch managers of engineering works (as I supposed—one had his back to me, the others were obvious) and the usual collection of unreadable papers. I didn't want to read until I went to bed, if then, and I wondered what to do with the next hour or so. I remembered the Close: how, long ago, having come on alone from Mells I had missed the man with whom I expected to stay, and wandered about Salisbury on a summer night, with few people in the sable-and-silver streets, golden lights in the upper windows, and come at last to the Close and seen that great spire fretted on the moonlight, and walked all round past the comfortable old houses, with here the soft music of a quartette behind blinds, and here an uncurtained window and a glimpse of shirt-fronts, mahogany and plate, and then walked off in the silence listening to the echo of my own foot-steps and thinking of a story, sad, but not altogether so, spring-ing from it all, which I wrote long afterwards. To-night there was no moon and I was tired; besides, one never should try to recapture perfection, though it should always be striven after, in any particular world, until it is attained.

I thought, feeling at once solitary and yet in no great need of actual talk (as the past and tenderness were upon me), that I might as well go through the corridor to the bar, sit in a corner, have a nightcap, and watch and listen to whatever habitués might be present. I threaded my way through, swung open a door, and there, confronting me as though I had come to my expected place, like the stars in the Ancient Mariner, were the rotund jocularity of Aubrey's face and the petite merriment of Sally's. Two tankards were waved at me. "Ha, ha, ha!" laughed Aubrey, his mouth wide, his eyes closed. "We've been waiting for you for an hour, but we knew you'd come. Where the devil were you when we passed you on the road?" He laughed again, as though his simple stratagem of recommending this hotel to me were an elaborate joke; I fully expected him to pull cold bacon or fish out of his pockets. But no, he had merely driven twenty-four miles or so (having presumably looked to his garden and done his quantum of the History of the Thoroughbred) in order to spring a small surprise; and when, just after, the barmaid announced: "Time, gentlemen, please!" he parted on the doorstep, and groaned off eastward quite happily, a warning against o'er-vaulting ambition and a testimonial to the simple life.

I went back to the wickerwork lounge. The two heavier of the Scotch engineering experts (if that they were) had gone off yawning to bed, having expressed all the usual opinions, doubts and alarms about France, Germany, the League, Italy and Signor Mussolini. The third remained, a major-in-the-Territorials-looking man, with tidy grey hair, bright sympathetic eyes, long vertical lines on his sallow cheeks, a close-cut grey moustache and an honest strong chin. He had obviously just ordered a last toddy and his glance invited conversation. I returned his look, pressed a bell, and came up and sat beside him, affecting to pick up an old number of an illustrated weekly. The waiter came in and I ordered. Asked the stranger: "Know this place well?"

"The town, yes," I said, "but this hotel, no. Staying long?"

"Only to-night; and you?"

"Only to-night. As a fact I'm walking to Devonshire. I suppose you and your friends are on a motor-tour?"

"In point of fact I'm alone. They're not my friends. I never set eyes on them until to-night. Very decent fellows, though. Scotchmen."

"I couldn't help overhearing you. You none of you seem to have been very cheerful about the situation."

"Well, who could be? It seemed to be getting brighter before this chap Musso began breathing fire and slaughter against these damned Abyssinians. I've not much use for the Abyssinians: I had a brother-in-law on the Somaliland frontier. They can't control their own people. Steal women, slaves, cattle, do any damn thing. But damn it all, they're in the League, and if people start breaking treaties at this hour of the day what the devil is the good of making them. Pity! A year or so ago Musso looked about the soundest of the lot. Now they're only waiting for the rains to stop and hell will be let loose. Another wretched European war, I suppose."

He jerked up his chin resignedly and took a long drink. He had obviously been through the last one. "What do you make of it?" he asked, turning to me, as I daresay one helpless Cabinet Minister, in *tête-à-tête,* has often turned to another.

There was stillness over the wickerwork and the engravings on the walls. There was a rattle and clink from the service department behind the shutter, and lights seemed to be going out beyond the lounge in which we sat. A waiter peered round the door: "Anything more before the bar closes, gentlemen?" he asked. "No," we replied, "good night." "Good night," came back as from one who had to see all hatches down after the last of us had passed to bed. "I suppose we had better go up," I said, sleepy, although he was an agreeable man.

"I suppose so," said the major (if such he was), "but I wish to God I could make out what the devil that fella Musso is up to. Did you ever meet anybody who'd talked to him?"

We were out of the door and at the foot of the stairs.

"As a matter of fact I have myself," I said. "It didn't amount to much, but I'll tell you about it in the morning if you like. What time do you breakfast?"

"Half-past eight."

"Call it nine and I'll join you."

FIFTH DAY

"I say," said the major, as I ordered a raw egg and milk, "is that all you ever have for breakfast?"

"As a rule," I assured him. "Tea and coffee are racial poisons." I had had my tea in bed.

The two Scotchmen, who had breakfasted early, walked out of the coffee-room with a reserved nod to their casual, though temporarily cordial, companion of the night before, and the door closed behind them for ever. They knew neither of our names, nor we each other's, nor ever would. Ships pass each other, with a hail, every night in country hotels, giving neither name nor port of destination. In two days the major and I would have discovered that we knew each other's cousins at school; but there were not two days, so it wasn't necessary.

We looked at the newspapers. The major finished his fish, his kidneys and bacon, his toast and marmalade, and his three cups of coffee. Looking at his watch and carefully folding his napkin: "Do you feel like a cigarette in the lounge?" he asked.

"Rather; my time's my own." Outside the window the sky looked none too promising. It was, in fact, a depressing mixture of yellow and indigo; a sky low and windless. We drew two chairs together in the fireless place, and lit cigarettes. "You said," remarked the major, "that you once talked to Mussolini. What's he like? Is he as grim as he looks?" "Not in the least," I assured him; "I found him thoroughly attractive. A lot of poetry and humour about him." Then I told him what I could remember.

It happened like this. About six years ago an Italian friend of mine, one of the veterans of Italian letters, was lunching with me in London; he heard I was going to Italy the following Easter and asked me if there was anybody I wanted to meet. I answered purely in jest, not thinking the thing practicable as I was not an interviewer and had no political mission: "Oh, Mussolini, of course." He replied: "Oh, I think *that* can be arranged," and proceeded to talk about pictures.

Three months later I was dining with him in Florence and he remarked, out of the blue, that when I got to Rome I was to let the Foreign Office know, for the interview had been arranged. I was thoroughly surprised, and also a little shy about invading the presence of the busiest man in Europe out of what began to appear to me as mere vulgar curiosity. "Are you sure that I shouldn't be making myself a nuisance?" I asked. "Certainly not," he replied, "I told them you were an Englishman who wrote poetry," and, as though the matter was closed, turned to exhibit the charms of a Greek marble head.

As soon as I got to my hotel in Rome I was informed that Signor X at the Palazzo Venezia wanted me on the telephone;

the news, I must say, being broken to me with a deference to which I am not accustomed. I rang up and a young and pleasant voice asked me if a certain hour next morning would suit me. I said: "Yes," and a written confirmation was sent.

Next day I took a cab along the old Appian Way, full of pot-holes, and lined with ancient tombs and broken fragments of pious inscriptions (for the old Romans were as polite on their tombstones as we are), and so to Lake Nemi, which the Government had recently half-drained in order to recover the state barge of Caligula which legend had asserted to have been full of treasure. Legend spoke truly in regard to the galley being there; but legend, with its usual passion for buried treasure, had overlooked the fact that even the maddest of rich men would hardly keep all his valuables in a house-boat, and all that was actually recovered with the framework of the vessel was some tiles and a few bronze heads of animals which were part of the decorations. But, turning from the venerable timbers and looking at the muddy ring of cliff which the drain-ing had left between the lowest belt of trees and the lake-surface, I suddenly thought: "Here have hundreds of thousands of pounds been spent on an enterprise which no previous Italian Government would have undertaken. The same thing is going on at Herculaneum which pre-war governments re-fused to do anything about, although it was far grander than Pompeii. Everybody says: 'Il Duce is doing this and Il Duce is doing that'. The man holds half the Cabinet posts. I wonder how much he really knows about what his subordinates are doing under his inspiration." So there was a notion as to con-versation; provided, that is, that Signor Mussolini was one of those rare eminences who allowed conversation to be two-sided. What could he know about his own alleged excavations when he was looking after Earth, Sea and Air, Industry, Roads and extremely-strained relations abroad? "Never mind the League of Nations," I thought; "let us see what he has to say about archæology."

I got back to Rome, and at half-past seven (if it was half-past seven) took a taxi through the rain to that majestic build-ing which used to be the Venetian Embassy and from the balcony of which Il Duce so frequently addresses the troops and anybody else who happens to be standing about. After passing various sentinels I reached an upper landing; was received by a most courteous young secretary who spoke perfect English; and was shown into an ante-chamber where two middle-aged Americans who looked like anxious business men with a "proposition" were already waiting. Il Duce, I was told, would be late. He was detained at the Chamber where he had to make a speech defending some Minister or other against an onslaught. This sounded odd to me at first: why can't the Whips look after the votes as they would in England? I wondered. But then I realized that where there is only one party there may be a special kind of freedom to criticize details of administration, for only one man's fate is at stake and nothing can rob the party of office or the government of power.

There for about an hour we sat, amid the marbles and the brocades and the busts of dead Venetians. The daylight faded, and now and then the business men murmured piteously together as though the waiting-room were that of a dentist. "They're before me," I mused from time to time, "but I do hope that when they are shown in His Excellency will say 'Nothing doing'—which is not very far from the Italian expression *far niente* though not used in quite so *dolce* a way, as a rule. Can they——" I wondered, "be armament manufacturers?" But no; I glanced at them unobtrusively, and concluded that they didn't look anything like rich enough for that. On the other hand it seemed to be unlikely that two salesmen of agricultural machinery (which I thought, since I had never seen one, they might possibly be) would be awaiting an audience with the Dictator. "Anyhow," I determined after another side-long look at their faces, "I'll swear they are not authors, not even popular ones, whatever they are!" With increasing frequency and poignancy I wished that I had brought a book by Mr. Wodehouse to while away the time.

However, time passed, as is its habit. A grave official arrived and conducted the two salesmen of harvesters through a side door and I settled down for a further long wait. Only a minute or two more and the pair came back for their hats and were

D

shown out. "Perhaps," I began to reflect, surprised at this brevity of reception, "they only wanted his autograph, after all," but further speculation was cut short by the grave one, who returned, said: "The Duce will see you now," led me out, showed me through a door, closed it, and left me standing.

Everybody who has ever enjoyed an audience with Signor Mussolini must have felt the same first shock at the vastness and severity of that long, many-windowed apartment. I felt as small as a mouse in a cathedral, though the mouse would not have had my added discomfort of feeling certain that I should fall down, in involuntary and overdone obeisance, on the polished marble floor. There, at the far end of the long bare salon, unadorned by any paintings, very cold to the eye, was a single desk and a small dark figure bending over papers. My feet, as I walked delicately up the slippery distance, made a loud ringing sound. "Dear, dear!" I thought, "how embarrassing is the spurious concentration of the Great, which I have often met with in statesmen elsewhere." As I approached he sprang up—looking much smaller in morning coat and politician's collar than he does in uniform—and advanced towards me with outstretched hands, and the rather baleful look which is familiar in the public prints.

I sat down opposite him. "Would you rather talk English or French?" he asked in English. "French," I replied in French, having heard, quite correctly, that he was very fluent in that language. Still stern and rigid, he asked one or two conventional questions, but, the moment we got going, all the apparently histrionic exterior was discarded like a glove, and for the rest of the time he was natural, vigorously animated, eloquent and extraordinarily quick; he moved from mood to mood and from jest to earnest.

Politics naturally had to be touched on first, particularly as there was supposed to be an especially serious international crisis: he talked with remarkable frankness and sense about foreign affairs; and as for his domestic régime he summarized his exposition with the remark, made with an engaging smile: "Moi, je suis démocrate, comme Jules César." He asked, with obvious genuineness, what was thought about him in England,

and at one point threw out the question: "Do you think we are a living people or a museum?"

"Both," I replied, noting here a probable key to his career. But the word "museum" reminded me of what I had wanted to hear him talk about. "How are the diggings going on at Herculaneum?" I asked.

Any illusion I may have had that he would not be familiar with the details of excavation was soon dispelled. He passed from Herculaneum (mentioning the chance of discovering lost classical manuscripts there), he described the discoveries at Ostia, he mentioned about a dozen Latin cities (which I had never heard mentioned since I last read Livy) as suitable places for later digging, and then he began to talk about his particular favourites—the diggings and clearances at Rome, in which important relics of the Empire have been unearthed at the expense of some of the remains of the Middle Ages. He suddenly brought me up abruptly by asking: "Did you hear about the Vestal Virgin's grave last week?" I said No, and he at once described the discovery of the interment. "And in her arms she had a wooden model of the baby she could never bear; isn't that touching?" I said it was, very, and he repeated his question, much more emphatically, until, I suppose, the right tinge of emotion came into my voice.

It was getting late. At a convenient pause I rose. He walked to the door with me. I said: "It was extremely kind of you to see me; you must be tired." He gazed at me with determination: "I—I am never tired," he growled, as though resenting a charge. Can this be true of anybody?

At the door he said: "Send me one of your books." I felt disappointed; the hollow compliment seemed unworthy of so real a person. When the man I had first seen greeted me and hoped I had had an enjoyable conversation, I replied: "Most varied and interesting, but I wish he hadn't told me to send him a book he will never open." The secretary looked pained. "No," he protested, "he doesn't ask for books he won't read." . . .

To all this the major in the Salisbury hotel listened attentively. When I had finished he was silent for some seconds and then said: "Well, I daresay he's a very pleasant fellow, since you say so; but why does·he go about with that scowl on? What about a glass of sherry before you take the road?"

"It might help to console us about the international situation," I said; so we had our glass of sherry.

When I was paying my bill I remembered an old intention of visiting the local museum, repository of many finds from the Plain and (I believe) the skeleton of a Giant. But no; I was not meant to see local museums; this happened to be the day the museum was shut. Mildly exasperated I thought I would get out of the town at once. I had half a mind to cut south-west to Broadchalke and the high downs. But I hadn't been there since Maurice Hewlett died there. I stayed there often with him in his old monastic building with the clear, weedy, chalk-stream full of small trout rippling along the bottom of the garden; the little fountain enclosed by cypresses to remind him of Tuscany; the small bridges across the stream; the quiet library where he wrote standing up at a lectern; and where I had sat up late while he and Robert Bridges had hammered at each other about æsthetics in a charming conversation of which I only remember Hewlett saying to him: "If you think that, you think damn nonsense, my dear chap," and receiving a blunt *tu quoque*. The books—he had some fine early things and a great collection of early chroniclers with whom he had lived in his mediæval (or, as he called it, "tushery") period—are all scattered. Strangers, I suppose, are living there now. I wonder if they take those long walks through the lovely outskirts of Cranborne Chase that we used to take, or know the empty house we came on in the woods, or (inspired by the lynchets on the sunny slopes of the down) try as he tried to grow English white wine, only to find all the bottles blowing to pieces just as he was going to drink it, or live passionately with the remote past of that very old country, with Saxon, Roman, and the men who worked the flints? Better not go there, I thought; it would be rather like visiting a graveyard. So I decided to go westward by the road through Wilton, and let chance lead me. It would probably mean Shaftesbury.

"Not a bad idea either," I reflected, as, under a menacing sky, I walked through the outskirts of the city. Shaftesbury, in a way, is disappointing; though it is full of churches and taverns, the chief ingredients of all noble towns, most of the buildings are not very old and not very beautiful. If one sees it from the plain, set high on its hill like a town of Umbria or Provence, one feels that only a dream city imagined by Mr. Frederick Griggs could do justice to the site. When one is in it one finds pleasant enough Georgian buildings but not pinnacles, bastions, buttresses, archways and arcades of ancient stone that should really be there. No; the two great things about Shaftesbury are the superb view from the terraced eminence—a great expanse of country which De Wint or Wilson Steer might have painted—and the Largest Sideboard in England.

It was that sideboard I thought of chiefly as I stepped westward to Shaston. It was some years since I had last made a pilgrimage to that sideboard, and, though Becket's shrine at Canterbury was doubtless finer in some ways, it can hardly have been much larger. It stands in the first-floor dining-room of the Grosvenor Hotel and nearly fills one long wall. It was carved (by a Swiss, I think) in the early eighteenth century, and was shown in the Great Exhibition. The whole front is covered with sanguinary battle-scenes in high relief, bearded and mailed mercenaries hacking and hewing each other in thousands: it might have been the father and mother of all the Victorian carvings, bronzes and ivory plaques. It is a monstrosity that no passing of the years will ever make anything else; but it is a monument of human patience and skill without taste, and produces a mixture of awe and amusement which is poignantly pleasant. Yes, mused I, the Shaftesbury Sideboard; and, if it rains, I will sit in front of it and contemplate those Teutonic ritters, stilled in their frenzies like the people on Keats's Urn.

"If it rains": I had just, at about eleven-thirty, got to the parting of the ways before Wilton and the gates of the great house when a heavy drop fell on my nose and another on my neck. It began to pelt, and cursing at having to undo my neatly-strapped bundle in order to get at my mackintosh cape, I was just getting my arms out of the straps when a car stopped in front of me. It was the most dilapidated Austin Seven I had ever seen. The front door was pushed open and an elderly weather-beaten parson's face was pushed out.

"Wouldn't you like to come in out of the rain?"

"Thank you very much——"—and I did.

"Which way are you going?"

"I really don't know. Almost anywhere—really."

"Can I give you a lift?"

"That would be extraordinarily kind of you, so long as you aren't going due east."

"Would it help you if I dropped you in the middle of the Plain?"

The rain was coming down in sheets. I thought I'd stick to the temporary shelter and find out later where I was to be deposited; the sideboard, the Cerne Abbas Giant, Portland Bill, Egdon Heath and all the other temptations in the south-westerly direction could wait to see me another time. Several flashes of lightning, more torrents, and with the water pouring down the wind-screen we set off on the road that leads north-west up the Wylye valley: a new road to me, though I knew both ends of it.

By this time I had noticed three things about my companion. One was that his rugged face had known tropic suns. Another was that his pipe had seen long service. And the third was that on his ancient hat there were those strings which are worn only by the upper ranks of the ecclesiastical profession. We were both of us rather shy for the first few minutes, and after we had both acutely observed that it was very wet, silence fell upon us, as we sped away from the English Channel, my destination, towards the Bristol Channel, which was once apostrophized by Mrs. Yearsley, the Bristol milkwoman poet, with "Hail, useful Channel!" After a while I felt it would be mannerly of me to break the ice, so I said: "Excuse me, sir, but are you a bishop?"

"Yes," he replied, "that is to say, I was."

"Colonial?"

"British Bongoland."

"Is there a nice cathedral there?"

"Not at all bad."

"It's in Edwardstown, isn't it?"

"Yes."

"Very few white people there, I imagine?"

"About seventy."

"Were all your choristers negroes?"

"Yes."

"Many earthquakes when you were there?"

"Some."

"How's mahogany?"

"Bad."

"How's coffee?"

"Bad."

"Rubber down, too?"

"Yes."

We rattled on through the moisture; I could remember nothing further about the industries of Bongoland, and my thoughts strayed to the Monosyllabic Friars in Rabelais. Suddenly we slowed up. There was a little inn with no other houses near; it bore the name of some unusual bird, as it might be the Dodo. "Visiting the sick," I thought to myself, and I said: "Parishioner?" "No," replied the bishop, shutting off the engine, "but I never pass this place without going in for a Guinness. Do you mind?"

"I think I'll join you," I answered, rejoicing in the rare opportunity of being led astray by a bishop. We went into the bar, the bishop hailed the landlord, who was discussing with two shepherds the effect of too much rain on potatoes, two Guinnesses were ordered, the right reverend gentleman refilled his pipe, and then, noticing the bandage on my hand, he said: "Hullo, cut your finger?" I told him that I had been damaged by a fast bowler and that my finger felt as though it would always be swollen and crooked. "I expect it will," said the bishop cheerfully; then, holding out a gnarled handful of fingers, added: "Wicket-keeping." "Bongoland?" I asked. "No," said he, "Tasmania and Saskatchewan"; then, before I had time to enquire about the chronological side of his travels, he surprisingly asked me if I knew anything about church plate, proceeding to inform me about Diocesan Surveys of such things now in process. Patens and chalices at one corner of the bar, potatoes at the other; Hudson's Bay and Australia at one corner, at the other, Wiltshire.

The bishop looked at his watch. "Would it be all right if I dropped you at Wylye?" he enquired. "Perfect," I said. "You see," he explained, "when I get there I have to turn east towards Amesbury." "That's all right, thanks very much," I said, and we resumed our drive. It poured incessantly, and it was still pouring when he drew up at the "Bell" at Wylye, the capital of the Plain, shook hands, raised his hat and left me.

I had some bread and cheese, put on my mackintosh cape which just came down to my knees, and started along the up-and-down road which runs for a dozen miles from Wylye to Mere, where the Plain ends. On a fine day it would have been better to leave the road and take the ridges, but visibility was bad, and I had no desire to get lost in the wet. There was little traffic; a car every quarter of an hour came out of the weeping road behind, and moaned away into the distance ahead. Copses and eminences which had tempted me to idle long since were not to be explored: *"patulæ recubans sub tegmine fagi"* was not for to-day nor teaching the woods to ring with Amaryllis's name. In such weather, when one's hat drips and the bottom of one's waterproof flaps loaded with water against one's trousers, and one's smoke will not keep alight, walking, with several hours in front of one, is a drudgery. Once only there was a thing I remember. Suddenly at a rise I heard a tinkle to my left, and there on a top of down, silhouetted like shadows against the grey skyless world, there was a long frieze—sheep, a few cattle, a dog and two men, which came and passed into obscurity. "Larger than human" it all looked, and the shepherds' heads were bowed; melancholy stirred in my heart and for some time I walked on without noticing where I was. The sheep had brought to my mind a memory of the picture "Love among the Ruins"; "the quiet coloured end of evening" and the sheep tinkling homeward in the twilight. I was far away in Italy. I saw across the Wiltshire rain that part of the Campagna which you cross when you come to Rome by road from Viterbo, and which surprises one by sudden little corners, dingle and cottage and stream, which might be Devonshire; and the plain south of Rome where the arches of the great aqueducts stride to the Alban Hills; and the marshy wilderness behind the coast north of Ostia, where great birds flap out of the desolation and the air swarms with noxious insects. And then in my mind I did many journeys again. I saw Florence from a terrace at Settingnano and watched the sunset fade and the lights come out; and Assisi from Perugia with one shaft of radiance gleaming on it out of a black thunderous sky; and Orvieto on its great crag; and the flag of flame above Stromboli at night streaming across the dark waters; and the church at Murano with the smoky Bellini; and the Giorgione at Castel Franco high in the hills; and the spectral mystery of Malcontenta, where the beautiful lady was imprisoned and died, and haunts the gardens at twilight in the manner of a poem by Poe. The horn of a car blew behind me and I got out of the way.

It was six o'clock when I came down into Mere, where are a fine church tower and two old coaching inns. I found the one best known to me much modernized, with a new lounge, a *table d'hôte* and waiters in white coats: I can dispense with all that, but I can suppose that the modern motor-tourist likes it. I did not want soup or fish: I had an immense plate of cold beef, with which I was persuaded, in the absence of pickled cabbage, to take pickled onions. It was the first time in my life, and very likely the last.

In bed that night, and early, at another inn where I met a man with a couple of greyhounds who asked me out duck-shooting on the morrow, I was reading Edward Hutton's *Highways and Byways of Somerset* which I had found lying about; a beautiful and learned book, by a man who was at Blundells just before me, the style seemingly influenced by Mr. Belloc, but that is no bad thing. Every page was starred with landscapes and buildings which I wanted to see again. Why not, I wondered, cut south again towards Crewkerne,

D*

and revisit the tombs of the Pouletts at Hinton St. George, an overwhelming muster of marbles and alabasters, armours and wigs which has few rivals but those of the Bolingbrokes at Lydiard Tregoze and those of the Russells, so severely barred off at Chenies? Or what about finding again that panorama from a crest which I once came across on a small road somewhere south of Langport and Somerton—sunshine, harvesting on the hill-top, and endless miles of fields and woods far below —a prospect which I have never been able to rediscover? Or I might even go to that other little town, where in a simple inn I slept long ago, and where I met a young barmaid who was fluent in ancient Greek (after taking her degree she had decided that a country barmaid's life was livelier than a schoolmistress's) and who, when I asked her for a book to take to bed, presented me with Trevelyan's *Early Life of Charles James Fox*. But no, I sighed, she's sure to have moved by now. Then a drawing of that noble thing, the Pulteney Bridge, settled it: I would go to Bath; and if the weather was still foul or the journey over twenty miles, I would take a bus or even stop at Frome.

Bath was due north; hardly on the way to Devonshire. However, by and large Somerset really was west of Wiltshire and marched with Devon, so I was moving on in a sense. Besides, I wanted to go to Bath, and why shouldn't I? With an extraordinary sense of new-found and unaccustomed freedom arising from a complete absence of arrangement with others, I decided that I would—unless I changed my mind in the morning. I shut the book, blew out the light and began to luxuriate in memories of "the English Florence."

"How long is it since I was there? Imagine letting five years go by without seeing Bath!" True, Chivers and George Saintsbury would no longer be there, and it wouldn't be quite the same thing; but the more I thought about it the more I was inclined once more to survey from Beechen Cliff that august amphitheatre, with its belfries clustering in the valley and its crescents climbing the hills: with eyes averted as far as possible from the modern red rash by Lansdowne. But five years?—no, I had forgotten, it was less than three years since I had been there, but then, that hadn't really been a visit to Bath but a gastronomic pilgrimage to Horace Vachell's lovely old manor just outside it and to Harveys' at Bristol.

It was a pious visit by certain members of the Saintsbury Club: André Simon, Colonel Ian Campbell, A. J. A. Symons and myself. At Bath we established contact with Evan Morgan, who was at that moment staying in a hotel, and whom we found in a vast room of which the windows were sealed and the floor covered with newspapers because he was travelling with a flock of small birds—there may have been some fish as well, but I don't remember. We dined in the evening with Vachell, a prince of connoisseurs, and next day went on to Bristol, where the Harvey family gave lunch to us and two or three of their friends. What a place! The cellars of these most ancient wine-merchants were once part of a mediæval monastery, and are still labelled "Crypt 1," "Crypt 2," and so on. The old panelled dining-room made a perfect setting for a lunch of which the central feature was a saddle of Southdown, and of which the wine list was composed of a series of clarets, including several of the '70's, some of them so rare as to be no longer in the market. We tried them all, and in the end voted on them by ballot without previous discussion; there was almost unanimity in the votes as to order of merit, and the Lafites led easily; and before we parted we drank the memory of the author of *Notes on a Cellar Book*, not to mention *A History of Prosody* and a hundred other works, as it is drunk at every dinner of the Club in London.

That was a man: one of the race of great professors. Bath knew only his later years. After a lusty life as scholar, teacher, combative Tory journalist, universal devourer of books and wine-drinker, he had to retire, on an age-limit, from his Edinburgh professorship just after the war broke out. His huge library was sold for very little, and he retired to a basement in Royal Crescent, with a bedridden wife, a small fraction of his books, failing health, very little money, and doctor's orders to drink nothing but champagne—which meant, thenceforth, total abstinence. His wife died and he was left alone. For a year or two he was still able to walk about the streets. I remember

Edmund Gosse (who had had some kind of feud with him) sitting on his balcony over Regent's Park and saying to me: "We were in Bath last week and a polar bear passed me in the street." "Really!" I exclaimed. "Yes," he said, "when it came quite close I saw it was George Saintsbury." He was white and stooped, and I suppose much bemuffled and begloved; but indoors he was too frail to remind one of bears, and his last years, after he had fallen in the street from vertigo, were spent entirely indoors.

Never did I know lonely old age and its ailments more bravely borne. There in his little basement study he would sit, black skull-cap, weak spectacled eyes, bulbous veined nose, thinned white beard, gnarled hands—looking, as an American friend* whom I took to see him remarked, "a mixture between the Rabelaisian and the Rabbinical." When well over eighty his enthusiasm for literature, great and small, was as ardent as ever: to hear him talk about Jane Austen, Sir Walter Scott, or indeed almost anybody, with his vast relish for character and memory for detail, to see his weak old eyes glitter and hear his high chuckle of glee, was to feel a Laodicean and ashamed.

His modesty was equal to his courtesy, which was gallant. Once Sir George Chrystal (who had been one of his pupils) and I went to Bath to sound him about a testimonial on his eightieth birthday. First, when he thought we wanted to do something for himself, he refused point-blank. Then, when he was reluctantly brought to see that people wanted to commemorate him, he said very emphatically that he did not want people, for his sake, to subscribe to anything useful, least of all scholarships, of which there were sufficient already. By degrees we worked the conversation round to a portrait for his old college at Oxford, and he ridiculed the idea that his college could possibly want to remember him. In the end William

---

* The American friend rewarded me later by taking me late at night, through woods full of the croaking of frogs, to see red wine bottled in the cellar of a seventeenth-century farmhouse in New York State when "Prohibition" was in its heyday. It was drinkable wine, carefully binned by vintages; and there, by a lanthorn's light, George Saintsbury's health was also pledged. I do not think that our farmer host knew much about the subject of the toast, but he obviously wished him well.

Nicholson painted a magnificent portrait, and it hangs in Merton now.

Another honour was offered him which no pressure could induce him to take. Bath is a city which is very chary about conferring its Freedom upon anybody: it will hardly sink below the level of a Prince of Wales. For some years after the war the perpetual Mayor (had he been still alive he might have been still mayor) was Cedric Chivers. He was scarcely a literary man, though the friend of many a one; and he rejoiced in two direct connections with literature in that he did wholesale bookbinding for public libraries and that his Mayoress, in his widowerhood, was Madame Sarah Grand, authoress of *The Heavenly Twins.* He showered treasures on the town, he was a magpie for gathering facts about its social and architectural history, and he thought it was only right and proper that all eminent persons should come to live at Bath when in retirement. So one day it "came to him in a flash" that George Saintsbury, being at the moment the city's chief ornament (intellectually, at all events), should be made a Freeman of Bath. "Preliminary soundings" were taken by myself. The old man was deeply grateful, but he couldn't leave his dwelling, disclaimed deserts, and probably detested the notion of accepting the honour unless he could go through the necessary ceremonies and celebrations. So Bath's Roll lost a good signature—why Saintsbury's name was never suggested for the O.M. is another matter.

But Cedric Chivers! What a character that was! He had gone to America young, made a fortune out of patent binding machines, returned and built a model factory on the northern heights above Bath, near the Lansdown Cricket Ground. To go over his works with him was a pleasure: all the girls seemed to regard him as an uncle. He supported every sort of charity and gave every sort of public entertainment, but his chief pleasure lay in collecting and showing his friends his extraordinary jumble of works of art. His last house, though substantial and stone-built, was small (he had given his large one to some cause), with a pleasant garden sloping towards the town. The garden was adorned by ornamental fishponds, statues, and a long wooden concert-cum-dining room, and the house was crowded with oil-paintings, water-colours, prints, china, bookcases, bronzes, busts, snuff-boxes and every kind of bijouterie. Some were good, some were very bad: his love for them all (especially for those which were the work of friends) was such that the guest would have been a prig and a cad who did not, at whatever sacrifice of principles and canons, lie roundly and profess a hearty admiration for the whole lot. He was small, grey, moustached, bright-eyed, birdlike, active and chattering; and when one was at his house his attention was divided between supplying one with cigars and refreshments and displaying his treasures. The apples of his eye were certain books which he had had made, partly because they were as marvellous as things should be on which no money had been spared, and partly to demonstrate that, although he supplied Public Libraries with cheap bindings by the ton, he was really a lover of binding as an art. They were elaborately tooled in gold; portraits were let into panels on the covers; the pages were adorned with water-colours of knights and undines and sylphs and innocent children in pale pink and blue—and he admired the artists employed on them as though they had been Derômes and Burne-Joneses. Next to these his chief delight was a light silver filigree box from the lid of which, when a button was pressed, an emerald bird sprang forth and circled and rapidly twittered in soprano, then going back with a sudden snap. It was a very pretty thing. Once, thought Chivers, it may have belonged to Marie Antoinette; later it certainly belonged to Mr. G. K. Chesterton.

Amongst his countless hospitalities was an annual entertainment to a touring cricket team. For many years in August, Clifford Bax used to take some fifteen people westward for a fortnight: Bath was used as a headquarters, and matches (when the rain permitted) were played against the local sides and against the elevens of towns and villages all around, such as Devizes, Chippenham, Melksham, Trowbridge, Lacock and Box—the village sides usually being the most difficult ones to beat. Nothing can have been more agreeable than these tours.

For one thing, the players were convivial, intelligent and

mixed; when off the field musicians like Arnold Bax, Armstrong Gibbs and Julius Harrison, and writers like the captain, Alec Waugh and Ralph Straus were active with pen and piano. For another, the cricket, though not all the best performers were eminent in the arts (or, so to speak, vice versa), was lively and good. And, for another, the country was perfect from a touring side's point of view; hilly, well-wooded, and covered with ancient things, so that an early start and a detour could easily secure a visit to a mediæval inn, to the Saxon church at Bradford or, as once happened, to dear old Lord Methuen's collection of pictures at Corsham, whilst any Sunday could take one to the riches of the Cotswolds. The opposing sides were the right kind of people, and some of the grounds were beautifully situated—especially that rustic field at Lacock, where fauna of all sorts, from donkeys to geese, used to graze, and behind which lay a long line of peaceful old buildings dominated by the church spire of one of the loveliest little towns in all England. It is off the track, it has not changed for centuries, it was beautifully laid out in a rectangle with delicious side alleys, and on its flank is the Abbey where Talbot started photography, and in the crypt of which is a gigantic bronze bowl made by an Italian in the fifteenth century, not to mention innumerable bats.

Every year, to this combination, Cedric Chivers gave at least one entertainment, flowing with the milk of human kindness and much else. In dinner clothes and blazers we drove up to his house and a long evening in his garden room—the garden itself being festooned with fairy-lamps, red, green, yellow and blue, the very fishpond having coloured lights beneath the water, and necklaces of light glittering from the terraces of Bath far below. Sometimes he had extra guests. Once it was old F. E. Weatherley, then eighty.

This charming and simple old man is, I suppose, now fading from memory. He came from North Devon, practised at the local bar, and took silk at an advanced age; but he was known in every villa of the suburbs and provinces as an incredibly prolific writer of lyrics for drawing-room songs, his only rival being his much weaker contemporary Clifton Bingham. Sea-songs, patriotic songs, love-songs, songs about roses in gardens, songs about Devon and Somerset, farmers and fishermen, they were all one to him: his collected poems would be awe-inspiring. His writing life reached far back to the days when all England languished in the evenings to the strains of Tosti and Pinsuti, Blumenthal and Löhr, and he was still active when he died, about ten years ago. A neat, chubby little rodent of a man, he was, at first, rather reticent in the company of boisterous juniors, all strange to him. But somebody remembered one of his songs, which must be fifty years old, called "Nancy Lee," and boldly asked him to sing it. A bardic fire flashed from his eyes and, on request, he piped it twice with a lusty chorus; he was a happy man for the rest of the evening and died within a twelvemonth. I think it was the last time Chivers was host that he did things on a grander scale, and took a large banqueting room and asked scores of people in honour of T. P. O'Connor, who had many interests, though cricket was probably not one of them.

A night or two afterwards I spent one of the oddest evenings of my life. Another man and I stayed on in Bath, and my eldest son also happened to be there; a message came from T. P., who was staying at the Grand Pump-Room Hotel, asking us to come over after dinner. When we got to his private sitting-room we found him with Lord Harris: the incongruity of the pair, although they had age and long political experience in common, was startling—but they had both taken their aged bones to Bath and come together, the impish Irish journalist with his shapeless face and sly eyes, and the tall, austere, aquiline, bewhiskered, correct cricketer and Indian governor. Lord Harris, who at nearly eighty had recently been making runs and taking wickets on the Fourth of June at Eton, welcomed every attempt to turn the conversation to cricket or imperial history, but T. P. was too much for him and for some hours monopolized the talk with reminiscences of Victorian worthies of the Jubilee Plunger type, and stories of the what-the-lady's-husband-said-to-the-duke sort, relating to past ornaments of Burke. Now and again, as he produced an especially impudent piece of ancient scandal, he turned with his brogue and said: "Ye'll remember that, Lord Harris?" Lord Harris was the perfect gentleman, and perhaps he was really enjoying the relaxation from decorum; but his nods of assent were of the slightest and his smiles had a trace of effort in them. It was rather as though an Archbishop should have found himself supping with the chorus, and was making the best of it. How much truth there was in T. P.'s stories I never could guess. He was the most incorrigible gossip I ever knew; and yet, when he was libelling the dead most outrageously, there never seemed to be any malice in him. He liked people and collected them and stories about them: in his own house, where he was a very gay host, he assembled the most extra-ordinarily variegated parties and managed to fuse them by his sheer common humanity. . . .

All gone, and irrecoverable. But Bath it should be; and with the rain pattering on the windows, I turned over.

SIXTH DAY

"BANG!"

The noise awoke me. I saw the wraith of a maid, and heard her say "Bath."

"No," I said muzzily, "it can't be——" and then realized that she wished to know when I wanted one. . . .

The rain had rained itself out and the morning was fresh and sunny as, after an examination of the map, I paid my bill and strolled into the bar to say good-bye to the landlord, of whom I had had a bare glimpse the night before, as I was tired and had had a drenching. "Glass of beer to set you on the road, sir?" he asked.

I was having it with him, and hearing what the *Daily Express* had to say about Foreign Affairs, when (the hour being now half-past ten) a car suddenly braked to a standstill outside the door, and a young man and a young woman, in their early twenties, poured in and demanded two gin and Frenches. The young man was short and slight, with inno-cent eyes, hollow pale cheeks, a little fair moustache, a khaki mackintosh, and, just visible behind the upturned collar, a tie which I diagnosed as Old Merchant Taylors or near it. The girl was the female of the species—fair, rosy, lipsticked and clad in a red oil-skin which would have put a pillar-box to the blush.

He was called George; she was called Olga; they were going from Weymouth to Bristol, and had started early; and the old "Morris" was running like a hare. This much, from their chatter to each other and the landlord, I learned within a minute; and within two minutes I had politely refused more refreshment, the young woman had gone upstairs to powder her nose, and I had learned that they were engaged. The young man was going strong with the landlord on the invention of an ideal England XI, when the girl reappeared, stared at me strangely, stepped up to me, hesitated, then asked me if I were myself.

"Yes," I said, "but what made you think that?"

"Oh," she replied, "I just noticed your name in the register. Besides, I once heard you make a speech."

"Where was that?"

"At an English Association meeting. I was at college then. I did so want to ask you a question afterwards."

"Why didn't you?"

"I felt so shy."

"Well, ask me now."

I spoke, I hope, with due gallantry, but my heart sank within me. I knew what was coming. I have not yet been on Greenland's icy mountains, in spite of a kind invitation from Mr. Augustine Courtauld, whom I have forgotten to ask about the literary fashions there prevailing. I have not been on India's coral strand, nor have my nostrils snuffed the spicy breezes of Ceylon's isle. But I am sure it would be just the same there as in Somerset: for in Paris and Cairo, and Haifa, Rhodes, and Copenhagen, in the Town Hall of Helsingfors and on the Pine Valley Golf Course in New Jersey, I heard that question asked and, somehow, seen it coming. It came: "Did you know D. H. Lawrence well?" and once more I had to answer: I corresponded with him a bit but only met him once, and that was in 1913. It was in somebody's Chelsea garden. Other people talked. He gloomed all the time. His face was shadowy; he looked impressive and ill.

The next question was about to follow when George, tossing off his drink and saying "Well, cheerio!" to the landlord, turned, rubbed his hands briskly and said: "Well, old girl, I think we'd better be moving along." "Do stop a moment, I must introduce you," exclaimed his fiancée. "Old friends, what?" he began. The introduction was made; we shook hands. "Hiking, what?" said George. "Well, walking——" I said.

The girl suggested that they should take me to Bath. I split the difference with my not very exacting pedestrian conscience and said that I should be grateful if they would drop me at the entrance to Frome. The girl told the young man that I was going in the back seat with her. This happened; and off we went.

There was no looking out of the window. Literary conversation must have been scarce in the maiden's home-circle, whether at Weymouth or Bristol, and she eagerly got in as many questions as she could in the time. The questions were none of them abstract: second-hand contact with esteemed personalities was what was wanted, and with as many of them as possible. I admitted my various degrees of acquaintanceship with Mr. T. S. Eliot, Mrs. Woolf, Mr. Aldous Huxley, several Sitwells, and various devastating and daring young authors of both sexes. I felt happy when I was able to claim old friendship, and unkind and mean when I had to throw a cold douche on her enthusiasm by confessing that I hardly knew the people or even, as happened with some poets, that I had not yet had the privilege of meeting them at all.

Her tastes and knowledge—though I doubted whether she had more than dipped into her authors—were emphatically contemporary. I felt that it would be a mistake to try to be polite by talking about Hardy, Conrad, or Augustine Birrell: I should have been greeted, as sometimes before, by the sort of puzzled stare which would also have greeted me if I had told her the joke which Charles Lamb made to me in the

Temple over the whist-table (though that, of course, was before the war) or (but that also was before the war) what the Duke of Wellington said to me on the field of Waterloo. The catechism failed. There was a pause. We both looked out of the window at the hedges hurrying back.

She had been meditating. Looking straight ahead, and with a slight trembling in her voice, she said: "Did you know Rupert Brooke?"

"Very well," I said; and I knew she was now speaking of a poet whom she had read and loved as a girl before she took up with the intellectual life. "What was he like?" she asked, as I was wondering where to begin. There suddenly came into my mind the silly reactions of fashion, the current jealousy of people who had hearts and died in the war, the smiling denigration by living dogs (some of whom knew Brooke), of dead lions, and I said angrily: "A damn nice man, damn good-looking, not a bit girlish, and would have been a damn good poet if he'd lived!" She looked surprised. I simmered down, and told her, rather jerkily, as the car bumped along the road, what came into my mind as I focused my eyes on the driver's back.

I had, I told her, first met Rupert in Green Street, Cambridge; and last, just before he sailed for the Dardanelles. . . .

*   *   *   *   *

"You're sure we can't take you on to Bath?" asked the girl as we drew up on the outskirts of Frome. "Quite certain, thank you," I said. "It's quite a pleasant walk from here. Good-bye. I hope we shall meet again." Off they went, but for a quarter of an hour I lingered. I was looking for something which I did not find.

Near Frome is Mells. Years ago, when that tall, grand, handsome, white-bearded old man Sir John Horner was alive, I turned up there for a week-end with a picture. I had picked it up in a "junk-shop" at Plymouth while changing trains; it was a lovely Italian lake-scene by Richard Wilson, and later on shown at the Tate Gallery when they had a Wilson Memorial Exhibition. Conversation naturally turned to the subject of picking up masterpieces, and Lady Horner told me that the late Sir Hugh Lane had laid the foundations of his career by picking up a blackened Romney in Frome. Returning thus, I thought I would look around Frome to see if there were another Romney. A shop, but not the old shop, with some pictures I did find, and some of them were black enough, in all conscience. There were some pudding-faced Georgian portraits. But there was nothing I wanted to buy.

Why should there be? Well, although it is said daily in the book and picture worlds that the day of bargains and discoveries is over, I don't believe it. Fashions change, pictures get dirty, fakes multiply so much that genuine things are suspected, hundreds of auctions take place daily all over Britain in which "pictures by or attributed to" anybody from Raphael to Sidney Cooper are exposed for sale, most of the owners, auctioneers and local dealers know very little—and a little knowledge is worse than none in such matters—about works of art; while, though the London men have their agents (whatever the intuition or connoisseurship of most of these may be like) on the road, they cannot be in all the shops all the time. And pictures are easier to come by than books: any bookseller can read a title-page or a colophon, but how many provincial furniture dealers (to take the most extremely identifiable style as an instance) would know a grubby or even a clean El Greco if they saw one? Hunting for pictures requires free movement in time and space and that is what most of us cannot get. Perhaps if I could have stayed in Frome for a month something might have turned up. But that's the catch.

As I left Frome and began to walk up the valley I thought again about the conversation in the car and wondered what would have happened had Rupert and all those others survived the war, or if there had been no war to survive. Would the fashion for eccentricity in the arts have gone to such lengths, and would the papers have been full of praises of poets who seem not to write for the ear at all? Nobody could prove anything, I reflected, but the fact that one generation does influence the next must mean that a generation missing makes a difference. But the thing, I thought again, is world-wide and began before: so perhaps we were, anyhow, in for an Age, which would, at the peril of having its works rapidly out-moded, make literature the servant of doctrine more thoroughly than ever. In two respectable papers I had just seen two determined young reviewers denouncing one poet for still hankering after Beauty and applauding another because his work, at any rate, wasn't emotional. All this can lead to is a small public getting the dry, unmelodious, intellectual husks it wants, the great public consoling itself with "Annie Laurie," and the hungry sheep in between, who are anxious to be up with the times and look for guidance where there is none, pretending to admire what it does not admire, affecting that the darkest and craggiest passages of Donne are sublime, and reading Shakespeare's songs in secret.

But as I walked along this gentle serene morning in that sequestered country unfevered by metropolitan debates, I re-membered a discussion some years before the war, or, rather, a monologue by T. E. Hulme, who was killed in the war and also knew Brooke. Hulme, a huge, ham-faced, idle man, but one of great wit and lightning intellect, was at St. John's in my time, was sent down with the longest mock funeral ever seen in the town, and, after a few years, reappeared in London as king of a weekly *salon* held in the fine drawing-room of a friend's house in Soho which used to be the Venetian embassy. Large numbers of people—writers, painters, philo-sophers, patrons—used to assemble there and smoke and drink liqueurs; while Hulme, as massive as Johnson but a non-smoker and a teetotaller, consumed sweets, argued with anybody who was willing to cope with him, or soliloquized on almost any theme, ancient or modern. Sometimes he talked great sense, sometimes great nonsense: when it was nonsense he was fully aware of the fact, but not all his listeners were. Always his talk was fluent, well shaped, subtle, various in allusion, full of illuminating simile; he was combative, fiery-tempered, intolerant of those who crossed him, catholic other-wise in his tastes in friends, an utter individualist in his habits, and afraid of nobody. As I say, he was idle: a few papers remain, and he translated, with some collaboration from me, one small book by Bergson, and one by Georges Sorel, who greatly influenced Mussolini and, incidentally, diagnosed in the exiled young revolutionary the fervent nationalist which Mussolini later became. He also wrote about six small un-rhymed poems as protests against woolliness and inexactitude. I had forgotten them until the other day when I saw that some solemn young man, at whom he would have jeered, had been alluding to him as "that important poet," and all I can recall of them are three phrases:

"Thine old star-eaten blanket of the sky."

"A tap of gold heels on the pavement hard."

"The moon looked over the hedge
Like a red-faced farmer."

At all events, whatever he was talking about, specialists and practising artists thought him worth listening to. None the less, perhaps, because there was, though his views fluctuated, always behind his thought an endeavour to relate things. He was really a philosopher—which reminds me that, after attend-ing a Philosophical Congress at Bologna, he swore to me that there had been a free fight in the Ethical Section.

Once he was discoursing on the changes in prevailing philosophical theory. He said that all the possible views were always there, like the diverse speakers at Marble Arch, but that the crowd was sometimes around one platform and some-times around another, illustrating the theory by a disquisition on everybody from Heraclitus onwards.

* * * * *

Through Beckington and Woolverton I walked the six miles or so to Norton St. Philip. It was nearly two when I got to the "George" Inn, one of the unspoilt mediæval inns of England. I refreshed myself, but the man I was looking for I did not find: a truly traditional and contented character. He was a basket-maker on his own, one of the few left—rarer now, I dare say, than the lace-makers in Bucks—and he asked me once if I needed anything in the basket or cradle way. I told him that all I wanted for my purposes was a larger wastepaper-basket than I had ever yet seen. He took the job on. I have it still. It comes up to my waist.

I roamed round the back of the "George" to have another look at the turret staircase in the mellow golden stone of these parts, which might have come from the back-premises of a cathedral, and then went on. I spoke to no one and I did not, as I had hoped, pass a cricket match in being.

So, by the way of the road that leads over Beechen Cliff, I came down into Bath. When the city first came into sight, below my feet, I paused and thought again of the time when, on foot or in a car, alone or in company, there were always two houses I would make for, and now there were none. No welcome. The mood was interrupted by a thought which made me laugh heartily aloud, much to the surprise of a spectacled passer-by who looked like Rudyard Kipling: I remembered what had been the greatest and most unexpected welcome of my life.

It was in April 1933; I was going to Denmark and Sweden to make a few speeches about literature which were intended to promote international friendship. A friend came with me part of the way and we crossed in the steamer from Harwich to Esbjerg; a peaceful journey, and, apparently, no other passengers. When evening fell, on the second day, we went on deck to watch the nearing shore. As we approached the quay-side we became aware, in the light of great white arc-lamps, of multitudes of people packed together and stretching away on either hand as far as the eye could reach, little pink upturned faces like sand on the seashore. I turned to my companion and said: "Dudley, authors don't get a welcome like this in England; these Continental peoples know how to do things." I found there was an eager-looking Danish steward standing next to me and said to him: "What on earth is all this about?"—for by this time a gangway had been thrown from ship to quay, and people looking like a Mayor and Corporation were standing at the other end of it. "It's the *Railway Queen*," replied the steward, in astonishment. "What *Railway Queen?*" I asked. "Why, your *English Rail-*

way Queen," said he, "she's come over to congratulate the Danish railways."

We didn't know what it all meant, so we just waited. About twenty minutes passed and all our attempts to leave the ship were baulked. Her Majesty had to come first. At long last there emerged on deck, followed by fathers, brothers and what not, a young girl, with bowed head, clad in a green bespangled dress and a coronet and veil. As she walked down the gangway the crowds cheered, the bands played, and the Mayor began to make a speech. Not until the *Railway Queen* had completed her progress were we allowed into the Customs House to declare nothing at all.

We got to Copenhagen in the morning. An extremely beautiful woman-journalist (if this isn't too much to swallow) met the train and asked me what I thought about Shakespeare and John Galsworthy. I told her about the *Railway Queen*. She said that the *Railway Queen* was the news of the day in Denmark and was going to have a Guildhall luncheon. I said, truly, that I didn't even know there was a *Railway Queen*, let alone knowing whether she was the Queen of one railway, or of all our systems, or who elected her. The interviewer grinned. That evening I saw her again. She said: "Well, I saw the *Railway Queen* and told her you'd never heard of her." "What did she say to that?" I naturally asked. "She said that she'd never heard of you."

That was a blow. However, the lady put things right next day, for she induced an undergraduate with fair hair, a pleasant smile and a fast car, to drive us out to Elsinore to see Hamlet's grave. Opposite that Hans Andersen castle there is a steep mound, freely sprinkled with tall trees, and on the top of it a vast granite sarcophagus with "Hamlet" incised on it. "This looks to me rather new?" I said. "Oh yes," replied my guide, "it was only put here a few years ago. The innkeeper buried his cat here." "But why," I went on, "did he get the sculptor to carve on it a leopard with a fish's tail?" "Perhaps," she responded brightly, "the cat had a fish's tail." After that I felt I could not cope with the Danes, and contented myself with looking about me; amongst the sights I saw being, from below the battlements, a solitary silhouetted sentinel with an inordinately long rifle and bayonet, keeping watch over the Sound for all the world as though he were a super at the Old Vic. . . .

But I was nearing Bath.

I descended the hill and crossed the railway. Where should I sleep? A walker with a kitbag could obviously not present himself at some of the hotels: the porters and book-keepers would look haughty, and perhaps pretend there was no room; and, even if one forced one's way in, the dinner-jackets and knitting bags would give one disdainful looks over shoulders. I remembered the time in 1923, when a party of us, including A. P. Herbert, in Belloc's aged, and now at last defunct *Nona* —about which he wrote a lovely book—had sailed in rough weather up the Channel, taken a quiet entry into the Solent through the dawn and landed at Ryde, unshaven and covered with fish-scales (though ready and eager to wash) and presented ourselves for breakfast at the nearest hotel. Foreigners were apparently in charge; pressed white flannels and yachting caps were everywhere in evidence; we were told there was no breakfast going. When the leader of the party made his presence felt and began talking about the laws (he had recently been a legislator) there were rapid conferences, and in the end a compromise was reached: we were given our bacon and eggs, but a screen was put round us (for we had really been sailing) in order that the people with yachting caps should not be contaminated. I did not want that sort of thing, as I was alone and unsupported, to be repeated at Bath. So I went to a humble middle-class hotel, discarded my superfluities in a bedroom, and dined on tomato soup, turbot, roast mutton and prunes and custard. Then I explored the hotel.

There was a large drawing-room with some ladies steadily knitting, but not smoking. I went down a passage and found a small lounge with some commercial travellers in it. It was only nine; why not go out? I got my hat, went to the parapet by the bridge, and looked at the weir in the twilight, turned round by the Abbey and aimlessly examined some second-hand furniture shops and then, somewhere at the back, found myself outside a cosy-looking tavern. I went in.

A plump landlady was sitting and sewing behind the bar. A clock ticked. A forlorn dart-board gazed on clean sawdust. I went up to the counter and ordered a pint of beer. The landlady gave me an old friend's smile and, as she was drawing it, said: "You'll be glad to hear that Douglas has started on his job." "Rather!" I answered, hastily, hoping she did not observe my start of surprise; and there followed one of those *solvitur loquendo* dialogues in which one has to go carefully for fear of hurting somebody's feelings. I could only suppose —as I put my face in the tankard in order to gain time—that she was mistaking me for somebody else. We all have our doubles. I once met mine in the Strand, and he gave me a very sinister grin, as though to imply that I didn't know what he was letting me in for. Perhaps the wretch was now infesting Bath. "Was it motor-work you said he was going to do?" I asked warily.

"Why no, the railway. Clerk on the railway."

"Let me see, is it seventeen he is now?"

"No, sixteen last birthday; but of course he's big for his age."

"Will you——?"

"Well, just this once. A glass of port, please. Thank you."

"Is Douglas still keen on football?"

"No, it's the music more, now. Always was, really."

"Of course. Wasn't it the accordion?"

"No, never that, but the banjo and the xylophone and the piano."

"I remember now. He was playing once when I came in. Jolly good, wasn't he?"

"He was that! Why, only on Sunday week he played the organ in church! He'd never touched the organ before, and he only played one note wrong!"

"I hope he's going on with it."

"I hope he's not. So does my husband. It would interfere with his career."

"Can't he practise in the evenings?"

"Evening classes for him! He's got his future to think of."

Poor Douglas and his career. I suppose that in ten years' time he will be carefully writing out Season Tickets at Fishguard. But perhaps the goddess will be imperative. He will break loose, all England will know Douglas Something and his Band, his hair will be blue-black and plastered, he will have a wide mouth and large teeth, and as a reward for filling the air with dreadful noises he will draw hundreds of pounds a week and marry an Afghan Princess.

Two more men, obvious familiars, came in. I said: "Good night," and hurried out lest complications about my double should ensue. He might even owe them money.

Up the hill and down: then I went back to the hotel to draw the lounge again. Three travellers were there, as so often in Dickens.

Two of the commercial travellers were not conversable: their backs were turned, brief-cases were beside them, and they were scribbling hard, perhaps to their wives, perhaps to their employers, reporting either progress or the lack of it. I picked up an old *Tatler* and sat down in one of the two wicker chairs in front of the crinkled-paper-stuffed fireplace; there was a small table between me and the third commercial traveller who, a gaunt man with a heavy moustache like Seddon, the murderer, in a desultory way was glancing at the local paper. He looked at me, as though he wished to speak; I returned his gaze sympathetically and he twiddled a table-bell. A worried waiter came in: "A double-Scotch and a Polly," said the traveller, and to me: "I always believe in a night-cap." "Quite right, too," I agreed, not knowing what else to say. "Had a good day?" "Saturday, you know," he replied, "but not a bad day yesterday. What about you?"

"Not bad," I attempted weakly, realizing that he thought me one of the fraternity. He bubbled the mineral-water into his glass, and waved waiter and tray away. "And what's your line?"

I was rather stuck, and said: "Books."

"Not bad here, I daresay," he nodded, and then, looking intently at me, raising his glass and quaffing with a murmured salutation, "but d'you know, I can put my hand on my heart and say that I've never read a book in my life."

Wordsworth's lines came into my head: "I travelled among unknown men." I didn't believe such a thing possible. "Not even a small one?" I asked.

"Not even a small one," he asserted, "when I'm home my hobby is singing in the choir."

"I used to," I agreed, "where is it?"

"Liverpool."

"Church of England?"

"Certainly."

"Baritone?"

"Yes. . . . Spot?"

"No, thanks very much."

I remembered something, rose, said good night, and walked out to the sort of buttery-hatch behind which the cashier kept herself. She came to my knock.

"What can I do for you, sir?"

"I say. I'd forgotten. Would you awfully mind? I want a shirt and two pairs of socks washed. I shan't be going till Monday."

"But to-morrow's Sunday!"

"I know. But I thought somebody in the hotel might oblige. I mean, I don't want any starch, or blue tissue-paper, or cellophane, or pins stuck in where I can't find them."

"Well, perhaps we can manage it."

"Thank you so much."

"You're welcome."

"Good night."

"Good night, sir."

Down went the frosted-glass hatch, for she was really shut. I climbed two pairs of stairs to my little back room, switched on the light and went to open the window. Below was a narrow court; a street-lamp shone on patches of peeling Georgian stone, architrave and pilaster and pedimented door. Light came from only one room down the alley: "Bath goes to sleep early," I thought.

I undressed, turned on the bedside light, and not feeling

sleepy—as I had had a short day and no great amount of walking—I left it for a while. With my head propped on my hand
I stared at the paper on the opposite wall, a charming thing
covered with rosebuds tied up with true-lovers' knots in blue
ribbon. Thinking of commercial travellers I remembered a
story Murray Allison told me long ago about them. There
were two, before a coffee-room fire, near bedtime, a sociable
A, just in from seeing friends, and a laconic B, who had been
reading. The conversation ran:

A: Taken any orders to-day?
B: No.
A: (after a pause) Have you taken any this week?
B: No.
A: Have you taken any this month?
B: No.
A: (desperately) Well, any this year?
B: One.
A: (leaping up) My God, man, what do you travel in?
B: (languidly) Battleships.

What a story-teller that man was! I used to suspect him of
making up most of his stories and most of the songs which he
said he had heard Spaniards singing in Havana and Italians in
New York. A neat, rosy, dapper, silver-haired man (who used,
as it were, to wink at one in apology for his conventional
appearance), he had been born in Australia of barn-storming
parents, emasculated (as he sometimes used to boast) more
sheep than any other man in the Dominion, written and drawn
for the *Sydney Bulletin,* come to England with no assets except
salesmanship, jumped into the Advertising Management of
The Times under Northcliffe, parted from that, acquired *Land
and Water* for a song, thought of Belloc as a military critic—
in fact, that is the way he went on, now with a fortune, now
with nothing, and dying just as he seemed safely in harbour.
One book of stories, *Mr. Franklyn's Adventure,* remains for
those who did not know him; to those who did know him he
will always be alive, and an encouragement. He took more

pleasure in his friends' performances than in his own, and there wasn't an art, from music to printing, about which he did not know enough to enable him to cheer on an expert.

Lights out, in a comfortable reverie, I went on thinking of Jimmy Allison, friend of all the world in general and artists in particular. Once, sitting up in his old farmhouse under the down's shoulder at Rodmell, with great logs burning, two more writing men present, and the women gone to bed, he had looked seriously at the fire and asked us—though in less pensive moments he could appear every kind of booster and thruster and, on his mind's surface, believed in a glorious future for every country that spoke English—if we knew what it meant to an Australian to come back to so temperate, so varied, and so kindly a country as this. He spoke of the Americans (I daresay he was thinking of American business and advertising friends whom he had met in Houston and such places, and in whom he had detected hidden feelings of which he himself made no secret) and how they simply (at least, those whom he knew) came to London hotels and notorious beauty-spots and said impatiently, and in language which our own reticence did not permit us to use, but which we understood: "They simply don't know it, boys. Can't you put it across, boys? Can't you paint England in words? Can't you do a gallery that'll just show 'em?" He could see what he wanted: in some of his spare time he painted in water-colours, and, for an amateur, boldly and well.

One at least of his companions did actually try to begin something that night, with the quiet dark beams overhead, and the casement curtains still in the night air—for to imaginative people contact with "rugged enthusiasts" may be more exciting and helpful than any amount of dry discussion with analytical folk who have read all the books in the world and are aware of all the changing theories (though they seldom see that their own will be superseded) of the ages. "Have a heart," said Jimmy Allison; it was a kind of ace of trumps which he could produce on the most diverse occasions, and always with effect. And that night, and in the morning (for one did not rise early on a Sunday there) I began a series of scattered stanzas in which I tried to crystallize aspects of the English scene. Snatches, at Bath, I could still remember. One began:

> And inns by evening waters broad and still
> Whose dark walls bear great browning pike and bream

which perhaps made too much of an effort with adjectives; and:

> And tidal creeks whose shrunken runlets gleam
> Where blackened hulls lie stranded far apart,
> Forlorn on miles of mudbanks. . . .

But it wouldn't work out. Describe I might in cameos. But a long poem could not be a series of framed water-colours, or even oils. Tennyson had done the best in that kind in the "Palace of Art"—pearls strung on a platitude, too fragile. Fusing was required and that depended on more than brain, observation, the gift of visualizing, ear, taste or whatnot, and one had to wait for it.

I forgot Allison and drifted into thoughts of the Muse and the way she takes people. Some, both among the great and the little, are poets all the time. Some are not; and of the great some are prepared to wait until what Housman calls the "continuous state of excitement" returns, while some are content, out of habit, conscience, or merely because a large public prefers made-up verses to inspired ones, to turn out something every day and publish the living and the dead work together.

Five years it was, I reflected, since I had for a month or two felt that nothing else in the world except poetry was worth having or doing; only to know again the hour when common day broke in once more, and the strange fires had gone from the mast-heads, and comfortable Philistinism seemed no bad thing, and I was even able, who had lived for weeks in an air where beauty and wit seemed one, and the people I knew like gracious forms walking on the rainbow banks of Paradise, to bid, with curled lips, a cold-blooded farewell to the Muse. In bits I reconstructed it. It ran, I remembered, rather like this:

> Lo, thus has ended all our escapade!
>   I must back to work, to grind until the end.
> "Poets," Lord Dewar said, "are born, not paid":
>   How right he was! now what have I to spend?
> Item, the income-tax; item, bills for schooling,
>   Item, the garage; item, railway fare. . . .
> You hear it all? A truce to all this fooling!
>   Vain now is even the witchery of your hair!
> Back, Muse, into your box; that fetching glance
>   'Neath lowered lids is useless! Do as you're bid,
> Get in and go to sleep—no, not a chance!
>   Sorry; good-bye; that's right—I'll shut the lid. . . .
> But, should I feel an intolerable strain,
> Why, Jill-in-the-Box, you may pop out again!

"Five years ago," I muttered in the darkness to my pillow. "It's extraordinarily odd. I simply don't understand it. Is it physical? It must be something in one's self, somehow. For Life goes on all the same. What a trite phrase."

A noise came from the dark court below. It was a quavering raucous voice, off the note, droning the monotonous maudlin refrain of a song about the Isle of Capri. "It hath a dying fall!" I groaned bitterly.

As it faded away, I remembered where, when it had already siroccoed the world for six months, I had last heard it.

Lunching in a quiet restaurant over the bay at Naples: a wide window, the sparkling sea, Capri a blue enchantment in the distance. The three of us had just ordered: Madame di Sermoneta and I an omelette, the enterprising Sir Basil Peto a plate of Neapolitan shellfish, which he had never before tasted.

As we waited, listening to the gentle susurrus of the local epicures behind us, there hove into hearing outside a light operatic tenor, passing on its way. It might have been singing "La Donna è mobile," but, very tunefully, in Italian, with the reproachful fairyland in sight, it was singing "The Isle of Capree." Sir Basil did not seem to know or notice. Madame di Sermoneta and I looked at each other wanly.

E.

And, oh yes; when Sir Basil's plate arrived it was crawling with things like great scarlet slugs with small shells on them. He did not move a muscle. As they quested and peered about, he harpooned them one by one and ate them. We watched fascinated and horror-struck. He, like the Colonel and Die-hard he is, admitted no error or regret, but said: "Very nice, too; I shall have some more of them some time."

I am sure he won't.

What a song can recall!

I slept, and did not dream.

SEVENTH DAY

I WOKE when the tea came and, Shanks's pony feeling lazy, asked for three Sunday papers and went through the familiar process of being astonished at the multitude of superb books in the publishers' advertisements, beginning and then dropping Mr. Torquemada's crossword puzzle, getting every light except one in an acrostic, noting with admiration that fifty-nine colonels in Bournemouth were able to inform the world as to the authorship of Casabianca, and wondering whether Mr. Ripley was a man or a League of Nations.

The bells of the city pealed for church. When I had gone through each sheet a second time, reduced to reading about women's clothes and what a good time Lord and Lady Some-thing were having with Lord and Lady Something Else on the Yorkshire moors, I began to think about how I should spend the day: a Sunday alone in Bath, no less.

Human frailty very nearly overcame me to the extent of hiring a car and going to see some people I knew in the neigh-bourhood. But that really would hardly be the Way to a Horse; and conscience, with difficulty, won.

"What about the waters?" I asked myself, remembering that warm liquid which, like so many modern novels, it just un-pleasant enough to be interesting, and no more. But, some-how, Sunday morning (even if the Pump Room was open) hardly seemed the time for Beau Nash's society. What else was there?

A voice came into my head: "Why not do absolutely nothing? Why exert yourself? Why think? Remember what Walt Whitman so truly said about animals. Fret not, but just let the time pass over you. To start with, you can take a short walk before lunch."

I took a short walk and sat on a seat in a public garden. A dapper-looking elderly man with an umbrella tucked under his arm, and a Cairn trotting behind him, joined me on the seat. "Fine morning," he said. "Yes, admiral," I replied. He looked puzzled, not realizing that his umbrella was descended from a long line of telescopes; then, realizing that, after all, I might know him by sight, he fell into familiar conversation.

What he said about sport, politics, and the neglect of the Navy I do not remember in detail; nor do I remember how we got on to horticulture—probably by noticing flowers in beds. But I do remember my astonishment when he shot out the remark: "I suppose you know that all flowers are constantly trying to become blue?" I said, timidly, that I saw no sign of it in the geraniums, and that roses, with the utmost encouragement from human beings, had never contrived to become blue. "No," he said, "but the fact remains that they all aspire to it." As human beings aspire after virtue, I mused; but he continued with a wealth of botanical detail which I could not follow to prove his thesis. Suddenly he looked at his watch and, with a cheery: "Good morning to you; come along, Jane," departed.

He may or may not have been correct; but he was evidently a keen gardener and if I ever see him again it will be at the Chelsea Flower Show—though I shan't speak to him, as he won't remember me.

What a delightful lot those gardeners are! Once a year they descend on London in their thousands, these retired men, and wrinkled sunburnt ladies with hands inured to grubbing in the earth, and press eagerly from stall to stall in the hot, shady grass-odorous tents and from rock-garden to rock-garden outside, eagerly discussing whether each primula and saxifrage which they haven't got will "do" with them. Then they depart for their fastnesses in Shropshire or Dorset, leaving the more senseless part of the population to stew in London for a "Season" which ought to be arranged for the winter, instead of for months when hawthorn, laburnum and lilac bloom and die, and the full prime of summer comes on with the rose. I usually go to the Show, though I do not know which dianthus is a rare one from Tibet and which is not. Each year I learn some Latin names and each year forget, and the same applies when I read the books. I believe I might even retain the umbelliferæ and the compositæ of the Alps (of which Reggie Farrer, who was reluctant to learn more Latin names than he had to, said in his lovely book on the Dolomites, there were hundreds of which he did not know the names) if they were called things like Yodeller's Carrot and Chamois Parsley. But the tendency is all the other way. Even bungaloid wives have learnt to say antirrhinum and nigella instead of the snapdragon and love-in-a-mist of their mothers, and the time may come when Perdita's catalogue of flowers may all have to be translated into Seedsmanese, and only the rose and the lily will be allowed to smell as sweet by their old names because the Latin ones are too much like the English ones to make really enigmatic jargon.

Thus thinking, I strolled past the Abbey up the hill, looked into shop windows, observed the decorous streams walking home from church, wondered what proportion of them were going to have roast beef, decided that, since it was Bath and traditional, I would, if I could, have some myself, and walked into the hall of a hotel. Roast beef was on the card all right, but as it was only half-past twelve I thought I would go into the bar and have an apéritif. There was one other man leaning on the counter, and as the barmaid left him to attend to my gin and French I could not help noticing that he stared at me rather intently. He was soldierly, sunburnt, with blue eyes, a plumpish face and a brown moustache. He came up and rather shyly said: "Excuse me, sir, isn't your name Squire?"

"Yes . . . I was sure your face was familiar, but . . ."

"Don't you remember I played cricket for you about ten

years ago? In Kent it was; you asked Lewis to bring a spare man. My name's Hopkinson."

"Oh, I remember. Weren't you in the Army?"

"Yes. I'm just back from Egypt now. Are you staying in Bath?"

"No, I'm passing through on a holiday. I'm walking."

"I'm in a car; going on to Taunton to stay with some people."

"Are you lunching here?"

"Thought of it."

"Why not let's lunch together. What will you have?"

"Oh, a dry sherry, thanks very much."

It came. "All the best," said he, and drank.

We talked awhile about India, Egyptian students and the dust of Mersa Matrouh. Then we went in to lunch in a coffee-room which was almost empty.

Harking back to the Near East over coffee and cigarettes he asked me if I had known T. E. Lawrence, who had been killed three months before. I said I had. The Arab Bureau, the Hedjaz, the War: various names were mentioned. Hopkinson paused; then said: "I say, Squire, you must have known an awful number of people."

"Yes," I replied weakly, "and a number of awful people."

"Have you ever thought of writing your memoirs?"

Steel engravings of dead statesmen and horses in walnut frames looked down gravely at me from the walls; their memories at least had been piously preserved; anyhow in Bath. "Well," I admitted, "people have suggested it occasionally and, under Providence, I expect I shall do it some time. In point of fact I'm by way of beginning now."

"How do you mean?"

"Well, I'm going to write a book about this holiday I'm on, and I shall put down anything I remember as I go, quite apart from what may happen at the time, such as meeting you during this Sabbath calm in Bath."

"But you won't have any notes or diaries with you. You may forget to put down all sorts of important things."

"That's quite true. For instance, I was once held up to see

Mr. Gladstone appear on a balcony. I don't know the date and I only dimly remember the enormous yelling crowd. If you hadn't provoked me to give him as an example I don't suppose I should have thought of him if I had sat upon every five-barred gate from here to Land's End. So his name, for one, will not appear in my index. . . . I don't suppose," I murmured to myself reminiscently, "he would have been a friend of mine, anyhow."

He laughed. "If I," he said, "wrote a book that way I should be afraid of finding when I finished it that I'd left everything out."

"There is something to be said," I argued, "in favour of the things which spontaneously recur to one's mind being the most important to oneself—or, at any rate, the truest, as it were. Also when I think of my diaries and fifty great boxes of letters I quail."

*   *   *   *   *

Late in the afternoon I was back in the little lounge. It was the hour when wireless Sunday services begin and the walker in suburban streets hears hymns moaning from many harmoniums. A provincial city at that hour might have inspired the early muse of Mr. T. S. Eliot. The travellers had gone; I had written a postcard; I had found Webster's Dictionary not so readable as it sometimes has been; and I had made a vow that never, never, never again would I decide to spend a day doing absolutely nothing in any place where there was not an out-of-door, whole-time café and, for spectacle, either a lively population of passers-by or a beautiful view. I smoked cigarette after cigarette, stared at the silent ink-stands and armchairs, and allowed my thoughts to stray over the habitable globe.

China, of course, was no good; it was not yet up, and America on Sunday morning was no more tempting than Bath—though I did remember one jovial hour before lunch in Philadelphia with certain Quakers, newly come from their meeting, who in the house of one of them very heartily defied the then law of their country and were full of good stories.

But from a solitary traveller's point of view, almost any town on the continent of Europe would be preferable—place, platz or piazza with sipping sitters and chattering walkers—to any town in England, where for centuries there has been a set and stubborn refusal to admit that the Sabbath was made for man, and not man for the Sabbath.

This globe, according to the latest theories, which are those of Copernicus and Galileo extended, is a speck of dust in the Universe. Alice Meynell wrote a poem, called "Christ in the Universe," in which she envisaged Our Lord, visiting planet after planet, betrayed by Judas after Judas, judged by Pilate after Pilate, and dying for star after star. Hers was one of the great imaginative feats; the answer of the astronomers was that the planets nearer than ourselves to the sun would be too hot, and that those farther than us from the sun would be too cold. But what an answer! Is the soul a matter of temperature?

Anatole France, a sceptic who had his lucid moments, suddenly (I think in *The Garden of Epicurus*) thought that all we are, and know and see, may be but a corpuscle in the blood of (to us) a giant, who contemplates, not only suns beyond our sun, but universes in which our sun and all our planets are but as corpuscles—and envisages worlds beyond, and beyond, and beyond—for, in point of fact, there is no end to infinity, and there is no end to eternity, and the human brain can comprehend neither of them, and all it can do is to fall down and worship the Greater Glory of God. When one gets into that remoteness of speculation, humble before the Eternal, bewildered about one's own existence, puzzled as to how anything can *be,* and trying to get behind *cogito ergo sum,* all the things of this world appear small.

One reads the papers. "Albania Annoyed at Italian Intrusion," "Canton at Issue with Nanking," "Mussolini and Malta." How preposterous it all appears! And how especially absurd such a thing as Sabbatarianism, and the desire, on one day in the week, to prevent other people from indulging in harmless amusements. . . .

"Well, why stay here the night?" came the voice of common sense. Inclination echoed "Why?" I yawned, stretched, remembered, went downstairs and telephoned; and within half an hour the car was at the door for me. I had forgotten Charles entirely: and, although he would probably insist on dressing for dinner, even although it was Sunday and he a bachelor and I was not in a position to do so, he was a hospitable soul and his house was full of books. He did dress.

We dined well and sat late, and for a brief evening I regretted that I had left long behind the mania for fine, early and rare editions. Before the war, when he and I were in London, we used to examine second-hand booksellers' catalogues in the luncheon hour, and compare in the evenings the things we had found in cellars and on barrows. Now in his retirement, he had gone on, and the shaded luxurious room was lined with leather bindings, old and new, with gold letters softly gleaming on them. As I turned over the early printed books, the old poets, the beautiful reprints by modern presses, a desire for material possessions came faintly, but poignantly, back which I thought I had lost for ever; and I was astonished to find how many dates, whether of Aldines or eighteenth-century quartos, had lain dormant in my mind, ready to spring to life like those mythical seeds which did but sleep in the tombs of the Pharaohs. In company with a man who never lived more than he had to in his own time, to whom foreign countries were chiefly places which had contained early presses at Venice, Florence, Basle, Strasbourg and the like, and the map of England was studded (as to others with towns, mines or golf-courses) with good second-hand bookshops, I returned for a while to an air in which Pynson and de Worde, Burton, Urquhart, Baskerville and Charles Lamb were "forms more real than mortal man" at present thumping and bellowing on the planet. Whisky, a siphon, and cut glasses were brought in; drinks were poured out; and Charles incessantly sat down and chatted and then, as something arose in talk, went to open glass-fronted shelves and brought out one more treasure, spreading out his hands in delight over red-morocco, gilt-tooled on the overlaps, armorial deckings on calf, presentation copies from Locke and Beckford, and paper, centuries old, as white as when, in those strange old strainers and vats and presses, it was made. As I turned over the pages of his trophies my thoughts were half there and half elsewhere. They kept on straying to things I had once possessed and the places in which I had found them. There was the volume of Goethe's songs, inscribed by Frau Goethe, which I had bought for threepence in Bridport when the weather made cricket impossible—gusts of rain and a south-wester that kept blowing the bails off the stumps. There was the first edition of Chapman's *Homer,* with George MacDonald's signature and Homeric drawings of Flaxman inserted which I had picked up in a bundle (also including first editions by Johnson and Defoe) in a London sale-room. There was that noble great encyclopædia of Vincentius Bellovacensis—Vincent of Beauvais—with its thick crinkled snowy paper and illuminated initials. There was the *Margarita Poetica* of Albertus de Eyb, which I could not afford to pay for in cash, and consequently asked the old Jew in Sicilian Avenue to Chiswick to take his money's worth in books—he taking his money's worth ten times over, again and again snatching one more first edition, knowing that I would not let the fine old tome go for the sake of just one more book I valued less. There was that almost complete collection of English poetry worth reading, some good copies, some ragged firsts, from folios of Jonson and Beaumont and Fletcher to the obscurest early Americans. There were the first Aldines of Catullus and Euripides (with goffered edges); there was that unrecorded pre-first piracy of Pascal; there were all those pretty French books, with the engravings of the eighteenth century, the Grécourts and Pirons and Dorats and *The Parrot* by the gentleman whose very name I have now forgotten and cannot be bothered to look up. When again, I mused, shall I ever see a copy of "Jane Squire on the Method of Determining the Longitude"—of George II's time she was, possibly a relative of mine, probably a termagant who frightened the Admiralty out of their wits—or the infamous compositions of Robbé de Beauveset which I should have wanted to be burned by the common hangman had they not been so excessively rare, or of Œcolampadius on the Gospel of St. John and several such which I treasured only (for no human being will ever again

E*

read them) because they were not mentioned in the catalogue of the British Museum? First editions of Keats, Shelley and Coleridge passed across my vision; great sets like Dodsley's Old Plays; all those Calendars, Catalogues, Short Lists and other reference books. They had all gone when I moved house, and I had not given them a thought since: yet here was Charles still eagerly pursuing, clutching and poring as once had I, who had moved on stepping-stones of my dead selves to, I hope, nothing worse, and was evidently no collector born but one who had merely wished to learn, and, having learned, willingly discarded his text-books. . . .

The last half-hour we sat in armchairs under the standard lamp, smoking with the tray between us. It suddenly occurred to Charles, who had taken for granted my reappearance after a long interval, to ask me what I had been doing lately. It is never an easy question to answer when relationship has been broken for several years: you don't know whether to begin with "Had I written any short stories when I last saw you?" "I saw the Eclipse at Sandown two years ago with a woman I don't suppose you've ever heard of," "How many children had I when we last met?" or "Just the same old things, you know." However, some remark or other brought up the subject of contemporary literature, and it dawned upon me that he had read almost nothing new (although he took up the weeklies) for thirty years and assumed that during that period nothing worth reading had been written—he has probably read *John Buncle,* but never *Kim,* one of the great novels of the world. He mentioned several much belauded novelists into whom he had dipped and asked me how on earth I could admire them. "I don't," said I; "I think they are clever shallow cheapjacks." "Well," he grumbled, "everybody seems to read them." "I don't care if they do," I replied, "but there are plenty of better writers than those." "Where are your poets?" he went on; "I tried a volume by So-and-so not long ago, and it was dreary pretentious rubbish." "I quite agree," I said. "Well, what did I say?" he continued; "they're all rotten." I was tempted to go for him and try to ram into his head all my admirations and try once more to make him see; but as I looked at his scholarly profile and greying hair I remembered old conversations and asked myself what was the good of disturbing him by exhortations which could never convince him. He was the immovable mass; he was quite resolved not to read his contemporaries; instinct led him to notice only those of them whom he would have disliked even had they been dead; and all of them were part of that hot living present from which he wished to flee. He will never read these lines, as I am a contemporary; though, were I to edit Fuller's *Worthies,* he would be enthusiastically interested and send me corrections and footnotes for a second edition which would never appear.

Undressing, in a large and Chippendalish room, I sang snatches of the most singable modern poems I could remember. I laughed aloud as I wondered what look of horror, as of one who fears a maniac, would come over Charles's bookworm's face were I to swing his bedroom door open and loudly exclaim:

> The Saracen's Head looks down the lane
> Where we shall never drink wine again. . . .

* * * * *

That was then; and now as I write, the "Saracen's Head" looks down the lane, and the world will never be the same again; for Chesterton is dead; and, just before him, the great lyric poet of whom he said when blowing away pessimism with great lusty puffs, that "The song of the cheerful Shropshire Lad is simply a perfectly horrid song." Charles, I am sure, can never have done more than dip into either of them with predetermined resistance: one to him was probably a journalist and the other a don. Yet, a hundred years hence, the Charleses of the period (provided the progress of science, trade, and dulce and decorum has not blown Europe to bits), will be busily searching shops in Bideford and Newcastle for obscure pamphlets which Chesterton himself did not remember writing, and the more jovial lovers of great men dead will assemble at the "Saracen's Head" in Beaconsfield (unless a bench of dissenting licensing magistrates and secret drinkers has abolished it as redundant) and quaff pints to Chesterton. The little Della Cruscans and Spasmodics of our day, with their fashionable modes of obscurity and sham violence, and their peevish hatred of love, laughter, jugs of wine, boughs, thous and song, will have whimpered and sneered their way into oblivion, but the hearts of boys and men will be braced by the lays of the laughing cavalier who at last left the lanes and the wild roses to go to Paradise by way of Kensal Green.

Thus I thought in bed, not realising that within a few months not Chesterton only but several others would have gone who seemed to have been always there and a world without whom one never contemplated—such men as he and Kipling seemed ageless and fixed, and now they are both gone, and there are only two or three remaining whose names were known when my generation was young, and after them there is almost a whole generation missing. It is strange to think that, if one lives for another twenty years, one will be regarded as a sort of Methuselah because of that gap, and they will wear a sort of "Did-you-once-see-Shelley-plain?" air when one admits to having had acquaintance with Hardy, Bridges, Housman, Alice Meynell and all that race, and to have met people who met people who knew Keats and Lamb. What will they look like if one mentions some of the peacocks of the hour such as Presidents of Boards of Trade, Education and so on? Bewildered, I expect; for, though the names of one or two of the Prime Ministers of our time will be kept alive with the Pitts and the Gladstones, those of others will be duly, if dully, handed down in the chronicles like those of Rockingham and Addington, Joash and Jehoahash.

EIGHTH DAY

"Which way are you going?" asked Charles after breakfast.

"I'm not quite sure," I said; "let's have a look at the map."

We spread it out on the table. "If you'd like to be dropped anywhere within reason you can be," he offered.

"Roughly anywhere except Radstock," I murmured as my forefinger roved over the red-veined tracts of brown and green, "or, for that matter, Midsomer Norton, in spite of its pretty name. The Fosse-Way is attractive, and if I went to Stratton I might have another look at their new chapel at Downside, though it does take the gilt off their old buildings, just as does the new chapel at Charterhouse which makes the rest of the place look like St. Pancras. There's a place here called Binegar. I must have been through it, I suppose, though it is strange that one shouldn't remember a place which rhymes to vinegar—though a rhyme to that is not needed so much as a rhyme to silver and a few more rhymes to love which might obviate the necessity of the eye-rhymes "move" and "prove." Well, never mind; drop me on to the top of the Mendips by Pen Hill, and I'll walk down through Wells."

He had had some catalogues by the morning's post, so he sent me by car. I stopped it on the top of the ridge, got out and sat down by the road-side; and there suddenly came into my head a thought of St. Clement of Alexandria.

Why?

Well, there is no evidence that St. Clement ever came to Wells, though some think, and I like to think it myself, that St. Joseph of Arimathea came to Glastonbury and planted there the Holy Thorn. But I was, as the crow flies (or flew), only two or three miles from Wookey Hole, and St. Clement of Alexandria said something.

The texts of the very early Fathers, apostolic and other, are growing dim in my memory, though the impression I derived from them when young, those men so nearly in touch with the great event, so overshadowed and overwhelmed by that recent thing, and mostly so simple in their language as they were certain in their belief, has not faded; to open their pages is to lift a curtain behind which dwells awe: they are half-way between the companions of Christ and those later men who more and more settled down to ecclesiasticism, theology, and the definition of heresies. The personality of only one of them has always remained alive to me, and that one is St. Clement; for amongst those good bishops and fishers of men he was the link with the cultivated world, a devout Christian so sensitive and well-read that he could have responded to the legend which arose some centuries after of the sailors who, passing the Morea, heard a voice calling from the hollows of the hills, "Great Pan is dead." He was, if I remember, an Athenian born, and brought up in the schools of pagan philosophy; he became Bishop of Alexandria and wrote discursively, amusingly, kindly, quoting (and here again I draw upon memory and refer to no more than I thought of on the Mendips) Homer and Euripides. He was probably an admirable missioner to the cultivated Greeks of the city, the frequenters of the great library which was burnt up in the prairie fire of Islam, the neo-Platonists, the scholar-successors of the unnecessary men who invented Greek accents, and of Callimachus, whose work has mostly sunk out of sight but who wrote that lovely address to the dead Heraclitus which Johnson Cory turned into a perfect English poem:

> Still are thy pleasant voices, thy nightingales, awake,
> For Death he taketh all away, but them he cannot take.

For Alexandria was not entirely populated by the characters of Pierre Louys.

I had not, I recalled, as I surveyed the great landscape below me, thought of St. Clement for a very long time when, a few years ago, he was suddenly and violently brought back in the most unexpected surroundings. It was a Sunday in August and another man and I went in my car for a "run round" the Mendips—Wookey Hole, the Cheddar Caves, lunch at Cheddar, up the gorge and along the hamlets on the Bristol side. It was a lovely sunny day; we saw some lonely churches with fine towers; even the swarm of holiday motors could not spoil the majesty of the Gorge, the great perpendicular cliffs coiling snakelike to the summit; and in the garden of the inn at Cheddar we caused pain by asking, with apparent sincerity, for Canadian Cheddar cheese. But the caves, for all the strings of electric lights and the murmurous company of stumbling trippers, were the thing; the pools, the smooth cataracts, the pillars and stalactites of many-coloured limestone, milky, golden and blue; and the moment of all to me was the moment when the guide made that remark.

He had done that tour through the underworld, I daresay, for many days in many summers: and, like the housekeepers in great half-shut country places and the vergers in cathedrals, he had his lesson by heart and probably said it perfectly every night in his sleep. In grotto after grotto he told us the romantic name of the cave and described whatever bones of men and beasts may have been found there: now and then he switched on lights which, human agency apart, would never have been on sea or land, let alone in the bowels of the Mendips. And then, somewhere in the course of his discourse, this grey official with the peaked cap, "doing" (as the saying goes) "his stuff," quoted St. Clement of Alexandria—possibly about caves at Delphi or Dodona, but I don't remember—and staggered me. My eyebrows went up and up, the transverse wrinkles in my brow deepened, my temple tightened, my mouth opened, and then I had to resist a temptation to make all the caverns of Mendip echo and re-echo to my laughter. For what had St. Clement to do with Wookey Hole, and where the devil had the official guide to Wookey Hole, who personally conducted through it parties of motor-cyclists who had never even heard of St. Ignatius Loyola, learnt about Clement of Alexandria?

Enlightenment came later. When we blinked back into the unscholastic light of day I bought a guide written by a gentleman—a prince of troglodytes or, as they call themselves, speleologists—and, amid all the anthropological and geological information there was embedded (as, according to Tennyson and fact, eggs are embedded and injellied in veal-and-ham pie) the very quotation from St. Clement which had passed so glibly, amid those Dantesque recesses, from the punctual and unamused lips of the guide. "England! my England!" I thought; and loved my fellow-countrymen for their solemnity. I hope I am not libelling the guide when I suppose that, out of that context, he knew very little of that Saint who inhabited, like Pater's Marius, both the groves of Academe and the Garden of Gethsemane; and I am quite sure that not once per annum is there amongst that throng of tourists, becapped and plus-foured, and temporarily sobered by the ancient and the subterranean, a man who ever heard of St. Clement, or of any of the popes Clement, or even of Clement Scott; yet never a one of them, and bless them for it, even in the neighbourhood of Cheddar would ever rise before the guide and shout out "Cheese it!" For, in certain surroundings, we respect learning, just·as we respect religion in church.

"Shall I go to Wookey Hole again?" I thought to myself: and then: "But why curtail the already curtailed cur?" And then: "What on earth is that to do with it—Wookey Hole is not a cur and you were not thinking of curtailing it. You were merely thinking that you didn't want to do the same thing twice, or at any rate this thing twice."

"Stop!" I said, to this daimon who will, day in, day out, and even in my sleep (for the phrase "night out" might be misleading) keep on rebuking me, correcting me, quibbling, splitting hairs, and checking me in full innocent career, "cannot a man be allowed his little harmless parallels of sound and meaning, and even his plays upon words?" I pulled up a bunch of grass and chewed it savagely. "For," said I, "where would all those wandering authors have been, Lucian, Rabelais and Sterne, if they had not been allowed (they hadn't you, you beast, to stop them) to give their tongues a loose rein occasionally? Anyhow, damn you, the phrase just came back to me."

Full summer; a slope at my feet; the mellow day gentling over that long stretch of Somerset: Wells, Glastonbury and all that isle of Avalon in which you can take your choice between Arthur and his last fight and Alfred and his cakes; but if you are wise, will be like Chesterton and accept both, both being certainly true symbolically and perhaps true in fact. But did, in these surroundings, Adam Smith, Cobden and Bright ever exist? I do not want to be profane, but can anybody imagine anybody else, divine or human, contemplating the Cobden statue in Mornington Crescent (quite properly placed amid all the dismalness into which false philosophies led us) and saying: "Consider Cobden in his bronze frock-coat and bronze trousers—was Solomon in all his glory arrayed like unto one of these?" *Sartor Resartus* was written too early; and drawn too early were Thackeray's pictures of Louis with his clothes and Louis without his clothes. The clothes of nineteenth-century England are its condemnation; and Lord Macaulay, for all his brilliance of style, never objected to them, but probably thought them a stage in progress towards God knows what. Think of Bright without his clothes. It isn't possible; and, if it were, we should shrink from it.

*   *   *   *   *

"It's quite easy to be wise after the event," said the daimon (perhaps it would save trouble if we began to spell him "demon"), "but weren't those people just as well-meaning as yourself?"

"I daresay they were," I reflected; and, unmeaningly again (and I dared not say the lines aloud because of the way in which the demon had reprimanded me when I quoted Calverley) there came into my mind the last lines of Thomas Ingoldsby which began with:

As I laye a-thynkynge, a-thynkynge, a-thynkynge,
There came a little bird and it sang upon the spraye.

The little bird came and sang to me: and it sang to me, and to all in all generations who deplore their elders: "Truly we are the children and wisdom shall die with us." It seems hardly possible to even ordinarily sensible minds of our generation that we could have done almost anything that, as a nation, we have done in the past. Why on earth did we wage the Hundred Years War or the Wars of the Roses? Why on earth did we allow ourselves to get to such a point as to have to stomach the Tudors? Why did we let Oliver Cromwell murder the king and then murder Parliament in the cause of Parliament versus the King? Why did we bring in that ghastly Dutchman? Why did we lose a reluctant America with Pitt, Fox and Burke telling us not to? How could we, throughout the nineteenth century, pretend to ourselves that

Charles II was a monster because he had mistresses (to whom, as to everybody else, he was kind), and regard it as an article of faith that none of his successors indulged themselves, and less openly and elegantly, in the same way? How could we have been conquered (it almost induces one to think that Marx's materialistic philosophy of History may be true) by the *laissez-faire* theory of economics, which suited the manufacturing middle classes, was reconciled to the crawling of women on all-fours in coal-mines and the sale of small children from the southern workhouses to cotton factories in the north, covered the country with slums and derelict factories and justified all the predictions of Disraeli? How could we have supposed that a League of Nations based on the doctrine of "One Nation One Vote" would work in a world so variegated in regard to race, climate, development and power, and with nations all of different sizes? Theory, theory: what crimes are committed in thy name! "That damned Rousseau!" I exclaimed to myself; and then I reminded myself that there had been a great deal of harm done in the world long before the Geneva watchmaker's son ever began writing operas about shepherdesses, fabricating fantastic origins for the State, pulling down pillars, or getting maidservants punished for thefts which he himself had committed. "The swine!" I thought; and then the demon mocked: "What about casting the first stone?" . . .

Unable, although I had more spare time than overworked Cabinet Ministers, who unravel all the mysteries of history or the problems of contemporary politics in an hour, I thought it better, squaring my pack, to resume my pilgrimage, reciting to myself the consoling line of the poet, A. Y. Campbell:

"God speaks in history, and man in myth."

"But even that," I reflected, as I lightly trod the downward way to Wells, "begs a question in the first part: it is a little determinist, is it not? It isn't so much 'God helps him who helps himself' as 'We can't help ourselves, God help us!' It is a little irrational to saddle 'a power not ourselves, making

for righteousness' with jerry-building and Hitler's 'purge.'"
I remembered the Tower of Siloam; and was comforted to
think that a greater than all of us left the mystery where it
was, so far as this world is concerned, and got himself crucified
not only for our redemption beyond, but for our strengthening
here. And then I thought how trivially my reflections had
begun, and the demon said: "Your thoughts wander superficially from this to that and you grin one moment and go
serious the next," and then I answered: "Fool demon, I believe
you are the Devil himself; for all things are interwoven; you
cannot move a grain of sand without troubling a star; a man
saw a ladder going to Heaven from Charing Cross; I shall let
my thoughts stray wherever they will and no imp of Satan
shall prevent me from cross-examining the past, the present,
the future, or myself. *Retro me!*"

Something departed; and I thought no more that day thus
introspectively, being a healthy body moving through scenes
of beauty and watching them with outward eyes.

As I came into Wells under the gate I was glad. I went to
an inn and left my baggage there; and unimpeded walked
across the Close and into the cathedral, looking again at the
strange arch and the great old clock. Then I went outside
again and wandered round the moat which surrounds the
bishop's palace. There is a bell-pull there which hangs down
into the water: it is there for the disdainful swans to tug on
when they feel hungry. The swan tugs, the bell jangles, the
food is forthcoming; and they have been doing it, father and
son, for centuries. And within the moat there is that old
palace, the oldest massive brick part of which dates from
King John.

It was about lunch-time. I wanted lunch, and I wanted to
see the inside of the bishop's palace; and I thought, though I
wasn't quite sure, that the Bishop of Bath and Wells was a
member of my own old College at Cambridge. He who hesi-
tates is lost. I hesitated and was lost. And now, unless the
bishop, by some incredible coincidence, happens to read this,
I shall never see the inside of that lovely place, which I con-
ceive to be full of illuminated missals, chained books, and

recumbent, mitred, effigies in alabaster or marble, removed from the church by King Henry's order but preserved (since it was so far from London) by the piety of the priests. The piety, I may add, was sporadic; the Historical Manuscripts Commission published, twenty years ago, volumes about the clerics of Wells before the Reformation which contain a good many funny stories, but harmless stories, and none so disgusting as the story of the fat, bewhiskered king who murdered Sir Thomas More and the aged and saintly abbot of Glaston.

I went back to lunch alone; and there came to me the thought, recorded by Rossetti: "When have I been here before?" I ordered some cutlets, remembered that I had been there many times, and then suddenly remembered that I had been there once significantly. Not in the years when I was merely walking back to Devon; not in the late years when I was taking cricketers round the counties, from Campden to Taunton, on Sundays when we were "not working"; but once when I went back to Devon with a fellow-Devonian, I suppose thirty, but it might be forty, years older than me.

The men (partly owing to the war which obliterated so many people who would be now between forty and sixty) who remember John Lane in his prime are now probably few. When I was at school I knew his name as the publisher of the *Yellow Book* and the *Keynotes Series*. I thought of him as a person mixed up with Aubrey Beardsley and Oscar Wilde: clever, audacious, and definitely *fin-de-siècle*. The odd thing is that John Lane simply detested all that.

To lead up to the time when I went to Wells with John Lane (I providing the car and he the petrol, for he always arranged things to the uttermost farthing and would bargain you out of a halfpenny and give you a champagne and lobster dinner afterwards) I am afraid that I must go some way back.

(Remember that we are still at Wells: that lovely cathedral, and that arch, and that close, the competing and ancient hotels, the swans, the libraries, the choristers, and the moats.)

Well, when I was at school (and I left school thirty years ago and still meet superior youths who think they have discovered Baudelaire for the first time in the Croydon Free

Library or the Oxford Union) I struck those *Fleurs de Mal* of Baudelaire with the spell-binding portrait of him in a smock, the head slightly bowed, the great melancholy eyes looking straight at one above the wide sensuous mouth, and Gautier's ample introduction. I used, after lights were out, to steal down from the dormitory to my study in a dressing-gown to translate him, carefully drawing the curtains so that no chink of light shone across the lawn to Mr. Francis's premises—I learned long afterwards that they knew all about it but assumed I was up to something innocuous of the sort, though I daresay their eyebrows might have gone up had they seen my industrious versions of *The Giantess, The Carrion* and the poem about the repulsive Jewess. My own natural imaginings were not in the least like Baudelaire's (he haunted me but he did not infect me), but most young writers go through intellectual measles of some sorts, and for a year or two I "experienced" all the grimmest literature I could find. Not that it was only the fact that his material was very unlike that of the approved poets with whom I was familiar and who were fit to be studied in schools. There was fascination in that strange mixture (to be found also in Flaubert) of realism and romance, in the wistful personality which stood in the mud and looked at the stars, in the marble purity of the style and the firm ring of the music. However, at school and later, I translated most of him (though a few were too horrible for me) and there came a time when I thought I would like to publish them— a few were ultimately published in a small book of verse which I rightly suppressed because of its falsity, which I did not perceive until it was printed: my late father-in-law, moreover, startled me by not realising that the translations were translations, and expressing the hope (not to me) that they did not record actual experiences of my own.

It was in the autumn of 1906, when I was twenty-two. I was sitting in an upstairs room in the office of the local daily (now extinct) at Plymouth where I worked for two years until I got a small job in London, and Mr. John Lane was suddenly announced—he had come up to gossip with Mr. (now Sir) Herbert Russell, the naval expert of the organ, with whom I shared the room. Lane was a little man with a round head, round bald forehead, shrewd narrow eyes, plump pink cheeks, and a neat pointed white beard; brisk in all his movements and full of chatter. I was any nameless young man in a provincial town; he gave me an Egyptian cigarette out of a gold case and began by rather coming it over me as a metropolitan veteran, speaking familiarly of literary lords and such, for whom he always had a harmless propensity. When he found I was not illiterate he changed his tone and was on the job (Chesterfield might turn in his grave at such a phrase) at once. Had I written a novel? Was I thinking of writing a novel? If so would I send it to him? No: but I wanted to publish a volume of verse translations from the French. The light was dimmed in his eyes; I could see him thinking: "What, one more of them?" for the vogue had passed of those Bodley Head poets of whom somebody wrote:

> Lo, where upon Parnassus' slopes they romp
> The sons of Wat, of David, John and Thomp.

Still, he said gallantly that I should send the manuscript to his London address.

I did. It came back, not to my surprise. He very civilly wrote to say that he had shown it to Mr. Arthur Symons, who had said that he preferred my translations to somebody else's: but that there was no demand for such things, but, as a fellow-Devonian, would I get in touch with him as soon as I came to London? This I did, and after some years he gave me manuscripts to read, and until his death I saw a great deal of him, frequently dining at his house (which was full of treasures he had picked up, including an excellent portrait by Gilbert Stuart) or lunching at the Reform or the Cocoa Tree Club—which was Queen Anne, the oldest club in London, had a blackened cocoa-palm trunk shooting up in the middle of it, and is now, unhappily, no more. At one such gathering, in 1924 (the last year of Lane's life), we were talking, as usual, about Devon (for Lane was born in a farmhouse near Hartland, a strange origin for the patron of the *Yellow Book*) and

I said that I was going to tour it by myself in August with an open car. He said he would like to come with me. That was arranged. I picked him up, I think, in Bath, and we spent a happy fortnight on the road, and I became very fond of him as we went circling and criss-crossing Devon, descending for meals on country houses with pictures, admiring views and investigating every church we saw: his eyesight was defective and I sometimes became almost exhausted reading out to him every old time-eaten epitaph in a churchyard.

Never did I hear (and I wish I had imbibed it all) so much information. Lane had a collector's memory. Everything in Devon was sacred to him, and he knew everything that was to be known about the smallest "worthies" the county had ever produced. "Stop!" he used to cry in some hamlet, "we must go into the little church here; there is a tablet to Joseph Skinner, the engraver." He had no idea that there are times, in a motor-car, when one should not divert the attention of the man at the wheel; constantly when I was threading the traffic of such places as Ashburton or Chudleigh, he would suddenly clutch my arm and exclaim: "Look at that little barber's shop on the left. It used to be the baker's shop where Solomon Toop, the portrait painter, was born"; Toop, as often as not, being some obscure eighteenth-century son-of-a-gun of whom I had never heard. Even on the lonely roads of Dartmoor, with the purple heather everywhere and the little streams tumbling down from the tors, and the bog-pools reflecting the blue of the sky, the excerpts from *Devon Notes and Queries* would come rattling from his tongue, for local lore meant far more to him than landscape and he would have liked the tors better had their rocky crowns been the birthplaces even of faded commentators on the Old Testament.

Wells, after we had left Bath, was the first place at which we had stopped: coming back alone, I thought of him, and his vitality quenched, of how he had been a legend to me before I ever met him, of how then I had known him for years, and now he was a legend, and a waning legend again. And I found myself reflecting on the strange phase of literature with which his name is associated.

I don't know who coined the phrase "The Naughty Nineties," but it was rather a silly one. There is at least as much to be said for "The Dirty Thirties" which I recently heard applied to our own decade. Queen Victoria was on the throne; Lords Wolseley, Roberts and Kitchener were national heroes; Kipling was expounding the duties of the Empire; Watts was at the apex of painting; Hardy, Meredith, Henry James, Gissing and Stevenson reached audiences who had never heard either of Hubert Crackanthorpe's stories or of his suicide; Conrad was beginning to be known; the characteristic entertainments of the period were Gilbert and Sullivan's operas; Austin Dobson had a great reputation; the dominant critics were Gosse, Saintsbury, Birrell, Dowden, Lang, "Q," and others who, had they been confronted with much of our own "modern" literature, would not have minded seeing it put in the furnace; the dreadful, crude, emancipated, middle-class "naughtiness" of our own day was unknown. Beardsley was no more typical of the age artistically than Wilde was socially. Still, there was something distinctive there and most adolescents were drawn to examine it, if not permanently to like it: for it was something new in England.

Even *The Yellow Book,* let alone Lane's General List, was not, atmospherically, all of a piece: Lane, for instance, published the poems of A. C. Benson, and it would be difficult indeed to think of Arthur Benson talking of "splendid sins" or describing in verse his travels from music-hall to gin-palace with a marauding lady in a feather boa. Lane, to the young, indeed, seemed to publish almost all the exciting new authors and to have a monopoly in poets. As a publisher, to certain ages and temperaments, just after his greater exploits, he dominated the sky. It was, of course, a false impression; not only were the great ancient saurians, the Longmans and Murrays and Macmillans there, as they still are, but very likely several publishers like Methuen actually did more business than Lane; yet Lane was the man for novelties. And though, as I have said, his authors were by no means all of the same kind, they appeared to be more of a kind than they were because they were all under the same distinctive umbrella.

Books published by Lane all had a common and pleasant idiosyncrasy of format: whether they were sacred or profane, they were printed, decorated and bound in an especially Laneish manner. And, although the contents of the *Yellow Book* included stories and articles by such respectable authors as James and Benson and at least one drawing by Lord Leighton, whose Greeks savoured more of the Court of Saint James's than of the Court of Argos, the fact remained that all were enveloped in a cover of a shockingly bold yellow and that the cover was originally adorned by an undoubtedly decadent drawing by Aubrey Beardsley.

"What," I thought to myself in that luncheon-room at Wells, while I sipped my coffee and (in order to help recover my youth) a liqueur brandy, "really was the art which gave rise to the theory about the Naughty Nineties, and what were its origins and who were at the centre of the movement, though it may have been a movement which preached anything but movement, and came in the end to very little." There came to my mind two lines of Canon Ainger's, who wrote:

> I would we had more of the godly heart,
> And less of the Bodley Head.

There did flourish, under the umbrella of that brisk farmer's son from Devon who collected antiques, loved dining out with the great, hardly ever read a book, but had a nose for fashions and for paid readers who could spot the potentially fashionable, a certain nucleus of authors and artists who were definitely Bodley Head and what (though the type is a permanent one) is now known as "ninetyish."

They mostly derive both manner and matter from the French: from Baudelaire, Verlaine, Gautier, Maupassant, the early Huysmans, Zola, Daumier, Toulouse-Lautrec and Félicien Rops—and it may be remarked that French influence is usually stifling to English art, turning our feet on to tracks which lead to dead-ends: or should I say culs-de-sac? They flaunted style like a banner; their view was that art should do anything in the world except conceal art; they were contemptuous of the industrial and bourgeois age into which they were born, but unlike Ruskin and Morris they did not thunder against it, but curled their lips against it and took refuge from it with their bars, stars, nenuphars and lupanars, all of which, in some sort, rhymed. They were the Romantic movement gone to seed, unable to fly from Les Villes Tentaculaires, and escaping into deliriums of sex, or sacerdotalism, finding consolation in the Latin of the Rite, or from cadences like grey evening over Thames or Seine, or patched, powdered, red-heeled prose like that of the *marquises* in *Under the Hill,* or apostrophes to suicide and annihilation. Linked to these by a common rebellion against convention were certain bold realists and reformers, mostly women, who wished to preach the glorious free future in language more frank than was then commonly used, but to us prudish to a fault, and challenging that view of "Reticence in Literature" which was so eloquently preached in the *Yellow Book* itself by the young father-to-be of Mr. Evelyn Waugh. With a centipede foot in every camp there was the young Mr. Max Beerbohm who made a first appearance in the *Yellow Book* with "A Defence of Cosmetics" (which, being incorrigibly healthy, he probably disliked) very far, in spirit, from those poems about rouge, henna and patchouli, which took strange pleasure in the painting of the cadaverous faces of consumption, dissipation and death, hollow under the pallor of glittering gas-light chandeliers. In retrospect, even now, they take a large place in the contemporary scene; to the young, thirty years ago, they seemed even more significant; yet to most of their own contemporaries and elders they really mattered very little. Dowson, a very typical one in point, was never "on the map" until Mr. Arthur Symons edited the pathetic invalid years after he and the *Yellow Book* were both dead. Wilde, as John Lane so often protested, never even wrote for the *Yellow Book:* "I couldn't stand the man," he used to say. But Beardsley illustrated "Salome," and there came that dreadful trial. I was too young, being ten or eleven, to know much about it. All I remember is hearing "Oscar" yelled by roughs after each other in the street, and one more thing. There were at that time certain pink sheets calling themselves "Police News" and such titles, which used to hang up in the little sweet-tobacco-newsagents' shops in the lower portions of the town. Usually the frontispieces displayed masked and bull's-eye-lanterned burglars shooting constables, who fell with outflung arms and crisped fingers, or else heavy-moustached murderers standing above prone women in shifts from whose gashed throats blood streamed to the floor. There came a week when my small eyes saw something, on my way back from a little school, of which I did not know the meaning. The headline was, "Sale of Oscar Wilde's Effects," and the effects appeared mostly to be opulent naked statues—doubtless of gods and goddesses, Aphrodite and Antinous, but at that age I didn't know even that much, though the image stuck and sticks still. All that must have made John Lane red in the face with anger: as the crude rhyme goes, "Everyone thought it was me." He never got quite away from the association; though I must admit that until his dying day he clung pitifully to the notion that since Beardsley succeeded, anybody who imitated Beardsley might succeed. The truth was that Beardsley's style and outlook—remember that terrible Messalina and those corpulent Jews shivering like jellies at the shivers of Wagner—were just tolerable in a genius, but that imitators without his genius were quite unbearable.

"Well," I thought, "eleven years ago on that trip, I used often to try to get Lane to talk about all the strange hierophants of sin whom he used to publish, but he would always change the subject and talk about Hayman or Opie instead." Suddenly there came back to me acutely the memory of a library of which I was given the run during the holidays when I was in my last years at school. It had belonged to a man (his young face was in Rugger groups of 1883 and 1884 in the dining-room of my house at school) who was, if this can be understood, the adopted nephew of an adopted great-aunt of mine, and whom I had known, in my childish lowliness, when, elegantly dressed and moustached, he loomed above me before he dropped dead on the Hoe from heart disease, brought on by excessive cigarette-smoking, which was the right end for a ninetyish man, if not for Sir Richard Grenville. Just before I was old enough to talk to him as man to man he died; his foster-mother, who had also a huge aviary in a conservatory, full of Java sparrows, waxbills, and parrakeets, and a parlour crowded with woolwork screens, canaries, solitaire boards, mahogany, parrots, filigree, fans, and elongated engravings of Nelson dying on deck, surrounded by spars and pig-tailed tars, and Wellington exchanging hearty greetings with Blücher after Waterloo, would not part with a single book that he had left behind him. His library, which was between hall and twittering aviary, was dusted and used as a passage; but it was never read until I, considered a promising youth with an eccentric taste for promiscuous reading, was let loose on it.

He must have been an odd man, and I wish I had been old enough before he died really to know him; I did not realize then (taking, as the young will, all things for granted) that he must have had certain sophisticated years in London before he came back to Plymouth (where such beings must have been scarce) as a rather opulent young auditor or solicitor or whatever he was—for I do not even remember that much. Everything that John Lane had ever published was in that book-lined chamber, and some of the books were inscribed by their authors (one at least is still alive) to this mysterious creature who to me was but a reserved proud face, a moustache and a cigarette. I thought when he died, for he was moderately portly and of a full complexion, that he was an ageing man, whose prime was over: he cannot have been much more than thirty-four when the cigarettes (but at that time coroners regarded cigarettes as next door to cocaine) stopped, or did not stop, his heart. But die he did; and a few years afterwards his adoptive aunt (who, when I was rising nineteen and had just spent a bitter snowy week at Cambridge trying to get a History Scholarship at King's and getting one at John's, stood me, on my way back to the West, a luncheon at the Arundel Hotel near Temple Station, that ancient if often rebuilt and redecorated hostelry which Dickens praised and at which she stayed for fifty consecutive years) died also. All she had, and his books which she so jealously kept dusted and in their places, was left to a brother of his, who was, as it might be, vicar of Eastbourne.

I remember that vicar well: he may be still alive, and I hope he is, even though he did tell me that (this is over thirty years ago) the speech of all my generation was slurred and slangy, and say to me, aged fifteen, "Of course we both agree about the paper constitutions of Carlyle." I agreed, like the devil: at any rate I knew who Carlyle was, and had made extracts from *Sartor Resartus* in a note-book. But what did the vicar think when his brother's books were sent on to him; and what did he do with them?

I have often wondered. The Lane publications: well enough. The autographed *Dorian Gray;* well enough: many a High Church parson probably flaunted it in the eyes of his parishioners in order to make them sit up, and God knows the moral was morality itself—we begin with face and features statically beautiful or ugly, and what we do and think will turn them, by heavenly or infernal light from within, into ugly or beautiful; an old Alcibiades would hardly have compared with an old Socrates, though he had ever so great a start: this Socrates knew, and it saddened him, for he loved the lad. All the works of Zola—how well I remember reading them in my holidays, the whole lot of them; over-rated then but under-rated now. He was a repulsive man in a way; boringly Republican, Rationalist and Realist, though he did let his suppressed self out a little in *La Faute de l'Abbé Mouret* and a great deal in *Le Rêve.* His *Rome* was documented in a fortnight. He arrived (*cf.* the *Cose Viste* of my friend Ugo Ojetti, who had the task of taking him round) with note-book and pencil, determined, like a reporter, to record the right cross-sections of Cardinals and Duchesses, and went back to Paris thinking he knew all about it. His *La Terre,* which (had the French cared to produce a companion to *Cold Comfort Farm*) could have been devastatingly burlesqued, was utterly humour-less, though doubtless many of the facts were inhumanly correct. His *Germinal* was justified by a drowning scene in a coal-mine which epitomised all the love and heroism which have come to a climax in all the drowned pits everywhere, and may again be witnessed, save by corpses in position, to-morrow. His *Débâcle* preached in vain the lesson of the foulness and futility of war. There was *Nana;* there was *The Rush for the Spoil,* there were all the volumes of the Rougon-Macquart series.

Well, all those the vicar may have gladly inherited; not very good literature, but morally most determined. He may also have gladly contracted the early novels of George Moore: *Esther Waters, A Drama in Muslin* and the rest. *Flames,* by Robert Hichens, would not have disturbed him, nor *A Yellow Aster,* nor the works of Ouida and Edna Lyall. He could safely have taken over Rabelais (illustrated by Doré), the *Contes Drolatiques* (illustrated by Doré), and the translations of Petronius and Lucian. But what about the books in the little room upstairs—the German psycho-physiologists and all that, *Le Moyen de Parvenir* and the utterly boring but undeniably corrupt compositions of Restif de la Bretonne? Vicar: what became of them?—for it is the deuce and all to destroy a prettily-bound book even if one wishes that the contents had never been written. . . .

It was getting on for four o'clock and the waiter, the lounge having emptied, was hovering around with the apparent desire that I should pay my bill. I paid it, picked up my pack by the straps, went out, found a seat, and began to reflect. I tried to hark back to the 'nineties, remembering at the same time a remark of Wilde's that "dialect is a method of re-creating a past that has never existed." Sitting in the sunshine I fished out of my pockets certain envelopes and a pencil, and began, having nothing better or worse to do, to try to write in the manner of those forty-years-gone people of "the 'nineties." Only beginnings came; for, truth to tell, I did not see why the originals should have been finished, let alone the imitations. There came a beginning:

> Rain drifted quickly down from a lilac sky. Miss Jones felt the child stir within her.

That would do for George Egerton, and (in matter at least) for Grant Allen.

The washing of the *blanchisseuse* fluttered on the line.
The leaves of the poplars trembled silver in the sad wind;
Gustave sipped his absinthe.

That would do for Crackanthorpe.

> Ah me, ah me, the quiet end of evening fades
> *Nunc it per iter tenebricosum,* to the shades
> Where all the roses, all the roses, roses go,
> Had it been otherwise, ah yea, I know, I know.

That would do for Dowson, and then, thought I, what on
earth am I doing here in Wells, thinking of all those and
of Mallarmé and Debussy when I might be setting my blood
coursing on foot? I forgot all about them as I sauntered
("strode" would be more powerful, but not true) out of the
town; but I still remembered Debussy. The miles between
Wells and Glastonbury are few. The Tor with its monument
can be seen all the way, and the expectation of that ancient
place felt. But, as I cast my eye to east and west, and thought
of the antiquity of the land, the pallid and urban, tense and
bearded face of Debussy came between me and the fields and
hills; for I had once seen him. One thing leads to another.

It was some day in the lost time before the war, and at the
Queen's Hall, that Debussy appeared to conduct a concert of
his own works. The place was full and somebody had taken
me to a box whence the conductor's face could be seen in
profile. The year I do not know, nor whether it was after or
before that first production of *Pelléas et Mélisande* at Covent
Garden, a perfect marriage of words and music which seems
to memory to have been one monotony of pale arms under
dark trees by old crumbling towers or in torchlit cavernous
corridors, with wan voices lamenting over an existence in
which the blind lead the blind from one dread enigma to
another. At any rate, *L'Après-midi d'un Faune* had for some
years been familiar to the adherents of Sir Henry Wood, joining that company of popular favourites, such as "1812," *Fin-
landia, L'Apprenti Sorcier,* the *Casse-Noisette Suite* and the
tone-poems of Richard Strauss, which still stoutly hold the

Promenade fort to-day. For some years, fascinated by what seemed the revolutionary extension of symbolism and impression from literature to music (for music crossed the Channel slowly then) young women, with mildly Socialist opinions and hair parted Madonna-wise, had been yearningly playing in the candle-lit, brown-paper-walled drawing-rooms of Hampstead and Chelsea, those wistful mysterious piano pieces about cathedrals under the sea and rain falling on places that never were, full of the sound of elfin horns, muffled bells and little winds wandering about the whole tone scale. At any rate, London was ready for him.

The place was packed, and the orchestra crowded in their serried tiers; amid a roar of applause Debussy stepped down to his desk, and the impression his face and mien made on me was unforgettable, there was such an intensity about him. He stood rigidly and his head was black and ivory, a wave of black hair falling over his right brow, his moustache and beard black, his face chiselled in ivory—deep sunken eyes with shadows under them, hollow shadowed cheeks, set mouth—a face bearing the marks of illness, of incessant labour, of passionate exactitude.

After a few bars of one of the "items" (perhaps the first, but certainly one of those short pieces such as *Nuages*, *Fêtes* and *La Mer*) his face suddenly contorted, he flung his baton on the ground, and simultaneously spat out some expression, undoubtedly contumelious, but inaudible in detail and probably incomprehensible to the orchestra, who were English. There was a pause as heart-stopping as a scream; and then the audience rustled like reeds. An appalling mistake had been made. Somebody, let us say the tenth bassoon, had either missed a note, played the wrong note, or played the right note in the wrong place. If that unhappy instrumentalist is still alive I daresay he is the only man except myself who remembers the disaster. But I remember also, when the baton had been resumed, the pale face composed, and the piece started all over again, thinking to myself, "How dreadful it must be to take things so seriously! And, my unhappy genius, who on earth in the audience would have noticed or minded such an error in such a shimmering tissue of sound any more than he would notice in a reproduction of a landscape by Monet if one pale-pink spot had appeared in a corner instead of one pale-green one."

"Those were the days," thought I. It isn't that they were necessarily any better than these: even this year at the Promenade Concerts swarms of youths and maidens are standing, smoking, moving from one foot to another with aching loins, have been shouting themselves hoarse after hearing for the first time the Ninth Symphony, or the *Jupiter* or the Mendelssohn Violin Concerto with the rapturous feeling of discovery which might be a blind man's who, on being given sight, should be confronted with his first moon or his first primrose. Thirty years hence they may be talking to each other about their first hearing of Respighi, Granados, Lambert or William Walton. It is a mistake to confuse the loss of one's own youthful freshness with a deterioration in the quality of the times. What cannot be helped, and should not foolishly be deplored, is that one cannot experience first love twice, any more than Cortes could twice see the Pacific for the first time from the peak in Darien. Even when in later life one hears a work, new to oneself, by a great composer, one already knows his language so well that there will never be the shock of utter novelty about it or the sense of overwhelming beauty and strangeness. And the same applies to new composers: they are never so surprising as everything was in youth unless they achieve complete novelty by eschewing euphony and throwing the baby out with the bath. Surprise I certainly had, but not delight, when I heard Bela Bartok play a piano concerto of his own, and I shall never forget the time, in 1913 or 1914, when Arnold Schönberg, saluted then as a new planet, came to London to conduct a Schönberg programme.

He was still, I daresay, a Professor of Counterpoint, though nobody would have guessed it, and he had given up his earlier manner, in which he was an ape of Wagner, as Richard Strauss is when he forgets he is a Viennese. The outstanding feature of the concert was a number of supposedly impressionistic works. Was it only fancy when one thought one saw

F

on the faces of the very orchestra bewilderment and a desire to laugh as they obediently produced an apparently disconnected series of little twangings, grunts and groans, poppings of corks and gratings of cart-wheels? About the audience at least there was no doubt. They exploded with laughter, ran out into the corridors to laugh with each other, imitated the noises, cheered ironically, and only just stopped short of barracking the conductor like a Sydney cricket crowd. For myself I enjoyed the audience, if not the music, and went away remembering a story I had heard about Rossini being taken by young friends to hear an opera by the new marvel, Richard Wagner. The dialogue, after the show, ran roughly like this:

DISCIPLES: What did you think of it, Master?

ROSSINI: I don't think it would be fair to express an opinion without hearing it a second time.

DISCIPLES (*eagerly*): And when are you going to hear it a second time, Master.

ROSSINI (*emphatically*): Never!

Both he and Wagner would doubtless have been surprised to hear that a century later their operas would be performed together at Covent Garden. For me I am of Rossini's party, because Wagner invented a din not known before, made voices bellow against instruments, was so anxious to reach a peak of noise which could only be achieved by the falling of the firmament that he piled climax after climax until he almost burst, was unbearably prolix, and took his silly allegories seriously, fit hero for the ex-Kaiser and Dr. Goebbels. There are people (some of them slaves of fashion, some liking violent assaults on their senses, perhaps) who would prefer *Siegfried* or *Tristan* at Covent Garden to *Figaro* or *Don Giovanni* at Glyndebourne, and who do not think the "Prize-Song" from the *Meistersingers* glutinous. I am not of them, nor ever was: and yet what powers he had!—as Schumann, who wrung his hands over him very early, recognized.

These things, I reflected, as I passed by dull fields, are as may be: both individuals and ages differ in their tastes. The only time I remember an audience so angry that it mostly walked out expostulating was when the Stage Society first produced Tchekov's *Cherry Orchard;* yet nowadays they all take it like lambs, and will even swallow that dismal Seagull. The time may come when those works of Schönberg's (though it must be remembered that even if good new composers often have a difficult passage, not every composer, or painter, or author, who has a difficult passage is necessarily destined for later fame) will be whistled in the streets by errand-boys who have heard them on the wireless, sandwiched between the *Peer Gynt* suite and Harry Finkel and his band. Anyhow, I wish I had Hazlitt's memory for detail and could write about musicians something like *My First Acquaintance with Poets*. To have seen and talked to so many, and to remember so little of what they said! What a pity! Bernard van Dieren, who died the other day, had the greatest intellect of all the composers I have known. In his profound and witty last book, *Down Among the Dead Men,* he records immense conversations between himself and Busoni, who was his intellectual equal and the greatest pianist of our time, in which every word rings true and in character, and I doubt if he took notes. Yet here am I, who have had conversations with Van Dieren since Busoni died, and remember little of them except that we usually agreed about the good, the beautiful, the comic, the pretentious and the vulgar, though never will the power and breeding in his eyes and features depart from me.

For music and faces, scenes, expressions and the atmosphere of men and poems, stay with me better than words. I should still remember, even had I never met it since, that grand opening theme of Elgar's First Symphony, heard at its first performance, conducted (unless that was another time) by himself, rather stiffly, in a square-shouldered frock-coat. I remember the breathlessness of the audience, wondering how the superbly elongated thing could be brought to a satisfactory close; and my own wonder as to whether the symphony could live up to it; and the tremendous applause at the end; and thinking, as I cheered with the rest, "I suppose this is partly unconscious relief because an Englishman has at last written a bearable symphony." Yet I met him not long afterwards, and talked to him frequently after that, and what remains? The image of a handsome colonel kind of man (who might, at sight, have written the bandmaster part of his music) with haughty eyes, aquiline nose and a heavy grey moustache, watching billiards and enjoying a good cigar. I once noticed one of his admirers saying that Elgar's music was as English as the Roast Beef of Old England—or Old Argentina, as we should now put it. As a compliment applied to any music not meant to be jolly and humorous it was hardly suitable: wild hyacinths and chalk downs are as English as roast beef, and much more like music, though one can imagine the Boar's Head being brought to Hall to the strains of "Land of Hope and Glory." But certainly to the casual fellow-member of a club the conventional side of him was uppermost. None the worse perhaps: A. E. Housman, unless one got him alone, preferred to talk about claret and the Navy. So, for that matter, often did old, stoutly Anglo-Irish, Sir Charles Villiers Stanford, whom I used to meet, though much more often and intimately, for he played bridge as regularly as he played it badly, at the Savile Club. Everything about him, in those later years, drooped: tumbled forelock, eyelids, cheeks, moustache, chin, shoulders. At the bridge table he was constantly disputatious in a lachrymose way: "Ah, me bhoy, whoy on earth did ye (or didn't ye) put me up?" was his regular remark to his partners. Nobody minded, for away from the table he was delightful, interlacing his fingers as the sparkle returned to his old eyes and he repeated old funny stories about Dublin, London and Cambridge. At Cambridge he was for long Professor of Music. He told me that once Tennyson (whose *Revenge* he set to music) was visiting him there and they were setting out for a walk to Coton. A clergyman hurried up to them and, saying to Tennyson, "May I join you, sir?" proceeded to do so. His chatter was incessant and boring; Tennyson, to Stanford's shock and surprise, began to use the foulest language. The cleric stood it for as long as he could, but grew paler and paler, and at last had to fly with a stammered farewell. "That's finished off that bloody parson," growled Tennyson, and resumed his normal style of conversation. Stanford knew that there were greater musicians about than himself, and was handsome to and about his abler pupils. He told me that one of them, whom I knew, was perhaps the most promising composer alive. I thought to myself that there was something both of Beethoven and Mozart about him, but the after-effects of the trenches did their work, and a breakdown came, which still continues.

I dodged a charabanc. Sibelius, I reflected, a greater than Elgar, is still alive. In Finland, not long ago, asked if there was anybody I wanted to see, I said "Sibelius." I was told that it was impossible; he was now a recluse. "Tell him," I suggested, "that it is an Englishman who writes verse." The result was favourable, and after lunch three of us motored for forty miles through that succession of up and down, pine and birch, lake and wooden chalet, which makes the northern countries so monotonously delightful. We were received with charming hospitality by Sibelius and his wife: he had not forgotten that England had given him his earliest and warmest welcome, though he could not commit himself to a date for that last long-promised symphony. His head was impressive; the mass of Strindberg's without the madness. That I remember little more is perhaps pardonable. There were five people present. Each knew two languages, but no two the same two. English, French, German, Swedish and Finnish had to be employed, and everybody politely tried to keep the conversation general. Lord Macaulay, doubtless, would have remembered every word in each language; Boswell or Eckermann would have out with note-book and pencil as soon as the car left the gate. To me it all seems to have passed in a dream, ending with a stirrup-cup of John Haig and the kindest of partings.

The newer composers may be better, as good, or worse than those who were new (Ravel, and Max Reger, the patternmaker, who seems to have faded out, were amongst them) before the war; or it may be that music has been gradually dwindling since Brahms: but can it be doubted that the great performers were better then than now? Sarasate and Joachim hardly belong to the period, though I heard them both. Nor Patti, though her old and cracking voice had brought tears to my eyes at the end of one of the last of her many farewells. But Calvé was still singing; Caruso and Melba were in their prime, and for those in London to whom singing meant above all *Lieder* there was Elena Gerhardt, at her greatest with Nikisch accompanying; George Henschel (who, when he was nearly eighty, used to descend on me at my office and warble Schubert with little power but all the old intelligence and sweetness) and, more modest, but perfect in a small hall, Plunket Greene, so full of human wit and understanding, and absolute master of his voice. Pachmann would return again and again, playing Chopin as nobody (except possibly Chopin) can ever have played him; more and more eccentric as the years went by, joking with the audience and telling them precisely what was what, but with fingers like rippling streams. But to me there was above all Ysaye, who magnetized me more than any player of any instrument whom I ever heard, and much more than Kubelik or Kreisler or any of the amazingly brilliant violin prodigies who have succeeded him.

I heard him many times before need drove him to become a conductor at Cincinnati or Milwaukee and stole him from Europe and the violin. Most of all I remember him when, with that firm, clear player the old bearded Pugno at the piano, he gave (about 1909) the whole of the Beethoven violin sonatas at a series of very badly attended concerts. There was no pose or panache about him. He appeared, calm and dignified, lending majesty even to a frock-coat, bowed, took up his fiddle and began. There was absolute mastery of technique, but a fusion with that of the highest qualities of brain and heart seldom found together. And his bended head, the heavy, impressive, yet sensitive, clean-shaven face, with the eyes smouldering over the music another had made and he was sharing had the power and the fascination of a Sphinx or a Rameses come to life, something ancient, experienced in all joys and sorrows and climes, yet resolved to be reticent save through the medium of the bow, with which he could sing the tenderest and the most tremendous things with utter conviction and no exaggeration. Often in the darkness I can see and hear him now.

*   *   *   *   *

"I say," said the demon, "where have you got?"

"Nearly to Glastonbury."

"Mooning along like that it is a wonder you haven't been run over."

"I was thinking of music."

"Do you mean Rutland Boughton?"

"If you like."

"Did you ever see *The Immortal Hour?*"

"Yes."

"What is the meaning of the title?"

"The first act, I suppose."

This insulting reflection cheered me up as I entered the town, and made for the "George," or "Pilgrimes" Inn, one of the few genuine mediæval hostelries, built as such, which survive in England. What a noble façade it is, with its bright heraldic shields, its mass-strong verticals and bold archways! That inn, and a few other things, suffice to dominate in Glastonbury the later pleasant things and the modern unpleasant excrescences. I went up the yard and had a tankard. But there seemed to be rather a lot of motor-cars and gin-and-Frenches about; so remembering that on the threshold of that place I had made my peace (after a gross misunderstanding) with that genuine, but (or and) suspicious Radical H. W. Massingham very shortly before I saw him buried in the Brompton Cemetery, that awful memorial to *laissez-faire,* I went elsewhere to find supper and a bed.

I had my supper. When I came out, dusk had fallen and it was steadily raining. I scuttled down the street and went into a humble bar. Three or four old men were sitting there. "Raining again, master?" "Yes," I admitted. A second butted in very slowly: "Not until them forty days are up," said he. The rest of us could not remember whether St. Swithin's Day had been wet or fine, so could hardly refute him. But the third produced a red herring: "It'll be full moon o' Sunday," he said, "and that do often make a change." But the first was not to be robbed of his gloom. "Then 'er wastes," he said, "and I remember the old folks tellin' me that when 'er's wastin' 'er spills it out."

I raised my glass to them and mused. There were they using such a phrase as "a wasting moon," suggestive of Coleridge and dim light on desolate seas, but suggestive of all wastings and declines of physical decay. Their roots are in the elementary facts of nature: birth, maturity, failing and death; they are never far from the churchyard. That is what made Thomas Hardy their one great representative spokesman. His celebrated gloom did not mean an abiding sadness in himself: he merely accepted. In his prime he drew a picture to one of his poems (for he commenced active life as an architect) representing a church and its floor above, and, below, a charnel-house full of open coffins with skeletons in them. In old age he took me out to "Mellstock" and, surveying the tombstones of his sires, asked me what I thought of the lettering. I commended it; and, with enthusiasm in his eyes he said: "If you ever want a good monumental mason, just drop me a postcard and I'll let you know where you can find one."

"A wasting moon." I remembered how many other words, generally supposed to be archaic or artistically affected, I had heard slipping from the mouths of old rustics; not thirty miles from London there are places where you may still hear, from settle and ingle-nook, old men saying that when young they were "lissome." Young ones too: for the old things die hard even when opposed by education and the wireless.

I talked to them a little about Somerset cricket (they all remembered Sammy Woods and Martyn) and then went back early to bed.

In my bedroom I found a Bible. By lamplight I read two chapters of St. John. But the print was too small for me; my eyes swam; I blew the light out and before I fell asleep cursed and damned a political system which is quite capable of taxing the whole population in order to provide children with free spectacles, but will not do the obvious thing which even the

oculists (who are not entirely selfish) would back up, and pro-
hibit, on pain of death (a justifiable thing where offences are
cold-blooded), the use, whether in book or newspaper, of type
below a certain size. Before literacy became general it didn't
matter so much; but now, every year, visiting schools of any
grade, travelling in any sort of conveyance, one cannot help
noticing that year after year the number of the young who
have been clapped into spectacles steadily increases. Reading
at all is probably bad for the eyes; but that cannot be helped,
it is the price we have to pay for the advance of knowledge
and the distant hope of civilization. But reading minute type
is the devil and all.

"Will they stop it? I doubt it——" I murmured to myself,
as I drifted into the fourth dimension and the world of J. W.
Dunne.

NINTH DAY

But what can one say about Glastonbury? If there is a county
in England where more than elsewhere an open-minded
person is forced to regret the Reformation, and its child the
Great Rebellion (both run by Welshmen in unconscious
revenge), it is Somerset. The whole county, still rich in
treasure, is covered with things destroyed, ruined, or despoiled:
and as one sees the brick suburbs crawling out along the roads,
and the tea-houses, and the petrol-stations, one wonders
whether the time is not in sight when almost everything worth
looking at in what was once the loveliest of all counties will
not have been made by Nature, with whom man, as lately
as the Wars of the Roses (during which Eton, King's and
thousands of parish churches were built), used happily to
co-operate.

Sanitation was not good in the Middle Ages. The Indian
proverb ("The nearer the village the greater the stink") would
have been applicable to England then. Lunatics were burnt
as witches. Plague and famine swept the country. So they do
now: the plague of ugliness and the starvation of the soul.

F*

Pathetically we rush about "saving" this, that, and the other, and trying to "stop" things, instead of releasing our creative energies for a further addition to the beauty of our earth; and the things we try to save are usually the work of those abused monks, against whom war is still being waged all over the world by fanatics who have no sense of any other life but this.

I went into an inn in Glastonbury expecting to find farmers talking about horses. Instead of that I found two Tappertits talking about foreign affairs. One of them preferred General Chow Chung to General Chung Chow, and President Lupez to ex-President Gomez. The other took the opposite view; and neither of them had ever seen China or South America, or realized that Glastonbury Tor was above them, the "Pilgrims" Inn near them, the ruins of the Abbey something to be cared for, and the shades of Arthur and Alfred dwelling over Avalon.

Then a man came in with a wrinkled, keen, horsy face, and a conspicuous check suit. He ordered himself a double brandy and soda and informed me that it was a fine morning. I agreed. Gradually we slid into conversation. He said he thought that Mr. Baldwin was the best of them but he was damned if he knew why; and I agreed to that. He then discoursed about various sports, blood and other, and I agreed to those. And then he suddenly said: "Are you a writing chap?" and I replied: "More or less, amongst other things, but I hope I don't look like one." "There's something about you," he remarked, "and I'd like to tell you a story, but, mind you, you mustn't mention any names or give people any clues."

"Really," I said, "I may be many bad things, but I am not a contemporary novelist."

"Well," he said, "you may or may not know it, but we doctors come across a lot of strange things, and it's odd that you writers don't make use of them."

"Why don't you write them yourselves?" I asked.

"Too damn busy," he replied, ordering two more drinks from a lady he called Maudie and appeared to know very well;

and then: "Do you happen to be a Roman Catholic?"

I said: "No," but I thought I understood what it was to be one.

"Well," he went on, "there was a patient of mine near here, a Frenchman with a French wife and several children. They weren't rich and they weren't poor; they lived in a little villa surrounded by rhododendrons and laurels; they didn't keep a car but when they wanted one they hired one. What will you have?"

"It's my turn," I protested, feeling as if I had got into one of the works of Mr. Ernest Hemingway. When he was satisfied he resumed, fixing me with an Ancient Mariner's eye, and waving his glass in the air. "Now this chap," he said, "an elderly man with a pasty, clean-shaven face, was always regarded as a mystery in the neighbourhood. There was nothing against him. He always paid his tradesmen's bills. But there it was.

"Just about a year ago I had a telephone message saying he was ill. I went out there and found he'd got a growth in the bowel. Even operation couldn't save him for long, but operation was obviously necessary. I told him so. D'you know what he said to me?"

"I don't see how I can, really," I replied, reasonably.

"Well," he proceeded, "what he said was, in his foreign accent, 'Do what you like, but I won't have an anæsthetic.' And I said, 'Damn it all, man, your heart's all right,' and he replied that his body was his own.

"To cut a long story short, I gave him a local which worked on his lower half, and he watched me doing it."

I suddenly had a vision of that horrible picture in Bruges of the flaying of Cambyses.

"Of course," he concluded, "it only postponed things for a few months, and it was only when he pegged out that I discovered what was wrong."

"What?" I enquired.

"He was a Roman Catholic priest and he still believed, and if he might die he ought to confess, and he didn't want to tell another priest that he'd broken his vows. And his wife, mind you, was a very nice woman, very quiet, and she looked after the children very well."

He pulled out his watch. "I've got a patient," he said, and ran out to his car.

*   *   *   *   *

I collected my baggage, and that day, by divers roads and field-paths, went to a small town which is set pleasantly on a hill. It lost me distance, but after all, I was not out for records and Lord Wakefield had not offered me a prize. I saw some good views and a church or two; and, ultimately, an excellent steak and a comfortable bedroom. But before I sought the solace of this last I met another odd man, who rushed into the bar very eagerly. He was touring by himself in a car, and was a convinced, philosophical, anti-feminist.

He was tall, thin, hollow-cheeked; a splash of black hair tumbled over his left brow and his eyes glittered with fanaticism. Drinking (an odd idea) a dry sherry after his dinner and leaning his right elbow on the counter, after a preliminary exchange of commonplaces, he suddenly shot at me the question: "What do you think about women?"

It was rather a surprise, and difficult, like being asked what one thought about the Equator; and I was only able to stumble out some remark to the effect that I thought women were quite all right, really. His reply was: "Well, I definitely don't."

He had a slight stammer and wagged his forefinger at me: there was a Regency touch about him, he seemed to have a stock on though he had not, his manners were elaborately ingratiating, he gesticulated with hand and eyebrow, and opened every paragraph with "But, my dear sir"; sometimes adding, "Of course, I don't know who you are, but——" I thought he must have made a regrettable marriage in early youth. He told me what had happened in Greece and Rome as soon as women were emancipated, he said that women were idiots for competing with men instead of being men's inspiration, he demanded to know why they should expect men to stand up for them in trains now that they had the vote, he said that he had seen two women in riding breeches the day

before in an inn and had played dominoes with one of them
for half an hour before realizing that she was not a man, he
denounced Lady Astor, he bedazzled me with illustrations
drawn from all ages and climes, and then, with a suggestion
that sooner or later the men of Britain would rise and re-
establish the harem, he shook hands hurriedly and ran out
with a final expression which suggested "You have been
warned."

"Who was that?" I asked of the plump barmaid.

"Don't know his name," she replied. "He calls here sometimes. We think he's batty."

So did I, but they say a man's all the happier for a hobby.
I was reflecting on that in a corner, having taken in all the
marrow from a battered edition of some Western evening
paper, when I suddenly asked myself: "What is your hobby,
then?" And it dawned on me that I no longer had one.

It wasn't for lack of encouragement. My mother, when I
was young, repeatedly gave me boxes of carpenter's tools, and
the *Boy's Own Paper* every week offered me instructions as
to how to build anything from a yawl to a fowl-house. Never,
so far as I remember, did I spoil a single foot of material with
chisel or plane; the tools, in time, merely got lost. But collect
I did, with a vengeance.

Collecting began with . . .

The large barmaid's voice interrupted me. "I bet your
thoughts are far away. You're thinking of something pretty
deep."

"As a matter of fact," I acknowledged, "I was thinking
of beetles."

"I bet you weren't," said she; "beastly things, I hate 'em."

I placated her with that abominable but widely-favoured
drink, a port and lemon, and resumed my memories. For I
really—and people seldom believe you when you are telling
the truth—was thinking of beetles.

They were the last things in my youth—before I reached
the age, now in its turn passed, when I searched the Minories
and the New Cut for incunabula and water-colours—at which
I arrived. It began with crests (there were albums for such

then), coins, and postage-stamps; I inherited a collection of each from my mother, and some time or other they took wing and departed. Then there were birds' eggs, butterflies and moths, all a camphory moulder in their cabinets, and at last it came to beetles—and, as a sideline, bugs—not the household variety but the delightfully diversified little flatirons which would be more popular did they not share that opprobrious name.

It all happened, one holiday, through going to buy an exercise book at a printer's and stationer's. It was not a busy morning, so I fell into conversation with the shopkeeper, a lively little man with spectacles and a big black moustache. Quite out of the blue he asked me if I would like to come into his back premises and see his beetles. I didn't know what he meant but naturally said yes; and in a minute I was surrounded by tens of thousands of them all neatly arranged on white boards in their sliding shelves.

I had to unlearn some things, of course. I was informed that a black-beetle was not a beetle at all, that there were many weevils, for all that Captain Marryat may have said, which did not live in ship's biscuits, and that a ladybird was a beetle, no more, no less. The printer was a propagandist and an enthusiast: no Mormon ever went after a "prospect" for the Latter Day Saints more zealously than this little man set out to draw me into the congregation of coleopterists. He was eminent in his world. If there is a Royal Beetle Society he was certainly a Fellow of it, and he showed back numbers of some Institution's Proceedings which recorded several beetles which he had added either to those known to science or to the recorded British species. He showed them to me: they were very small and I was not surprised that they had been overlooked. All the same, when I left that shop, with a present of Ray's *British Beetles* under my arm and a promise to be a faithful beetler on my lips, I was a convert, and, I firmly believed, for life.

And how distant is one's past! Was it really I who turned over all those stones on Dartmoor and in the woods looking for the bombardiers, who parted the branches of gorse for the

Jew-beetle, who netted the ponds for the dityscus and his larva, the beastliest thing ever seen outside Bloomsbury, who counted the spots and noted the hues of the ladybirds, and peered through lenses to differentiate between species of the long-necked weevils? Well, actually it was. But when did I stop? I simply don't remember. And why? I don't know.

"Suppose," I said to myself in that corner at Wincanton, "I were to start all over again to-morrow. Either Sir Josiah Stamp or somebody else says daily that every man ought to have a hobby, and here is one of the easiest. There are beetles everywhere, infinitely cheaper than Picassos and Matisses, and much more beautiful. If to-morrow morning, when I set out for Camelot or wherever (for Cadbury may have been Camelot) I hop over a hedge occasionally and turn over a stone I can begin collecting all over again, and shall have things over which I can pore lovingly in winter and old age. Why miss such a chance? Why not, at any rate, collect something?"

"No," I replied to the demon (for such it again was), "never again! I am content to know that the beetles are there and to look at them alive when so inclined.

> What wondrous things
> Thy hand hath made

is what I now feel about beetles, if not about our latest coins and postage-stamps. What is the use of possessions, and why, above all, prefer a dead animal in a cupboard to a live one in its haunts? There was something to be said for collecting in one's boyhood; it took one about and made one look out for things."

"Have it your own way," said the demon, "but the time may come when you have nothing to do at home except listen to the wireless, and you know what that's like as a rule."

"I shall play patience," I said; and the demon retired bored, at least for the time being, though ready, as always, to return at odd moments with suggestions about gardening or book-plates.

"Anyhow," I said to myself, "merely living is a hobby in its

way." I had unintentionally spoken aloud. An emphatic
"Ah!" came from my left, and turning, I saw the period piece
with whom I had been conversing earlier in the evening.
"Hullo," I said, with no great originality, "are you back?"

"My dear sir," he confided, "I found your conversation so
interesting that I thought I might as well come back for an
hour. I've just put the car-lights on." It would hardly have
been civil to say that I had barely opened my mouth to him,
but I saw no reason why I shouldn't go on listening and I
wondered what would be his next text. "We were talking
about women," he said.

I nodded.

"Well, are you fond of mushrooms?"

He had chosen his own ground, and I thought it was time I
made a stand. "I think," I said, "they are amongst the most
beautiful things in nature. No dancer ever had such exquisite
pleats as their pink gills, and, in spite of their seeming solidity,
they are so exquisitely light. And the other fungi too . . ."

"But, my dear sir," he interrupted, "I didn't mean that at . . ."

"No," I said, as with instant comprehension, "I didn't mean
to say that I entirely agree with this propaganda in favour of
edible fungi. After all, there are only a few score of those,
whereas there are thousands of the others. It simply isn't safe
unless you are an expert. All I meant was that, poisonous or
not, when you see those lovely splashes of orange and red and
purple in the autumn beech-woods you wonder . . ."

"I'm so sorry, sir," he exclaimed, still polite and eager, "but
I mean, don't you think they're good . . ."

"Good, and remarkable," I assured him; "a man told me
that in Hawaii another man watched a fungus grow three
inches vertically in five-and-twenty minutes. It belonged, I
think, to the Stinkhorn tribe. We have some of them in this
country. But fungi, of course, are very cosmopolitan; they are
much less local than plants and . . ."

"But what I mean," he returned with a despairing precision
of speech, "is, do you like them to eat?"

"Stinkhorns?"

"No, mushrooms."

"I like them better than almost anything else, but I hardly ever touch them."

"Do you mean they don't agree with you?"

"No, they agree with me perfectly."

"Then I'm afraid, my dear sir, your remarks seem a little paradoxical."

"It was in this county of Somerset, I believe," I continued, and curiosity made him keep silence, "that . . . but have you heard of André Simon?"

"Do you mean the wine man?"

"Yes, and the food man, and the book man, and the garden man and a very fine man. Well, in one of his books he gives a list of menus he has had. Once he told a man he liked mushrooms. He came all this way to dine with him. What did he have? Mushroom soup, sole with mushrooms, chicken with mushrooms, and mushrooms on toast. I forget the rest, but that was enough; there may or may not have been a mushroom sweet."

"Ah, I see, so you were merely joking."

"Not at all. Nine times out of ten they come on as a savoury. I have a very moderate appetite and by the time they are reached I have stopped eating. So I have to admire them from a distance."

He looked as one who had forgotten what he had meant to say. He glanced at his watch and then, crying: "I must get on, good night, sir, good night," ran out.

*   *   *   *   *

The matronly barmaid was wiping a glass. She followed his exit with a compassionate smile, and then turned to me with an upward jerk of her head. I asked why on earth he had suddenly started talking about mushrooms. "Oh," she said, "he always preaches about something or other and then he forgets all about it. Before you came in there was a chap telling him about people down here growing mushrooms so as to keep the foreign ones out."

"A very good idea," I said; "I think there's a tariff now."

"It's a pity they can't put on more of them," she sensibly remarked; "I suppose they want us to starve in the next war."

"I suppose they do."

"Look at wheat!"

"Look at potatoes!"

"Look at bacon!"

"Look at eggs!"

"Look at fruit!"

"Look at vegetables!"

"Look at cheese!"

With a unanimity to be found everywhere in farming England we looked at all these things and others, and wondered what vengeance the populace would wreak upon the politicians should another war bring us to the verge of starvation. None, of course. Probably there will be a new lot in, who will say that it wasn't their fault.

*　　　*　　　*　　　*　　　*

"Time!" said the barmaid. The last revellers said their nightly good night and she locked up. "Would you like anything before you go to bed?" she asked. "Just one," I said, "won't you?"

"Thank you very much," she said, "I should like a port and lemon." She poured out the night-caps and sat down with a sigh of relief. "Well, there's another day over."

"Tired?"

"Not more than usual. But I don't think most people realize the amount of work there is in a place like this. You see, it isn't so much the serving, it's the endless washing up and dusting. You see all those bottles and glasses? I dusted them all before we opened this morning."

"Have a cigarette?"

"Thanks."

"Been at this job long?"

"Since the war."

"Oh."

"My husband was killed."

It was a bit too late to say that one was sorry. But I was.

*　　　*　　　*　　　*　　　*

She lent me an old "shocker." It was so very unconvincing
and illiterate that I thought I would turn the light out and
think of something. Hardly tariffs in bed, I reflected, so turned
to the beauty of fungi, those brilliant slabs and spikes and
domes. Why were some of the most venomous so magnificent?
Had I heard somebody say "as a warning to men and beasts."
But some poisonous things are not splendid, and the peacock
is eminently edible. It's like the old business of protective
colouring: if some have it, why not all? Why should the
partridge and the leaf-insect be so especially favoured? No;
Nature's hand was as indiscriminate as it was lavish.

Idly in the darkness I thought of the hues and patterns
bestowed on giant serpents, and on tigers as well as on the
gentle innocent spotted deer. And on the mackerel: was there
anything more resplendent than the blue-green-silver sheen on
a mackerel freshly taken from the water? When I got to
Devon I would go out and catch some, bait hooks, watch
bright spinners crumple enlarged and dimming out of sight,
feel the dripping line thrill through my fingers, watch the far
pale cliffs over the blue ripples as we tacked to and fro in the
bay. A grizzled fisherman who wouldn't talk much. When
had I last been fishing at sea? No, I didn't fish. It was two
years ago in Plymouth Sound when I went out with the official
trawlers and we scoured the bottom because a hospital urgently
wanted starfish. Twice we brought up the trawl and poured
great mounds of heaving fish and weeds on the deck, monk-
fish with their angles, plaice with their yellow spots, poor-
man's cod, whiting, red ribbon-fish, sea-slugs, crabs of all
sizes, weeds—red-brown, green-brown—all colours, spreading,
wobbling, writhing, streaming, flapping, slipping, sliding,
banging on the deck in the clear sunlight. Oh, to plunge one's
arms into them! I thought in a way: and in a way, I shrank.

We took them back to the Aquarium. There in shallow
tanks were "transients," dogfish and others living in temporary
amity, nothing of strife except when the lobster near death was
deliberately picked at the joints by the giant crabs.

Aquariums. The Naples one. The Monte Carlo one, out on
the Prince's Rock. The New York one at Battery Point, with

the shoal of little moving moonbeams from the Bermudas and that ghastly great Jew-fish with his nose, who stared at me with bulging marble eyes. I was with a girl. "I don't like your face," she said quietly to the fish.

The fish either did not hear or did not care.

I laughed at the memory, and sank into a bottomless sea of sleep.

TENTH DAY

It was a filthy morning, much too bad for going on until it cleared. I thought I would lie in bed and have breakfast for once. The maid came with the tea. "I think I should like to have some breakfast up here."

"Very well, sir. What would you like?"

"What have you got?"

"Bacon and eggs? . . . or bacon and tomato?"

In English country inns that dialogue is as standardized as any of the ceremonies of the Roman rite—I don't mention the Church of England, which offers more latitude. What follows is almost as regular.

"Bacon and eggs, then; and could you possibly let me have a morning paper?"

"I'm afraid there's only the *Mail*."

"That will do perfectly."

"I'll get it now if it's come."

The *Mail* came and I glanced over its pages, comparatively so much more sober than they used to be. There were rumours of war in it, and I remembered the remark Voltaire made when a general war seemed imminent. "Won't it be necessary to make peace after the war? Why the devil don't they make it at once, then?" There were remarks about home-grown food. I heartily agreed, not merely on grounds of prospective starvation but because I knew what my bacon would be like; the decline of British farming seems to have taken the heart out of British cooking and housekeeping. In the old books bacon was always "crisp." Who ever sees crisp bacon now?

Soggy leathery strips; and as often as not further waterlogged
by the presence of tomatoes reduced to wet pulp by frying—
an indignity almost as great as the frying of peaches. Then I
saw something about modern French painting and began
wondering, sipping my tea the while, as to whether the
influence of science, and in particular the doctrine of evolution, upon the arts wasn't responsible for the modern lack of
emotional depth and sensuous appeal. As A. E. Housman remarked, it takes "neither pains nor brains" to be in the fashion,
and there always have been fashions, which have always been
superseded.

"Ripple-ripple-ripple" went the rain in the gutters; the roof
across the sky's lid was covered with dripping hair and eyebrows.

"They are much more concerned about changing things than
with seeing or feeling them," I reflected, "and they are
encouraged to think that the only object of art is to have a
perpetually evolving technique."

"You're getting stuck fast in the past," said the demon.

"I'm not going to be taken in by that, my friend," I replied.

The door opened. "Your breakfast, sir," said the little maid.

"Still pelting," I remarked.

"Oh, it's dreadful, sir," said she, arranging the bedside table,
"I shouldn't go on in this weather if I were you."

"I don't think I will. Will it matter if I stay here till twelve?"

"Oh no, sir, missus told me to tell you."

"Could you by any chance get me a writing-block?"

"Oh yes, sir."

I had eaten my egg and drunk my coffee when she returned.
"Will this do?" she asked, thrusting on me a dainty packet of
violet envelopes and notepaper smelling of scented soap.

"Perfectly," I assured her, "if I wanted to write letters. But
I wanted something much larger and no envelopes."

"Do you mean scribble?"

"I expect so."

In five minutes she was back with the very thing: it had
lines on and was called "Champion Pine White Wove." I got
her to fetch me two supplementary cushions and settled down

to write a story exhibiting the absurdity of fashions in Art. Feeling very ironical I began by writing across the first page in large capitals the title (using my second and third fingers still):

A PLAIN UNVARNISHED TALE

and off I started.

Thus I began, and the tarnished pages are with me now. But before I went any farther I rang the bell. "Mary," I said, "bring me twenty Gold Flakes now, a whisky-and-soda at twelve o'clock, my lunch at one, and, if it isn't inconvenient, call me and get me a bath ready at half-past five o'clock." "Very well, sir," she said, as though this sort of thing happened every day; she carried out instructions and at five I was finished.

I

Tony Buckley kept a small Art Gallery. He had not always kept an Art Gallery, and although interested in Art he didn't really want to keep an Art Gallery; his fundamental desire being to live on his father's means, do no work at all, have a small flat in Half Moon Street, buy an occasional modern painting or etching, collect an occasional piece of old Chinese porcelain or modern Swedish or Lalique glass, have a shiny black-and-white bathroom with glass shelves to support any number of oils, scents, salts, and even medicines, give an occasional cocktail-party which would bring into service his numerous occasional tables, belong to two or three decent clubs with enough pale-faced, horn-rimmed spectacled Oxford friends in them (the poor employed in Museums, the rich Museum-minded) to provide him with intelligent, languid, high-voiced conversation, go out to intellectual cinemas with a few girls who did not too tiresomely insist that he should be a male, take tea occasionally with aged and sympathetic widows who adored him as a person of taste and feeling, have a polite, if taciturn, manservant, silk sheets, a silver tray and translucent porcelain for his morning tea, an enormous press for his coats and trousers, with shelves for his socks, handkerchiefs, collars and ties—and, indeed, everything that a young man about town should have. In youth he had every expectation that such would be his lot. He was an only son; his mother doted on him; his father was immensely rich and had a noble mansion, park and shoot in Northamptonshire and in Scotland a river and forest second to none. He went to Eton, where he did not distinguish himself but made intelligent friends. He went to Oxford, where he did not take a degree but made intelligent friends. When he had been at Oxford a year the war broke out. Tony, with a wry face, joined the 25th battalion of a county regiment and made ultimately, if with more resignation than enthusiasm, a quite good infantry officer. He was not wounded, but he was mentioned once in despatches—of which even he was a little proud, though he preferred Sheraton chairs very much as against the makeshifts he had to sit upon in dug-outs. But he was intensely distressed when he learnt that the Germans had burned the Roumanian oil-wells, and distressed even more, later on, when he learnt that the Bolsheviks had seized both the oilfields of the Caucasus and the mines of Siberia. For in all those quarters his father's investments lay: and on Armistice Day his father died.

Tony came back to England to find nothing left for him. His mother had retired to a Bournemouth private hotel on a small annuity. All that was saved from the wreck for himself was a paltry two thousand pounds, the interest on which would be barely sufficient to pay for his ties and his club subscriptions, let alone Merry and Berry and Lock, who still so venerably juxtapose their saddles and wines and hats at the bottom of St. James's Street. The point was: what was he to do? Dreadful though it was, he had to earn a living.

2

He tried several things, after he had definitely discovered that his mother simply couldn't spare another penny. Motor-salesmanship was his first attempt; but the slump had hit the trade hard and Eton and Harrow Motors, Ltd., sounded so expensive that most people did not dare enter the place and latest-acquired old school-fellows had to be the first to be dismissed. He had a dip into old furniture, and even for a week travelled biscuits in an Austin Seven. Then he suddenly saw an avenue. A Cézanne was coming up at Christie's. An old and rich friend, who had villas in Rome, Florence and Venice, but only an occasional perch at Claridge's in London, wanted to buy it. In a generous moment Bertie Finch said: "Tony, old thing, I shall have to pay somebody a commission for buying it for me, why shouldn't it be you? You've got your head screwed on; one or two of them have let me down; the thing's right enough—it will just fit into my little drawing-room over the Forum—my limit is five thousand." Tony went; he bid; he conquered; he collected his commission. He saw an opening at last. "After all," he meditated, "somebody has to get a profit on all the pictures which happen to be fashionable at the moment, so why shouldn't it be I?" He mobilized his capital, jeopardized his income, took a little shop in Earl Street, and started his series of exhibitions with a scratch lot of Matisse and Picasso drawings which he had picked up luckily and cheaply (apart from which, some of them were doubtful!) at the end of the autumn auctioneering season, and a roomful of woodcuts, angular and daring, by a young woman who paid for her show herself and knew everybody in London. Everybody she knew bought one of Mavis's drawings (though towards the end there were wry faces because all the cheapest ones had gone) and Tony, though he had not yet learned how exorbitant a commission a gallery proprietor should charge if he is really to be in the first rank, made enough out of them to pay for his first year's rent. Nothing succeeds (as may possibly have been remarked before) like success, and, thenceforward, Tony found no difficulty in keeping his galleries full and the Press interested. First, he got, without effort on his own part, all the rich semi-amateurs; then he got the kind of well, if garishly, dressed young artist whose clothes, looks, or connections (or all of them) make him "Willy" or "Hamish" at all the cocktail-parties about which the snob-columnists write; then he collected and launched a successful show of the survivors of the Post-Impressionist Movement; then he dared a Barbizon show; then he joined in the Boudin revival; and at last, having accumulated some money and a great reputation for taste, acumen, and honesty of dealing, he began to glimpse that Eldorado in which dwell those who (keeping eagle eyes open for death and death-duties) buy Primitives (Italian or Flemish), Titians, Rembrandts and portraits by Reynolds, Gainsborough and Lawrence for anything up to £80,000 apiece and sell them for anything up to £100,000 apiece. After which, why have a shop? You just hang a few things in your private house and ask Mr. Huggenheimer to dinner.

Tony Buckley had just reached this verge of the ultimate prosperity and happiness, and was sitting in his little back office (like Alnaschar with his tray) dreaming of a recovered freedom and a final farewell to commerce, like Wolsey's to greatness, when his dreams were rudely shattered. James came in: "Sorry, sir," he said, "but there's a lady to see you with some pictures and she won't go away."

"Who is she?" asked Tony.

"She says she's called Agrippina Mandeville," said James.

"I'm busy," said Tony, impatiently if mendaciously; "tell her to come back some other time."

"I did, sir," said James, a distant beaten look on his pale thin, prematurely old face, "but she said, 'Go to blazes! I've got to see Mr. Buckley.'"

"Oh, tell her I'm not here!" snapped Tony, with as near an approximation to anger so mild and well-bred a young man as he could achieve.

"I did, sir," answered James, "but she only said, 'Tell that to the marines! I can see him through the glass door. You can't take me in, my man—my brother was at school with him, and I've seen him often.'"

"Oh, bring her in then," remarked Tony wearily; "I suppose I can get rid of her somehow!"

James brought her in. She sat down in the spare chair without being asked, took a cigarette from the box on the table, fumbled in her bag for a match which the surprised Tony, remembering his manners, at last produced, closed her eyes, puffed several times in order to make sure that her cigarette was drawing, and then looked at Tony with large, brilliant dark eyes. He was fascinated.

It wasn't her beauty that fascinated him—though in her thin, hectic, aquiline, red cheek-boned, sensitive-lipped, untidy yet distinguished way she was certainly beautiful. No: it was her madness that fascinated him. He was alone with a madwoman and did not even dare to call for James.

All this passed through his mind in a second which seemed like an age. Then, staring at him with almost loving eyes and a slow compelling smile, she said: "Of course, you know what I've come for?"

He pulled himself together with a jerk.

"Well, of course, yes," said he. "Your name is Miss Agrippina Mandeville, and James tells me you've brought some pictures to show me. Naturally, I shall be delighted to see them."

"You'd better be," she observed quietly, as she lowered her lids and opened her portfolio, "for you've got to both show 'em and sell 'em."

Her specimens were produced. She had oil-paintings too, she explained; these were only a few examples of her unframed water-colours: but by no means the best, but quite enough to show what she could do. Tony took them and turned them over, bewildered, staggered. In his youth, he dimly remembered, he had seen things like these in the windows of provincial art-shops (which were also picture-frame makers); local products, the grand metropolitan windows being occupied by coloured engravings of "The Roll-Call," "The Thin Red Line" and "Floreat Etona!"

There were herbaceous borders, every flower dabbed in most recognizable; there were little maids in pinafores plucking primroses or, aprons extended, looking up ladders on the top of which their brothers or sisters were plucking apples; there were goose-girls on commons, and tinies playing with bunnies —all were painted in the exact and unimaginative style of the ladies who once got hung in a Minor Room at the Academy in 1870. Tony hated being rude to women; and he guessed that this particular woman was an especially sad and luckless one. Also he was beginning, in a curious vague way, to be afraid of her. But his connoisseur's conscience was fully awake, and he bravely said:

"I'm extraordinarily sorry, Miss Mandeville, these things are very lovely in their way. But we dealers are obliged rather to specialize—my own clients prefer either Old Masters or ultra-modern pictures—and though I myself much prefer the straightforward kind of representation of really beautiful things that you do, I think you would be much better advised to go to Cohen's in Bond Street or Jones's in Leicester Square."

Quite suddenly he found himself looking into the dark cavernous mouth of a revolver, held in an unflinching hand, behind which was Miss Mandeville's beautiful, consumptive, mocking, maniacal face.

"Oh, is that how the land lies?" she observed, with icy precision. "I will give you exactly sixty seconds to think again. I have a wrist-watch, but I shan't bother to look at it. One . . . two . . . three . . . four . . ."

"I say!" said Tony feverishly, "can't you let me think for a minute or two? I mean, I might ring somebody up—and there's . . ."

"Ten . . . eleven . . . twelve . . ." counted Miss Mandeville.

"But—I mean, there's always this, that, and the . . ."

"Sixteen . . . seventeen . . . eighteen . . ." said Miss Mandeville.

"Look here!" cried Tony, "can't you, for a moment, put that beastly thing down, and just let's talk together and see what's best to be done——"

"Twenty-three . . . twenty-four . . . twenty-five . . ." said Miss Mandeville.

Tony screamed. "Oh, stop, stop, stop! I'll do anything!"

The revolver was still three feet from his head and pointing straight.

"Do you really mean that?" asked Miss Mandeville, screwing her eyes together and smiling with her lips.

"I do! I do! I do!" protested Tony.

The revolver was still levelled.

"On your word of honour as a gentleman?" asked Miss Mandeville, "I don't mean picture-dealer, but gentleman?"

Tony flung both arms into the air.

"I promise anything you want!" he shouted.

She was pacified. She put the revolver into her bag with lipstick, handkerchief, pocket-mirror and keys, and quietly observed:

"Well, now we're getting down to business. To-morrow, which is the 13th, I shall send you fifty oil-paintings and ninety-four water-colours, and my show opens on the 28th. Ever since your Gallery opened I've meant to have a show here. I leave it to you to fix the prices—you know far more about that kind of thing than I do. Have you got a match?"

He gave her one, and she went. He put his head between his hands.

3

Ten o'clock in Earl Street, St. James's. Tony arrived from Ryder Street punctual to the moment—as he was punctual with his morning tea, his rising, his use of the lemon-verbena bath salts which could only be bought in the Royal Opera Arcade, his consumption of kidneys and bacon, his donning of a carnation, and his ringing for the lift. He paused for a moment, in intense gloom, outside his shop. Yes, James had been punctual too; the bills were already up on the discreet little hoarding outside the shop. They were fresh as paint ("Paint indeed!" he reflected bitterly) and they announced that within was to be seen an Exhibition of Paintings and Drawings by Agrippina Mandeville. Ruin stared him in the face, though Honour was saved. His friends, dropping casually in one by one, would look astonished at the ghastly show, assume the appearance of dying codfish, shake hands limply with their eyes wandering and walk out, never to see him again, but to tell their friends (over dry sherries in their clubs) either that Tony Buckley had suddenly gone off his head or that Tony Buckley had always really been a pretender and that his bogusness (or should it be "bogusity?" he reflected with a despairing curl of the lip) had been exposed at last. At any rate, he was done for; and all his hopes of gradually, through good taste, tact, social connections and an ability to talk to Americans, becoming another Colnaghi, Agnew, Duveen or Hugh Lane scattered to the winds. Hope slightly revived when he remembered that he had never engaged when he made the fatal promise to send out cards either to the public or to the Press. Usually his Private Views were crowded with dowager duchesses, Prime Ministers' widows, middle-aged Foreign Office men with monocles, young fashionables who had gone on the stage in order to earn the wherewithal for oysters, lobsters, caviare and cocktails, under-secretaries, and resolute old ladies who were jolly well determined that, until extreme unction was given them, they were not going to be left out of anything where everybody else, who was anybody, was. They none of them ever bought anything. They just smoked cigarettes (in spite of the "No Smoking" notice), grabbed each other by the biceps, made hasty luncheon and dinner dates, and generally shouted, "Emily, darling!" and "Bob, darling!" all over the place. But although they did not —and most of them, poor things, no longer could—buy anything themselves, they did tell other people.

Time and again, after an unprofitable Private View, sitting alone like Marius amid the ruins of Rome, Tony had leapt to his feet as a frog-faced, fussy, bespectacled financial magnate had stridden into the Gallery, all astrakhan and Rolls, and— in the self-conscious manner in which the uneducated opulent address their superior inferiors, the educated poor—informed him that the Duchess of Dorset or Mrs. Portcullis had told him to buy a picture from Mr. Buckley's remarkable show. "I've got a little place up the river—I should like something about three feet by two; have you got any sunsets?" They usually took something and Tony always kicked himself when he remembered their suspicious faces as he told them the real prices he was charging instead of asking the preposterously large sums that they were accustomed to give to the worst daubers in the Royal Academy.

"All over," thought Tony. "I haven't asked anybody, but somebody's sure to turn up. And then I shall have to fly the country, and go to one of the Colonies, if there is still any Colony willing to take anybody from this country, I wonder if there are any openings in Mauritius or the Falkland Islands?"

He was wandering aimlessly about, after vaguely fingering some unsold modern sculptures by a young Chelsea artist who reduced birds and beasts to their quite unrecognizable, but highly convincing and symbolical, essentials when he heard a gust at the swing-door. And there, pouring in, a turbulence of rakish hat, darting eyes, aquiline nose, about-to-be-double chin, ample bosom, and a general clutter of necklaces, rings, bracelets, amber drop ear-rings and just possible red hair, was Lady Margarine Dunlop—most noted of all patrons of the latest developments in the perpetually progressing evolution on Art, which has advanced from Michelangelo to Finkelstein in next to no time.

"This is the end," thought Tony; but, remembering the trenches, he pulled himself together and moved towards the door with the sympathetic smile and welcoming hand of the professional dealer in works of art.

4

Lady Margarine Dunlop, that large, talkative, effusive, dominating woman, who knew all about everything which had happened in the last twenty years, liked modern pictures and intellectual young men—and was quite able to pay for both. Rich in her own right, she had married Sir Guy Dunlop, a hereditary City magnate, who was richer still and gave her all she wanted. Her parties were the most celebrated of all in that quarter of London where fashion, art, letters, and the most intelligent parts of both Toryism and Bolshevism meet; her cook was excellent; her wines were good; she could always offer her guests the best cigars, though they seldom smoked them; and her husband was invariably absent. Occasionally some visitor got a glimpse of him. He was such a very great magnate that it really did not matter if he went to the City at all; he had, what we are told is the greatest of all gifts in a great genius, the power of Delegation. The result was that, now and then, some guest of Lady Margarine's turning up early, either because the taxi-man had been forgetfully quick,

or because he hadn't a watch, or because he really wanted a
private word with and further invitations from his hostess,
would catch a glimpse of Sir Guy nipping out of the hall into
his car, clad in plus-fours on his way to a golf-course, and
receive from him a hazy nod of pretended recognition. The
Dunlops went their own ways. That they had met on occasion
there were no fewer than four pieces of evidence—three girls
and the heir to the baronetcy. When, in the ordinary way,
they conversed, nobody could suggest. It certainly couldn't
have been at breakfast; with her tray and the telephone Lady
Margarine was fully occupied until it was time for her hair-
dresser, her milliner, or an early call at an art exhibition. It
couldn't be at lunch, tea, or dinner, because she was always
either out or entertaining. The only possible assumption was
that they occasionally got thrown together when they were
away for week-ends in the country. At all events, it is highly
unlikely that Sir Guy cared for the pictures and *objets d'art*
with which his wife filled their house, and just as likely that
he never noticed them.

Lady Margarine playfully slapped Tony's hand. "You
naughty man," she reproached him. "Why didn't you tell
me you had a new show on?" Tony writhed.

"I don't mind telling you, in confidence," he said, "that I
don't want you to see it. I'm just having a quiet week with
some awful rustic paintings—just to oblige a friend—well, a
kind of relation, I mean. Look at them if you must, but at
your own risk!"

She sailed to the main wall, and he followed, watching her
peer at "A Surrey Garden," "A Garden in Surrey," "Hollyhocks," and "The Pet Calf" through her lorgnette and then
she suddenly screamed with delight.

"But, Tony!" she screamed, "they're absolutely lovely!
They're *period!* The painter's a genius—nobody could possibly
guess they weren't done fifty years ago. And me just
going to do up the back drawing-room as a Mid-Victorian
Room!"

To Tony's surprise, and dawning delight, she ran to his
desk and telephoned to four people in quick succession, tell-

ing them they simply must come at once to Earl Street. She bought six pictures at once; in the afternoon the Gallery was quite full of elegant women and indolent young men, all exclaiming: "Aren't they perfect!" "Aren't they marvellous!" "Aren't they absolutely 1870!" "Aren't they too sweet!" and "Tony, you simply must bring her to lunch."

For two days picture after picture went at steadily rising prices, and people simply couldn't tire of saying how wonderful was Tony's flair for the very latest thing.

Nor was this all: far from it. Sir Guy, strolling through his drawing-room, found his attention caught by a little picture which tore at his heart-strings, so strongly did the "Cottage Garden" (with white palings and old lady complete) remind him of the dawn of sentiment in his boyhood's home at Surbiton. He had a library in which there were no books; he sent his wife a note, got an answer, and within an hour he was at Tony's, buying hard; while by the end of the week a golf-club, full of his opulent friends, who had never dared protest to their wives about being surrounded by Cubism and Expressionism, had cleaned out the Show, and embarked on that slippery slope that always awaits rich brokers who begin cordial relations with a picture-dealer.

Miss Mandeville was vindicated and pacified; Tony had made a large profit; he had realized once and for all that it was his job to discover what people wanted, rightly or wrongly. He has already led up to several Sir Joshuas, with very good hopes, and actually sold many old Academy pictures normally unsaleable in the auction-rooms, and he lives in expectation of ultimately giving a wing to the National Gallery and becoming a peer.

The moral of this story has so often been pointed that it is hardly worth while pointing it again.

"There now," I said to myself as I finished, "nobody can say you have been idle to-day."

"Nonsense!" sneered the demon, "it was all an excuse for staying in bed, and you didn't take any real trouble about it."

I searched for my answer among the usual roses and true-lovers'-knots of the wallpaper. "Anyhow, I *was* doing something," I answered lamely.

"Only because you hadn't anything to read and you would have been too bored to stay in bed if you hadn't written. You only worked for laziness' sake."

"Have it your own way. I was never any good at arguing with quibblers."

As I dressed I took consolation to myself. I remembered a remark which had haunted me for nearly twenty years. I was at a luncheon-party in Cavendish Square at Mr. Asquith's, then newly fallen from his high estate, but sage and humorous as ever. Somebody, I think the blind Sir Arthur Pearson, observed that a scientist had said that if somebody in South Africa should discover a lump of radium the size of a man's head it would do all the work in the world. "I am not sure that it would be a good idea," said Mr. Asquith. Often since I have wondered whether it could really be true that we should all be up to mischief if we hadn't to work: the corollary being that the ideal state of things would compel every man to sleep for eight hours and dig or what-not for sixteen.

"No," I said to myself, "I at least could safely be released from all necessity of labour."

* * * * *

When I got down to the bar, which had just opened, with a watery afternoon sunlight filtering through the windows, the barmaid greeted me with, "Good evening. Had a nice night's rest?" "Yes," I said, "a pint of bitter, please. And perhaps this gentleman would like one too," I added, noticing that the only other occupant of the bar, an obvious lorryman, was draining his glass. "Thanks," he said, approaching me, "are you the gent wot's hikin'?"

"Yes."

"Going on to-night?"

"To-morrow, I think."

"Where?"

"Taunton."

"I'm going there now if you'd like a lift?"

G

"Could you wait five minutes?"

"Ten if you like."

I packed, paid, apologized, and was ready; the driver courteously accepted "one for the road." We went out and mounted a gigantic covered van. As soon as we had rattled out of the town he cheerfully said that, of course, he wasn't allowed to give me a lift, really. The insurance companies didn't like it, he said, as we whizzed round a corner, and wouldn't pay up if there was an accident. Besides, there were all those girls chaps picked up at coffee-stalls on the main roads. A bad lot they were.

There was, what with the jolting and the conversation, not much chance of admiring the landscape. Just before Taunton he asked me to dismount, though he was quite willing for me to go on if I would masquerade as one of his directors on a holiday. I was glad to get off.

I did not feel like an early couch, and played snooker late with some men who were Freemasons in the house of one of them some miles from the town. It was a good distance, and I was taken to and fro in a car in the dark. They introduced each other to me, but I don't think remembered to ask my name. One of them, whichever it was, was a very open-handed host. The billiard-room was full of the heads of koodoo, sable antelope, eland, and dik-dik, and on each side of the marker was the vast open-mouthed club-toothed visage of a hippopotamus. But it hardly seemed the time and place to express my opinions about the wantonness of shooting harmless wild beasts.

ELEVENTH DAY

I DON'T know what time the lark got up, but, as for me, I rose pretty early, all things considered. After a quick walk to the two great rose-pink towers, noble though rebuilt, I set out on the last stage of my journey on the road through Wellington to Tiverton, which I had taken so many times before, not sorry to be strapping my now shapeless pack on my back for the last time, its bulk having greatly swollen through the periodic acquisition of new minor garments.

I had just reached the tangled junction of roads at the west end of the town when I thought to myself that the first part of the walk was not very interesting, that I wanted to saunter through the second part, and that I must get to Tiverton by tea-time. So I took the next train that stopped at Wellington and had but thirteen or fourteen miles to go.

I was tempted by the climb to the Wellington Monument on the edge of the Black Down Hills, but forwent it and pushed on along a road a great deal more frequented by motors than it used to be.

Now I looked around me at the country, growing more and more like Devonshire every mile, and now (though it is seldom I indulge in the luxury of enjoyments or otherwise to come) I thought how certain I was as to how I should spend the evening. The school would be shut. The only people I knew in the neighbourhood would be away, and anyhow I could not call dinner-jackets from the vasty deep. It was all Lombard Street to a China Orange (I wish someone would explain that phrase to me!) that I should, after dining, spend the evening, whether joining-in or merely overhearing, with a number of men in real or imagined riding-breeches talking about the Devon and Somerset Staghounds.

I came to a gate on a rise, went inside, sat down, and began to eat my sandwiches, looking at the distant hills. I was on the border of the county and already I could almost smell the washes, pink, yellow, cream and white, of the cob houses and the flowers in the rich cottage-gardens. "Why," thought I to myself, thinking of my story of the day before, "should cottage gardens be left to the bad painters? Why should apples on a tree not be painted and flowers as they grow, nodding to each other behind the palings, blue and yellow and red; but only flowers, boldly generalized, in urban glass or china, and apples, anæmic on trays with beer bottles beside them, tamed, bled and sicklied by the denizens of Charlotte Street and the Café du Dôme, all aping that able man who had a mania for reducing all things to structure, to anatomy, to bone and plane?"

Countless cottage gardens, farm gardens, gardens of modest old houses, I remembered from my youth, secluded by walls, half-screened by fences, or merging hedgeless into long orchard grass where jonquils grew under the spangled shadows of the apple-trees. It is almost unbearable pain to see them now; the Canterbury bells and sweet-williams in their season, the hollyhocks in theirs, the asters and dahlias in theirs, the marigolds gallantly living till autumn tears their last rags away; for their timelessness so forcibly contrasts with irrecoverable memories of days when they were first seen and stared at. But it would be worse if they went too; if one knew that the last wrinkled old dame in the last sun-bonnet had tended the last red amaryllis in a cottage window. I thought, with tears in my eyes, of all the long holidays of youth, moss-roses in the gardens, shells on the beaches, bluebells in the deep woods, heather, furze and whortleberries under the rocks of the great tors, black pools, boys, dead or scattered, with whom I had wandered everywhere, knowing nothing at all except the things worth knowing. I stared across the valley not counting time.

A car stopped behind the hedge. People laughed. They had the wireless on.

"Pascal avait son gouffre avec lui se mouvant."

*   *   *   *   *

I left the main Exeter Road at Sampford Peverell, where the street is worthy of the name. I had half a mind to turn north to Holcombe Rogus, where is that rare thing in Devon, a late fifteenth-century stone house with tower and hall; only in our day has the family which built it left it, as another left Montacute. But I went on, and came to Holberton, which was almost as far as one could walk on half-holidays between lunch and roll-call or roll-call and tea; and then, on the top of a hill, which used to be the turning-point of our practice runs for rugger, I could see the whole valley and the wooded hills all around and glimpses of buildings which were the school.

Every hedge and turning brought back the past more vividly than unassisted memory ever will.

*   *   *   *   *

I walked past the playing-fields and the houses. I passed the Chapel and Big School. I wanted to go in by the main gates.

I went in. There was nobody about. The square tower still stood there, its red sandstone as calm and kind as ever; and the great high trees on their lawns on the hither side of it, and the long line of mullioned windows, sunlit or blue-bough-shadowed, stretching away to the right, and the chapel far back on the left, with a new memorial cross in front of it that had no need to be there in my time.

There was no sound from beyond the roofs of a ball being kicked or bumping, no echoes of the old cries of "Take it with you, forwards," no distant shrillness of whistle.

The stones and the leaves were the same. Other boys would be there in a month. The man who used to blow the whistle would be there no more.

A mist came in front of me and I saw forms long dead or strayed. Boys swarmed up the drive in strange bowler hats. Boys ran out at the news of motor-cars. Boys sat late in their studies making coffee. Boys told stories to each other in dark dormitories, creepy stories which made them spring up with stopped hearts when strange wailings came from gas-meter or radiator. Fags came back from farms loaded with eggs, cream and flowers. People, over beyond the Tower, played fives. Others were in the tuck-shop. And Willy was there.

*   *   *   *   *

I pulled myself up. It was I that had changed. The old things would endure. Even now there were boys who would return thirty years hence and not a stick or stone would have altered. Only themselves. Less merry, less confident, with older hearts and knowing too late the meaning of words that sounded empty to boyish ears: "if youth but knew." And sad will be the song within them if they come, as I, when the place is empty. It is better to come when there is distraction.

I found someone who let me into School House. I went down the zigzagging corridor past studies with strange names on the doors, and at last, feeling like a burglar, opened the door of the one at the end, which was ours.

Some of the chairs seemed to be familiar. Football and cricket groups did not seem to be so much in favour as of old. There was little difference in the books on the shelves; the fevers of London seemed to have left this study at least unscathed. Whatever photographs of handsome mothers, plump sisters, and fathers in uniform there may have been had been stored away in cupboards.

There wasn't much to see. And then I suddenly remembered. With a pocket-knife (for the yellow dressing stone was almost as soft as the red sandstone) I had carved my name on the window-sill. Could it still be there?"

It was. I could read "J. C. SQ"; and a few strokes were still visible after it.

EPILOGUE

It was just a year after. I had finished that last sentence, musing after I had set it down on an earlier youth now much more vivid and present than it was in my late teens, when childhood would have seemed very far behind and very dim had I ever even have thought of it—much reading of other and more grown men's experiences having superseded and overlaid the fresh experiences, discoveries of friendship, of love, of beauty in sky, sea, earth, shell, weed and caterpillar, then so neglected because they had belonged to an outgrown and despised infancy. It was time to take a holiday again, and I obtained the horse.

First, since I was going off in the train of Celia Fiennes, of Lord Torrington and of Cobbett, I had to have some saddlebags. I suppose they may still be purchasable in that district between St. James's and Lower Regent Street which still contains Merry, Berry and Lock, like pretty maids all in a row, Mr. McMaster the print-dealer, certain eminent dealers in anglers' gear, and certain merchants of wine and cigars; and which till very recently even housed a firm which proudly displayed in its window nothing but a few royal heads of red deer and dealt in nothing but braces, which it had probably sold to

Pierce Egan, John Barclay, Lord Frederick Beauclerk and Squire Osbaldestone.

But the necessity of searching that pleasantly antediluvian district was removed from me. For Tschiffely offered to lend me some saddle-bags.

They were not the great packs which accompanied him when he took two years going from Buenos Ayres to New York, with two stout horses which alternately bore the burden of this Cowboy Swiss himself and that of his food, blankets and bags of doubloons—facing wild Indians, climbing the Andes, swimming the rivers full of alligators, penetrating to jungle-buried cities of the Aztecs, and, in the end, risking their lives on the main motor-roads of the United States, where an equestrian traveller was regarded as one cocking an antiquated snook at the modern moving world. No: it was a humble pair which he had used on his little mare Violet when he went through England; two little sacs like those in which the bees carry honey, which were strapped to the front of the saddle—one of them having room for the toilet apparatus of the horse and the other for my own tooth-brush, spare pyjamas, spare shirt, spare socks, and map. Even that amount of apparatus is sufficient to attract attention and even to arouse wonderment on an English road to-day. And all the more so if you go off on the sort of horse I took. For he was a huge flea-bitten grey, as distinctive in appearance as in character.

I first saw him in a field with several others. The owner pointed out one or two quiet-looking cobs grazing around as being suitable for my purpose, which was that of a walking-pace holiday.

Suddenly I caught his rolling eye. He was larger and older than any of them and, ceasing to munch, peered sidelong towards us. I caught his eye. He at once turned, came trotting up, and put his nose into my pocket, where there was neither carrot nor sugar. "This is the one I must have," I said. "Well," replied the owner, "I didn't think I'd let him go, but you can have him." He had been in the Scots Greys; nobody knew what his original name was, so they called him "Grandfather"; he could still jump, was hacked about a bit by bank-managers' wives, and occasionally had a day out with the Old Berkeley and enjoyed it. But for some years he had always slept at home.

I looked at the horse; he looked back at me with the intelligence of one of Swift's Houhnhyms; intelligent co-operation seemed to be promised; and it was arranged that he should come to me three days before I was to start in order that I, who had not been on a horse for fifteen years, should get used to him. I took him out for an hour each day, and his set convictions were soon revealed. He was quite all right if he was going towards his home, and, with a sigh, could be urged to go along a road which led away from it. But as soon as there was a turning which led back to his quarters he stopped dead, peered round in enquiry, and only proceeded when lustily jabbed in the ribs by my spurless heels.

I rode him for a week or so. I left Chesham on the first hot day of the first hot week of the year; and, as long as it lasted, for all his propensity to be as faithful to his home as the magnet to the pole, and to fight his martingale, it was enjoyable. The road, that first day, was too heavily metalled for anything but a walk or an occasional jog-trot; that I did not mind, as I was seeing the beechwoods, and hill and valley over the hedges. But already, going down the long steep hill into Great Missenden, I realized that there were more motors on the road than there used to be, and, at the bottom, another modern complication set in. There was a road leading back sharply southwards; there was a single-line stream of heavy lorries coming towards us; workmen were laying drains behind lines of ropes; and there was a cumbersome "Stop-Go" board which a man periodically tilted round.

He tried to turn home. With two gyrations I got him back, and addressed him to the green "Go." Just as we were entering the narrow defile the red "Stop" came round, and the great vans clanking through, and I had to haul him round. I wouldn't let him go forward and I wouldn't let him go back: reined up he mused, "What kind of undecided idiot am I carrying?" I couldn't explain to him about County Councils and one-way traffic; I simply had to appear a lunatic to him, and call him an ass until, at last, after several repetitions of the pantomime (for lorries don't wait), time, place and loved one all came together and I got him through into the street. At the far end, up the hill, I turned left on the Hampden and Risborough road. It was a beautiful ride. All those miles there is scarcely a cottage; nothing more than an occasional farmhouse or two, the steep undulations of the Chilterns, and sometimes deep woods on both sides. With a loose rein I went on.

Late in the afternoon, on the high hill above Whyteleafe, I turned him through a gap of the ragged hedges and stopped for five minutes above one of the noblest views in the Home Counties. All the wide vale of Aylesbury was spread below us, with a group of trees to the left emphasizing the height of the escarpment and the vastness of the distance, the chalk overlooking the clay as it does from the North and South Downs over the Weald. The bastions of Chinnor and Bledlow were on the left; I realized that in an afternoon I had come from the new England to the old, that in all the miles below me, with tiny roofs spaced among fields and woods, away and away till the haze veiled all, the little towns were as they had always been, except for half-hearted fringes, and the cows infinitely more numerous than the season-ticket-holders. And this was still Buckinghamshire which in one corner, near London, had its Slough of Despond, and in another its scabrous gash of High Wycombe, but here drifted off towards Oxfordshire and Northants, primitive still, with Thame and Bicester near its borders, the height of Brill in its north-western corner, and, north of Aylesbury the fenny, empty lands, full of slow streams, that lead to Olney where Cowper's house still stands, in which he kept his tame hares and boiled his watch while carefully observing the egg in his hand; a land where it was "always afternoon" and still is, in Brill and Long Crendon, and the remote parish with the perfect Norman church.

"Old Horse," I said, "I don't believe they can spoil this. The trains won't be able to get them to London in time."

He turned his head. "I don't mind waiting a little," observed his great eye, "but could I nibble a little of that bush?"

"Have it your own way," I agreed. "It looks rather poisonous. But animals are supposed to know what is good

G*

for them." I checked, remembering certain cattle with yew trees; and my three goats who died years ago, in agony, because the garden-boy, wishing to give them a treat, had fed them with rhododendron and laurel in a kind of mash or mine-strone. However, "Mithridates he died old," and this grey knew his way about.

He wrenched out great sprays with determined teeth; the deep hollows above his eyes worked as he chewed. He was content and I consoled. In the big towns and in committee rooms, on the arterial roads and the Sussex coast, it seems as though nothing can be done to stop the pollution of the populations; but here, no more than forty miles from London, the prospect was untainted and still slept in peace.

Down the long hill we wound. I asked my way of a digni-fied old man with side-whiskers and a stick, and, after thread-ing two lanes full of thatched cottages and little gardens full of flowers, found the entrance to a friend's house. I rode up the path between palings, dismounted, and knocked. My in-voluntary hostess-to-be came to the door. "What on earth have you got there?" she asked.

"A horse," I said. "Can you put us up for the night?"

"We can put *you* up, since we know you don't mind rough-ing it, but we haven't any place for a horse."

"Aren't there any stables at the pub?"

"There was one, but it's been turned into a garage."

"Isn't there a farmer near?"

"I daresay Mr. Jinks would put him up. Could he stay out in a field?"

"Rather!"

We led him a quarter of a mile and found a farmer; un-saddled him, groomed him, watered him and turned him out into an immense acreage containing several cows, several horses and the lushest of grass. He began eating at once.

My host was a politician of definitely Left propensities; it says much for his hospitality that we managed to talk about Spain (which, in a world full of snarls, had now superseded Abyssinia) without acerbity. After dinner I began to realize that I was getting stiffer and stiffer. At ten I asked if I might go to bed. I could hardly get up the stairs. I had not remembered that it was fifteen years since I had bestridden a steed and that one couldn't resume such pastimes as though there had been no interval. I read two pages of a pamphlet about reconstructing the League of Nations; hardly needing that assistance, I fell into deep and unbroken sleep.

*   *   *   *   *

"Your tea, sir, and madam says would you like your breakfast in bed?"

"I would, but I don't have any breakfast as a rule."

"Not just some eggs?"

"Well, yes, I think I will." I didn't want the eggs, but I wanted to stay in bed.

I read the papers. Even another scalding bath did not unstiffen my thighs or take the ache out of my hip-bones unaccustomed to the stretch of a horse now too wide for them. When I came downstairs my friend had retired to his study to work; his wife said brightly: "Well, are you going to do your twenty miles to-day?"

"I think not," I replied, as one who was on holiday and was entitled capriciously to change his mind.

"Why not stay another night?"

"No, I simply must work this stiffness off."

"What about staying for lunch and going on afterwards?"

The company was congenial, the armchairs comfortable, the prints on the walls pleasant, the books reassuring, the sunlit branches through the windows enchanting.

"Your horse is quite all right," my hostess resumed. "We've been to see him already. Mr. Jinks says he's made friends with the other horses and looks as if he'd settled down for life. Have a look at the papers while I talk to cook and then come up and see our local landlord."

With great strength of mind I said "Yes"; before long we were going slowly uphill through a village that would have appealed to Birket Foster or Mr. Blunden, and found an empty tap-room looking across the road to a rose-garden. The landlord, a grave and preoccupied man, brought my pint; but I had been warned that he was a retired officer who had served long in India, and by an easy transit through my horse we got to polo. His face was illumined; he visited the back premises and brought out portraits of ponies and groups of moustached men with helmets, and sticks, sitting under verandahs at Peshawar or Ootacamund. But when I asked him how he liked being an innkeeper his face fell again. The villagers were a good lot but the visitors for meals were all wrong.

"Why?" I asked. "Are they noisy?"

"Oh no, it's not that; it's simply that they won't take the slightest interest in their food. Here am I, keen about cooking and liking cooking myself, prepared to give a variety of soups, fish, omelettes, vegetables, but I have given up asking 'em. They all demand hot roast beef, baked potatoes and cabbage."

"Never anything else?"

"Cold roast beef, sometimes." His eyes gazed absently out of the window as those of Zoo camels seem to gaze at lost desert sands. His thoughts had gone back to jungle, nullah and dak-bungalow, and curries he would never see again.

"It's annoying," he protested, "to find the newspapers always going for the food in inns when it's all the public's fault."

This was a new point of view to me, but on the whole I could not think of the country as being full of hotel-keepers passionate about cuisine and reduced to despair by a dull public which daily and mechanically demands beef and would feel lost without the smell of cabbage; however, it was no good arguing with one of the redeemed.

After lunch and coffee I said good-bye, and went down to the farm to recover the horse. The field was too large, the grass too good, his companions too congenial. Later on he was out twice in smaller fields and was as docile as a lamb; but here, with a rich prairie around him, he was resolved not to be caught. He would graze until we were near enough to see the sidelong roll of his eye, and then swerve round us at full tilt to some far hedge and start grazing again with cows all round him. Reinforcements had to be fetched, and, after he had showed in several runs what a fine three-quarter he would make, he was cornered by a cordon, given an undeserved lump of sugar, and led back to the barn to be saddled.

By the time we were on our way again it was four o'clock; overcast and spitting with rain. I had been told to go to a large old village, an easy distance of six or seven miles, which was notable for its maze of streets, its several central piazzas, the alleged (but unreal) stupidity of its inhabitants and the high mud walls along its lanes which I was assured made it the nearest thing in England to a Nigerian town. The reader may find it himself; it is a long way from its nominal railway station and the motorists haven't yet discovered it: there is local life there.

During the morning a plasterer had told me of an inn to go to. I had to chance it, for it wasn't on the telephone. I found it. The landlord, who had never been visited by a horse, looked at my mount as though it were a giraffe; as we debated, a circle of children gathered round with their fingers in their mouths.

The modesty of my needs was explained. We led the horse into the stable-yard. The stable contained perambulators, timber, and sundries, but the landlord said he would fetch two young men who kept a horse and cart and they would do everything I required.

He fetched them and went back to his quarters. At first sight it was clear that they resembled neither Alexander the master of Bucephalus nor Aristotle the instructor of Alexander. They ineffectively assisted the clearance of the stall, they watched me take off saddle and bridle, they fetched some bedding, they stood vacant while I found, up the yard, a bucket and a pump and brought water down with slop-slop: and when I asked them where I could buy corn they made street-ward motions with their thumbs. However, I got the corn; dined; went for a walk through the dim-lit streets and lanes; and got lost as had been forecast.

*   *   *   *   *

But this book is not about that journey. By short stages I sauntered round the fringes of Bucks, Northants and Oxfordshire. I sat, one lovely morning, on the horse by the windmill at Brill, looking across the valley to that great wall of the

Chilterns, and east and west into near infinity. Stopping for lunch in a Northamptonshire hamlet I had this conversation with a lady:

"Can I have lunch?"

"Afraid I cannot manage it."

"Haven't you *any*thing?"

"No; it's a pity you didn't come yesterday; we had a chicken."

"But isn't there a village shop where they sell stamps and tinned pressed beef?"

"I could get you some of that. But you'd have to wait half an hour, as my husband's got to have his dinner first."

I waited, playing desultory darts with the only other customer. I then enjoyed a luncheon of pressed beef, lettuce, tomatoes, and cheese which I should never have obtained without importunity. There was some excuse there; callers were probably almost unknown. But eggs are available everywhere. It is commonly remarked that in some regards the tests for publicans are more severe than those for clergymen. For myself I should like to see it laid down that no one should have a licence without passing an examination in omelettes and salads and guaranteeing to keep grated Parmesan cheese, and not to charge high prices for these things either.

In Hertfordshire I know a man who must be one of the few Italian publicans in the English countryside. He is an aged man, a retired chef who was at Claridge's, and to see his pleasure in serving minestrone and whatever else one wants, evoked by his own skilled hand, is to have one's own pleasure doubled. This quite apart from his charming frankness and humour, his admirable wife, and the superb pictures of birds and foliage which he makes out of gold, azure, vermilion and green snippets of cigar-bands. Where is there an Anglo-Saxon host like that, jolly companions though many of them are when they talk about racing or the foibles of politicians? But I draw to an end, and closing time.

*   *   *   *   *

There came, and for the first time in this rainy dismal

summer, some days of intense heat. Riding by day in breeches and gaiters was no pleasure, with spectacles having to be wiped and brow constantly mopped. I stayed one night with friends who inhabit an old tower, last relic, with its moat, of a castle destroyed like so much else of our heritage, by Oliver Williams, alias Cromwell. We tired not merely the sun but almost the stars with talking, and next day lounged under the cedars in deck-chairs, shirt-sleeves and muslin frocks, doing nothing more strenuous between light collations than watching wasps getting entrapped in a row of jam-jars full of beer, sugar, and wine, mixed.

Lazily, towards twilight, I rode off. Seven miles away, I remembered, in a market-town, there was a hostelry where I had been kindly treated over thirty years before, arriving late, on foot, dead tired and without luggage. There would be at least no difficulty about stabling in that town—a hunting centre—and I could certainly find a bed for myself somewhere.

It grew dark. A procession of cars approached me from both directions, blazing with lights, and swerving around my charger, who had no red light on his tail. It was towards closing-time when I drew up at the bar-door and shouted (there was a marked susurrus of conversation coming from within) the unnecessary question: "Is there anybody there?" A lusty voice answered back: "Why can't you come in?" "I can't bring a horse in, can I?" I remarked reasonably.

Out came the landlord, and I got off. Yes, he could put me up, but the horse would have to go somewhere else. "Do you mean to say you haven't got a stable even here?" "We put the grand piano in it last month," he said.

We took the horse elsewhere and tucked him up in a place full of thoroughbreds. Then I returned, ate bacon and eggs, and went to bed with an omnibus volume of shockers, property of the landlady.

Betimes I went to see the horse. Heat had softened and moistened his skin; the girth had worked forward, and he had a nasty raw gall. "Keep him here until he's healed," I said.

Twice a day I went to see him, to the profit of grocers and

fruiterers; as I walked up the yard his vast impassive head awaited me over his door.

At the end of a week he was quite well again.

But meanwhile life had not been standing still with me. I met men with cars who were delighted to drive me to see friends in neighbouring counties. I had been persuaded that I simply must stay for the Horse Show. I had been invited to go to Warwick Races. I had made friends with the Vicar, sat up late with him over a decanter, and found that his chief trouble in life was a plague of bats, who defiled his church and frightened his congregation, and I urged him to write a letter to the Press headed "Bats in the Belfry." I had been lent a gun by a sporting auctioneer and asked out to shoot partridges by friendly farmers. I had fallen into a daily routine of shopping, paper-buying, and dropping in on coteries of leisurely cronies. "Why should I not remain," I thought, "until my holiday is over? I might go further and fare worse."

Besides, the Fair was coming on in the market-place and I might (in the upshot I won three) win a watch at one of the games of skill. I felt a nostalgia for the blare of a merry-go round.

In the morning quietude of the bar I consulted the manageress.

"I'm enjoying myself so much here," I said.

"We're so glad."

"I've got into the habits of the place."

"There are worse."

"If I go on with that horse there will only be the same old troubles. Big roads swarming with traffic and too hard for trotting. Side-roads with inns off the telephone, no stabling, and fodder to be fetched."

"Sure to be. Nobody expects horses now and the roads aren't made for them."

"Do you know what I think I'll do? That horse is very fond of his home. I believe I'll telegraph and tell them that I want him boxed back."

"Why don't you?" said she.

To

WILLIAM BLISS

*This narrative as vagrant as our meandering
streams*

NOTE

*The lighter verses in Water-Music have
appeared in "Punch," whose proprietors
I thank for permission to reprint.*

PRELUDE

It was one of those glorious warm days we had in March 1938, to which posterity may refuse to give credence. Whether or not Bliss had tired him with talking I do not know, but the sun was certainly setting behind the poplars. We stood on the garden steps looking at the orb, now weary of well-doing. "Yes, Bliss," I said, "I've read all your books on canoeing and waterways, and I envy your sixty years of it. I don't know that I want to shoot rapids; that isn't my idea of a rest. But I've always wanted to take a holiday on quiet rivers and canals, seeing places to which roads and railways don't go; with no noise except the sound of water, and paddles, and the birds. Of course, I never shall now. . . ."

"Do you mean you've never been canoeing?" he said.

"Of course," I said, "I've idled in canoes hundreds of times, largely in backwaters, but I've never travelled with one, though I once did a week's sailing on the Ouse, and was wakened by cows."

"Have you got a diary on you?" said Bliss, knitting his brows, pulling at his grey moustache and gleaming at me through his spectacles.

"Yes," I said, pulling it out. Me unresisting, he laid hands on it. He opened it and flipped the pages over.

"Here," he announced, "this is when you are coming," and efficiently drew long strokes through the last four pages of May, concluding with the inscription "Home very cheerful and happy."

To me it seemed revolutionary. It was all very well not to get into a rut, but a holiday in England in May was completely unorthodox. Abroad, yes; but in England, since I became a householder, I could not remember taking more than a week-end except in late summer or early autumn. It seemed almost like truancy to go away when everybody else was working and all the millions of children were at school, to idle through a busy England meeting no other idlers; and in such a season not, for weeks, to take the chair once at the annual meeting of the Society for God knows What, to see a desk or a committee or to listen to speeches at any Public Dinner. However, he held me with his glittering eye and it was arranged.

Next week he turned up, having walked across half Buckinghamshire, with a lot of one-inch maps with azure waterways networked all over them. "We are going," said he—"yes, thanks, there's nothing like beer after a long walk—to start from Oxford. I'll see to the hiring of the canoe from Salter's. We shall go up the Cherwell; portage to the Oxford Canal; portage to the Avon at Warwick; come down the Avon, which may be very low in places owing to the drought, send the canoe by train to the upper Thames and then come down the Thames and return to Salter's. And don't you bring too much baggage."

"You are my skipper," I said, "and I am perfectly prepared to fall in with your wishes. But do you mean that I can't bring spare shirts, socks and handkerchiefs, or merely that there won't be room for a dinner-jacket?"

"Oh," he conceded, "you can bring a suitcase so long as it's of a reasonable size; you can even sit on it in the canoe; but there won't be room for cabin trunks."

"Well," I thought to myself, "I have known Bliss for a good many years, but he has seen me chiefly in London and in the company of people who do London things. He hasn't the least idea that I'm even more of a provincial than he is, he coming from Gloucestershire and I from Devonshire, that I can produce as solid and broad-spoken a line of rural ancestry as he, and that, although I know nothing more about Canadian canoes than can be learnt by lazing with one paddle and *Marius the Epicurean* under the willows by Trinity Bridge in the Cambridge Backs, I was mucking about outside Rame Head, sailing, and fishing for mackerel or breasting the waves in out-rigged double scullers, when I was twelve. He will, I suppose," continued I, all in one flash of thought, "expect me to call the bow of a canoe the radiator."

Letter.

Dear Bliss,   *May 18th, 1938.*

This is really an S O S.

I told you I would pick you up in X's car at midday on the 20th prox.—which I think is the lingo you talked when you were a solicitor in London, before you were a history coach in Oxford, and after you were (long before I was born) the son of a man in the Vatican Library and an enquiring lad who accosted the then Pope in the Vatican Gardens, and asked him why he, with his faith, should worry about death and received the reply: "My child, I am a human being."

The point is this: I have just met an Oxford man and he tells me that what they call "Eights Week" is beginning on May 20th. You are seventy-three, old though not venerable, utterly careless as to the figure you cut, completely free from self-consciousness or inferiority-complexes, and so on.

But, for me, I don't mind telling you that I have no desire to paddle a canoe, whether my own or yours, past all those barges, with the Eights going on, and all those young men in blazers and all those young women doing their sartorial best. We obviously couldn't go down from Salter's to the Cherwell while a race was on, whatever our legal rights; and, between divisions, looked on by all those disdainful eyes, we should be no better than Derby Dogs—animals invading the course, and ludicrous.

So it is a question of early-rising. Will you please be ready?

CHAPTER 1

Oxford to Kidlington

READY he was. He lives in a little farm-house with a large sloping garden and barns behind, some seven miles north-west of High Wycombe. It is six hundred and fifty feet up and the views are tremendous. The water comes from a well, the drive consists of steep turf and gorse-bushes, there is an inn called the "Peacock" within easy reach, there is a multitude of flowers outside the house and the right old furniture and china within.

At nine sharp we bumped up to the trellised gate. I went up the bordered path; Mrs. Bliss was at the door.

"You will find William gardening," she said. "He will be sitting on the wheelbarrow smoking his pipe."

He was, but with an alert and expectant air. He had on a disgraceful hat, a ginger coat, experienced grey flannel trousers, but a resplendent tie.

"Weren't you at Stonyhurst, Bliss?" I asked.

"Yes," he admitted, with a puzzled gaze.

"Well," I felt bound to say, as men have been sent to prison for less than this, "why are you wearing an Old Salopian tie?"

"It isn't!" he replied hotly. "It is the tie of my daughter's Hockey Club."

I said "Sorry!" not knowing what else would fit the occasion.

He went in to fetch his things. He had a huge walker's knapsack which would have made a guardsman faint. There was also a smaller canvas bag from which a map was protruding.

"Is that bag all maps?" I asked.

"No," he said, "mostly books."

This was true, but they were all his own books. Most serviceable to him they were, too. Whenever there was any doubt as to conditions of portage, distances, numbers of locks in a stretch, and so on, he at once resorted to the best authority, placing implicit trust in his own assertions. I only once found reason to question his infallibility, but, afloat, I was clay in his hands.

We said the last good-byes. A doubt, as we were parting, assailed Bliss's almost inured wife.

"I suppose you *are* going where you say you're going?"*

* It reminded me of another complication. A Russian Jew told me that two Jewish salesmen met in some desolate plain near Brest-Litovsk. The dialogue, in that immense inane, was:
"Vare are you going?"
"Varsaw."
  (Pause.)
"You liar, you *are* going to Varsaw."

Bliss was hurt.

"What on earth . . ." he asked.

"Don't you remember," she continued in a level voice, "that time when you told me that you and your brother were going for a little calm holiday on the Grand Trunk Canal, and then I opened my *Daily Mail* one morning and saw a whole column saying that three men had, in a foolhardy manner, gone down through all the rocks and races of the Eden, which nobody had ever done before?"

"That was a long time ago, my dear," said Bliss meekly, "and I've only told you two lies since."

"And that," remarked Mrs. Bliss, with a solid wave of farewell, "is the biggest one yet. Now you two can get on."

I sympathized with him, in a way; my sex are always misunderstood. I sympathized with her in a way; my sex are rather elusive, and I suspect that the apparently stable politicians and bankers are even more elusive than the rest of us, unimaginative though they may look. At all events, Mr. Bliss will be canoeing, prevaricating, and going to Early Mass until he is ninety, or I will eat my hat. . . .

Nothing would induce me to eat Bliss's.

*   *   *   *   *

The car got moving; Mrs. Bliss and her daughter forgivingly waved to us; we conquered a new series of gorse-bushes and bumps of grass and arrived at the corner by the "Peacock" where there was a road of sorts.

"Please stop!" shouted Bliss to the chauffeur.

"What's up now?" I asked.

"There's something I must pick up," said he, sauntered into the inn, remained for a time, just long enough to be suspect, and came out burdened with a yellow-brown jar encased in wickerwork. "I thought," he explained, "we might have some cider in our canoe."

The cider was packed in the rear of the car with Bliss, his knapsacks, and my aged brown suitcase—it was bought in Newhaven (Yale), Conn., in 1921 for the outrageous sum of sixteen pounds (the exchange was against us and that was a

University town) and I have never regretted its price, for it has been half over the world with me, and is still unbowed though battered, and might repeat Henley's amazing defiance with much more assurance than I.

I thought it was very considerate of Bliss to have arranged for that cider. There might be parching afternoons, when inns were out of reach or even closed, and stagnant canal water uninviting, and that cider, to dusty tongues, might be as grateful as evening dew. But, in the end, it became a mere symbol. We had a glass each before we set off from Salter's; and then it became a sort of fixture in the boat, a basket with a nozzle lying asleep behind the pointed prow, and never remembered except when it wasn't needed. At the end of a fortnight it was still almost unbroached.

The cider packed, we set out for Oxford, by an empty wooded road that led to Stokenchurch. All the blossoms were out together, and the hedge-bottoms crowded with the white cow-parsley. It was a heavenly sunny day—almost the last we were to see—and invited indolence and vagrancy. Forgetting the menace of the Eights I said to Bliss: "Can't we turn aside for a few minutes to Fingest?" I hadn't seen that church, with its great square Norman tower, for years.

"I know your mania for looking at churches," said Bliss, "and you can see plenty of them when we have got off, but I'm not going to let you hold us up now."

I remembered Gibbon's sentence in his *Autobiography,* about the time when his father induced him to throw over his girl because she was a foreigner and a "strange alliance"; "I sighed as a lover and obeyed as a son." What a noble artist as an historian (though nobody yet has been in the same street as Thucydides), and what a stylistic stylist—but, Phœbus! what a lover! But, perhaps, had she been different he would have behaved differently. She, on her part, ambitious to the core, did not sigh for long, but married Necker from Geneva, banker, financier, economist, chancellor of the exchequer, and became the mother of Madame de Staël, a heavy responsibility.

We rolled into Oxford, exchanging sympathetic views about the majority of the ales in that town and district. We approached Magdalen Bridge and that soaring tower which always makes my heart lose a beat by its beauty as many taller buildings fail to do. We went down the High, and crossed Carfax, and then Bliss shouted to the chauffeur: "Go on to the railway station and then stop; I shall have to look at my map."

We went on, and Bliss hopped out. He addressed the first party who passed, an elderly and leisurely man. "Can you tell me where the offices of the Oxford Canal Company are?" he asked.

"Mr. Bliss, I think," said the old gentleman—who proved to be by no means the last who had loved Bliss long since and lost him merely awhile. We obeyed instructions, opened a rusty great gate, drove up through an arbour of ash and ilex, lilac and laburnum, and arrived at a yellow classic temple out of Bath—pillars, pediments, steps, wistaria, blue sky and pigeons.

"Look here, Bliss," I said, "this must be the back of Worcester College, or else somebody's house; no limited liability company could possibly think of usury or shares in such a place as this."

We rang, expecting a flunkey in livery; but no, these really were the offices of the Oxford Canal.

We were shown into a spacious office. While Bliss was negotiating with the Canal, embodied in a very courteous secretary, about the dues we had to pay and winches with which to handle the locks, I smoked a cigarette and examined a large wall-map produced by the Royal Commission on Canals and Waterways. It was depressing to see how many were described as derelict, and to realize again the dreadful waste and lack of foresight of the nineteenth century in this regard as in many others, the railways being allowed deliberately to ruin a national system of transport, which to-day might be relieving the roads far more than it is. What a tremendous effort was made, I thought, in the two generations after the last Duke of Bridgwater, "the father of inland navigation," made his first canal in Lancashire. What enthusiasm, expenditure and labour was put into the canals; the labour—for everything was done by hand in those days—was colossal. And now hundreds of miles are choked or dry or even in process of being filled up. . . .

Bliss finished the business. We pocketed our passports and shook hands with the secretary, whose last words were that we should find the Cherwell very dry and difficult of navigation about Islip. Then we went out, Bliss carrying a large iron winch.

"Do we go to Salter's now?" I asked.

"Well," he explained, "I have just one more call to pay. I want to see a chap off Beaumont Street. It's about our Village Hall and I'm told we may squeeze some money for an extension out of these National Fitness people."

"Good luck to you," I said, "I'm sure they had much better waste their money on your Village Hall than on those awful photographs of jumping girls and men that they're sticking up everywhere, which at best can only make the ordinary person think 'What is the good of me trying.' "

We crawled up to Carfax, then to the left, then to the left again by the Randolph, down a sombre little stone street. Bliss got out and for some minutes (with apologies to the shades of Edward Elgar and Arthur Benson) I endeavoured to compose a New National Fitness Anthem, beginning:

> League of Health and Beauty
> League we love so well. . . .

Then I thought I would stretch my legs, and began to stroll up the forlorn street towards the Corn. There is always something odd to be found in our ancient University towns. There, in a humble and sooty dwelling which was labelled "Oxford Society of Art," there was a modest poster saying "Exhibition of Buddhist Sculpture from Siam, and Greek Embroideries. Entrance to non-members, sixpence." I didn't know whether this was a lost cause or a last enchantment; certainly no crowd was surging around the portal and I longed to go in and give the strange little exhibition sixpennyworth of leg-up. But I dared not get out of sight of the car lest I should hold up our expedition. . . .

Bliss came out; after we had bought some tobacco we went to Salter's, at Folly Bridge. There was the handsome Canadian canoe ready for us, cushions and all. The luggage, including the cider-keg, was stored, and we were just going to move off when Bliss said: "By Jove, we shan't be able to get anything to eat on the Cherwell. We must get something for lunch."

Off we went, and into a largish store. Little chance did it offer us to encourage British agriculture. Everywhere were labels encouraging us to buy Danish bacon, New Zealand butter and Australian Cheddar, for even Australia now seems to have joined Canada and the U.S.A. in pirating the name of what is one of the best of cheeses when it is genuine. When I asked them if they had any Chinese eggs they seemed offended; in the end we made shift with a box of those sticky little cheese triangles wrapped in silver paper, a loaf of bread, some slices of sausage and tongue, a pork pie, a packet of genuine (i.e. kitchen) salt and a twopenny tin of mustard. Laden with these we returned to the canoe. Just as we were setting forth Bliss remembered once more: "By Jove," he said, "we have nothing to drink our cider out of," so the two of us went up to the neighbouring inn and induced them to sell us a glass—it lasted precisely one day and Bliss replaced it with a cracked mug which he bought from a village alehouse for a penny. Once more we went back to the long-suffering Mr. Salter's floating hard. This time we really got away, and a few minutes' brisk paddling past the still dormant barges (so soon to turn into hundreds of yards, if not a whole league, of Health and Beauty) brought us to the Cherwell mouth and our northward journey had begun.

Northward, I say; well, in a sense. For sheer lack of settled direction all the streams round Oxford could give the celebrated Meander points and a beating. That it seems an age since one gets away from the last of Oxford is perhaps not the Cherwell's fault. As we slowly paddled by wall, pasture, and thicket, past Christ Church Meadows and the Botanic Gardens, no sound except the zip of our paddles and the tinkling of water, it seemed that we should never get out of the town.

It was all pleasant enough; the green water under the branches cool to the hand; lilac and laburnum out, and pink and white hawthorn; all like an interminable extension of the pleasant riparian outskirts of a Cathedral city. But "How much longer, Bliss," I said, "is it before we get away from Oxford?"

"You seem to forget," said he, paddling away behind me, "that Oxford is a long rectangle running north and south."

I suddenly realized that that was true; that the backbone of Oxford was not the High but the Banbury Road.

"Why be in such a hurry to get away from Oxford," whispered my Demon to me, as, as in the "Canadian Boat Song," our oars kept time, "for you've often been eager enough to get there? Look," he went on, "there is even wild life here" —and ahead, standing immobile, like a grey-blue china figure, on a shadowy grassy verge behind somebody's back-garden, stood a heron, who rose as we came near him and slowly and heavily flapped up stream and away.

"I suppose you are right," I mused, "there was always a certain amount of wild life about these parts."

It came into my mind that it was thirty-one years since I had last gone drowsily up the Cherwell on just such a sunny day, though late in the afternoon, with another man. I had been down from Cambridge nearly a year, and was staying in Balliol for a week, doing whatever was suggested to me with whomsoever suggested it.

So I went up the Cherwell in a boat with a new, quiet, and interesting acquaintance reputed to be a brilliant scholar and full of still, deep, waters. We talked a little, without excitement, of Petronius, Rabelais, and later, if less literate, friends of ours, and then he suddenly leapt to life. "Look!" he cried, as nearly as cry he could, for his face seldom moved and his voice seldom rose, and one felt that he hardly dared smile lest his pince-nez, which were part of his disillusioned outfit, should drop off and leave but blinking eyes beneath an unexceptionable dome of brow.

He was pointing: straddling a field was a huge painted sign advertising a forthcoming Oxford Pageant, giving names and dates and announcing a book of the words by Robert Bridges.

"Look," he said, with the acute economic reasoning which he has exhibited ever since, "do you think that that is doing any good here?"

"No," I admitted, remembering how promiscuously I had seen advertisements scattered about by bill-posters-in-a-hurry in the unlikeliest wildernesses, and even fading posters in rustic blind-alleys inviting non-existent passers-by to join the Army. "No, I shouldn't think that if it stayed here for a year it would sell a single ticket."

"In that event," he replied with quiet decision, "it had better come to my rooms in Balliol; far more people will see it there."

I cannot say how large it really was; in retrospect it seems about twelve by five, and it was certainly numbingly heavy and very cumbersome. We stepped ashore, up-rooted it, got it aboard without collapsing our craft and turned down-stream, delivered the boat and landed. As we went off, the boat-house keeper saluted; we were obviously bent on important business concerning the Oxford Pageant.

My ringleader ringled, and I meekly followed. He ahead, I behind, with this vast congeries of painted planks supported by our crushed palms and leaning on our aching shoulders, paraded through the crowded streets of Oxford. We were weary and very responsible Titans, with bowed heads and aspiring eyes gazing upwards towards some unguessed dawn. Once a policeman saluted; nobody spoke to us; we were respected.

Edward Shanks says that he was once in some recondite sun-dusty village street, and lost. An old man came along between the thatched cottages, roses, and elms, holding his hands apart at a fixed distance. Shanks asked him the way to the place where he would be, and received from the half-paralysed creature, who wouldn't even move his head, only this reply: "Doan't 'ee speak to Oi, Oi be carryin' a door."

Nobody spoke to us; not even when we reached the portal of that ugly Balliol building which faces on the Broad. The porter also saluted; if he thought at all he probably thought that them young gentlemen were carrying that there board into College in order to paint some of them there funny pictures on it.

Crab-wise we got it up the staircase and into his sitting-room. He took off his pince-nez, wiped them, mopped his forehead, and said, "Let's have a sherry—I think we've earned it." What became of the structure I know not; what became of him I know; with every year the number of reputations for lifelong solemnity which one could blow up increases. . . .

"Wake up, Squire," called Bliss from behind me, "we're just coming to Magdalen Bridge."

"Good Lord, haven't we passed that yet?"—on the parapet were numerous down-staring heads, travelling canoeists in those parts being as surprising in May as cuckoos in December. Under it we went, glided past Mesopotamia and Parson's Pleasure with little stream against us, and over the rollers, and then came to a grassy fringe with cows peering over. A cuckoo in the distance was expressing its opinion of foster-parents.

"The Parks are in there," said Bliss.

"I'd forgotten. I believe there's a match on; I believe it's the University and Leicestershire; do come and see ten minutes of it."

"This is one of your obsessions; it's as bad as the churches," said Mr. Bliss, looking at the damp herbs, the slippery muddy bank, his canvas shoes and the keg of cider.

"If you'll only come ashore for a few minutes we can have lunch here immediately after."

He agreed; we scrambled up the bank; for a dry and hayless year the grass was long and damp, and the cows had emphasized their presence. However, we traversed the moist steppe and got to the ground. Lomas and Walford were batting, the latter of whom I was later to see make at Lord's on an off-day one of the liveliest and loveliest two-hundreds I have ever seen.

Nobody was watching them on this occasion either. There were about sixteen spectators on the townward side, that stately side so full of great trees, and one lorn man from an agency in the Press-box; otherwise there were no signs of life except on the wicket, and little there. "Your trick," I said. We went back, I made mustard with Cherwell water, in the absence of Official Inspectors, and suffered no ill effects. We lunched and then we proceeded. "Here, or hereabouts," said Bliss, "we should see a kingfisher." We did not; but we put up herons all day.

The sun shone; the water rippled; high harmless clouds dropped light shadows; nothing happened except Nature. Once, in a coppice which dipped to the water's edge—for March had been early and April late—we saw kingcups, blue-bells and primroses all flowering together. Once we paused by a stone wall to look at the little purplish ivy-leaved toad-flax, strangely called mother-of-thousands, most delicate of the snap-dragons, though the common orange-and-yellow one of our hedgerows takes some beating.

"We ought to see a kingfisher, here or hereabouts," said Bliss. We saw no kingfishers, but still a heron or two rose leisurely, and moor-hens at every ten yards or so scuttled alarmed across to their nests, giving themselves away completely, as innocent as the lapwings and all sorts of other creatures who pathetically and, alas, mistakenly, believe that their cunning can match ours. Their cause is just. "How can a man," said Philip Gosse once to me, who had endured France, Mesopotamia and India, "take away from a bird the only things it has—its nest and its eggs?" I didn't know the answer. There isn't any answer.

As I write these lines I have just read an article in the *Field* by a big-game shooter who appears genuinely interested in the variety and richness of God-given life in this world and says that a shooter's dream should be to go to the Soudan, and bag a bongo and a giant-eland, so rare a combination, like a double on the Cambridgeshire and the Cesarewitch. If they are pests, keep them down; if they are not pests let them live in peace. Birds and rabbits apart I don't want to shoot anything or any-body; but, other things being equal, I had much rather shoot a bongo-hunter than a bongo. . . .

The stream was very low, the wind dead ahead and we had

to keep a look-out for stumps. At Marston Ferry, where an inn overlooks the river on the right, mute glances passed between us: we moored the canoe, and walked to the inn and ordered a pint apiece of the Morrell's which the inn provided. It was a simple, pleasant room, but it was not long before a morose expression came over Bliss's face.

In a corner drinking beer were four undergraduates, two of the large disdainful man-of-the-world type and two humbler worshippers with pale faces, fair fluffy hair and high affected voices, who carried an atmosphere of chromium chairs and scarlet leather with them.

"I say, Charles," said one of the latter to his hero, "you were frightfully blind on Wednesday."

"Tight as an owl!"

"We were all most frightfully tight."

"A good binge; who took me home?"

"Why, we all took you home, and then you took us home!"

"God, I mixed 'em!" (shouting) "Four more pints, please."

Had they recalled their excesses in undertones we might not have minded, though their faces were not winning. But squeaky or husky, they all talked with such a rude and indifferent loudness that there was no room for both parties in the inn and we retreated to the more congenial company of the water-rats.

"Modern Oxford, I suppose," grunted Bliss, who had lived in the town years gone by.

"Not really," I said, "there were just as appalling people about when we were young, only one managed to forget them."

"Why can't they get drunk without boasting about it?"

But perhaps they were boasting without having got drunk. I remembered the old story of the freshman who assembled a dozen of his contemporaries after Hall, put a bottle of Bass on the table and said: "Now, boys, we don't break up until we have killed that bottle!"

Leaving these desperate dogs to their debauches we went on paddling under branches, past meadows and little hanging copses. "We shall see a kingfisher about here," remarked Bliss

to my back from time to time, but the answer was usually a
heron—not a day on that whole trip but we saw at least half
a dozen herons. There was as thick a rise of may-fly all day
as ever I saw; the slow stream was covered with little dabbles
where the fat white moth-like things rose to the surface and
clumsily disengaged their wings; the lower air was full of
flutterings and they tumbled into the boat in dozens.

"A happy time for the trout," I said.

"There are no trout in the Cherwell," said Bliss.

"What a waste of may-fly," I remarked.

"Your thoughts are purely animal," he murmured; "Come
along, paddle up—put some beef into it."

We swished along for two or three miles, pausing now and
then to be green thoughts in a green shade. The whole lovely
secluded wilderness might have been our own; neither on
that day nor on any other, except for the barges on the canal,
did we see any moving craft.

"This is the time to canoe," said Bliss, reading my thoughts;
"in August clubs of canoeists go about in droves on some of
the rivers, and make camps at night. Wireless, too, I expect."

"That seems a contradiction in terms," I said, "but I wouldn't
mind trying one tent with one canoe like ours."

"Not at this time of year," he replied. "Anyhow, I've tried
it often enough and what with the rain and the wind, the
fetching of water and buying of food, the cooking and the
packing, there's not much to be said for it after a hard day's
work in the canoe."

On the left a willowed pasture sloped down to the grassy
bank. At the top of it, against trees and the sky, stood a noble
stone Jacobean house, with classic touches, unimpaired. Behind
it rose a church spire; in front an ancient row of barns sloped
towards the stream; on the rough grass were cropping a horse,
a donkey, and some white geese. There were no signs of a
hamlet or of inhabitants.

"What is this place?" I asked.

"Water Eaton House."

"We must land and sit down. I want to have a good look
at it."

"Here, it's only our first day and your mania for architecture is getting the better of you already."

"At any rate I warned you I couldn't pass an old church."

"If you want to see old churches you can see all you want to after you've done your ration of paddling for the day. We must go on, or we shall never get anywhere."

We landed; Bliss read one of his own standard works to find out how long it would take us to get to Islip; I lay face downwards, chewing grass and watching the grey-yellow lichened old house in the sun against the clear sky. "How happy I could be if I lived there and were always there," I thought, as one so often does. But? There are enchanting places where "*coelum non animum mutant*" comes as a kind of consolation, even if there is a kind of deadly finality about getting to know one's inescapable self as the years pass by. Also with houses as with all beautiful works of art it is perhaps better to love them than to possess them. They are the quintessence of their makers whose frailties have died with them; they are a reproach to ourselves; we lose something if we become inured to them and they if they grow mingled with our daily doings. Or is that again solace for frustrated covetousness? I did not address the question to the grey donkey and the geese who were taking all things, including ourselves, for granted. . . .

Bliss tugged at his moustache.

"Not much more than a mile to Islip," he observed, "but it will be slow going with the river so low. Come along."

The river was shallow, sluggish and full of weed; now and then we grazed the bottom. There were no kingfishers yet but we flushed a pair of mallard which quacked, flapped splashing along the water, and then beat into the beyond. In a half hour or so we bore in sight of Islip Mill astride its arch, still, unlike most old mills in those parts, working. There was no hope of paddling up the main stream of the Cherwell, which was one ripple of shallows; there was nothing for it but evacuation and a portage.

I was landed. Bliss took off his shoes, rolled up his trouser-legs, and began to tow the reluctant canoe round the bend, while a cuckoo in the distance made suitable comments. I

H

scrambled up to the mill-house and knocked at the door.

"Can I——" I asked, "go through your garden? My friend and I want to take a canoe over into the mill-stream."

"You're welcome; and thank you for asking leave."

"Doesn't everybody?"

"No, they just walk through the place as if it were their own."

I thanked him, traversed a chiaroscuro cavern full of sacks and flour, went through a pretty garden and a wicket, and then on to a rough humpy peninsula of field with a few old trees on it. The portage was longer than usual, owing to the difficulty of finding a landing-place for the canoe. But we ultimately made the journey with the luggage, hauled her up the mud-bank, and dragged and lifted her over the field and into the mill-stream. There we left her (Bliss having given up all hope of reaching the Oxford Canal that night) and he was persuaded to come with me to see Islip Church. It has a simple solid tower, as is the manner in those parts—towers are more elaborate farther west until the grey starknesses of Dartmoor and Cornwall are met with—and it was given by Edward the Confessor to St. Peter's at Westminster, namely, the Abbey, in whose hands it still remains. His effigy stands there with beard, crown and sceptre, saying "I have given to Christ and to St. Peter in Westminster ye little toun of Islippe wherein I was born with all things which belong therewith"—it all comes out of his will, though not in his English.

A few hundred yards of smooth still mill-stream, reed-fringed and populous with swimming birds and voles, and we joined the river again. The wooded reaches were beautiful; the water so low as to make progress very slow. Once we stuck amid several swans, though they made no attempt to break our legs with their wings. Once, the wind blowing cold and fiercely in our faces, we stranded under an arch of Kidlington Bridge, and there was more wading. "It is about five," said Bliss, "we had better moor at Kidlington."

Works were going on there; we ran into the mill-pool and landed in a garden by a summer-house. The Old Mill had been turned into a very pleasant residence; the owner, when produced by a puzzled small boy, was most hospitable and allowed us to leave the canoe at the sluice and our gear in the summer-house while we went hunting for quarters—for we had nowhere made arrangements for them, though I dare say that Bliss, more of a man of programmes, might have stuck to a schedule had he been on his determined own.

As a straggler the village of Kidlington would be hard to beat. It rambles over a square mile or so. While Bliss conversed in a small tavern which had no accommodation, whither we had wearily dragged our bags, I rambled about the village, seeking beds. Tourists wanting beds must be almost as rare there as in St. Kilda. One hostelry might conceivably have put up one person had there not been illness in the family; others held out not even a hypothetical hope; only one kindly passer-by made a suggestion.

Returning after half an hour I found Bliss with a tankard talking about Lord Nuffield. "What have you found, Squire?" he asked.

"Not a bed in any inn."

"But we must sleep somewhere."

"A passer-by did tell me that there was a Miss Somebody, a retired schoolmistress, who might put us up."

"Well, failing anything else, I suppose we'd better try that."

"I'm hanged if I will, Bliss. This is the first day of a holiday and I refuse point-blank to spend the evening under the roof of an unlicensed schoolmistress."

"But she may be a first-class cook and a very cultivated person."

"Yes, her board may groan, there may be Brahms on the piano, Stevenson and Galsworthy on the shelves, and photographs of the Acropolis on the bedroom walls. I'm not saying anything against her, but I'm not going there."

"Please yourself, but what do you suggest?"

"May I have a look at that map in your pocket? . . . Yes, about twelve miles."

"What's about twelve miles?"

"Bicester."

"But we can't go all that way!"

"I certainly can't pass it without calling there. We shall sleep at the 'Crown'."

There was a car for hire round the corner; I telephoned; we shipped the luggage; we noticed, as we went, that in those parts aeroplanes were plentiful and strong on the wing, and in half an hour we were in the broad main street of Bicester, pulled up before the comfortable Georgian front of the Crown Hotel. The rosy face and stalwart form of Mr. Ben Tilt advanced from the door-way. He had known me arrive on foot, by car, by train and on a horse. "What have you come in this time?" he asked.

"A canoe."

"It'll be an aeroplane next time."

But it won't.

The best of hostesses was perfectly prepared to do anything for us. But when you are taking a great deal of exercise in the open air breakfast is a good meal at any hour. We had bacon, eggs, and fried potatoes, and the mustard—this is for the benefit of half the inns in England—was of course freshly made.

We were alone in the dining-room. Distant murmurs reached us from the dart-players in the bar; mingled with these were occasional muffled waves of orchestral music.

"What on earth is that concert?" enquired Bliss as the coffee came.

"This is a peculiar place," I told him, "one of the only two inns in England which has a cinema attached. The people go up the stable yard and in by a side door so that there is no contamination of the innocent by licensed premises. One of the shows to-night has Shirley Temple. All the children come to see her and presently I expect we shall hear their yells of delight."

"Do you know all about these damned film stars?"

"Only the names of most of them; the photographs are usually quite enough for me. I did once see Greta Garbo. It was in Rome and the film in Italian. A very sad film it was and her eyes were full of tears. There was a thunderstorm on, but I had to go out in the middle, preferring to be drenched by rain outside rather than by tears inside. All the same, film-stars did once inspire me to song. It was all owing to a poster."

"How was that?"

"Did you ever hear of the poster

> ALLEGED BOGUS
> WEST-END MAJOR'S
> FATAL FALL
> OVER CAT
> IN FLAT?"

"No."

"Well, it was done by an evening paper before the war. I never thought I should see an odder one. I was walking along Pall Mall not long ago when, near the Carlton, I saw a seedy red-nosed man holding up the poster of a popular weekly. It ran:

> FILM STARS
> NEARLY BLOWN UP
> BY TIN OF
> SARDINES."

"Of course you bought the paper."

"Of course I did not. I preferred to let my fancy wander rather than to be disillusioned by some quite commonplace explanation. I wrote a folk-song about it. Do you know the tune of 'I come from the country, my name it is Giles'?" I hummed it.

"Yes," said Bliss.

"Well, listen:

> Now come all you lads and you lassies so fine
> And hark to this doleful sad ditty of mine,
> How a beautiful bevy of Hollywood queens
> Were nearly blown up by a tin of sardines!

CHORUS.

> Ri-tooral, li-tooral, li-tooral, li-tay,
> Ri-tooral, li-tooral, li-tooral, li-tay,

> Ri-tooral, li-tooral, li-tooral, li-tay,
> They were nearly blown up by a tin of sardines."

I paused. "Shall I go on?"

"Carry on," said Bliss, lighting another cigarette and taking a swig at his tankard. I remembered it as best I could:

> And how did it happen? Well, that I don't know;
> And how many were there—a dozen or so,
> Or a score or a hundred unfortunate weans
> Who were nearly blown up by a tin of sardines.
>
> > Ri-tooral, etc., etc.,
> > They'd a narrow escape from that tin of sardines.
>
> 'Twould be quite comprehensible after a dish
> Of that super-charged monster the tor-pe-do fish;
> But who'd have the face to inform the Marines
> He was nearly blown up by a tin of sardines?
>
> > Ri-tooral, etc., etc.,
> > How *is* one blown up by a tin of sardines?
>
> I was blown up by parents when I was a boy,
> And blowing me up was my schoolmaster's joy;
> Though "blown up by bank-managers," I know what
> > that means,
> I was never blown up by a tin of sardines.
>
> > Ri-tooral, etc., etc.,
> > I was never blown up by a tin of sardines!
>
> I brought a large tin to my humble abode
> And I sat on the lid and it didn't explode;
> It never would rank with the best magazines:
> I seemed quite immune to that tin of sardines.
>
> > Ri-tooral, etc., etc.,
> > I seemed quite immune to that tin of sardines.

What size of tin's needed, and what special brand
Of sardines will go up at the sight of a band
Of the Shebas and Sheilas and Janets and Jeans
Who appear to incite so the wrath of sardines?

Ri-tooral, etc., etc.,
Who are bitterly hated by certain sardines.

Oh, what is this whisper? What is it I hear?
Alas, there's no question; in future, I fear,
When I see all those goggling great eyes on the screens
I may wish they could all be blown up by sardines.

Ri-tooral, etc., etc.,
If they only could *all* be blown up by sardines!

Bliss gazed musingly into the distance; whether or not he liked the song he evidently shared the sentiments.

"Let us go into the bar," he said.

We did not stay long. I at least was tired. I asked after one or two friends of two years ago. "Oh," was the answer, "she's left the district," or "No, he doesn't come here much now." It was a microcosm of life with its perpetual partings. One notices these things more forcibly when one has been absent for a time and several changes come together.

In bed I briefly perused the only book I had brought with me. It was Viscount Harberton's *How to Lengthen our Ears,* which has been my frequent consolation since it first appeared twenty years ago. In any serious company I should have to admit it to be preposterous and indefensible. It is a jovial attack on all book-learning and all learned men with the exception of those, like Schopenhauer and Herbert Spencer, of whom the author approves. Once more I looked at the pleasant frontispiece. There is a "surround" of portraits of Swinburne, Wordsworth, Goldsmith and Gibbon, the last three in solemn and half-witted profiles, and in the centre is the beaming and bewhiskered mug of William Whiteley, the Universal Provider, whom Lord Harberton considers to have

been a far more sensible and useful man. I looked at the
Preface. "The aim of these pages is to show that we owe more
to unlearned people than to the sons of learning, and that the
whole education craze is a wicked mistake," says Lord
Harberton, putting all his cards on the table at once. "Suppose you wanted your child to become stupider than was intended by nature, how would you proceed? The best way, I
fancy, would be to make the child learn to read as early as five
years of age, and go to school at least five and a half hours a
day. This is now compulsory. Next, you might, by means of
cheap publications and free libraries, do all you could to make
him spend every minute of his spare time in reading, till the
feat had become a habit. This is now encouraged. On those
lines, there is the best possible method of lengthening your
child's ears, and my aim is to provide you with plenty of
evidence that you would have every chance of succeeding
beyond all reasonable expectations. My book commences with
the great principle of aural development; after that, evidence
is given of the actual process, followed by some typical developments; I then turn to a few of those who escaped or resisted
education."

I began to turn over the pages for sentences marked either
because of their unorthodox sagacity or because of their
amusing extravagance. There was the delightful passage in
which a public school curriculum was outlined, under which
the boys should cook, mend, make and build all day and "their
evenings, instead of being spent in preparation, were devoted
to Auction Bridge." There was that in which the author,
having quoted all the most banal and bathetic lines from
"aural" poets, including Wordsworth's

> The wretched parents all the night
> Went shouting far and wide

expressed a preference for the bereaved husband, recorded by
"Pitcher," who thus put into poetry what he had been robbed
of "by the tomb." ("Mr. Binstead, all honour to him, has preserved for us the fragment, but it is only a fragment"):

I gazed at the sad reminder,
　　Of the form that had made me weep;
Then I swallowed a useful "binder"
　　And suddenly fell asleep.

There was the imposing catalogue of great men without education, on the lines of "Dr. Livingstone worked in a cotton
factory as a boy of ten. And probably all the better for it.
Would that Viscounts Bryce, Morley and Haldane had had
plenty of factory work when young!" There was the scathing
"If any young Wordsworths are found to-day imbibing
impulses 'from a vernal wood' during school hours, some
education prowler will summon them and have them fined a
pound, and if they do it again they will, under Samuel's
Children's Act, be packed off to an industrial school to herd
with embryo thieves till the age of sixteen. English law, A.D.
1916." Doctors, divines, lawyers, all come under the lash and
there is a whole chapter on Lord Macaulay's Ears.

"At any rate a fine direct style," I reflected. . . .

There came a gentle knock at the door.

"Come in!" I called.

"I thought you might like something to read," said Bliss.

"Oh, thanks awfully; it's extraordinarily kind of you."

"I thought you might like to look up to-morrow's trip. Good
night."

"Good night."

The door closed. The book was one of his own treatises on
canoeing.

"He means to get me properly educated," I thought, and
switched off the light.

　　Flocks of the memories of the days draw near
　　　　The dovecot doors of sleep.

For a little while in the darkness I remembered boughs and
sliding green waters, marsh-marigolds, bluebells and lady-
smocks. But I did not dream of them; nor of anything, until
the maid came with tea in the morning.

H*

CHAPTER II

KIDLINGTON TO AYNHO

I TELEPHONED, and went into the coffee-room. Bliss had got over several hurdles and was spooning out marmalade. "Short journey to-day," he said, "and we can stay at the inn by the canal at Aynho."

"I've told them we're coming back here for the night; Aynho's no farther than Kidlington and Mr. Tilt says he'll fetch us."

"It will be Sunday," he went on; "is there a Catholic Church here?"

"Of course there is," said I, subsequently finding out that there was, of course. "And we must have a shortish day to-morrow."

"Why?" he asked.

"Because the Cartwrights have very kindly offered to fetch us to lunch at Aynho House to-morrow."

"I last," ruminated Bliss, "dined at Aynho House over fifty years ago, in old Mr. Cartwright's day; he was a magnificent old man, with a very fine taste in everything, including port."

I read the papers, while Bliss went out and bought things. The car came and we retraced our tracks.

"The Cherwell," said Bliss, "will be quite impossible above Kidlington. It's almost dry in parts. While you were looking for rooms last evening I arranged that a hand-cart should be ready to take the canoe across to the Canal. It's about a mile and a half to the Pits, a mile below Thrup."

At the inn at Kidlington the hand-cart was ready. We loaded it (by kind permission of the owner's wife) with the help of the gardener at the Mill House, and the three of us set off with our large and unusual burden. As we doggedly trudged along eyes peered from cottage windows as through the lattices of harems, and an increasing horde of children followed us. There was a weak sun and a cold north wind, but what with work and embarrassment we kept warm enough. It was about noon when we reached the Canal, and under the gaze of the infantry, stowed our gear and went off on waters where we should find no snags nor shallows.

"It is a mile to Thrup," came the voice from behind me, as we briskly paddled, "and then a mile to Shipton-on-Cherwell. Then there is a lock, and the river and the canal are one for a mile. Then the river goes off on our left."

This was true enough, but let him who wishes to follow the strange wanderings of the Cherwell, by, with, and under the Canal, study them in the map.

Occasionally, while Bliss, left, right, left, right, kept her forging ahead, I paused, spread the map on my knees, and tried to memorize it all myself. As we neared Thrup I noticed that a church was marked in the village.

"Couldn't we stop here a little while," I ventured, "and look at the church?"

"You carry on," said Bliss, "you can look at churches when you have done your day's work."

"But," I said, trying the bait, "it says there is an inn, too."

"There is an inn two or three miles farther up; you carry on."

Many times it was like that. Some days half a dozen times in a morning we would pass church towers, embosomed in thatched roofs or woods or beckoning from distant hill-tops, with who knows what Norman doorways, clerestories, crusaders' effigies or family tombs, but this ruthless lover of the treadmill and the day's ration of miles would plunge on, and you cannot safely have a struggle in a canoe. Doubtless they were all far nobler than the churches I did see.

River and canal ran cheek by jowl. We approached the first lock. "I hope you like working locks," said Bliss.

"Aren't there lock-keepers?" I asked, forgetfully.

"Their cottages are still there, but not the keepers," he replied. "What do you think I brought that winch for?"

It suddenly occurred to me that although I had often enough stood over canal locks and watched water dripping out of them, and languidly felt myself rising or falling between the slimy walls of Boulter's Lock and such places, I had always taken the mechanism for granted and assumed that working locks was the sort of thing other men were paid to do, with the criminal insouciance of people who have always rung a bell if they wanted more coal put on the fire. After those scores of locks we worked on the Oxford Canal I shall never be quite content to pass through a lock which a keeper is working while the traveller idles.

You are ascending, let us say, to the canal summit. Far ahead, at the end of the silver calm perspective of water there grows upon the sight a barrier of darkness with small uprights cut against the sky. You paddle gradually up to it, its outlines become clearer, its height grows, and as you come close you see it "open and empty," the higher water above penned up by a massive gate of blackened wood. You draw the canoe to the bank. One of you steps on to the tow-path with the winch, the other paddles swiftly in to wait at the base of the glistening, muddy, black-weed-hung perpendicular walls—brick with a stone coping.

The one ashore shoves at a great arm which closes the lower gate. Then he goes to the upper one, fixes his winch to a bolt on a pillar, winds hard at the pinion wheel as the jagged iron rod or rack shoots up indicating his progress, and wedges it; crosses back, winds up the other sluice, and waits as the water gradually pours in at the depth, heaving up the surface, and with hiss and rumble fills and fills the basin until no more can come in. The upper gate, which could never be shifted against a weight of higher water, will now open outwards almost at a touch. The canoe is stroked out; and the voyage goes on. There is a perpetual satisfaction and a sense of power in so easily controlling so mighty a mass of water; and there is wonder in the fact that no one ever seems to leave both sets of gates open, empty a summit reach and flood a countryside. . . .

Yet, sometimes, as I was standing on a gate looking down at the depth and the moving power an old trouble came back to me and I had to retire, an old creepy fascination.

I was thirteen. I was staying at Morwenstow with the son of the curate in charge—the vicar, Hawker's successor, being a dear old man past his duties. One day we went nesting on some high cliffs near Welcombe, between Morwenstow and

Hartland, cliffs higher, grimmer and dizzier than anything known to Shakespeare's gatherer of samphire.* There came a place where a rusty-red splodge with greenish specks on it was visible not very far from the top of a cliff hundreds of feet high. I went down the slightly sloping and grass-tufted upper portion—the lower part was sheer stone—and reached a point whence I could easily drop to the ledge on which the nest lay; the mother bird (if she indeed it was) by this time screaming uneuphoniously around my head. I pocketed a pair of eggs, looked up and found that I couldn't possibly get up, looked down at the far shingle, rocks and Atlantic foam, and decided that I certainly could not go down. I was stuck.

I bellowed to Eric at the top. He bellowed back. "You must get a rope" (happily there was no wind to swallow our voices), I shouted. "All right," he shouted back.

I wasn't aware of fear. I waited phlegmatically, nursing my eggs, and looking over the rolling waste towards an invisible Ireland to the left, Wales ahead, and Lundy to the right. It seemed a long time before I heard a far halloo and dangling down in front of me came what was obviously a length, or several joined lengths, of clothes-line from a neighbouring farm-house. I knotted the end round my waist, hung on above with my hands, and began to be hauled up, helping by jabbing my toes into every possible crevice and shoving. Then I began to use my hands as well and grass and earth came into my mouth with scratchy and dusty taste. I did not think: "If this cord breaks I shall be hurled into the dreadful abyss below"; I was a young animal preoccupied with a job and with no time for reflection; I wasn't frightened at all.

But when I got over the brink at the top I collapsed. I lay face downwards on the grass and shuddered and shuddered. Something elementary in me protected the eggs from breaking; but my subconscious (of which I had never heard) must

* The collection of the cliff-root samphire in order to get an ingredient for pickles is one of the oddest of excuses for a dangerous trade. But perhaps it has gone out with the chilis and peppercorns which used to add heat and variety to pre-War Piccalilli, which relish (unless there is a brand unknown to me) for the robuster cold meats is now reduced to the simplicity of cucumber, gherkin, onion and cauliflower.

have been profoundly disturbed by the thinness of that rope, and my nerve had gone for the day.

Not only for that day. I don't know how long it was before I began to realize that I could no longer bear even looking down from a height, let alone climbing down one. It was still longer before I began to think that that experience dated the origin of my now chronic propensity to vertigo. For some years I could not even stand on a railway station when a train was coming in without going to the back of the platform and hanging on to a pillar for fear of flinging myself in front of the whirling engine. That simply could not be; trains one had to face daily; I cured myself by always standing on the edge of the platform with my hands in my pockets and looking at the approaching engine with deliberate indifference and even disdain.

But height is another matter; one hasn't to face it every day; its attraction is even more terrible; even as I write these lines, on a ground-floor, and merely think of looking down from a top-floor, my feet tingle and everything below my knees turns to jelly. It isn't the fear of falling; were it that I should never have gone up in an aeroplane. It is a spell. Once, when a man had noticed how gingerly I crept along over a precipice (with things looking so dizzingly small below, as Shakespeare saw), and he walking lightfoot as a goat, he asked me what was the matter.

"I'm a victim of vertigo," I said.

"You merely mean giddiness," said he.

"Don't you deceive yourself, I know what giddiness is."

You can get giddy in a ball-room if you go round the same way too many times too fast; the lights turn into flashing streamers, your brain swims like tea in a cup whizzed round by a spoon. But then you feel only like falling; not like throwing yourself down. With me, from building, cliff or ladder, if I look down I have to clench both hands and fists to prevent myself from flinging myself out and down; I shrink, if I may so say without irreverence, from the mere memory of Christ on the pinnacle of the Temple.

There is no question of a suicidal impulse. I have a con-

firmed desire to live as long as I can (at least until I am utterly
"sans everything"), and there are a great many people in the
world to-day whom I should like to survive; I could not contemplate suicide unless driven insane by worry. What I have
is a terrible attraction which at once paralyses and draws to
the inviting abyss; one is afflicted by a kind of agoraphobia in
an expanse of air, and it is possible to get it in the gallery of a
Club library as well as on a cliff or high steeple. "Don't look
down," they tell climbers; but I don't have to look down;
what's there is all too painfully present without looking. One
dreads the exercise of its influence even in sleep. I shall never
forget the first night I slept—if slept is the word—in America.
It was in 1921; A. P. Herbert and I took a two months' holiday together and very enjoyably toured the land. But the first
night was not at all enjoyable.

We shared a large room on the twelfth floor of an old hotel,
shortly afterwards demolished. It was autumn and the "heat"
was on; the place was like a brick-kiln; we could neither adjust
the radiator nor get an answer to the bell, which earlier in the
day had produced a negro boy of notable stupidity. So we
opened the window, and even at that required only single
sheets over us. But that window began to draw me as soon as
I had begun to doze; I thought of the stone ravine outside,
remembered that I had sleep-walked in youth. "See Naples
and die" was good enough, but "Die just before you are going
to see the U.S.A." seemed to be overdoing it; so I got out of
bed and shut the window again. This alternation went on all
night, and we were not greatly rested in the morning; however, as it is not easy for a visitor to New York to sleep in any
event, it perhaps didn't much matter.

It was not until long after I was grown up that I learnt,
through a newspaper correspondence, that my malady was not
unique. Until then I thought of myself as singularly handi-
capped and even especially cowardly, and forced myself to the
tops of the Dome of St. Paul's and the Belfry of Bruges and
scores of village church towers, with staircases stinking of bats,
merely because I shrank from it, though longing for the views.
Only three years ago I whizzed up the Campanile at Venice,

up the sloping staircase of which Napoleon rode his horse, thinking "I simply mustn't be a poltroon and miss this." But it was no good; I leant over the parapets long enough to verify the astounding fact that, for all the height of the tower and the vastness of the prospect, not a single inch of Venice's countless canals (so screened by tall palaces) can be seen from it; and then retired to the middle for support and was glad when I got below again and could go for a cognac to Florian's.

We went through the lock, Bliss operating ashore to make certain that I had taken in the technique. We sailed out.

The village of Shipton was on our left; Hampton Gay—alas, with such a name, unvisited—on our right, and the lifted waterway gave us good views. River and canal for a mile were married, but before we came to our next lock and the river's parting we drew up at a little wharf on the right with a flower-beset inn on a gentle eminence above it.

"This," said my companion, "is The Rock of Gibraltar, and this is where we lunch." I was delighted to hear it as I had begun to fear that we might not land before closing-time. It was a near thing, but a miss is as good as a mile.

In the pleasant empty tap-room, with a pretty view from its windows, we settled down to bread, beer and cheese. I asked for pickled red cabbage; there was none; I rather regretted my rashness, as it reminded Bliss of pickled onions, which he got.

Silence reigned awhile. Then I said, rather vapidly, "Why is this place called 'The Rock of Gibraltar'?"

The reply was almost equally vapid: "I don't know; there is no village called Gibraltar here."

"Possibly there was a landlord here once who fought with Admiral Rooke or in the three years' siege under General Elliott, when our men dropped three thousand red-hot shots on the enemy fleets in one day."

"Possibly," he said, absently looking out of the window. "Hallo, there's an unusual iris."

He vanished; I heard talk about cos lettuces and cabbages floating in. It died away. "Once let him loose in a garden," I thought, "and goodness knows when he'll come back."

I fell into a reverie about the names and signs of inns. They are sometimes written about and even exhibited because of their beauty, oddity or antiquity, but a survey of them would throw a great deal of light on social history and the popular mind. The mediæval signs were mostly religious like the "Cross Keys" and the "Lamb and Flag," or heraldic like all the "Lions" and "Bears." It was not, I think, until the eighteenth century that retired soldiers and sailors began to name their inns after battles and their heroes—"Admiral Rodney," "Admiral Benbow," the "Duke of Cumberland," with the "Marquis of Granby" (who had a special care for the rank and file) predominant over all. The "Iron Duke" and the "Hero of Waterloo" are known; near Aldershot there is a "Hero of Inkerman" (the private soldier, I think).* Another legacy of the Crimea, I remember, I saw once in Essex. It was the name, not of an inn, but of its landlord; the lintel, in Francis Thompson's words, was "armed with the crested and prevailing name" of "Adam Sebastopol Smith." The old soldiers and sailors, in that way, are still loyal to their revered commanders; there are plenty of "Jellicoe Browns," "Haig Joneses," not to mention "Jubilee Robinsons." But, since there are no new free houses now under the genuine proprietorship of pensioners, we are not likely to find the best-beloved captains commemorated with a crop of "Plumer's Heads" and "Allenby's Arms"; the brewers, who are now masters, may think as far as "King George V" or "Haig" but no farther, preferring, as a rule, to be even more conventional than that. However, there are brewers and brewers, as may be realized if one tours the Home Counties and notices how one will take care to keep a historic name and sign in the ascendant, and another will relegate history to the background, splash his own name about with

* Anybody looking at a large-scale map may discover that not only inns but farms commemorate our battles. Looking up the map around Aynho I notice within a few miles an Inkerman Farm; also a Waterloo Farm. There is also a Troy Farm, though I can hardly suppose that a survivor from the siege came to that neighbourhood, unless it be true, after all, that we Britons spring from Prince Brut of Troy, sometime supposed to have founded the University of Cambridge, though Gibbon seems to ascribe the foundation rather to the Vandals than to the Trojans.

maddening redundancy, and even give every inn under his
control the same mass-produced enamel sign with no Blue
Boar or coat-of-arms on it but only his own beastly trade-mark,
as void of individuality as his beer. . . .

Having examined every head of cabbage Bliss returned, and
we set off again from the little wharf. How many locks we
passed that day I cannot be sure: Bliss says ten, his book gives
seven and the map indicates eight: at all events there were
enough in the thirteen miles to give variety to the trip and
there was quite enough work to keep us warm in the bitter
north wind under the low grey sky. Sometimes the wind was
so strong and dead ahead that one or other of us had to go
ashore with a long tow-rope over a shoulder, warped round
the boat-hook stuck through a hole forward, and plod along
like a barge-horse while the other, forty yards behind, kept the
boat's head straight with his paddle. To begin with it seemed
dreary work and I counted my footsteps to count the quarter-
miles; later I became accustomed and enjoyed the solitude and
the freedom of fancy and memory while back and legs were
doing their task, and realized why bargees' horses looked so
meditative and inured.

Now and then one of them came along, "nid-nid-nodding,"
as Mr. de la Mare would put it, and behind it on the steely
water the low, broad, flat, slowly-swimming, black barge, with
its little cabin superstructure, smoke coming out of the galley-
pipe, and its long mound of sand or coal. As it approached, the
gay colours on its prow would become clear, flowers and
diamond patterns in crude red blue and yellow, bright ochreous
and traditional as the paintings of knights on Sicilian carts.
Passing we would see the name, sometimes a simple *Emma* or
Mary Rose, such names as fishermen use and sailors get tattooed
on their forearms, sometimes exotic names like *Brahmapootra*
or *Jordan,* fruit of some company's liking for categories; and
then at the tiller with a dog, some peaceful man, or brown
woman or girl, whose home was the canal. They greeted us as
they passed, and silently receded towards Oxford.

Almost always, straight ahead, or visible round a corner
across the high flats was a bridge. They are massive edifices

built of that desolate, timeless Midland brick which is only at home in the smutty suburbs of industrial towns, and they are lost and lonely in the fields. A bridge over a river means a road, and usually a hamlet near; rivers came before bridges or roads. But a new canal winding its calculated way, cutting through the pastures of this man and that, could not be allowed unless its constructors gave access from bank to bank to those whose land they were severing. Large solid bridges, with but a few yards of bare track leading to them, can therefore be seen in the middle of empty wastes out of sight of a farm. We never saw anybody crossing them, though once the great heavy immobile head of a horse hung over a parapet and stared at us as we came up and under. Every bridge had an iron plate on it with a number: 125, 124, 123, they passed, and one wished they had been differentiated by names such as one sees in accounts of runs of hounds, Foxfield Farm Bridge, Haggis Copse Bridge, or what not—and perhaps by the local peasantry they are known by such names. But doubtless they had been planned lock, stock and barrel by engineers in a town; and engineers, as a rule, have little play of imagination. I should, I think, make one exception. The Anglican Cathedral at Gibraltar (Spain, not Oxon) was, as a tablet in it proclaims, built in the early nineteenth century by a Colonel of H.M. Royal Engineers and his men. Such a wild blend of tame Gothic and tame Moorish has never been seen elsewhere. If ever Mr. John Betjeman publishes, as I hope he will, a folio compendium of comic architecture as comprehensive as Dugdale's *Monasticon*, this, rather than Sezincote or any such Beckfordian thing, should give him his frontispiece. . . .

"We were talking of Quakers," once remarked Mrs. Warre Cornish to me after two minutes' silence by a drawing-room mantelpiece. We had been talking about no such thing, but her thoughts were accustomed to stray, and her remarks came up, like the Atlantic islands, which are connected under the sea, but of which the connections are not visible. Well, we were talking about canoeing.

The afternoon wore on; the canal rising lock by lock, about a hundred feet. Hamlets with spires were sometimes visible

in the background; men were absent, birds were many, every
hedge-foot was thick with cow-parsley. A pair of herons
flapped north; there were no kingfishers. Now and then a
coot crossed us, the white parchment strip of "baldness" coming
over its brow like the nose-guard of a Norman knight; moor-
hens were plentiful in the rushes and sedge and under the
small trees. Sometimes they were swimming with that peculiar
nodding of their heads. Usually we saw them first when, at
our approach, they rushed out from one margin and fluttered
across to the other, legs hanging, and leaving a spattered silver
wake behind them from their splashing flight. There never
seems to be any point in the manœuvre. If they are afraid of
disclosing their ribbon nests in water-plant beds or in alder-
roots they would do better to sit tight.

We passed the Heyfords, Steeple Aston, where there is said
to be an embroidered cope of the fourteenth century, and
Somerton in easy drudgery, and at last just beyond the bridge
came to Aynho Wharf and Inn at half-past six. Over the bridge
hung the heads of Mr. Tilt and a friend. We drew up at the
wharf. Bliss got out, I handed him my stained leather bag, his
shapeless sacks and the cider-keg which we had forgotten all
day and prepared to disembark.

As I stood I waved to Mr. Tilt and began to spring ashore.
I forgot for the moment in what a frail and mobile craft I was.
Pressing hard with my back foot as though I were emerging
from some stout sea-dinghy or perhaps that buoyant stone
coffin in which the Saint found his way from Brittany to Cornwall, I found the canoe going off like a leaf and myself astride
between higher bank and lower canoe, tried to return, and fell
over backward into the water as the canoe turned keel upward. My head, through some instinct, remained unwetted.
An anxious voice from the bridge, as Mr. Tilt prepared to dive,
called "Can you swim?" "Like a bird," I replied thought-
lessly and gave, since I *was* in, a little demonstration. Then I
swam to the bank and hoisted myself out, feeling as heavy as
a walrus.

There I stood, streams of canal sluicing from me. The
others, between laughs, got the canoe out, drained her, restored

her and moored her. "How lucky," I thought, as I watched them, "that the luggage had been taken out; I might never have found another copy of Lord Harberton."

I wrung out every accessible fold of my clothing. In the inn, as I dripped on the stone-flagged floor, I had some brandy. We squeezed into the car, I beside Mr. Tilt; every time he laughed, for no apparent reason, I thought he was going to swerve into the hedge. At the "Crown" I had a boiling bath, changed, and came down feeling extremely fit. We had some more eggs and bacon, and enjoyed an hour in the atmosphere of smoke and darts.

In the lounge, after the outside world had passed through the doors, though distant voices still crooned from the cinema, we sat in wicker chairs with a night-cap. Bliss, while I was having a bath, had apparently been brooding. He took from his pocket a much-stained and crumpled copy of a superior weekly, unfolded it, turned over some pages, and then, passing it to me, remarked: "What on earth do you make of that?"

"That," was a review of some verses, all too characteristic of contemporary reviews in that it aired the reviewer's opinions without quoting anything to show the quality of the author reviewed. But quoted with admiration approaching awe were two excerpts from Mr. T. S. Eliot—one about the "damp souls of housemaids" and one in which the evening was compared to "a patient lying anæsthetized upon a table." "As if God Almighty made sunsets for that!" exploded Bliss; "damn it all, Squire, you've read these moderns and I haven't; what the devil do they do it for?"

"Don't lump them all together just because the press does," I said, "those sentences at least are not obscure and pretentious gibberish. And they aren't really typical. They date from his early period when he was a depressed and frustrated romantic. He is a churchwarden now. Anyhow the proper way in which to regard it is as urban and local, a sort of peevish *vers-de-société.*"

"*Vers-de-société* be hanged!" ejaculated Bliss, "the chap ought to have a good dinner or go canoeing or something. If you want *vers-de-société* give me Horace. I should like," he went on bitterly, "to translate Horace into Eliotese." I thought it a good idea and made a note of it.

Bliss's eyes wandered. He was seeking comfort and found it. "Let them listen to this," he said, and began reciting impressively:

> "As some grave Tyrian trader, from the sea,
>   Descried at sunrise an emerging prow
>   Lifting the cool-haired creepers stealthily
>   The fringes of a southward-facing brow
>   Among the Aegean isles;
>   And saw the merry Grecian coaster come,
>   Freighted with amber grapes, and Chian wine,
>   Green, bursting figs, and tunnies steep'd in brine
>   And knew the intruders on his ancient home."

"Yes," I said, "the bit about Phoenician and Greek sailors at the end of *The Scholar Gypsy.*"

"There were no such things as Phoenicians," he said, surprisingly.

"But Tyre and Sidon and Carthage, surely all those places were inhabited by Phoenicians. Cousins of the Jews, I've always understood. They came to the Scilly Isles for tin."

"No," insisted Bliss, "the Egyptians came to the Scilly Islands for tin. Anyhow, even Matthew Arnold could have done with a bit more Philistine in him. There are too many of these Manicheans about. They're afraid of letting their bodies enjoy themselves. All the same, Matthew Arnold did once."

"When was that?"

"My father told me that somebody once asked Arnold up to stay on the Tay and sent him off with a ghillie to fish. He hooked a salmon, broke his rod, jumped into the river and came out spluttering and panting with the fish in his arms. He was so excited that he wanted to go on doing it all day, broken rod and all."

"Did Matthew Arnold tell your father that?"

"No, another man did; I forget his name."

"Well, Bliss, I don't know if you're sleepy, but I am. Good night."

"Good night."

*   *   *   *   *

"Dear, dear," I mused, as I turned over my book in bed, "some people contrive to avoid these troublesome literary debates. 'A day will dawn,' says Lord Harberton, 'when "well-read", of a mind, will be a term of contempt, something resembling "boose-born" as applied to an ode. My hope,' he piously proceeds, 'is to help the arrival of this wished-for day'."

CHAPTER III

Aynho to Banbury

When I came down Bliss had gone to Mass. There was no hurry, but, I thought, if we get a decent morning, some day we ought to make a really early start. Dawn would hardly be possible unless in some house or inn we should descend in socks and escape like malefactors, with Bliss breakfastless. Yet dawn, even on a pastoral stretch of the canal, would have the exquisite and noble quality that it has over water. I thought of the many times I had seen the light tremble up the east and the sun's rim rise at sea. Twice, especially, when I was at the tiller alone and the others below. Once, as day broke, we were passing the Needles and the ship gently made her way up the Solent in still water, past sleeping wide shores, until we dropped into Ryde and all its moored craft to see the men stirring to life and work. The other time was coming out of Cherbourg Harbour after a long, lumbering, almost windless crossing. With the light a freshening following breeze sprang up; the air was cold; colour came into the dark blue choppy sea; then in the east the thinnest rind of the sun's globe, and in a few minutes there was a bar of broken gold across the waters, gleaming on sail and metal, gradually warming the clean and lonely waters in a world far from human speech.

"However," I reflected, "it is Sunday and the canoe has not a right to reproach us this morning." As a rule, if Shelley is to be believed, it might have done so. In *The Boat on the Serchio,* one of the most personal if not one of the most polished of his fragments, a somewhat similar expedition is sketched. On more dangerous waters (again if Shelley is to be believed) with fierce torrent and dread chasm, but much the same sort of things, "What think you," says Lionel,

> "as she lies in her green cove
> Our little sleeping boat is thinking of?"

and Melchior replies:

> "If morning dreams are true, why I should guess
> That she was dreaming of our idleness,
>   And of the miles of watery way
> We should have led her by this time of day. . . .
> She dreams that we are not yet out of bed."

After this Shelley becomes the hearty mariner:

> "Ay, heave the ballast overboard,
> And stow the eatables in the aft locker."
> "Would not this keg be best a little lowered?"
> "No, now all's right." "Those bottles of warm tea—
> (give me some straw)—must be stowed tenderly."

The bottles of tea, it might be assumed, were for Shelley, even without the confirmation of the later lines:

> "With a bottle in one hand—
>   As if his very soul were at a stand,
>   Lionel stood."

The keg, presumably, was for his companion. We too had a keg though we had forgotten all about it. . . .

After breakfast I read the Sunday papers. Another book-reviewer drew me back to the subject of Bliss's remarks in the evening. I found a solemn examination of verses which seemed to me cacophonous gibberish. "What on earth *is* happening?" I asked myself, as somebody asks me about once a week. What; and why?

What *is* happening? One plays with theories about religious decay, politics, economics, urbanization, to account for the occlusion of style and manners, the ear and the heart, in so much literature and painting. What accounts for the shades of the prison-house closing in so much more severely than of old? the worse things are, the greater, surely, should be the consolations of sound, imagery and pure love. Don't boys muse as they did, or do they forget later?

I drifted off into thoughts of childhood. Active and gregarious as I was, when I was much too young to reflect upon my interests, let alone define them, my chief delights lay elsewhere, my spirit and my senses feeding incessantly on Nature and on books, on colour, form, scent and sound. I could always be happy alone, and I had my private and unspoken pleasures when not alone.

I will not apply to myself Vaughan's lines:

> Happy those early days when I
> Shined in my angel infancy
> Before I understood this place,
> Appointed for my second race,

for I doubt if ever I looked like Reynolds' cherub heads, or his Infant Samuel, or his Age of Innocence. I feel humbled before Traherne's famous description of early childhood:

> The corn was orient and immortal wheat, which never should be reaped, nor was ever sown. I thought it had stood from everlasting to everlasting. The dust and stones of the street were as precious as gold; the gates were at first the end of the world. The green trees, when I saw them first through one of the gates, transported and

ravished me; their sweetness and unusual beauty made
my heart to leap, and almost mad with ecstacy. The Men!
O what venerable and reverend creatures did the aged
seem! Immortal Cherubims! And young men glittering
and sparkling Angels, and maids strange seraphic pieces
of life and beauty! Boys and girls, tumbling in the streets
and playing, were moving jewels. I knew not that they
were born or should die; but all things abided eternally as
they were in their proper places.

I cannot impute to my childhood so pure and mystic a vision
as that—perhaps indeed even the elder and saintly Traherne,
while lamenting things lost, forgot things gained, including
the power of perceiving through childish perceptions a vision
which childhood itself had not perceived. But I can apply to
myself those lovely and concise lines of Mr. W. H. Davies:

> I saw this day sweet flowers grow thick—
> But not one like the child did pick . . .
>
> A hundred butterflies saw I—
> But not one like the child saw fly.
>
> I saw the horses roll in grass—
> But no horse like the child saw pass.
>
> My world this day has lovely been—
> But not like what the child has seen.

For I remember as far back as I remember anything, the
intensity with which I stared at colour and form, feeling
mystery though unacquainted with the word for it, even in
my first remembered toys—not the rag-dolls, over whom I
wept when they got dirty (a Crusoe and a Red Riding Hood)
and were burnt, for it was living people I loved in them, but
the glass marbles with spiral colours within them and the
brilliant rainbow strands of wool from which I was taught,
with the aid of pins and cotton-reels, to weave reins for my
wooden horses. The glass marbles, I take it, contained dyed

paper or metal-foil—I have never brought myself to break one
and see. The wool, shading from vermilion to orange, blue,
indigo, pink, yellow, all burning-bright as Blake's tiger, was I
daresay produced from aniline dyes—of which Solferino and
Magenta, named in my mother's youth after two battles, as
though we were to call two modern colours Loos, and Third
Ypres, were among the first.

I know now that aniline dyes come from coal-tar; until I
progress a little farther in my philosophy, as I hope to do, that
must take some of the gilt off—coal-tar has a scarcely flower-
like smell and so many associations with roads, traffic, and
limited liability companies. Had I heard the word "aniline"
then it would probably have enchanted my not-quite-angelic
but receptive ear. For a lovely word it is, and so are many
whose sounds do not quite reach us because of intercepting
associations. Long ago I noted how ugly in themselves were
some of the consecrated names of poets and how exquisite the
names of many of the most dreadful diseases. What a "crested
and resounding name" would have Sir Erysipelas, stout and
grey-bearded compeer of Sir Isumbras at the Ford; what an
Amazon Queen Pyorrhea would make; and how delicate, sad
and Maeterlinckian a girl, nightgowned and candle-lit in a
turret, the forsaken Princess Anæmia.

With those wools I played; and I stared at playing-cards,
back and front; and I was happy with a box of old lace Valen-
tines, which my mother had, frail punctured things whose thin
leaves opened one after another like the shimmering layers of
a Transformation Scene, to disclose in the centre an arrow-
stricken heart or a many-coloured bouquet in a long-handled
concave basket or that sweetest of almost vanished things, the
image of a rich red moss-rose. . . .

And later there were so many things—primroses spilt over
woodland banks, bluebells and lent-lilies, smooth beech-trunks,
acorns—all the flowers and trees and hedges; deep moist lanes
full of wild strawberries and hart's-tongue ferns; stone walls
with crevices from which sprouted wild geranium and the flat
round leaves and ivory flowers of the pennywort. There were
days on sands finding fine white scallop shells, days on pebbly

beaches full of shells, winkle-shape or cockle-shape, or whorled, black, yellow, orange, brown, green, or checkered purple, green and grey; waves with prickly sea-urchins and pale transparent violet jelly-fish; rock-pools with delicate anemones and darting fish; days on the water where the woods came down to the strip of yellow weed left by the tide. There was a dark evening in a lonely church by the sea, oil-lamps hanging, "Through the Night of Doubt and Sorrow," and the steady melancholy crash of the breakers heard in all the intervals of the service. There was a drive in a trap one June night, the air heavy with the scent of honeysuckle, the hedges sprinkled with quiet glow-worms, shining greeny-yellow, when I caught some glow-worms and put them in a tin full of holes—but they weren't there in the morning, which is a way that such things have. There were corn-chandlers' shops fragrant with oats and peas and mice; provision shops piled with the colours of lemons, oranges, tomatoes, pomegranates, cucumbers, sugar by the sackful. . . . There were brilliant brown horse-chestnuts in their prickly sheaths and autumnal leaves, and hips, smooth ellipses of vermilion chinese lacquer, to be treasured till they wrinkled and faded. . . . There was a "waste" on the fringes of the moor where the yellow wild iris grew and cotton-rushes which, peeled, produced soft snow-white rods, worth days of staring, and there were peaty still pools and a trembling brook, frogs and newts with ridged backs, and the lonely moor in the background, lying patient under the sky through all the seasons with its rock-crowned tors, and old funereal barrows and monuments and gorse, heather, and bog, and crying plover. And there were sunsets over the sea which gave a child who had no words a pleasure that was married to pain and led to gropings after eternity and grief.

*   *   *   *   *

An hour had flown.

Bliss came in from the coffee-room, a map and his chief textbook on Canoeing with him.

"Look here, Squire," he said, his forefinger waggling along a maze of blue lines on the map; "to-morrow night we ought to get to the junction with the Napton and Warwick Canal. To do that we ought to get to Cropredy to-night."

It was a pleasant name to get to; King Charles beat Waller there, although, because of Marston Moor, it was little use. But how far was it?

"Banbury is just under seven, Cropredy just over eleven."

"How many locks?"

"Eight, perhaps."

"There'll be a strong head-wind and we're lunching out."

"We can leave soon after lunch."

I said nothing, though I knew that once he got into a house with a history, books, pictures, furniture, gardens and good conversation, Bliss would be no more Spartan and time-tabulistic than I. Anyhow a few days' training would break him in. We needn't, as the event turned out, have bothered our heads as to where we should get that night. The mailed fist of the Corporation of Banbury settled the matter for us.

At twelve the car came to fetch us, and we drove through country full of memories of the Civil War, Edgehill itself not being far away, to that pretty village dominated by house and church, as a village should be. It is a classic stone house of the mid-seventeenth century; the Cartwright of the day was, lamentably, a Roundhead; his old home was burnt down in the wars, but his descendants to-day have no reason to be dis-satisfied with the new house which the Parliament built for him. Generations of collectors have filled it with treasures, including some noble pictures: my opinion that Bliss would be in no hurry to go away from that hospitable place was con-firmed. Go, in the end, we did, were driven to the wharf, un-moored the canoe, and embarked with a definite feeling of well-being.

It was four o'clock. We still hoped to get to Cropredy, though what with the head-wind and the locks, our arrival there was bound to be late. Paddling hard, but making not much more than three miles an hour, we went through the lock at Alderbury where we crossed the Cherwell, leaving it on our right, mounting through locks at King's Sutton and Bodicot. Banbury Lock (seven miles) we approached through the customary outskirts at seven, and there we had a shock. The towering lock gates were shut; and between them and us was an assembly of barges with one, as it might be the *Brahmapootra,* lying broadside on, straight ahead, blocking all access.

A man sat on the deck smoking, a terrier sitting beside him. "We want to get on," shouted Bliss.

"You can't," sang the man back.

"Why?"

"It's Sunday."

"What the devil has that got to do with it?"

"This is Banbury."

*   *   *   *   *

A whole past of associations flashed across my memory. Why of course, if there were places where you wouldn't be allowed even to go through a lock on Sunday Banbury would be one of them.

It is a very extraordinary thing. Most country towns of just that size and even less than that antiquity are the pleasantest places in the world, full of tradition and good-fellowship. But there is Banbury, in the heart of rural England and Shakespeare's special England at that, and there is, and has been for centuries, a pall of grimness over it. In our infancy we were brought up to think of it as a dream-place out of fairy-land, like Norwich with its especial links with the Man in the Moon, and London Bridge which broke down. Thither, to its Cross, we were summoned, on our cock-horses, to see the fine lady riding her horse, with his proudly arched neck, with her bells on finger and toes, and music always travelling with her wherever she went. We did not know that all the pageantry of Banbury disappeared long ago, when its Puritans rose, broke up all its crosses with hammer and pick, and smashed all the glass and statuary in the church, in the true spirit of iconoclasm, old and new. We heard of Banbury buns, not knowing that long ago Shakespeare's "cakes and ale" was altered, jestingly as applied to Banbury, into "cakes and zeal."

"Zeal-of-the-land Busy," out of Ben Jonson's *Bartholomew*

Fair, was a Banbury baker. Drunken Barnaby's lines are celebrated;

> To Banbury came I, O profane one!
> There I saw a Puritane one,
> Hanging of his cat on Monday,
> For killing of a mouse on Sunday.

Seventeenth-century popular literature is full of scathing remarks about the mentality of Banbury; at the end of the eighteenth century its citizens, probably for reasons of "graft," destroyed their magnificent great mediæval church; and the blight of Puritanism hangs over Banbury to this day. Doubtless there are exceptions there; the descendants of the beaten minority may survive as well as those of the truculent majority. The test applied to Sodom and Gomorrah was a pretty lenient one and I daresay that Banbury would pass it with ease. . . .

Meanwhile we had to spend the night there and what were we to do? On our left there was a mixture of sheds and open spaces which was formidably labelled "Corporation Wharf."

"Where on earth are we to leave the canoe?" asked Bliss, rather angrily.

"Here," I said.

"But the whole place is obviously locked up."

"Never mind; I'm sure I can find a way out and get a taxi from somewhere."

Bliss, whose supremacy afloat was unquestioned, gave in. We tipped the luggage out, and hauled the canoe up the bank and on to the gravel. "Over there'll do," he said, and as soon as we had lugged it to the indicated place we saw that it would be in the way of the Corporation dust-carts when they wanted to go out in the morning. From spot to spot we carried it, each time finding that we were obstructing the hypothetical passage of the Borough Surveyor or the Fire Brigade. In the end Bliss set his mind: "We'll dump it here and leave it here," he said. As soon as we straightened it against a shed I noticed an inscription over a door just amidships. "I say, Bliss," I said, "this won't do, we're blocking up the Sanitary Inspector's door."

"If," exclaimed Bliss with impatient finality, "a man can't

step over a canoe he's not fit to be a Sanitary Inspector."

It sounded like one of those remarks which are classified as "Sayings of the Week" in the Sunday papers. There's nothing like a *non sequitur* after all; it was Sergeant Arabin who said, "Prisoner at the bar, you had excellent parents and a very good education, instead of which you go around the country stealing ducks."

I left Bliss sitting on the baggage and walked to the gates. They were locked right enough, but on the inside. It is enough to say that I got out, ordered a taxi by telephone, fetched Bliss and left the place precisely as I found it.

We went to a hostelry. Perhaps we had been spoilt by our previous entertainment, but we found the amenities less noticeable than the prices, no company, and a general air of chill and indifference. I won't say the menu was in French but it seemed like it, and we were obviously Numbers and even my companion could have got no small-talk out of the landlord or the staff. It would have suited some people very well, very likely.

"I say," said Bliss, as we stood about on the pavement, after we had eaten our Banburian Sunday tomato soup, fish and mutton, "this place seems pretty bleak. I think I'll go and look up a man I know . . . he wasn't born in Banbury."

"All right," I replied, thinking I would go back to my bedroom and the single-minded enthusiasm of Lord Harberton, "I shall turn in early—I'm rather tired."

But as soon as he had gone, I remembered that I had friends in an ancient house near Banbury. I rang up. F. came in and fetched me. There were five of them. While four played bridge, the fifth talked to me, and very late one of them drove me home. All Banbury was in bed. . . .

Why, I wondered, do I never even want to play bridge now? Memory went back over countless games.

I was much alone with my mother in early days; my father and she parted when I was six or seven; so I cannot vie with Edmund Gosse's *Father and Son* for intimacy of domestic revelation, especially as my father erred as far in the non-rigid direction as Gosse's in the rigid. There are certainly drawbacks in being brought up entirely by a mother; she can't

share all one's interests and her mind (whatever the goodness
of her heart) can't work like one's own; "they have their
dreams and do not think of us," as Flecker's sorrowful women
lament when their men are setting out for Samarkand.

But mine infected me with cards. She and her friends used
to play whist in each other's houses, and, having been taught
in the afternoons when I was very small, I was allowed sometimes to join in for a rubber before I went to bed and the
serious business began. Cowrie shells (at so much a dozen),
I remember, were used as counters (I associate them with woolwork screens, canary cages, plush photograph frames, Bohemian
vases hung with lustres, countless little tables and pieces of
bric-à-brac, and water-colours of raging Cornish seas). Other
games I knew as far back as I can remember—solo whist, nap,
cribbage, piquet, bezique, and games now wholly or partly
extinct like écarté and even loo.

We had a backgammon board but I never saw it used, and,
until the recent feverish revival, thought the game gone for
ever. Neither then nor ever did my mother gamble for more
than the little she could afford (she had seen too much of that
in her brief married life), but she regarded moderate gambling
as giving a spice to life, which it certainly is, and more and
more so as the vast multitudes who go in for their humble
sweeps and pools realize that nothing but chance could possibly
bring a fairy-tale change into their lives, penuriously fixed
from cradle to grave, and usually in dim, smoky, surroundings.

Cards I continued to play until Contract and Mr. Culbertson
came in, with the books, the commercialization, the elaborate
signalling, the wooden taught partners with hard-and-fast
rules, and the vast penalties subject to the aberrations of wild
partners. Now I play only when it is sociable so to do. But I
am sorry for those who haven't bridge at their disposal, have
churlishly to say they cannot make a fourth, are compelled to
read books in corners in the country when everybody else is
at the tables, and miss the extraordinary contacts with varied
humanity which cards provide. Too varied sometimes, perhaps. Once, in bad weather in a large Swiss hotel, I was roped
into a Whist Drive held for the benefit of a Conducted Tour,

I

which seemed chiefly to consist of Dissenting ministers and their wives; and when the M.C. announced from a chair in the middle "Ladies and Gentlemen, Clubs is Trumps," the Sheba who had fallen to my lot leant across to me and eagerly whispered: "Are those the little things like shamrocks?" Thus far, she guessed right; but not much farther, and we didn't win the plated teapot.

But there have been many and delightful other occasions in liners and hotels when cards have led to conversations with all sorts of persons to whom I might never have spoken. Once I was coming home from the Baltic in a small ship. The first day I spent entirely with two Salvation Army officers (who happened to sit with me at meals) and we had almost exhausted the sanitation of Latvia when a steward approached me from three disconsolate men in a corner of the smoke-room and said: "Those gentlemen wonder whether you would make a fourth at bridge?" They were commercial travellers, each one after his kind; we played all day for two days, and in the evenings I sat up with one of them, a quiet man who told me all about wool, and with whom I corresponded later about books. Playing cards will gradually break ice and prise people; through it I have heard the "shop" of soldiers, engineers, manufacturers, prospectors, grocers, foreign countesses and all sorts. One chance I missed. The man was a little old fat Jew, very likeable, but too shy to talk. Too late, just as we were berthing at Southampton he stood me a cock-tail, and as we parted, handed me a card saying, "Here's my card; when you're next in N'York I'd be pleased if you'd come and see me." We shook hands and he vanished; when I looked at his card in the train it bore this inscription: "Israel Abrahams. President Pan-American Insecticide Corporation Inc." I smiled, I admit; subconsciously, perhaps, I felt that a Corporation Inc. sounded too large and cumbersome a thing to be dealing with creatures so small and sprightly as insects. But I lamented also; I don't suppose I shall ever again meet a man who might give me the inside information about insecticides, or talk about them with a President's evangelistic zeal.

*   *   *   *   *

And I was taught early the charms of gambling on the race-course, and the delights of racing itself. Every year with a number of relations we went to the local races and sometimes further afield in a brake with luncheon baskets and a view from the top, and I would struggle through the crowds clutch-ing my silver to sympathetic-looking bookies on whom, during the races, I kept a close watch. That taste I have never lost and I still go racing when I can—though I daresay I should get heartily sick of it if I went every day like some people. Racing at places like Newbury where there is comfort and you can see the running from anywhere is still great fun; and so are the remoter meetings where you get a strange Dickensian mix-ture of rustics and invading urban toughs. The crowds change little, the bookmakers not at all; what one who began as early as I misses are the horses. I saw a good old traditional journalist the other day describing the Derby as "The Feast of St. Horse," and so it is in a way. But I knew the meetings when there were no cars and plenty of turnpike gates, and a whole countryside would assemble in wagonettes, carriages, gigs, traps, governess-carts, drags; every sort of vehicle drawn by every size, shape, and colour of horse, with glisten and shine and clank of harness, and the air full of the smell of horse and trampled grass. I feel about those old occasions with some-thing of the nostalgia of John Nyren remembering Hambledon long after; when the old cricket matches came back to his ancient memory mingled with the scents of ale and roses and the cries of countrymen shouting, "Tich and turn," "Tich and turn." And there is an added poignancy which comes from my obstinate belief that when I was a small boy my luck was in. Reason says that my gains stuck in my memory because I was allowed to keep them and that my losses did not because I was kindly recouped for them by uncles. However, though never a confirmed plunger, I must admit that as a rule, when I have betted or played for stakes, I have been lucky. One painful exception occurs to me.

In the beginning of August 1923 Louis Marlow and I (we had been friends for twenty years) decided to go to Monte Carlo, at that time unfrequented in the summer, with small

capitals and try a mild, slow, cautious system. Before we went,
conversations with friends took this sort of line:

"What on earth do you want to go to Monte Carlo for at
this time of year?"

"We thought we'd like some sun and we want to try a
system."

"But you won't find anyone there."

"We don't want to find anyone there."

"But it's out of the season and all the decent hotels will
be shut."

"We don't want the Hôtel de Paris; we shall be sure to find
a place good enough for us."

"All right; please yourselves; go and get roasted to death."

So we went, and were not roasted to death. The usual
temperature was 104 degrees, but it was a dry heat; hotel and
Casino were airy, and the only place in which we suffered from
heat was the train as it rattled past the blinding chalky slopes
of Provence. We found the Hotel Terminus open and got
communicating rooms with a balcony sheer over the Mediterranean; everything, since it was the dead season, was cheap;
and champagne and peaches, to which we felt much inclined,
were going for next to nothing on the exchange. The Sporting Club was shut, but the Casino was open, and we had no
hankering for brilliant assemblies of the Phillips Oppenheim
type, full of Grand Dukes, ambassadors with pointed white
beards, dark adventurers, lithe adventuresses, and peerless
peeresses who would lean over us with their fabulous emerald
necklaces bumping against the backs of our heads. The General
Rooms, as was predicted, were sparsely populated; there were
a few residents who "went to the office," as they call it, each
morning. Day visitors from Milan or Marseilles, mostly looking like respectable civil servants or schoolmistresses, formed
now and then a queue at the ticket office, as it were an army
of sheep besieging a butcher's; while now and again an expen-
sive-looking party from a cruising yacht would break in chattering, plaster a table with discs for half an hour, and then, in
a flock, bustle out leaving the Room at peace again. On the
whole the place had an atmosphere of rest and emptiness, and

one wondered what the Monegasque police in their white had to do. The hotel was cheaper than a Margate boarding-house; the shops were asleep and contained little summer-wear; the Casino was like a Sunday-school with timid punters putting on one-and-threepence a time, and a dim murmur around the teachers, those philosophic croupiers who might well have been giving lessons in deportment.

It was a pleasant time. We rose early in the tonic air and saw the sun rise from Italy. It came up very red on the grey sea verge, the water in the harbour greenish-yellow with pale blue ripples. Then it rose swiftly, turning orange, deep orange, gold, and brighter, stronger, gold laying a long dazzling wavy spear across the water. We breakfasted on our balcony, and then spent the morning in the Casino, now and then dropping out to report progress. We lunched in the Hotel Garden under a sunshade. In the afternoons, like two old ladies, in a decayed carriage, we crawled along white roads mottled with blue shadows up to little hill-towns, Eze or Roquebrune, and drank wine outside mountain inns looking down over woods and villas and blue sea; or we bathed in the warm sea, and dressed in cabins through the walls of which came the voices of the local tenority singing "La Donna è Mobile" or "Ah Che la Morte." Then dinner and an apéritif in the twilight outside the Café de Paris, where "Yes, We Have No Bananas" dawned upon our as yet unaccustomed ears, then to the rooms again until closing time.

It was all perfect. It is true that the architecture of modern Monte Carlo is mostly not beautiful. But it is only a narrow strip; "the mountains look on Monte Carlo, and Monte Carlo looks on the sea"; the elements dominate the works of man there, at any rate when the place is summer-sleepy and almost empty. The gambling, up to a point, was perfect, too. There was no wild plunging. Louis modified our system, as will presently be learned. But I plugged on with it, with certainly not less than an average eight-hours day, backing red and black both, odd and even both, high and low both (or rather the differences between them in my six columns of figures) simultaneously, and always starting again when the tower of possible loss looked like mounting to toppling-point. For a week it worked with a regularity that beat Bradshaw. Never less than eleven pounds did I make in a day and never more than thirteen. But there came an evening when Louis, who had been in a corner, joined me and said: "Look here, I've had enough of this. It's all too slow for me. I've only made thirty bob the whole week. I will, of course, stay the other week I said I'd come for. But do you mind coming up here alone while I go out driving or bathing? There are several people I should like to look up in Cannes and Cap Ferrat and I like those little hill-towns."

The prospect dismayed me. Solitary working over those green cloths with no companion to confide in was not at all to my taste. So I made him an extravagant offer. "Look here," I said, echoing his words, "suppose I raise you a good capital which will enable you to play higher, will you come here again to-morrow?"

"If you'd like me to."

"All right, wait here for me for two minutes."

I wandered off and found a table where there was a loud murmur: there had been a run of sixteen on black. I have no illusions about the Theory of Probability (though it must be remembered that there *is* such a thing as a record run, a limit in practice, if not in theory), but I thought, "This is as likely a chance as any," and put one third of my substantial winnings on red.

Black turned up. I pulled out my remaining roll of milles and staked the rest of my winnings, again on red. The table span round; the little white pill tinkled round in the opposite direction; the wheel slowed; the pill slowed; it hesitated on knife-edge after knife-edge; and then came down in a black number again.

My winnings were gone. Though not given much to crying over spilt milk (a grotesque habit) I admit I did not wait to see if black's run was going to end at eighteen. I rejoined my friend. "I'm sorry," he said, in a sympathetic drawl, "but we can go for drives and drop in here occasionally when we feel inclined." So we went out and had a drink, under the lamps and the stars, at one of the little tables across the square, and walked down to the hotel.

When we got there, there was a telegram for him. It said: "Come back at once. Mother seriously ill." My gamble, entirely against my principles, had been utterly thrown away. He had to go; I, not wishing to be solitary there, went with him. His mother, happily, survived for many years and died in serene old age. I spent my remaining week in Wales flogging a river for salmon. I never even heard of a salmon; but the wet woods, the wet rocks, the crashing, bubbling, singing waters, the smell of moss and damp, were lovely and consoling.

> "I have been there and fain would go,
> 'Twas like a little Heaven below"

saith the poet. To apply that to Monte Carlo would perhaps be going too far. But I must say I enjoyed it. I have never been there since. But I have often thought of it, especially when lingering in one of those dismal dim Swiss casinos, which the Swiss Government keeps open in order to attract visitors, and overloads with zeros in order to show its disapproval of gambling. And I thought of it again this very morning as I wrote these pages. For I saw in a popular paper (I have noticed no obituaries elsewhere) a few lines about one whom I met there. I should like to record the event and to use the little headline, in honour of one who had long disappeared from public view:

THE STORY OF ZAZEL.

It was the second morning of my stay in Monte Carlo. I had had a very good two hours at the roulette table. The system moved extraordinarily fast; nothing went wrong; there were nice short runs; I simply scooped in the counters and all my pockets were stuffed with them. Suddenly I was touched on the arm by somebody on the left. . . .

I was not, at this stage, surprised. The evening before I had had ten minutes of trente-et-quarante which moved so quickly that I could hardly keep up with my pencilled accounts. I won heavily, but gave up exhausted. Throughout the brief session a plump well-preserved woman in lilac sitting next over me had poked her face across my reluctant one and whispered: "You vinning," "You losing," and "Ah, you vill play goot!" As I rose, she pinched me in the biceps, followed me to the bar, and made me celebrate the good luck she said she had brought me with a bottle of champagne; which was a little hard, as I didn't know her from Adam, or perhaps Eve. She had little French, and her principal language, which may have been Yiddish or Roumanian, was to me Double-Dutch. However, I bowed and departed. . . .

Anyhow, this wasn't like that. I turned; there was a dear little old woman, refined and gentle-looking, although faintly bearded and slightly bleary, dressed in shabby black with a grey scarf round her neck.

"Would you mind," she said timidly, with the faintest touch of Cockney in her voice, "if I followed your play?"

This was rather embarrassing, of course. I'd rather she had done it without asking, as I might have crashed at any moment. Still I naturally said: "Delighted, but of course I hope I shan't let you down."

"You're in luck to-day," she replied, with a charming smile, as she settled in the next seat to me.

Happily, the luck lasted. She played very low, but she won what was obviously to her a great deal, if not the wealth of the Indies, and occasionally her gratitude bubbled out excitedly.

After a while she said she was going to stop. It is always a good thing to do occasionally: to go to the little bar and have a drink, to go outside and look at the red blossoms of the oleanders with the Mediterranean behind; that green cloth and wheel tire the eyes, and even the crooning of the stiff-faced croupiers gets a bit wearisome, rather like being in a church of somebody else's religion listening to a monotonous ritual. So I said: "I shall take a rest, too. Would you care for a drink?" She said, looking up at me (for she was very tiny), that she seldom took anything, but that an occasion like this should be celebrated, so we made our way to the small bar. There sat the Lilac Woman (whom I suspected to be really Scarlet) drinking champagne again, and making eyes at a ghastly fat man with no hair and four necks, afterwards described to me by the barman (an Italian) as "un roi, ou un pacha, ou quelquechose." Luckily she made no attempt at recognition.

Much to my surprise, my frail old lady asked for a whisky and a cigarette; she didn't look as if she had ever heard of either. She didn't quite wear a bonnet, though, conjuring up her face, I see her in one. She certainly had a black satin dress, a grey misty scarf, a gold locket on a thin chain, silver hair, a crinkled grandmotherly face and innocent blue eyes—all like a Victorian dowager gone a little dowdy and dusty but with traces of former grace. After we had had our drinks, wanting to get out of sight of that appalling couple, I suggested a seat outside in the shade of a tree.

"Don't you want to go back to the tables?" she asked.

"Not in the least," I protested. "I'd much rather sit outside with you. It's very quiet and pleasant, and there's a breeze to-day." A champagne cork popped; she rose suddenly.

"Very well, then," she said, "let us go outside and talk."

*   *   *   *   *

Thereafter, we met in the mornings, played a little, and then went outside to the seat above that lovely harbour and sea. She did not arrive till after opening hours, as she had to come by train from somewhere along the coast. Gradually her story came out. She was a widow living in rooms on a small annuity. She had very little margin but roulette was her one amusement, and whenever she could (as a rule once or twice a week) she came over to Monte Carlo with a few francs in her reticule and, I think, lost them. Then one day I suggested she might come over next day and dine, as I knew my companion was dining out. She agreed and the whole story came out. . . .

It was evening, but still warm, the lights twinkling against the fading sky, the moon just risen, the air heavy with scent. I had given her dinner, and we were sitting alone over coffee in my hotel garden. We had dressed. She was in an ash-blue

I*

frock, looking twenty years younger; her eyes had a soft light in them and her cheeks the echo of the roses of youth. I was aware for the first time of her strong and perfect, though very small figure. We had been talking about the past and travel, she seeming to have known, long ago, every town in Europe from Lille to Kiev. After the coffee there was a moment's silence; she looked past me to the ship-lights in the harbour and the Old Town on its rock, and said: "But I don't suppose you would know who I used to be even if I were to tell you?"

She turned and smiled at me rather sadly.

"Do tell me," I said.

She took a photograph out of her bag, and passed it over. It was old, had been taken in Norwood, and represented a handsome girl in tights.

I looked enquiringly.

"It's me," she said, "the 'uman Cannon-ball. I was Zazel."

*   *   *   *   *

The name seemed instantaneously familiar; then I wondered if I were not making a confusion with Voltaire's Zadig. Then the truth came to me with a shock as though I had suddenly found myself living with remote celebrities like Grimaldi, Taglioni, the Infant Roscius, the Calculating Boy, or the Learned Pig—though this last comparison is hardly kind to one who must have been a pretty girl. Zazel! Why, she had been famous before I was born. Still alive, having coffee with me! "Good Lord!" I exclaimed, "you don't say so!"

But she did say so, and so it was. In 1880 or so, she was the talk of Britain, if not of Europe, as elderly people still remember, and when I was small I was always seeing or hearing references to her. She was the young artiste who was shot daily out of a cannon at the Royal Aquarium,* curving resplendent into air in tinselled tights to fall into a net, a puff of smoke following her some minutes later.

---

* A music-hall which stood opposite the Abbey where now stands the ornate Central Hall. The Methodists built this, largely out of a Million Shillings Fund. They might raise a few more shillings to face with stone the remaining bare brick surface of the building—which at present shows very bad manners to the Abbey.

"And then," she said, "they stopped me. A lot of those inter-fering men in Parliament started a Committee about it and they passed a Law forbidding me to do it. Oh, I was wretched!"

"Were you very fond of it?" I asked.

"I loved it. They'd just no right to take away me living if I loved it. I was ambitious. I wanted to be great. You see, it was me Art!"

I confess I had heard of many arts, but the Art of being Shot out of a Cannon was not one of them. However, I knew what she meant; she had had her technique of bravery and control and was proud of it and her elegance. And I shared her hatred of those who stopped her charming performance, which gave such pleasure to multitudes and to herself, merely because somebody might occasionally be killed at it; probably the very same merciless, mercenary Puritans who fought tooth and nail against attempts, at the expense of their precious pockets, to reduce the ghastly and wanton mortality in mines and merchant-vessels. But they're still at their old games, in other directions.

Well, her career as a cannon-ball was ended, and shortly afterwards she married a Mr. Starr, an Englishman from Ash-ford who was European manager of Barnum and Bailey's and brought the show to England. "Me and me dear husband lived together without grousing for forty years. He oughtn't to have been in the show business reely," she said, "his people were gentlefolk in Kent, but had lost their money. Here" (showing me a signet ring) "is his crest. We travelled a lot and were very happy, but he is dead now, and I came down here."

I pictured those wanderings in a world of dwarfs, giants, bearded women, dog-faced men, performing seals, boxing kangaroos, ringmasters, equestriennes, jugglers, acrobats and lion-tamers, and thought of the contrast with this second starry garden above the gentle wash of the sea. "I suppose," I said, "you have many mementoes of the old days?"

"I haven't much," she replied, "but I've got one picture I'm fond of. It's me at seventeen. Did you ever hear of a painter called Mr. Watts?"

Shade of George Frederick Watts, O.M., R.A.! She wouldn't have been surprised if I had answered "No!" Shades of the National Portrait Gallery, of the Tate, of Compton; of all those bearded Victorian portraits, of all those allegorical infants, monsters, and bowed repentant backs; of Love, Life and Death; Life, Death and Hope; Death, Hope and Faith; Life embracing Faith, Death embracing Hope; of the projected frescoes for the Hall of Euston Station, of acres of canvas spread with fading paint! "Why, yes," I assured her. "He was a very famous man indeed. Everybody knows about Mr. Watts."

"Well," she went on, relieved, "he painted my portrait when I was doing that act at the Aquarium. He came behind one day and said he wanted to paint me. I said could he do it there and he said no I had to come to his studio. I said I'd ask mother and asked him what I should wear. He said I should wear what I had on, and of course that made me feel awkward as the dress I performed in was cut low and it seemed different. I couldn't have a man looking so close at my flesh, especially because when I put my head back sometimes things didn't stay where they ought to be. Oh," she went on inconsequently, "I did look like a boy; they used to bet on it. So I asked mother and she said 'You can go if Maggie goes with you'—Maggie was my elder sister, you see."

So off the two went, to Little Holland House in Melbury Road and that vast studio, and Mr. Watts, in his prime, painted the circus-girl, in tights, when he could spare time from Love, Mammon, Matthew Arnold and Cardinal Manning, and I daresay it was one of his liveliest works. Anyhow he had given it to Zazel, and she had taken it about with her as she travelled and aged, and here it was in cheap Riviera lodgings. "I wish," she sighed, interrupting our shared musings over the past, "I knew what to do with it after I'm gone."

"Haven't you anybody to leave it to?"

"Nobody at all."

"Why not leave it to the National Gallery?"

"I did try to suggest that to my solicitor when I was last

in London, but all he said was 'Pooh! They wouldn't want a picture of you!' "

"They'd jump at it!" I exclaimed indignantly. "I don't suppose your wretched solicitor knows anything about it at all. Let me see it some time next week."

I never saw her again. Our departure was sudden and unexpected, and I hadn't her address. Year after year, in all these fifteen, I have meant to go back and look for her and her treasure, but the winds and waves have carried me elsewhere, and I have done no more than pass through Monte Carlo in the train, in the dark.

And now I see in the paper a small paragraph saying that "a few days ago, in the late 'seventies," she has died, and now I can never see her again.

*   *   *   *   *

At this point I hear the voice of that whispering Demon who, if he had his way, would always be making things so difficult for me. Thus:

DEMON: I thought you were canoeing. You can hardly persuade people that what happened to you at a casino in 1923 helped you to navigate in 1938.

MYSELF: I gave myself licence to wander. You don't seem to have read my Dedication.

DEMON: Yes, I did; but there is a mean in all things. You seem to be following the method of Sterne who said he wrote down one sentence and trusted to God for the next.

MYSELF: Sterne knew exactly what he was doing and so do I.

DEMON: Nobody would think so.

MYSELF: Have you ever kept goats?

DEMON: What's that to do with it? No, I haven't.

MYSELF: Well, I have. As for you, I daresay your own horns and hoofs are enough to be going on with. I had three beauties—father and mother and kid. They were delightful. If I went into the paddock where they were kept, half of which was an orchard, and lay on the grass to read a book, they would climb upon me as though they were chamois and I an Alpine peak. The kid was like an affectionate puppy, the mother like an affectionate pony, and even the old billy, who had black-and-yellow jewels of eyes, as keen as a crocodile's but not repulsive, proud as he was of his head and size and shaggy coat and masculinity, was willing to be my friend and followed me to the end of his tether, especially if I brought him boughs of apple-leaves. I should have had those goats still if it hadn't been for the garden-boy.

DEMON: And what, pray, did the garden-boy do?

MYSELF: He used his private judgment, having never heard of conscience and being too stupid to consult authority.

DEMON: But what did he actually do?

MYSELF: If you want to know, he made them a great mash of laurel and rhododendron leaves; that he admitted, and I strongly suspect (although he denied it) that he added a certain amount of yew. The goats died, poor things.

DEMON: I'm sorry, of course, but I don't see the relevance of those goats.

MYSELF: You never do see when I'm leading up to something.

DEMON: You take such a damn long time doing it.

MYSELF: You must be one of those hard-boiled moderns. For myself, I prefer an easy progress, a prose as melodious as may be, a straying over hedges and a chasing after butterflies. Facts for me are flies but style is amber. The point is that I want you, for the moment, to consider me as a goat.

DEMON: That's easy.

MYSELF: Oh dear, I knew you'd say that. The worst of you underbred moderns is that you will interrupt a man when you haven't the least idea as to what he's going to say. I am using a simile or, if you prefer it, a metaphor, though I daresay they are the same thing to you.

DEMON: Yes.

MYSELF: Well, when I kept my great goat with the slanting eyes of agate and aquamarine, I, of course, tethered him on a long chain fastened to a stout iron stave driven into the ground. Sometimes, if the ground was especially sodden or the old goat especially wanton, he would escape at night or under the roseate hues of early dawn, and when I went out, footmarking the morning dew, I would find him ever so far away from his allotted place, dragging chain and picket after him in a far corner under the elms, with all the lower branches of the apple-trees stripped clean of leaves and some of the trunk barked and he looking innocent and oblivious.

DEMON: That last phrase sounds modern Irish.

MYSELF: If that's so, I'm sorry. I associate such locutions with people who call themselves Sean MacGaoilain and Liam O' Faighloaivain, and expect me to remember their names well enough to order their books. They're worse than the Czechs. Czech to me is Czech but Ye Olde Irisshe is Czech-mate. I will say this in favour of Mr. James Joyce: he has never, for all the temptation to the pedant and the schoolmaster in him, attempted to call himself Seumas O' Jehoiahoaish.

DEMON: I rather admire Joyce.

MYSELF: Oh yes, and Donne, and Gerard Hopkins and D. H. Lawrence, and all the other people who have nothing in common with each other except that they have flashes of genius and are often obscure. Half those people wouldn't have been seen dead in a field with the other half. I saw in a "literary organ" the other day a leading article saying these people were the only people now read, that the Elizabethan poets dealt only in clichés, and that the Elizabethan adventurers and dramatists (with the strange exceptions of Webster and Tourneur) appealed only to sadists. I thought not only of the great; I thought of Drake, his hands unstained by innocent blood, I thought of Raleigh and his dreams and his long imprisonment and his History, and his eloquent address to Death from the Tower of London, "Whom none has persuaded, thou hast persuaded," and his last letter to his wife before James murdered him; I thought of Gilbert going into the unknown; I thought of the stainless Sidney and the death at Zutphen and the song which begins:

> Who is this that this dark night
>   Underneath my window plaineth?

I thought of all those; and of Nicholas Breton, the tender and infinitely varied, and his Astrophel's Song, with its quick beginning followed up so breathlessly and lovingly:

> Fair in a morn (O fairest morn!)
>   Was never morn so fair.
> There shone a sun, tho' not the sun
>   That shineth in the air.
> For the earth and from the earth,
>   (Was never such a creature!)
> Did come this face (was never face
>   That carried such a feature).
> Upon a hill (O blessed hill,
>   Was never hill so blessed!)
> There stood a man (was never man
>   For woman so distressed).

Are we sadists that we should love Grenville's last fight in Tudor prose or Tennyson's verse? The monks of Mount Athos, Gibbon says, stared at their navels and saw a great light; you modern introverts stare at your navels and see a great darkness.

DEMON: Have you finished? What about that goat?

MYSELF: The point is that in the pasturing of goats may be found an emblem of my kind of reminiscences. You stake the goat, and his long tether allows him to roam in a circle which takes him behind his fixed point and ahead of it; you move his stake and the same thing happens. He always seems to be going backwards and forwards, but the stake shifts steadily on and in the end the whole field is cropped.

DEMON: Crop some, then.

CHAPTER IV

BANBURY TO FENNY COMPTON

NEXT morning Bliss went off to take the canoe through Banbury Lock, recovered from its Sabbath sleep, while I, with a car, took the luggage to a wharf above. We were glad to go. However thickly honours, in my old age, may cluster round my brow, I don't think I shall be made a freeman of the borough of Banbury.

At eleven we set out; about one—five miles and several locks —we were at Cropredy. There we tethered her and went up to a cosy inn. In the tap the landlord was sitting with another ancient: "Mr. Bliss, I think," he said. "I haven't been here for thirteen years," replied the pleased but astounded Bliss. The landlord made no answer but went off to fetch our beer, bread, cheese and pickled cabbage, the wan "nature" kind, not stained a cheerful red by the introduction of a little beetroot or wine. Conversation was chiefly about the poor prospects of the hay-harvest; drought and cold, no rain, no sun.

The tap-room looked across to the churchyard. There is a good squat tower. At the entrance to the church were hints:

"Go straight into church. . . . Kneel down. . . . Do not look round every time the door opens." There was a brass in the floor: "Here rests the body of Priscilla Plant, the only daughter of Thomas and Ione Plant of Great Boston, who deceased the 25th day of Februarie 1637. The maid is not dead but sleepeth" —I took it down because of the name of Ione, which is like something out of Landor—but then it occurred to me that it was probably Joan spelt Jone, with an I for a J. In the tower base was a notice from a bell-maker, founded in 1700, asking us to "please note change of address." There was an Eagle lectern, reminiscent of the cockyolly bird; it was Pre-Reformation and had spent a hundred and fifty years in the river; perhaps the bun-makers of Banbury put it there; the church was rebuilt in 1320.

At three we started again; for the next two and three-quarter hours we were chiefly occupied in opening and shutting locks, being several times held up by leisurely barges. At Clayton Top Lock (about our thirteenth so far, in rather more than that number of miles), the lockless "summit level" of twelve miles began, at about four hundred feet above sea-level. There comes a time when a canal reaches as high in a watershed as it can go with a hope of being recruited by leats drawn from higher reaches of adjoining rivers (for every boat passing through a lock "wastes" a lock-full of water) and must follow one high contour line, even at the expense of cuttings and tunnels, replenishing itself from rivulets and reservoirs.

"All the time," remarks my companion, "they are meandering thus among the contours of the hills their course is marked out for them by the law of gravity and not by the will of the engineer, and you will see that they must necessarily take you (as they do) into places remote from man and the habitations of man. It is here on their summit-levels that our canals give you their wildest beauty and show you a sort of landscape that no river nor everyday road can give. You pass no villages or farms, you are alone among the hills, and will meet no one unless it is a barge, towed by a sleepy horse, pushing the quiet water away in front of its square bows and lifting the long water-weeds along the banks; and when it has passed and the undulations have ceased to chuckle in the sedges, everything is still again. There is nothing quite like the summit-levels of our English canals anywhere else in England."

We were high, but there were higher hills in the background over both banks.

At a pause Bliss said: "But you should see the top of the Kennet and Avon."

"Isn't that the one that is now all choked up and derelict?"

"No, you're thinking of the Thames and Severn which runs up the Golden Valley and through the great Sapperton Tunnel. We shall never see that in action again; parts of it are even being filled up. But the Kennet and Avon has been cleared. By Devizes you get one of the finest views in the world. The canal drops two hundred feet in a mile; you look down on a precipice of twenty-nine locks, all the Avon valley below you. . . ."

There was a reservoir on the right; we went through a deep cutting; Bliss began in that solitude to think about inns. "I think," he said, after studying the map and his Collected Works, "we had better stop at Fenny Compton; there is an inn marked there, right by the Canal Bridge."

When we got there it was about half-past six. We moored the canoe, unloaded, and went into the bar; there was a solitary man meditating over a pint, and a friendly landlord behind the counter. As country inns go the place looked vast; there simply must be spare rooms there unless the Old Woman who Lived in a Shoe had migrated to those parts. But no, said the landlady, with unfeigned regret, we couldn't be put up, they never could put anybody up.

"But why? You must have the rooms?"

"Yes, we have the rooms."

"Why, then?"

"All our water has to be brought a mile and a half."

"Can't you sink a well?"

"We did, but they won't let us use it."

"Why?"

"The Sanitary Inspector said that canal water got into it."

Bliss here intervened, his face showing that he savagely remembered his remarks about Sanitary Inspectors on the previous evening.

"This is absurd. Here are we canoeing. Nobody can stop us drinking canal water in our canoe. Anyhow, why is it worse to have a bath in one per cent of canal water when anybody on the bank can dive into a hundred per cent of it? It doesn't make sense," he muttered.

It seemed a deadlock. "Anyhow," said Bliss, reluctantly resigned, "have you got such a thing as a pipe-cleaner?"

"No," admitted the landlady, "you see we never have a demand for them."

"Haven't you even got a feather?"

She had a bright idea. "We keep chickens," she said, with an eager smile. She went to a side-door, and said something to her husband Sam; in two seconds he was back with a handful of noble feathers. Whether they had been picked up, or plucked from the living fowl, as the steaks were alleged to be cut from the living Abyssinian cows, Bliss did not enquire and I do not know.

We got friendly and our kind hostess relented as far as she was able. We were to take a car to the village where there was an inn (with water) and if they couldn't accommodate us there, one of us was to return to the Canal and she would do her best.

We hired the car and set out for Fenny Compton. Yes, they had two rooms but they could only let us have one, as one was always kept for a regular traveller who might (he didn't that night) turn up any time. So I went back to the wharf, a delightful large bedroom, a splendid early supper and then some conversation.

The man who had been brooding over the bar was still there when I returned. He was a native of those parts revisiting the glimpses; he was sombre about agriculture and lamented the days of Lord Spencer—not the last one who had the large collar (and told the House of Commons that he was "not an agricultural labourer"), but the one before who had a large red beard. One hears these regrets everywhere for the country estate owners of a former time; but to our urban majority the word "landlord" means an usurious screw who sends somebody round every week to collect an exorbitant rent for a leaky house.

More cheerful company presently arrived; a buxom lady from a barge which we had seen to be tied up there when we arrived.

"Well, how did you and your friend get on?" she enquired over her Guinness.

I suppose I stared uncomprehendingly.

"In your canoe, I mean," she explained.

"Oh, did you see us?"

"We was the barge what was in your way last night at Banbury."

"Are you the *Brahmapootra?*"

"Yes, that's us; we was off by six this morning."

"Why is your barge called that?"

"Our company's got a hundred, and they're all called after rivers."

She took me aboard in the evening sunlight, and introduced me to her peaceable husband, who was smoking his pipe after supper. The children and the dog were playing with a football in a field by the water. Then we went back to the inn and she talked about their life while he played darts. It was a strangely equable existence she described, mostly up and down that canal and adjoining ones; only once had they been sent on the Grand Junction to London. They didn't like it; the children in big towns shouted vile abuse and threw stones at them. Birmingham was the worst. The country children were always friendly and polite. . . .

She went. I retired to a corner with the *Daily Mail* and the Saturday's cricket. Two men from a lorry came in and began talking about the news, with especial reference to the bulletins of the B.B.C.

"Ole 'Itler," said one, "I reckon 'e's got to keep on shoutin' to make 'em think 'e's doin' somethin'." As Herr Hitler had just walked into Austria I wondered what the speaker's notion of a deed was. . . .

"Too much of all that on the wireless," said the other, "all this 'ere political stuff. Why can't they give us a good ole murder now and then?"

Something they had said turned my thoughts back to the Germany of nearly a quarter of a century ago. I suddenly found that memories which had long seemed effaced came back vividly—perhaps because of the very contrast between the peace of this countryside and its avocations with the rhetoric, the marchings and trumpetings which were once more filling the German air.

It was in May, 1914. I was there the whole month, and had luck with the weather; I had taken some introductions; I had never been to Germany before. I knew just enough German to get what I wanted; four years of instruction at school had made me realize that my brain simply couldn't cope with it.

It was not taxed on my way from Flushing to Berlin; the only person in my carriage was a fat dark young Jewess with a rack full of luggage with which she fussed continually. She had come from Canada and spoke poor but emotional English with an American-German accent. Her excitement was due to the fact that she had not seen Uncle Solomon and Aunt Rebecca for two years and was concerned about the safety of the presents she was bringing them. No wonder: they were a live canary in a cage from Canada and a live lobster in a basket from Flushing; her repeated scramblings in the rack were to make sure that the little pets were still alive. At eleven —I remember I was reading Mrs. Barrington's *Life* of Walter Bagehot—we curled up on our seats by agreement; somewhere about two we jolted to a stop at Goch on the frontier, and I still remember the *douanier's* shrug when she anxiously declared the lobster and the canary.

The journey next day seemed endless. There were one or two wide rivers to look for; otherwise the monotony of the great European Plain, which roughly runs from the Cambridge Gog-Magogs to the Urals, was unbroken except by the Hill of Minden. Rumble, rumble, rumble, we went. At welcome intervals I worked my way to the dining-car. The lady was nervous, she was not going to risk anybody stealing the

canary which was to elicit *"Das ist schön"* from Aunt Rebecca
nor the lobster which would certainly get its equal due from
Uncle Solomon. I volunteered to look after them for her.
Thereafter, about once an hour she went off and came back
saying: "I 'ave 'ad bifsteck. . . . I dawn't like bifsteck," and
lifted the green curtain to say "Cheep, cheep, eesn't 'e a lofly
bird," to the unresponsive canary. I wondered, as I took my
turn for the corridor, how she would contend with food that
she really liked.

One meal I hurried over owing to the vainglorious boastings
and shoutings and jests of four colossal sweating business
men, with cropped heads and a plethora of necks and chins,
whose noise was intolerable. At the next I sat with a tall,
lean, straggly-bearded, vulture-throated person who might
have been a professor—of sorts, I mean—as it might be
Metallurgy, certainly not Classics. A civil and disillusioned
waiter bent over me with a large plated tureen full of the legs,
wings and trunks of grilled chickens; I took a liver-wing and
waited for the vegetables. My *vis-à-vis* took another; I hardly
noticed it. He took a second; so might I have done, had I been
hungry. He took a third, and I thought: "This old boy has
a hearty appetite." But when he proceeded to a fourth and
fifth section, until he reached a seventh and his platter was
heaped with about one and three-quarters chickens, I was
staggered. Had he beamed lustrously, patted a Falstaffian
paunch, bubbled: *"Das ist schön"* and settled down to it in
a Rabelaisian way, understanding and even affection might
have been mingled with my astonishment. I had rejoiced in
my time at the beeves and tripes and coiro meadows of
Grangousier; I had regretted not knowing that friend of
Brillat-Savarin's who ate 144 oysters at hors-d'œuvres, then
pulled down the points of his waistcoat and said: "Now I am
ready for my dinner"; and I remembered, though she would
hardly have done as a permanent guest, King George III's
Queen Charlotte who said of a goose that it was "an unsatis-
factory bird—too much for one and not enough for two." But
this cadaverous man showed no gross pleasure; he had only
barely grunted in reply to my *"Guten Abend."* He merely

glared at his heap as though it was something under a microscope; refused vegetables; neglected his bread; and ploughed relentlessly through all. As I toyed with my ladylike portions and sipped my half-bottle of Rheinwein I remembered the long procession of history and the durability of racial memories. "Perhaps," I thought, along the lines of *tout comprendre est tout pardonner,* "this is all owing to the dreadful privations of the Thirty Years War." "Don't be so romantic," muttered my Demon to me, "this chap is probably underpaid for his Academic Work and is merely getting his money's worth."

Back in my carriage I found my charming companion getting ready for Berlin. Everything else was on the seat; her largest case she could not manage. I took it down for her. Her eyes sparkled with gratitude. She raised the green shroud of the canary's cage and said: "Tweet, tweet," to it. Then she lifted the cage against my face and attempted to persuade the apathetic bird, which had already made a longer non-stop journey than ever made Columbus, to say "tweet, tweet" to me. It would not. It remained as still as Niobe and I don't blame it. . . .

Lights glittered through the darkness. We were in a big city. We were slowing. We were in a crowded station. It was Berlin. . . .

She lurched out of the window, filling it. We passed a swarm of her relations and they ran in a pack to catch her up. We jerked to a stop. I was forgotten. Out she tumbled into multitudinous arms, stretched as over some joyous Acheron; and when at last I got away there was an admiring ring around the lobster and the canary.

*   *   *   *   *

I stayed in a humble, clean, new hotel. I saw little of it except at bed-time; the guests were provincial and inoffensive, pastors and such, with smiling solicitous wives. "Strange," thought I, "that I am in the middle of this Mark of Brandenburg, which has for centuries been eating Europe up like a maggot in a nut and is most certainly going to have a war with us soon,"—for I had been convinced since the Bosnian affair that there would be a fight over the inevitable break-up of the Dual Monarchy even if the flushed German rulers did not have their fling at us without an excuse from that quarter —"and all these people look as mild as old Herr Deutsch at school." But the more I talked to them the more childlike and lacking in sophistication I found them, especially the men; it dawned on me gradually, as I went from place to place, that their cheerfulness and even merriment was childlike, and their capacity for simple and unselfish obedience could be a vice rather than a virtue. Opinions seemed to sweep through them, like winds over a wheat field. The individual did not think for himself, though he thought he did; from one end of the country to the other people of all types, even pacific liberal old dons, told me that "the Cossacks" were going to attack them; when, later, they were told that "the Cossacks" had actually done so they were perfectly ready, Socialists and all, to believe it and that a "ring" had been formed round the injured innocents that they were. Even the best men amongst them seemed to be passionately convinced that it was enough to be German to be right, and that a guttural quotation from Goethe would make everything go down. . . .

Rupert Brooke had been there not long before and written *Grantchester* in the Café des Westens, now (for all I know) closed up, like other haunts of his "temperamentvoll German Jews." His cool radiance had passed through those smoky nocturnal haunts; the eager little journalists and poets all asked after him. A man was usually there, to whom I often talked in a corner while the others laughed over their wine, tall, fair, scholarly, moderate, a thoughtful Socialist. "You should get somewhere," I thought. After the post-war chaos I noticed that he was in the Cabinet. Where is he now? Dead? Exiled? In a concentration camp? . . .

I went to the Kaiser Friedrich Museum. The Flemish pictures were beautiful; but so, thought I, was the celebrated "Leonardo" bust of Flora.

Dr. Bode, the Director, discovered it; after a world-wide sensation some still small voice in England observed: "that was made in Portsmouth by Richard Cockle Lucas; he was a friend of mine and I saw him making it." There was the usual spate of comparative illustrations showing the Lucas style and the Leonardo smile; then, reluctantly, the Berlin authorities consented to an inquest, and, when the bust was opened, there was found, as it might be, a loud check waist-coat of sound British make. Dr. Bode stuck to his guns. The Kaiser (who had also adhered, through thick and thin, to the view that the twentieth century began in nineteen hundred) loyally backed him up. This was, perhaps, German Transcen-dentalism. . . .

One day, as I was walking down Unter den Linden, I saw cars speed to the Royal Palace. Out sprang a little thin uni-formed figure, saluted, and tripped up the steps between an avenue of uniformed Titans. It was the Crown Prince. . . .

One day I took tea with the Socialist Party at the Reichstag and "went on" to a Debate. Tea at the Reichstag was not at all like tea on the terrace at the House of Commons, where men of all parties, passing along the tables with relatives, friends or boring but useful constituents, will exchange greet-ings and call each other "Bill." In the great refectory of the Reichstag each party had a long table. Here was the Centre, there was a block of bristling Conservatives looking like little Hindenburgs, and the Jews, as it were, had no dealings with the Samaritans; it seemed strange to anyone fresh from Eng-land accustomed to seeing members of the Front Bench staring across the floor at their cousins and school friends.

An uglier lot than those Socialists I never set eyes on. Those who weren't Jewish professional men were, I suppose, Trade Union leaders. For that matter a row of British Trade Union M.P.s would hardly, at first sight, appeal to Praxiteles; but this lot appeared a case for Epstein. The truth is, I suppose, that as soon as one is confronted with gross ugliness in men of another breed it strikes one more forcibly than a similar degree of it in one's own more familiar countrymen. . . .

The Chamber presented to English eyes as strange a sight as the tea-room. Below me, in a circular theatre, ranged from Left to Right the Parties. Above them on the left was a Presidential desk; behind the President was a row of tall impassive officers, glittering with epaulettes and decorations, and looking as though they were prepared at any moment to emulate that great Parliamentarian Cromwell (whose statue so comically stands outside the House of Commons) and summon in troopers to turn out those members and take away their bauble. Probably they felt it, for, at great length, the wild Socialist Liebknecht was speaking. He was denouncing, and his facts were correct, grandees who had been selling military dignities. Every now and then there would be an angry roar. Little men would leap up. The Presidential bell would ring. Liebknecht would go on with his hoarse invective, shaking his fists. When I realized that, as this was not the French Chamber, there would not be a free fight, I departed.

My host on that occasion was Ludwig Frank, undisputed leader of the Socialist Party. He was a swarthy Jewish barrister in early middle age, with a handsome heavyish face, a considerable moustache, and dark penetrating secretive eyes. He had something of the withdrawn air of Ramsay Macdonald, but there seemed a surer brain behind his reserve; some resemblance in mien and manner to Karl Marx's French grandson Jean Longuet, but more resolution, power, and, perhaps, integrity. I was not surprised when he, who might, I suppose, easily have avoided service, was reported killed, a lieutenant, at Lunéville, in the first weeks of the war.

Three years after that he might have inadvertently given me a bad quarter of an hour. I was going over a shipyard, looking at some of the latest vessels, and was dubiously scrutinized both coming in and departing. I had an old coat on. As I left I felt in my pocket for a match and pulled out an unstamped envelope. My name, with a Berlin address, was on it. I was bewildered until I opened it. Inside, dateless and in German script and on Reichstag notepaper, was a letter from Frank asking me to come and see him. Had that been a day for some routine search I should have been badly incriminated. And would those rough men have paused in manhandling me to have allowed me to say: "Do please ring up Mr. Eddie Marsh at the Admiralty"? . . .

I saw, I think in a private house, a Vermeer of which I have
lost trace. I went to a music-hall and was told that the chief
jokes were about mothers-in-law and a suburb corresponding to
our Tooting. But after a week I had had enough of Berlin;
most of the works of man there, unless you can include the
Tiergarten, were so unprepossessing. I went to several
picture shows; they were full of feeble imitations of French
modernists, and hideous caricatures of purely local origin.
This was everywhere so; even the New Pinakothek at Munich
contained hardly a picture worth skying at the Academy. Of
the Victorian "classics" Böcklin, so celebrated because of his
Maeterlinckian "Toteninsel," turned out to be a ghastly oleo-
graphist when seen in colour, and Max Liebermann and his
modern peers quite third-rate. I still wonder if there has ever
been a good painter in Germany since Dürer and Altdorfer—
and those came, like the musicians, from places very, very far
from Berlin and Prussia.

The Sieges-Allée, that incredible avenue of patriotic sculptures, was so funny as to be worth keeping; the streets were
mechanically dull. There was a height limit for buildings
in Berlin; everybody built up to the limit and individuality
was forced to blossom out in a violent variety of façades. . . .

There was that melancholy East Prussian plain. At Dresden
there was the Madonna and the row of riverside palaces
marvellously duplicated indoors by Canaletto. At Leipzig
there was the Book Exhibition; even a German exhibition was
a wilderness of mud and unfinished buildings on the day, and
even then the English were put to shame by their rivals, the
English pavilion being a little mock Tudor thing adorned
with a few noble books like the Kelmscott Chaucer, but otherwise mainly filled with dingy leavings like *Jones on the Penta-
teuch,* which publishers hoped to sell, I suppose, to passers-by.
There was Nuremberg, the town, the foul Iron Maiden, and
the Germania Museum, where I passed two huge Germans and
a fair comfortable *Frau.* The lady bowed and smiled; the men
scowled—I suppose because the day before, on a slow run, she
had given me a banana, and some chocolate in the train. There
was Munich, the writhing red great Rubenses, like pictures

of fishermen's worms under a microscope, the superb *Battle of Issus* by Altdorfer, and the English Garden, a great flowery grass meadow, better than all shaven pleasaunces. There were evenings in cellars with students; there were dinners with dear little bearded Professor Sieper, who knew English Literature but talked of Cossack invasions. He it was who, when my money was lost in the still royal posts of Bavaria, lent me £20 to get home with. I returned it; not knowing then that that was prospectively an unpatriotic action. His memory was to keep me from a quite wholesale denunciation of "German Professors" during the war. I should have liked to have written to him later. It was impossible. By the end of the war he was dead.

There were the line after line of dark crags and castles by the Rhine. It was 1914 and the kings were on their thrones.

CHAPTER V

FENNY COMPTON TO STOCKTON LOCKS

I BREAKFASTED early and went out into the sun; it had risen and the wind had not yet.

Left and right along the canal nothing was in sight; the barge *Brahmapootra* had made her usual early start. Bliss had probably got into a conversation with his landlord; at all events, I had not arranged to call for him until ten and I walked up and down the tow-path smoking cigarettes and staring at the water.

I was longing for a swim in that far from pellucid canal. Swimming, I reflected, was in early years my chief amusement. It ran in the family. My mother was a strong swimmer; my sister, until she broke a leg on Dartmoor, was one of the best in the West, and still possesses cups for seven-mile races and for the swim from Plymouth Breakwater, for which she broke the record. I could never swim very fast but could go on a long time. The other day I cast eyes on a pretty gilded document, signed by a German gymnastic instructor, attesting that at eleven I had swum half a mile in the sea. This I tore up; one can't keep everything. But I still possess books (chosen by me with an allocation of a pound or two) which were a prize won in the quarter-mile race at school. One of them is a volume of Rossetti's Poems. I remember a master pretending to be mildly shocked and telling me I would get over it— Rossetti, I mean, not poetry. Swimming was the thing I most missed when I left the west. What is a swimming bath or a slow flat river to one who has smelt the freshness of deep pools under green boughs in the wooded rivers of Devon with their mossy boulders, foaming falls, and clear brown water? And how dull it is to wade slowly into the grey muddied seas of Sussex and the East Coast when all one's youth one has dived from rocks at the cliff base into green water, translucent many feet down with shells and pebbles inviting the plunge: And when, with change of scene from the wild to the tame, there came also a rapid increase in near-sightedness which, for the old clear images of tree and stream, rock and wave and distant shipping, substituted but unfocused blurs of the colours of sun, sky and sea, much more of the old joy went. . . .

So why, I thought, not have a swim, since I hadn't been able to have a bath, and defy all Sanitary Inspectors?

I went into the landlady and said: "I should like to swim in the Canal: is there any sort of bathing dress you could lend me?"

"Nothing of the sort, I'm afraid," she regretted, "unless I could dig out an old one of mine."

"But you were so resourceful about Mr. Bliss's pipe-cleaners from the hens; haven't you a few peacocks whose tails might do for a dress for me?"

"What time did you say you'd fetch your friend?" she asked.

"Ten," I said.

"It's about that now," she remarked, looking at the moon-faced timepiece above the bottles.

*   *   *   *   *

So it was. Consoled by the sudden reflection that I *had* swum at least once in the Oxford Canal, though not in pea-cocks' feathers, I packed my things, saw that Lord Harberton was not missing, and went to the garage. At the village inn, as I had surmised, Bliss was holding a little circle spell-bound. I had noticed a church spire above trees. "Do you mind," I ventured, "if I just go up to the church?"

"No," he said, not having looked at it, "it's no good at all. Quite modern and all restored," he added sweepingly. The time which I might have spent verifying his statements was spent on trying to make out the Latin inscription of a sundial which he had discovered stuck high up on a side wall. After this he took me inside again and went up for his kit.

I ordered a tankard for the wait. There was a countryman present, small, wrinkled and red. "What's the weather going to be like?" I asked him—the only possible gambit, for I knew it wouldn't be the slightest use asking him whether he had been to any theatres or picture-galleries lately.

He screwed his face up, unsteadily lifted his pot, looked like Sir Oracle, announced:

"Rain before seven
Shine before eleven,"

and drank deep.

"Come along, Squire," called Bliss as he scrambled into the room, "there's no time to waste. We must get on. A lot of locks to-day."

We said good-bye and drove back to the "George and Dragon" by the canal.

There was sunshine of sorts. Bliss remembered his camera which, hitherto, had been as neglected as the cider-keg and my own sketch-book—it really is better to "travel light." He brought out the landlord and landlady, stood me between them, bent over his box with peering eyes and shading hand, and snapped us three times—possibly all on the same film, but I don't know.

Once more we got afloat. There were eight miles to Marston Doles, the first lock of descent to the Avon Valley, and no

possible port of call before we got there. A head wind had
sprung up, and before long it freshened to such an extent that
we had to resort to towing. We towed all that morning, first
Bliss, then myself. All around the great bend by Worm-
leighton I took her. There were no villages, no houses, no
barges, no people; nothing but cows, birds, the wayside flowers,
and the steady wind under a sky which had become evenly,
greyly, overcast. For a quiet hour at a stretch I pulled her,
with my head down, for the wind was in my eyes. At first
I looked at the flowers by my feet, and listened to the distant
ripple behind me. Then the noise of the water talking made
me think of a story I had tried to write long ago and never
finished, in which trees and waters spoke in communion in
just such a lonely place and the rare human visitors were the
observed. . . .

A writhen old alder leant over a steep river, throwing a deep
shadow. Beyond the shadow the water poured over grey
boulders in the sun, and at the side of the largest there was
always a falling wave. It changed in shape and size and colour.
In winter when the branches of the tree were bared and
groaned in the wind it was a roaring cascade above lashing
rapids of foam and brown water. In summer it was a small
bubbling curve, with a wash of froth below it, twisting but a
little and tinkling peacefully day and night. But it was always
the same waterfall, which had not changed its shape or music,
except seasonably, since beyond the memory of man. It had
for company the great boulder. But the stone never spoke. In
winter it was wet with the torrent, and, anyhow, its voice could
not have been heard above the din; in summer, when its great
round head was high above the shrunken river, it was content with the warmth, and glistened speckily, and drowsed in
the sun. It was only to the tree that the waterfall talked, for
the flowers and grasses on the brim were small children of
a day, and the fish and water-rats were of another world
and had their own thoughts.

Naiad and dryad, not resentful of their imprisonment by
root and rock, they talked gently to each other whenever they
felt inclined. "What can you see?" the waterfall would ask,

for itself could see but little except the rocks, a fringe of fern and forget-me-not, and the changing sky above. And the alder would answer: "The cows are going home through the butter-cups and the evening smoke is rising from the farm." Men seldom came there, for there was neither road nor bridge, and behind the alder was a high wilderness of wood.

One afternoon in spring, when the air was as fresh as the earth, the waterfall asked: "What can you see?" and the alder answered: "The swallows are skimming the fields, there are geese by the farther gate. A car has stopped by the gate. Two people have opened the gate. They are coming this way. . . ."

Bliss's voice came from behind me, a distant halloo: "Squire."

I turned and shouted: "Yes."

"Shall I take on now?"

"Don't bother."

"Sure?"

"Yes, I'm quite happy. I'm trying to remember something."

"Anything I can help in?" cried the solicitous encyclopaedia.

"No, thank you."

*   *   *   *   *

For the moment I was back on the Oxford Canal. But the mechanical movement soon took me away again. I tried to recall what the end of that story had been intended to be. I think it was only that the young man and the girl came often, and talked quietly there, but in the end came no more. "Why hadn't I finished it?" I wondered.

Perhaps it was because I was too close to childhood then, too newly sophisticated, and had but a dim contact with my early animism. The child heard voices and could not repeat them; with the power of writing the vision was dimmed and the faith snapped. Perhaps I was afraid that it might be but a reflection of Hans Andersen, who remained such a child that he could never, for all his vanity, realize how unique was his genius.

There was nothing wrong with the animism and I need never have minded repaying my debt to Hans Andersen. As

I trudged on I remembered, as I never can except in solitude, away from towns, or sleepless at night, the imaginative discoveries, and aids to discovery, of early youth. Fairy-tales and tin-soldiers. Each of these institutions is now condemned by the sort of Public Asses who will solemnly tell solemn congresses that it is to-day definitely established that the human frame cannot flourish without a certain minimum of food and sleep. But the tin-soldiers gave me no desire to kill or be killed and the fairy-tales left me with sufficient incredulity to question many modern thinkers. It was always the romantic, the beautiful, the sad that I loved, never the macabre such as renders terrible the starker folk-tales of Grimm. It was one thing to wander through the forests of fairyland, the huts of woodcutters and the caves of kindly gnomes with Snow-White, or a young son of King or Tailor setting out to make his fortune; but it was another to creep under gnarled and darkling branches to the baleful lit windows of a charnel-house of sugar where babies were baked and eaten by an old woman. It was one thing to rescue Sabra from a dragon pre-destined to defeat, or to struggle through thickets of briar and thorn to wake the Sleeping Beauty with a kiss, but another to shiver all night with the Unshivering Man in that grim uninhabited Keep while the devils from hell dropped down the chimney dissected trunks, heads, legs and arms which joined together at the bottom. The wicked in Grimm had a real touch of the infernal about them; the ogres and giants of British legend were a clumsy and gullible crew who were no match at all for the various Jacks who climbed bean-stalks after them or sounded challenges at their donjon-gates. But after all, it should be remembered that to the brothers Grimm the nursery public was a fortuitous side-line. They were learned and industrious philologists, grammarians and comparative folklorists and no more inspired in their labours by the wide eyes of enchanted children than was their namesake, the encyclopaedic Baron.

The more brutal horrors, such tales as *The Man Who Could Not Shudder,* can never be mistaken for anyone but Grimm; many of the others are so mixed up in memory that I should hesitate ascription.. But I think that almost any paragraph from her writings would give me a clue to Madame d'Aulnoy, whose *The White Cat* was as good a fairy-tale by a sophisticated professional as anything except *Cinderella*. I never see her mentioned now; I don't know if she is even in print; my own copy was an old one of my mother's, and I naturally didn't notice, between six and eight or so, the name of the translator. But I read her over and over again, moved by the genuine light manner she had .of depicting tender and faithful love, delighted by her animals, and relishing (for her elaboration of décor was a novelty to me in books) her glittering trousseaux and the gold, diamonds, rubies, emeralds and pearls which she showered upon her palaces and people. I daresay, were I to look at them again now, I might find them oddly suggestive of fêtes at Versailles and the perukes and patches of her period. But I shall certainly take a chance again with *The White Cat* and *The Yellow Dwarf* if they come my way.

Hans Andersen came gradually, the shorter and simpler stories being loved first, the longer and more elaborate later. *The Ugly Duckling* and *What the Moon Saw* can be understood by very young children. They are all little animists (most poets retain something of that as of other childish traits) and find not only no difficulty in believing that ducks talk to each other in the water-meadows and mice in cathedrals at night, but naturally accept every object in Nature as alive, sentient and capable of human benignity and malevolence. The child who abuses a stone over which he has tripped as "a naughty stone" is not, or is not wholly, pretending or being facetious: the stone is alive and has power. So deep-rooted is this in us—and with what obscure connections with ultimate reality?—that I for one, if alone (especially in the country), exposing myself to all perception and instinct, and honestly examining myself, must admit (and not without a sense of mystery and awe) that, under the skin of reason and acquired "knowledge," there is an I who not only thinks of every tree and flower as a person, but of every leaf as a person (and no two of them, through all eternity, have ever been the same), and even of every stone as a person. I pick up a rounded pebble or a jagged stone and it is itself, with its own shape and its own obstinate vitality. If I split a stone in two there are two persons; if I pound it into sand every grain of the sand exists still as an individual; as I naturally perceive things there is no boundary between organic and inorganic, but merely a graduation of qualities like the graduation of colours in the spectrum; a music-hall line like the old "Pretty little pansy faces" (though I might have worded it better and given it a better tune) doesn't appear to me in the least peculiar when I am looking at the flowers. All sailors feel of the sea as a person—the feeling permeates the writings of Conrad—but so seems each separate wave breaking over the bows or crashing and spreading and fading and receding and regathering on the sands. The waves, the winds, the stars to children, savages, saints, lunatics, lovers and poets all talk together; and it is nothing that lead soldiers at night should strut about and chat with china shepherdesses.

The longer, more serious stories of Andersen became more and more loved as I grew older, could feel pathos, and the exaltation of tragedy and luxuriate in descriptions of landscape as background and as a thing in itself. Even were I to wander in chill winter twilights by woodland and marshland and sea, lamenting reeds and sky-reflective lakes, in the more solitary parts of Jutland, I should never see it all more vividly than I do already because of Andersen read in childhood, when it was all a setting for sad Kings and lost lovers, ice-maidens, mermaids and wild swans.

*   *   *   *   *

There was a shout from Bliss: "Look ahead." Subconsciously I had seen it, though my thoughts had been far away; men have been known to drive cars quite safely in their sleep. We went through the first lock at Marston Doles; as we approached the second he said: "Hi! Let's get in to the bank here and see if we can find some lunch."

Set back from the left bank were two brick cottages with barns behind. "You go and ask," suggested Bliss. "You're younger than I am."

I went up, knocked at one front door, then at the other, and had no response from either. Wandering round the back I got an answer at last. A door opened and a pretty young woman appeared with a blond boy of one in her arms.

"I'm so sorry to trouble you, but could you conceivably let us have something for lunch. There are two of us in a canoe."

"I'm dreadfully sorry, but there's nothing in the house. I've got to fetch everything on my bicycle, and to-morrow's my day."

"But it's miles before we can get anything. Haven't you even bread and cheese?"

"Well, yes, we've got that. But are you sure that would be enough for you?"

"Rather! Just what we wanted."

"And I've nothing but cider."

"It's exactly what we like; we've been drinking it all the way in our canoe."

"Well, I'm sure you're welcome, if you don't really mind."

Cheered, I fetched Bliss. "Well done," he said. In the kitchen he shook hands with the girl, and patted the baby on the head. In the parlour he looked at the music on the piano and admired some floral designs in coloured silks and gold thread which were hanging on the walls. When the cloth was laid, he sat himself at the head of the table, rubbed his hands and said: "This is splendid. There isn't a pub within miles. We're in clover."

We certainly were. This Samaritan woman had a great gift for meiosis. She walked in time after time with dishes, plates, knives, forks and cruets. We weren't in the least taking the last crust from a cupboard which would be bare until the next bicycle expedition. The bread and the cheese were there; but so were butter and pickles; so were biscuits; so was a salad of lettuce, tomatoes and hard-boiled eggs; and so was a dish filled with cut pieces of chicken and ham; and so were certain bottles of cider.

"Magnificent," said Bliss, as the lady closed the door, asking, as she went, if we would like coffee; "Good Lord, Squire, this is far better than anything we should have found in the pubs round here." Then we set to, he especially.

The coffee came; the door closed again; we settled down in comfortable chairs for a smoke.

"And what," asked Bliss, "was it that you were thinking about all that time on the tow-path?"

"Oh, childhood, and Hans Andersen. This sort of trip rather throws one back to it all. In the normal rush one never thinks of anything but the present."

"Farther off from heaven than when you were a boy," suggested Bliss, encouragingly.

"In a way, yes," I replied. "Did you ever see my adaptation of that?"

"I can't say I did," he replied. "I don't read you modern chaps much."

I told him verses which I had written which were entitled merely *Metempsychosis,* but which German psychoanalysts might diagnose as expressing an even deeper-seated ganglion than Hood's:

> I remember, I remember,
> The last time I was born.
> I had four feet, I had a tail,
> I had a crumpled horn;
> And what a placid life I led!
> I never laughed or wept,
> All day, head down, I munched the grass,
> At night I simply slept.
>
> I did not drink, I did not smoke
> Too many cigarettes,
> Nor gamble on the Stock Exchange,
> I never ran up debts;
> I never sat up much too late,
> Holding the worst of cards,
> I did not try to understand
> The works of modern bards.
>
> My thoughts were white and innocent,
> As was my language too;

I never was provoked beyond
   A mild melodious moo.
In fact I was impeccable,
   And sorry am I now
To think I'm farther off from heaven
   Than when I was a cow.

Bliss knitted his brows. "I'm very fond," he said ruminatively, "of that laburnum, and the little window where the
sun came peeping in at morn."

"So am I," I assured him, "and I've seldom sinned to the
extent of parodying an actual good poem. I can't approve of
what Harry Graham did, for instance."

"What did Harry Graham do?"

"What he did was this:

I will arise and go now, and go to Inverness,
And a small villa rent there, of lath and plaster
   built;
Nine golf-clubs will I have there, and don my
   native dress,
And walk aloud in a b—— loud kilt.

Bliss laughed heartily. Then "We must be going on," he
said.

When we went into the kitchen we were asked if we had
been satisfied. "Splendid," we replied in chorus. "How much
do we owe you?" I asked.

"Would a shilling be too much?" shyly enquired the mistress
of the house, blushing, the baby in her arms and its cheek to
hers.

"Good heavens," protested Bliss, "but the cider cost that."

"Oh, I forgot the cider," was the meek reply. "You see, I've
never done this before." We settled it somehow.

     *   *   *   *   *

After that lunch we laboured. There were eight locks down-
hill to Napton. There we went ashore, though there was a

slight drizzle of rain. It is a picturesque place. There are two high lumps, on one a windmill, on the other a church with a village straggling down from its foot. It is a fine church; sadly finer than other churches which are to be built in the diocese, if one is to judge from a garish pink sketch of one attached to a Building Fund Appeal which we found everywhere in those parts. Back on the Canal we found ourselves after two miles unpleasant paddling in the rain at the junction of the Napton and Warwick Canal, now a section of the Grand Union. The wind was terrific, and, even when we were towing, the canoe kept on blowing into the bank. Three-quarters of a mile in those broader waters and we encountered the first three of the Calcott locks—it was a day of locks, and a strenuous day, for, with a head wind, we did about twenty-one miles and almost as many locks.

We were now, until we should reach the portage to the Avon, on a different, more imposing, and less attractive stretch of water, and Bliss (but of that later) stopped prophesying Kingfishers. The Grand Union Canal is now a great water highway, which, for a space, the Oxford Canal joins. Barges in pairs, petrol-driven, one tugging the other, come up from London, via Uxbridge, Rickmansworth, Berkhamsted, Tring, Fenny Stratford and Wolverton (where the infant Ouse is crossed) to Blisworth and so to the five miles which is shared with the Oxford Canal, and so to Warwick and Birmingham. No longer on that common stretch did we find ourselves high in a solitary land, with sedgy banks, rare horse-drawn barges and venerable locks. Here the locks have been rebuilt. The old narrow locks are closed; locks double their size are built alongside—why they couldn't have widened the old ones I cannot say. The banks are stiffened with concrete; we were reminded of the industrial England which we had forgotten.

We had been aiming at Long Itchington, the first village. But locks take time, and at Stockton there are eleven close together, descending in a ladder, a hill-forest of uprights. After the fifth or sixth, it being past six and the wind chill, we came to an inn on the left, and stopped in the hope of beds. It was a hospitable place, the bar populous with dogs; but they had no room, and recommended "The Blue Lias" beyond the next bank. At the name we looked at each other; I spoke for both: "Is Lias a misprint or some outlandish heraldic beast?"

Then it dawned on us simultaneously that it was a kind of limestone; the name was odd, all the same, as though an inn were to be called "The Ham Stone" or "The Purbeck Marble."

We paddled fiercely on, landed again, and found ourselves in a little bar-parlour with a roaring fire. Grandmother was playing patience on a bare table, mother was knitting, granddaughter was playing with toys by the fire. One workman was in a corner with a pint of beer. We joined him. Yes, we were told, there were plenty of rooms; the place used to drive a fine trade and so did the several inns thereabouts; but it was quiet now, all the hundreds of quarrymen having gone with the closing of the quarry.

"Foreign competition, I suppose," I said jumping to a conclusion usually safe.

"No," explained the landlady, "the blue lias was worked out."

Bliss was now in two moods about finishing all that series of locks that night, late or not. He stepped outside with his pipe for reflection, and I followed. No sooner had we got out than a barge came by. There was a man standing on it who shouted: "Bliss!"

"Lawrence," Bliss shouted back.

Lawrence landed and joined us. "I thought," he said, "from your letter that I might find you somewhere hereabouts. I've arranged for you to be put up at the bottom of the locks."

That settled it; we said good-bye to the "Blue Lias." Lawrence got into the canoe, and I went across to the tow-path, now on the right. As they laboured through the locks I continued to count them. Bliss thought there were so many locks at Stockton, his book seemed to say something else, my own count of eleven differed from both.

At the inn we moored the canoe under a road-bridge wall. Inside, while our bacon and eggs were being prepared, we peered into a smoky crowded bar. The crew of the *Brahma-*

K*

pootra were playing darts with others; they waved to us.

Supper was enjoyable. At ten Lawrence said good-night and went off in his car to Leamington. We thought we might turn in. The crowd had gone, and we asked the landlord to show us our rooms.

He was astonished: "Rooms? Why, we haven't got any rooms here."

"But our friend said he had arranged for us to stay here."

"He said you were coming but nothing about sleeping. There must be a misunderstanding."

"Can't you give us some kind of a shakedown?"

"We've no accommodation. Nobody's ever stayed here."

We couldn't plod back to the "Blue Lias" and knock them up in the dark. "We shall have to tow on to Warwick all night," I said to Bliss.

The landlord relented. He arranged for us somehow. Residential amenities were deplorably lacking; but, in the circumstances, all we could do was to thank our stars for beds, and the landlord for his kindness.

CHAPTER VI

Stockton Locks to Warwick

In the morning there was no water to wash in but there were pools of it on the ground and plenty more in the sky; it had rained all night.

Bliss at breakfast pored over his manual *Canoeing.*

"I have promised," said he, "to meet Lawrence on the towpath where we have to make the portage down from the canal into the Avon. He'll be there between twelve and one and he'll help us down with the canoe. There's a hill, very steep, bumpy, and covered with trees and bushes."

"How far is that from here?"

"Seven or eight miles."

"With this wind we shall have to tow a lot to make the distance."

"I'm afraid we shall; apart from anything else there are a lot of locks. How many are there? I should think ten," he went on, warming up to one of his favourite themes. "There's the five Bascot locks, the three Fosse Way locks, the two Radford Semele locks. The second of the Bascot locks is a double or "two-step" lock, as they call it. Two-step locks are fairly common. But on the Leeds and Liverpool Canal there are several three-step locks and one five-step lock. . . ."

I thought of Hamlet's father and "thy knotted and combinèd locks."

    *   *   *   *   *

It rained intermittently. We paddled with difficulty as far as the Bascot locks; after that I towed. At first the canal (which at one point crossed the Itchen by aqueduct) was pretty enough. After the last lock there were three or four miles of increasing ugliness, and I towed doggedly, occasionally wiping my spectacles and throwing away a cigarette dowsed by a fat plunk of rain. Once I boarded to see if we could possibly make headway paddling. It was a dreary stretch with one concrete bank and the horizon ahead dominated by a great mass which looked like a brewery, and occasional patches of scrubby overhanging bushes the only signs of a kindlier nature. Then an odd thing happened.

Not all that morning had Bliss said "Here or hereabouts we ought to see a kingfisher." It hadn't even occurred to him. But suddenly in front of me I saw a blue flash above the water. "Look, Bliss," I sang out, "there's a kingfisher!"

"Where?" he said, as it disappeared.

"There!" I said, as it reappeared.

"God bless my soul, so it is," said he.

"And there's another, and another, and another."

It was true. There, in the one ugly and semi-industrial stretch we had seen, with a constant traffic of motor-barges, were four kingfishers quartering the canal, moving ahead at our pace, their many colours merging in a sort of even Cambridge blue. They were in sight for a full two hundred yards and then vanished. "All I can say," muttered Bliss, "is that they've got a strange taste in scenery."

"All that remains now, Bliss," I said, "is for us to see our first yellow iris growing under the brewery wall." We did not. That did not come until we were being stranded and swirled about in a rapid on the Avon.

I landed and resumed the tow-rope. It was raining; the scenery was depressing; one was merely doing a job. The tow-path ran through a part of Leamington. There were foundries, brick-works and smutty little bridges; machinery clanked and pipes jetted clouds of white steam against the drizzly sky. Bedraggled women stared at us from the doors of squalid houses; three sinister children marched with me shouting and sneering; the canal was scattered with motionless cabbage-leaves, sheets of dirty paper, and skins of fruit. I remembered what the mistress of the *Brahmapootra* had said to me about the manners of town children.

Surprise mingled with my disgust. I wonder how many of the inhabitants of Leamington know of the existence of such a quarter. Royal Leamington Spa, indeed! The British Hom-burg, with its springs and pump-rooms and assembly-rooms, stucco terraces, palm-lounges and antique shops; its utterly decorous gout, obesity, neuritis, eczema, and dyspepsia! It was odd to think of my last visit there, and sitting, in a large lounge full of colonels and old knitting ladies, discussing Thackeray over sherries.

The squalor at last faded behind us. Soon we approached the aqueduct and saw Lawrence waiting on the right bank. He stepped aboard gingerly (for the canoe was not intended for three men and luggage) and we gently paddled across. A barge approached. We watched it go by—for we should see canal barges no more.

There is a touch of grandeur about that spot. Far below, the Avon runs through a rocky wooded ravine; the canal carries over a miniature Pont du Gard. We got out, decanted the luggage on the verge, and proceeded to take the canoe down the embankment. It was a difficult job; she had, except when she got stuck in a bush or against a trunk, to be held back. The others were ahead, I hanging on at the rear. The sodden slopes were not made for rubber soles; twice I slithered and fell down unpleasantly. The embarkation from a high slimy bank (after we had scrambled up and down again for the baggage) was awkward also. However, it was managed and we waved good-bye.

"I say!" exclaimed Bliss, when we were well afloat and paddling hard towards Warwick, "we forgot and he forgot! How on earth is Lawrence going to get back to his own side of the canal and his car!"

"I suppose he'll manage it somehow and some time."

I suppose he did.

*　　　*　　　*　　　*　　　*

It is not much over a mile from the aqueduct to Warwick Bridge and, although the stream scarcely moved over its weeds, we were there in less than a quarter of an hour. We saw no ordinary boat-house; but above the bridge there was a sort of Corporation Club House on the water-front of the trim public gardens. The keeper was absent, doubtless at lunch, so we couldn't ask permission; but we left her with the luggage and climbed up the steps into the town.

"Do you know Warwick well?" enquired Bliss as we walked towards the hill.

"Fairly well," I admitted.

"I know it like the palm of my hand," he remarked. "Where is this 'Crown' place you said you knew?"

"In the middle of the town."

"In that case we turn down here to the left," he asserted, pointing to the lovely lane of half-timbered houses which shelters under the castle rock.

"We don't. That leads to a dead end."

"You're wrong, my dear chap. Come along."

I let him have his way. We came to the dead end. He stared, tugged at his moustache, looked abashed, for the first time since I have known him, and mumbled "I was wrong and you were right." I exercised iron self-control and kindly said, "But aren't these old houses lovely?" My only reward was that he said: "What's come over you? You are strangely forbearing!"

As we got back into the main road he stopped and, as one seeing dawn, said: "We are now in the Flower's country; come, hurry now, it's nearly two," and led me into the "Castle Inn" for a pint of Sir Archibald's brew, which is worthy of Shakespeare's birthplace, whence it comes. Then we went to the "Crown," where the welcome was cheerful and the rooms booked. We lunched and I fetched the luggage in a taxi.

Bliss had arranged to spend the rest of the day and evening with friends in Leamington; and I was left, till next morning, at what the unresourceful call "a loose end," but which I think of as a space of absolute freedom which only finds us unprepared because, in an age so cramped by diaries and "dates" and obligations, so inured to running on rails, it comes so rarely. Habit, indeed, did at first lead to me wonder whom I would ring up and go to see. I got so far as fetching the local telephone-book. Then I suddenly said to myself: "I'm hanged if I do. I can dine out whenever I like at home. Until I go to bed I do whatever, and go wherever, I feel at the moment inclined."

Just then I found that the inclination (I was in a cosy corner of the now deserted bar with a shining tankard by me) was to go on perusing the telephone-book. There is a good deal of instruction and amusement to be got out of telephone-books. There are the strange trades: I once encountered in the London Book a subscriber who entered himself as "bug-eradicator." There are the strange names of people. There are the very peculiar titles of companies. At one time in the London Book there was one entitled, if my memory is accurate, "Abandoned Artesian Wells Reclaimed and Successfully Completed Ltd." It must have been difficult for its clients to remember that they had to look it up under "Abandoned," not under "Artesian," and annoying to find that when they had got its whole title off their chests their three minutes was nearly up. The entry has now, like the wells, been abandoned; either the company has succumbed under its load of nomenclature or else, as I trust, it has flourished and merely taken a briefer alias. I find consolation now in "Activated Sludge Ltd." When I first discovered it, thoughts of Browning and possessed mediums crossed my mind; later I was, and am, bewildered. Doubting my eyes I went to Victoria Street to verify the fact. There it was right enough: a brass plate at the foot of one of those grimly metallurgical staircases. I didn't like to go in and ask them what they did; so I walked away thinking that, perhaps, if anything stood in need of activation it would be sludge.

That "Ltd." reminds me of more sport which one can have with these directories. The Postmaster-General is a Pastmaster-General in the art of Abbreviation. The old inventors of "Jno.," "Jas.," "Wm.," and "Thos." would have welcomed him to their company. Years ago, wanting to go to see a friend, I looked his address up in the Telephone Book and found it was "Ptrs" something; I had to trouble a toll-call to him to find out which was the correct solution. I then broke into song on the subject of Post Office Shorthand, thus:

> To-day I thought I'd like to look
>   Once more at Cousin Jane;
> I sought her st. in the Telephone bk,
>   They said 'twas Ptrs. la.
> But was it Potter's, Peter's, what?
>   How was a man to know?
> I had to wander to the spot
>   And ask the G.P.O.
>
> Had there not been a G.P.O.
>   Which knew of Cousin Jane
> (If I may slangily put it so)
>   I'd have been dn. the drn.
> Well "drn" should be written "dra," maybe,
>   For a pretty little lump like "stn."
> Officially works out, you see,
>   To rhyme with "destination."
>
> "Works," do I write? No, "wks" I mean,
>   For "Wks" are everywhere—
> Mtr. and lthr. and mrgrn.,
>   In av. pl. and sq.

The engrs. have wks. galore,
 And he who has no wks.
Keeps a gnl. shp. or a gnl. sto.,
 Or perhaps in a grg. lurks.

Oh, what a swarming life persists
 In the English countryside!—
The dntsts., the tbcnsts.,
 The frmrs., England's pride;
The mdcl. practnrs.,
 The dlrs. and the drprs.,
And those useful men, the bkslrs.,
 Who are agts. for nwsprs.

My solr. lives in chambrs. packed,
 My landlord in a gnge.,
Which rhymes (surprising, but a fact)
 In this wk. to Crn. Exch.:
My plmbr. he dwells in Bggns Ct.,
 My srgn. in Knlwth. ho.,
And I fear that, if pressed, in the last resort,
 They'd sink to "Mcky. Mo."!

But the Telephone-Book is for casual dipping, not for sustained reading; it would not, I think, be anyone's choice, as some choose Shakespeare or Montaigne, for sole refreshment on a desert island. I put it back, and sauntered out into the street and made vaguely for St. Mary's Church. I did not want to revisit the Castle. The exterior of that great mass, perched on its woody precipice over river and park, is one of the most majestic things in Europe; the countless rooms inside are mostly later and their contents mostly much later. But there was a tomb in the church which I wanted to see again for admiration of a man and recovery of an inscription.

The tomb is that of Fulke Greville, Lord Brooke, from whose cousin Robert spring the modern Earls of Warwick, and a poet of sombre intellectual magnificence. The inscription he wrote for himself, describes himself as "Servant to

Queene Elizabeth, Concellor to King James, Frend to Sir Philip Sidney." What a tribute to both Sidney and Greville is that! When Greville died, Sidney had been in his grave for forty-two years, but his memory was still cherished after great lapse of time and change of fortune, for Greville became Chancellor of the Exchequer and died at seventy-four.

The two went to school at Shrewsbury on the same day; Sidney proceeded to Oxford, Greville to Cambridge; later, they united in London in that circle of courtly poets which included Sir Edward Dyer and centred round the pedantic and pugnacious Gabriel Harvey. They might have fallen together at Zutphen; but Elizabeth forbade Greville to go; he lived to write Sidney's life and died piteously, murdered by a servant whom he had omitted from his will.

Sitting in those solitary shades I thought of Sidney cut off so young and the futility of mankind's perpetual wars. We have known one on a scale of which Sidney never dreamed. I thought of school friends and college friends in that far time before an end was made of our youth—the end of young manhood, the end of a world and the end of a sodality. To people who were fifty when the war broke out it came as an interruption, however long, terrible and fraught with change. To us, who were thirty or less, it came as an end. We had no careers or long associations behind us, only beginnings, first sortings and plans, discoveries of friendship. The war broke on us, destroying, invalidating. Our youth went prematurely, we were scarred before our time by the griefs of age, we had to face a new world when we were just beginning to be acclimatized to an old one. And for half of us the parting from youth was more bitter and final, for to those bones there is no return, even in imagination, to lost things; no remembering, with every pang and outline softened in the gold-dusty air of illusion, the joys and sorrows that were, and the faces, serious or laughing, of those who strayed through courts that strangers now inhabit and by streams that still so brightly and indifferently flow. Sometimes to those of my generation who survived—only sometimes, and those who died would never have wished it so—sad retrospect is an irresistible temptation

and our minds are full of useless "ifs." The mood was habitual
with Edward Thomas who was killed at forty as a gunner,
having written, hacking and neglected, as good prose as any
man of his time, and bloomed into lovely poetry in his last few
years. He talked of the village cross-roads, the smithy and the
aspen:

> That ceaselessly, unreasonably, grieves,
> Or so men think who like a different tree.

But there is something in the spirit of man which has survived
the Dark Ages, the Tartar invasions, the floods of the Yellow
River and God knows what calamities before, which still holds
to hope and thinks the fight worth waging, mysterious though
may be our destiny beyond Time, and vile though the visages
of hatred, fear and the lust for pain and blood.

Meanwhile, I thought, in that noiseless haunt of generations,
men, when weary of fighting in the eternal struggle between
love and justice, hate, violence and fear, fall back on the consolations of the grave, lacking the larger hope, the faith which
can ignore the mountains of iniquity in the world. Those
phrases of Landor—though they are not from the dialogue he
wrote between those actual two, Greville and Sidney—returned
to my ear: "There are no fields of amaranth on this side of the
grave; there are no voices, oh Rhodope, that are not soon mute,
however tuneful; there is no name, with whatever emphasis of
passionate love repeated, of which the echo is not faint at last."

I wondered, as I contemplated the emblems of Fulke
Greville's mortality, who had written that majestic chant "O
miserable condition of humanity," where that passage had last
come into my mind. It was in the downstairs smoking-room
of the Athenæum Club.

I had gone there to lunch alone one day late in 1935; the
place was full and I was lucky to find an empty table-for-two
near the windows. Just after I had sat down I felt a hand on
my shoulder and heard a gentle voice saying: "Do you mind if
I join you?" "Of course not," I said, not realizing who it was;
there appeared before me the short figure of Kipling, and that
celebrated face, with the bushy tricorne of eyebrows and

moustache and the eyes peering curiously behind the thick lenses of his spectacles. He sat down.

"This is most. extraordinary!" I exclaimed, "for only last night I finished reading the whole of your works in the pocket edition."

"What on earth," he laughed, "did you want to do that for?" I did not lamely explain that *Kim* was one of the greatest novels in the language and that. . . . We began talking of the books of other men.

When we had finished he suggested coffee in the smoking-room, and the talk went on briskly. At three, when the crowd had vanished and left us alone in the room with one somnolent elder, he said: "Why not stay and have some tea?" "All right," I replied, "but I'd better ring up my secretary," which I did. At half-past four we had tea; at half-past five he ordered sherry; in short, I just managed to catch my train that winter's eve at half-past six. I never spent a more agreeable five hours' tête-à-tête in my life.

I had first met him many years before at a garden-party, met him then at rare intervals in London, and had sometimes corresponded with him, but I had never been alone with him before.

He shunned public appearances and the popular idea of him as a tough and arrogant flag-wagger was very false. His delight in physical prowess and daredevilry was probably accentuated by the fact that, small and very short-sighted, he had from boyhood never been much good at the sports and games in which he would have liked to excel. The vigour of his invective (which in life was mingled with a disarming humour) and the lusty heartiness of his Imperial opinions were made more emphatic by reaction against æsthetes, library doctrinaires, sentimentalists, and Padgett M.P.s, who feared, shrank from, evaded, or ignored what seemed to him the facts of life created by "the God of Things as they Are." These people, those who disdained the beauty of strength and courage, those who corrupted the ignorant with political theories evolved in libraries, those who laid down the law about peoples and countries they had never seen, those who despised men of action, those of whom he asked, "What can they know of

England who only England know?" annoyed him so much
that he had to annoy them back, causing the æsthetic flesh to
creep with his lusty journalistic jingles and maddening his
political bugbears with his scathing contempt and his ostenta-
tious admiration for all the "he-men" whom they hated and of
whom they were secretly jealous.

That surface of him, so amusingly caricatured by Mr. Max
Beerbohm in his drawing of him with "Britannyer 'is gurl,"
dancing on Hampstead Heath, she wearing his bowler, he
wearing her helmet and blowing blasts on a tin-trumpet, was
but a surface. Underneath was a vigorous thinker with a soft
heart, a lyric poet with a touch of Puck; the utterer of so many
salutes to adventure had a streak of the quietist; the popular
journalist was deeply and widely read in all our old literature.

In his writings he wore his learning so lightly that most
people never noticed it. I remember when he wrote his story
about "Janeites" a critic saying to me: "Whoever would have
thought that Kipling read Jane Austen!"

But that day (he must have been an omnivorous reader
in youth) we talked of every sort of author, including the
obscurest Elizabethan and eighteenth-century poets. There
was nothing he did not remember; the talk was fully shared;
and his modesty equalled his still youthful enthusiasm. In the
end we got to the poems of Landor, whose craftsmanship, we
agreed, was not to be surpassed. He glowed with pleasure
when I said that his epigram, "To Lyde" was worthy of
Landor. Then he leant towards me, looked round in mock
fear of being overheard in a monstrous confession, and whispered: "His poems, yes; but, though I know it's dreadful to
say so, his prose bores me stiff."

I admitted that for the rest of my life I should probably
admire most of it from a distance. Then came back to me
that address of Rhodope which had long haunted me, and I
quoted it.

"Yes," he said, "if that kind of artificial prose has to be
written it couldn't be done more beautifully"; and we fell to
talk about Pater, Burton and Sir Thomas Browne, most
elaborate of all but least self-conscious. . . .

Six o'clock approached. I got up. "Well," he said, "I hope we shan't miss each other next year in Sussex as we did last summer."

"We might have met long before next year if you hadn't refused."

"When was that?"

"The Savile Club wanted to give you a dinner this Christmas. After all, in the days of R.L.S. and Henley it was your home. Can't you come?"

"No, I can't."

"Why?"

"The place is too full of ghosts."

I did not dream that within a few weeks he, too, would be a ghost, and his voice, too, a dying echo.

*   *   *   *   *

I left the church thinking of that talk, of Greville's Poems (the Folio of which I once possessed before I shed at once my old books and my desire for them), and of that talk which had revived in us both, the older poet and the younger, our early zest in books and the sounds of words. I strayed to the river again and, leaning over the parapet, smoking uncounted cigarettes, tried to recover early experiences; thinking of the first books, not school-books, which had made impression on me, the dawn of the literary sense and the collecting passion. But I could get my memories into no sort of order.

My first books were those of my time, apart from those fairy tales which were so much more in vogue then than now. There were the usual childish stories and pretty picture books; Caldecotts and Kate Greenaways I had in plenty. Of the books about machines with which the modern child is familiar there were none, unless one can count a volume from which I used to copy drawings of the rigs of schooners, brigantines, cutters, ketches and yawls. With engines I had but one brief connection and that a bitter one. I had seen a "real" one, a solid-looking affair demanding "real" steam in a window, begged for it, and was commended to the money-box. Altogether too much went into the money-box, including a golden sovereign which a tall man gave me at Queen Victoria's First Jubilee and which I imagined I should be allowed to "bust." In time the pounds were accumulated and the engine was bought. I was too young to be allowed to handle it myself, so a neighbour's coachman was called in to get steam up. He must have done something wrong with valves; anyhow there was an explosion, and engine and tender went into a cupboard which was the limbo of broken toys.

My martial side was ministered to by a book called *Land Fights and Sea Battles;* at seven I knew a sight more about Sluys, Crécy, Van Tromp, Opdam, the Glorious First of June, Badajoz, Talavera, the Chesapeake and Shannon, and the Malakoff Redoubt than I ever shall know again.

The dawn of a literary sense I think I can precisely fix, so far as concerned the colour and sound of words; in each instance I believe I was encountering for the first time the words which fascinated me.

I was staying in the country with relatives and there was a room, little used, full of books. There was a good deal of litter from the eighteenth century, of which I remember only Stackhouse's Bible (familiar also to Charles Lamb's childhood) with its naïve pictures of the spiral Tower of Babel, of a cradled Moses in luxuriant bulrushes, of a Noah's Ark with booby animals looking out of the portholes, and of the Israelites worshipping a peculiarly asinine Golden calf, who looked sideways, as though abashed at being set on so undeserved a pedestal, and, in spite of an adequate festoon of leaves, screened his middle in the pudent manner of the Venus de' Medici. There were books about The Horse and The Dog and one called the *Muck Manual,* of which I was recently delighted to buy, from a sixpenny box, a copy for the sheer delight of its title, which would do for so very many modern novels. But mainly I remember great sets. There was the *Dictionary of National Biography.* I doubt if anybody in the house had opened it before myself, but a book was a book to me and I dabbled freely in it, though all I can remember is finding that persons of my own name had cut very little figure in the national life. There were one or two obscure bishops, I think, but the most outstanding celebrity was one Richard Squire, of Squire's Plot. He attempted to poison Queen Elizabeth by putting an envenomed pin upside down on her saddle. Considering the bulk of Gloriana's petticoats the gentleman must have been an optimist. Anyhow he was caught and suffered the usual fate of such.* There were also complete ranges of *Punch* and *The Illustrated London News,* of which last I retain pictures of the launch of the *Great Eastern* and of the American Civil War with its Frenchified uniforms, and of the end of Maximilian of Mexico. And there was a set of bound volumes of what I think was the *Graphic*.

At all events, in one of the last volumes—I suppose it was in 1890 or 1891, and I was six or seven—I came across Rider Haggard's *Cleopatra* as a serial. I can hardly have heard of either Haggard or Cleopatra (unless in connection with pearls in vinegar) at that time. I must have read all day; I was blamed afterwards for not turning up at meals; everybody thought I had gone out, and expeditions to scour the country-side for me were being organized. But I had read the story through (the only serial, I think, that ever I did read, and back numbers hardly count) and returned again and again to a picture with a sentence inscribed. The picture showed an aged Egyptian priest staring blankly at the heavens; the inscription beneath said, I think, "He gazed at the skies with sightless orbs," and it was the word "orbs" which hypnotized me, by virtue of something inherently suitable and sinister in it.

Some time later I stayed just outside Exeter with a widowed great-aunt. She wore black satin, a locket of jet and gold, and a lace cap; she spent most of her time doing crochet in her crowded drawing-room. The whole house was early Victorian; the dining-room dominated by a vast oil painting full of helmed, kilted and bearded warriors carrying off screaming

---

* History is so full of cruelty and blood that I was once cheered to read a Royal Proclamation of Elizabeth bound up with a contemporary edition of Holinshed. The populace was assured that the executed were unconscious before they suffered the last barbarities of the law. It seems that public opinion was ahead of the law in those days as later, under the Georges, when in order to avoid capital sentences juries used to decide that valuable things were only worth a shilling or so.

and exposed women. On the frame was written "The Rape of the Sabines"—a puzzler for me, as there were two words in it of which I did not know the meaning. Perhaps the painter's name was on it. Perhaps, even, the inscription said "after Rubens," but I didn't know at that stage that painters had names, except for one's aunts who signed water-colours "all very fine and large," as the song of the time had it. I can even feel pretty sure of the first eminent painter's name I did know. In a window, at Exeter or elsewhere, I saw a large dark picture of some brigandish and hairy men with flagons and glasses before them and the chiaroscuro doing its uttermost with one tall glass of deep red wine; and underneath was the name "M. A. Caravaggio," and my mind recorded it. So, though Michael Angelo Caravaggio was not as great as his predecessor Michael Angelo Buonarroti, I heard of him first, and he stirred me first, never see his name without emotion, and for his sake like all the dark painters of his period, and keep a Bassano in my study.

Well, at my great-aunt's there was no one else but a middle-aged daughter, and I cannot remember another child coming. There was a garden to play in where time doubtless passed quickly as I ate bay-leaves, watched spiders spinning on the dusty bushes, stared at bees and wasps on syringa blossoms and sundry shrubs, noticed the glossiness of some leaves and the soft wrinkles of others, searched for "woolly bears," and the fat green purple-and-white striped caterpillars of the privet-hawk, shook out currant moths and others from bushes, looked for small insects on grass stems and rummaged in the tool-shed. But there was also an attic full of things disused, broken-down chairs, tarnished mirrors, picture-frames chipped and plastery, and hundreds of superannuated books.

Years later, when I was passing through as an elderly school-boy, she (then nearly ninety) told me I could "take the lot," as nobody else wanted 'em. I spent an agreeable time with *Drelincourt on Death,* Hervey's *Meditations among the Tombs,* Klopstock's *Messiah,* Solomon Gessner's *Death of Abel, The Saint's Everlasting Rest, A Sentimental Journey, Rasselas,* Robertson's *George III,* Voltaire's *Charles XII,* Rollin, Rapin,

and others of all degrees. Lord! What bran I was then able
to chew! The *pièce de résistance* was an edifice in leather, brass,
wood and glass, built, pediment and all, to resemble a temple.
But along the architrave there was no inscription to the Senate
and People of Rome, or to a Pontifex Maximus, or to any of
the gods of Olympus: in letters of gold ran this—"Jones's
Diamond Classics." Inside, bound in faded and crinkled silks,
red, green, blue and gamboge, were a hundred midget volumes
printed in tiny type which, read by candlelight at home, helped
to send my eyesight on the downward path. Pope's *Iliad* and
Odyssey were there; Cowper, Blair's *Grave, Falconer's Ship-
wreck;* Langhorne; sundry novels about Edwins and Leonoras;
and I know not what else save that the *Sorrows of Werther*
was amongst them and I was as bewildered at seventeen as I
am now to know how, even when the Romantic Revival was
having the measles, such a song could have been made about
such a book.

The temple, as temples will, crumbled; the books, deprived
of their proper shelter, fell to pieces; I have none left. But one
book in that strange collection stayed with me until recently,
when, at a price, it passed to a more ardent collector of rarities
than I have ever been. It was a superb tall copy, finely bound
in gold-tooled red morocco, of *Boulter's Monument,* by the
Rev. Dr. Madden.

"And what, pray, was that?" said my Uncle Toby.

Well may the question be asked! Boulter, the poetically
commemorated, was Archbishop of Armagh and died in 1742.
The interest in the book, apart from its extreme rarity, lies in
the fact that it was submitted to Dr. Johnson's "castigation, or
revision."

But that was later. What stands out from that childish visit
is that it was then that I first came upon *Robinson Crusoe,* in
a dumpy volume with very small type and illustrations. The
second part did not excite me; the first woke the almost
universally latent desire to live on a temperate island with
muskets, a sufficiency of powder and shot, goats and plenty of
birds and fish. I still feel it acutely; to fly to solitude and
summer skies away from what Horace calls *"fumum et opes*

strepitumque Romae"—the roar, the traffic and the reek of
Rome. But there again one picture and one sentence fascinated
me. The castaway, amid the breakers, was clinging to a rock,
and underneath was the legend, "I held my hold till the storm
abated," and "abated" riveted me.

There was power in it and I felt it long before I ever learned
how in a deadlier context "abatement" would have a new and
blissful meaning to me. That one unfamiliar word made as
deep an impression on me, by its sheer musical conveyance of
crisis and assuagement, storm and settlement, as the discovery
of the savage's footprint or any other dramatic moment in the
book; and I still recover my early emotion whenever I see it
in print—I remember the throb I felt when I encountered it
the second time in the sentence "And Moses was a hundred
and twenty years old when he died: his eye was not dim, nor
his natural force abated." The whole first half of *Crusoe* (the
second rather bored me) I read over and over. When not
reading I did not take it literally, for there was one of those
little prefaces about Alexander Selkirk and Defoe's gift for
convincing lying; but, reading, I completely surrendered, and
still can be so to any stirring tale, however fantastic.

I suppose that the authors whom a small boy read then,
Henty and Kingston, Cooper, Mayne Reid, Cockton and
Ballantyne, are little read now. They have gone the way of
the school-stories of their time; their material is old-fashioned,
the cinema has undermined the position of what successors
they may have had, and the newspapers are full of current
adventure. Most boys who read at all read those, and some
of Stevenson and Marryat, and so did I. But I was early
acquainted with Dickens and *Tom Jones* and . . .

But what is the use of giving a catalogue? It is not my business to compress as much information as I can in a small
compass. Nor, if I pretended to record some steady development in my taste and widening in my reading could I do it
accurately, as I never was one of those sedulous youths, often
encountered in the early pages of Victorian biographies, who
made in their diaries such entries as: "Jan. 23rd: Read only
Dante, Purgatorio, Canto 2, Mill on Liberty, Chapter X,

Butler's *Analogy* thirty pages, and a little Homer, Corneille and Shelley. Truly an idle day."

I never read systematically but I read incessantly for pleasure, instinctively finding my natural sustenance through libraries and histories of literature; as a boy I knew my Montaigne, Rabelais, Lucian, Sterne, Swift and Malory much better than I do now. I must have done some official work, I suppose, though an aptitude for picking up rapidly the minimum necessary helped me. I wasn't bone-lazy, nor inspired like the old man I knew in a Cornish village who did literally nothing for sixty years because (as he put it), "I was working in the fields and I heard a Voice from Heaven saying, 'Work no More!'" But work left no impression in me; so far as mere memory, not reinforced by outside knowledge, is concerned I might have spent almost my whole time doing what I wanted to do, and a great deal of it reading poetry. How glad I am that nobody ever tried to make me read it.

Keats addressed Cowden Clarke: "You who first taught me all the sweets of song"; but there is teaching and teaching; I am thankful that nobody ever told me it was a solemn duty to be acquainted with the poets or their lives and English Literature had no place in my formal education. "They will read me in schools and they will call me that horrible Tennyson," said the Laureate. Not long ago somebody showed me a University examination paper in which some lines of my own were set for discussion in one of the questions. I forget whether the examinees were to discuss the metre (to which I doubt whether myself could give a name), to parse the passage (in which event they probably had a difficult time), or to explain the underlying meaning—in which event they probably produced fine symbolic notions which never occurred to me. Literary scholars we must have; but they are not produced by cramming the young in thousands with footnotes to literature which doesn't suit them, or against which (as is evident in much contemporary writing) they may react through too much familiarity of the wrong kind. . . .

I cannot remember a time when the simpler sort of poetry could not move me to smiles and tears, or the obscurer kind excite me with music and bright imagery. My very first book of verses, after the nursery-rhymes with their charming basic English tunes, was called *Poetry for the Young*. It was published by a firm called Griffith and Farran—I always noticed publishers' names, perhaps innocently thinking that they were philanthropists, kind men to produce such pleasant books for me—and it had a bright green cover with a gold Oriental fan on it, rather like a tennis-racket. There were plenty of the usual Victorian things to begin with—Jane and Ann Taylor, the Howitts and other worthies now occluded, a sufficiency of Mrs. Hemans and Longfellow, plenty of Southey, the right stirring things of Campbell, *The Destruction of Sennacherib*—and then, suddenly, the whole of *The Ancient Mariner,* which was quite another matter. Little of the argument did I follow. I did not know what an albatross looked like, and the allegorical part I found bewildering. But the images held me spellbound—the glittering eye, the ribbed sea-sand, the copper sun, the painted ship and ocean, the water-snakes—and the grave inexorable rhythm haunted me, as a little later did the music of "The Forsaken Merman."

Those early books have gone. I have no earlier possession than the first edition of the *Oxford Book of English Verse,* given to me when it first appeared and I was sixteen. This generation, familiar with it, takes it too much for granted. "All can grow the flower now, For all have got the seed"; I even noticed an impertinent young silly the other day describing it and its companions as "Reach-me-downs." But it crystallized and carried on (deficient though its last pages were), the taste of a generation, and I wish I could find amongst our younger writers poems worthy to be added to it.

*   *   *   *   *

A child misthrew a ball straight at me, and called for it back. I returned from the past, was alone by the Warwick Avon, and had no more cigarettes; it must also be six o'clock if, perchance, that was the time at which the Law, in Warwick, allowed a stranger to enter the only sort of club open to him. I did not feel like a large place; in a back street, taking an evening paper in with me, I went into a quiet and humble inn, adorned only by framed advertisements and a forlorn pin-table, ordered a pint of Sir Archibald's, leant upon the counter and looked around me.

A man and woman sat at a small table in a corner—he with a small whisky, she with a port; they were resting after the day's labours, husband and wife, saying little, at amity with each other and the world. Nobody else was present (except the landlord, who was in his shirt-sleeves and meditatively wiping glasses) when there entered a strange group of three who settled on my right. What had brought them together I do not know, unless there had been a race-meeting near, for they were oddly assorted. Next to me stood a short pathetic shabby little scrub, a diffident hanger-on. In the middle was a taller, broader, unshaven man who might have been a struggling horse-coper. But at the far side, facing me, half-turning away from the bar, with propped right elbow, and the free arm making impressive gestures as he airily talked from his superior wisdom, was a very flashy young personage of a type common in London but a rare visitant, like the oriole and the hoopoe, to country places.

He was large, but not yet fat; about thirty. He had a smart tilted hat, a smart blue suit, a fresh carnation and a bright and fresh club tie, with probably ten different ones at his hotel. Good looks of a kind which would later be coarsened were still with him, lustrous brown eyes which smiled superciliously under drooping lids, ruddy cheeks, a straight, rather fleshy nose, a well-carved chin, and a brown moustache whose hairs were carefully combed and whose ends bristled upwards and were constantly being brushed by a superior finger. Whether he was running through the money of some deceased manu-facturer, whether he was keeping up grandeur on very little, or whether he was living on his wits, I could not decide; either conjecture might have been correct; but he certainly liked lord-ing it in circles where a swaggering ass might pass as a lavish man-of-the-world.

The landlord stood awaiting their orders, the Man of the World standing the round. "You will have a sherry, perhaps?"

he said to the horse-coper. That laconic man grunted, "Scotch, if yer don't mind," with the air of one who never took anything else if he could help it. "Same-for-me-please," trembled the little shabby man, with the timid air of one who rarely dared ask for so expensive a thing. "Two double whiskies," said their grand friend to the landlord, in a sedulous drawl, "and for me, let me see, well, a large glass of the dryest of your dry sherries, and a dry biscuit."

"Only got cheese crackers and potato crisps," said the landlord.

"Never mind," said he.

The tray came and the usual greetings were exchanged, kindly, casually, and admiringly, in that order. The sherry, which was doubtless the landlord's dryest and only, was brown in colour. I remembered George Saintsbury's advice about public-house sherry: that one shouldn't even sip it until one has put a lump of bi-carbonate of soda into it to see if it foams over. However, the gesture of connoisseurship had been made; though, however impressed the little man may have been, I think the horse-coper had his doubts. He had, perhaps, seen the type before; they had talked promisingly of buying hunters at £300 a time, but in the end had said that probably they would be buzzing off to Switzerland, so perhaps would go on hacking just for this season.

The Man of the World caught my eye, leant over, and in a tone slightly modified for the benefit of myself and the others, said: "Excuse me, sir, but I wonder if you'd allow me to have just a glance at your evening paper." "By all means," I said, and passed it. He screwed in an eye-glass and perused it. "As I thought," he said, with a nod, "they're not doing too well. . . . Thank you, sir," and returned the paper.

The horse-coper looked indifferent. "You—mean—the—Austrylians?" asked the Little Man.

"Yes, of course they've only really got one bat."

The Big Man took an indifferent draught.

"Bradm—man," said the Little Man, acutely.

"And one bowler."

"O—Rei—lly," was the diagnosis.

I forgot them for a minute. Then I found that they had got
to racing. The Man of the World was comparing Punchestown
with Aintree. Though, of course, he said, he wasn't in a position to compare really, for although he had ridden often
enough at Punchestown he had never actually ridden in the
National.

"That so?" said the Big Man.

"Be—cher's—Brook," said the Little Man.

"I'm glad Bliss isn't here," I mused; "he would have torn
me away. He would have said: 'Good Lord, Squire, I can't
stand this chap any more. I shall be sick presently. Come
along, let's go somewhere else.'" Then once more the subject
changed; the theme of the fourth movement of this Trio was
the relative malignancy of drinks, the Big Man occasionally
providing a ground-bass to the discourse of the Man of the
World. Fierier and fierier were the cordials mentioned, until
at last the Little Man surprisingly said: "If—you—want—to—
rot—your—inside—give—me—Absint."

The Man of the World raised his eyebrows in amusement
and surprise. "Oh, yes, absinthe; Pernod."

"Stuff you drop through sugar and it makes the water
cloudy," said the Coper.

"But," said the Man of the World, recovering his pose,
"you know you can't get it even in Switzerland now. It's
illegal."

At this the Little Man dropped his one and only bombshell
of contradiction.

"You can," he stated firmly, "get—it—in—Swisserland—if—
they—know you."

Even the phlegm of the Coper was momentarily disturbed.
As for the Man of the World, his mouth opened, and his eyes,
already slightly protuberant, achieved the state of ophthalmic
goitre. He made as if to speak . . . and stopped himself.
"Could it be that this little wretch really had some. . . . ?"

The drinks were getting low. The Coper noticed it. He
finished his rapidly, gave a rapid hand-shake to his host of the
former round, muttered "I must go," and hastened through
the door. The Little Man, alarmed at being left with the

Grandee whom he had contradicted, said "Good night," and scuttled after him.

Left alone, the Swell fastened his gaze upon myself. I knew that if he caught an answering look from me he would at once open conversation. Probably he would begin with "You know, of course, those sort of fellows are . . . but speaking as one Man of the World to another——" Response to that gambit, I felt sure, would lead to a flood of crude stories which I shouldn't want to hear, and I might even be inveigled into a dinner for which I should, somehow or other, pay. During dinner he would explain why he hadn't thought it worth while to go to "the Varsity" and introduce sundry references to Lord's, the Brigade, the Foresters, I. Z., Le Touquet, and goodness knows what else, and he would end by saying: "Well, this has been very kind of you, sir, very kind indeed; and I hope that next time we meet you'll come and have dinner at *my* place."

Knowing my vulnerability, I, too, nodded and fled.

On the way home to dinner I wondered what on earth the small man had meant about getting absinthe "if they knew you." It couldn't be the worm turning; he was too subservient for that.

Somewhere he must have overheard something. I don't know the name of the President of Switzerland (that "tall but thin republic"), though perhaps some of the Swiss do. But I can't suppose that that dingy little man was a friend of his.

*   *   *   *   *

When I asked Bliss to send me his notes all he had to say about that afternoon and evening was that he went off to Leamington; adding "Forget what S. did." S.'s evening was much like his afternoon.

It might, I thought after I had taken my solitary meal, have been better; but there was no moon. Had there been a moon I should have gone to the bridge and been quite content to watch her radiance shed all around her sky, touching the rippled waters, and the trees, and turning the Castle into a majestic phantasmal mass of towering lights and darks; or strayed slowly down alleys transformed to chequers of silver and velvet black. There is good authority for saying that it is no use sighing after the moon; but I missed her, although I believe that Virgil, Shakespeare, Schumann, and all her dead lovers are regarded as having been extremely silly about her by those new writers over whose rhythms, cacophonies and rhymes one could almost break one's shins.

I went out after dinner, nevertheless, tempted by the thought of a solitary ramble through dark and unfamiliar streets. After a time I found myself in a quiet road of the outskirts, with scattered lamps and chinks of light coming through curtained windows. After fifty yards or so there was a gate, a lit and open window, and a plump little figure standing by the gate. He turned to me, a man of sixty with a cloth cap, and lifted his hand. " 'Ush," he said, " 'ere comes the nine o'clock noos."

I 'ushed, and it came; calamity after calamity in kindly domestic towns, with here an earthquake, here an explosion, and there a threat of war; train accidents in America, and turmoils in the Near East and Central Europe. When they reached those trite snippets from political speeches which are arranged to give fair play to all the various brands of platitu-dinizers, we spontaneously stepped off into the night together. My companion was evidently disappointed. "Always them politics," he complained. "Gimme a good ole murder." I had heard it a night or two before.

It was a pious opinion; events proved it a pious hope, and what a hope! Or a cry from a heart in dread, arising from a hope desperately clung to.

Someone might make an anthology of such things. It could begin with this dialogue from Mrs. Markham:

"Pray, mamma, what was a Druid?"
"A Druid, my dear, was a kind of clergyman."

It was nearly ten when I got back. I was tired and stiff, did not wait up for Bliss, and did not read in bed.

L

CHAPTER VII

WARWICK

In the morning I was still tired. So, I learned, was Bliss, when
he joined me in the doorway whence I was watching the local
Yeomanry marching off to camp through a grey deluge of rain.

"I vote we stay here to-night and go to Stratford to-morrow,"
said Bliss. "Right," I said.

He went off to the Warwick Park Estate to arrange about
getting the canoe over the Castle Weir next day and paid the
necessary three-and-sixpence; I took a taxi to the bridge to
explain things to the boatman, who was amiable and helpful.

The attraction of Leamington still held Bliss and he fled
thither again; I spent the rest of the morning reviewing some
infernal book. When I had posted it off and had my lunch, I
settled myself down in an arm-chair in an upstairs writing-
room with a box of cigarettes and a Bible I had found. It was
still pouring.

For two or three hours I sat there, now reading, now staring
out at the wet houses and sky and thinking. I kept on looking
at the Old Testament, that extraordinary compost. I do not go
so far as the eminent Catholic who described it to me as "a
horrible book full of stories about a lot of disgusting tribes,"
and, though I think that much of it should be reserved for the
mature, and even for anthropologists, I cannot understand the
desire of the Nazis to suppress it altogether. Parts of it are
the most exalted of man's works, spiritually and poetically;
and of the rest much is fit for anybody to read. All that it is
quite understandable that the Nazis should wish to ban. But
I cannot for the life of me see why they should suppress the
savage portions, which have always inspired the Fanatical
Elect who have gone forth with book and sword to persecute
those who differed from them—unless indeed they are jealous
that the heroes of a folk, historically so small and insignificant
as the ancient Jews, should enjoy so great a renown for their

comparatively petty butcheries and robberies and their merely primitive bigotries.

Nevertheless, I confess that I often wonder, as I wondered that afternoon, how it was that in youth I had taken so little notice of the viler parts of the Old Testament, and whether they might not be injurious to more sensitive minds than mine; and why I had not been (having as yet no inkling of theories of progressive revelation) bewildered by finding Jehovah and Christ talking in such contradictory manner within the covers of the same book; adultery (for instance) in the Old Testament being so much worse a crime than the massacre of innocents, whereas in the Gospels. . . .

From boyhood I knew the Bible very well, and should have known it well even if I had not spent many years in choirs and habitually read it during the sermons. It puzzled me again, in that Warwickshire hotel, how I could have read and listened to large portions of the Old Testament without being either brutalized or suffering a revulsion. Large portions of it show an appalling tolerance, and even advocacy, of treachery, cruelty, self-righteousness and hate, and the acceptance of its verbal inspiration has led to untold perversions of Christianity. Take the thirty-fourth chapter of Genesis. Take the appalling nineteenth chapter of Judges with its Trunk Murder ending. Or take the thirty-first chapter of Numbers after those precious Children of Israel had swooped upon the Midianites and taken great "prey and booty."

'And Moses, and Eleazar the priest, and all the princes of the congregation, went forth to meet them without the camp.

And Moses was wroth with the officers of the host, with the captains over thousands, and captains over hundreds, which came from the battle.

And Moses said unto them, Have ye saved the women alive?

Behold, these caused the children of Israel, through the counsel of Balaam, to commit trespass against the Lord in the matter of Peor, and there was a plague among the congregation of the Lord.

Now therefore kill every male among the little ones, and kill every woman that hath known man by lying with him.

But all the women children, that have not known man by lying with him, keep alive for yourselves.'

Not long before the Lord had spoken unto Moses, saying: "He that killeth a man he shall be put to death"; still, the killing of women and children, not Israelites, was a worthy action.

It is astonishing what things we will listen to in church. People who are horrified at the story of Iphigenia will complacently take the similar story of Jephthah, who offered his daughter up as a burnt offering to the Lord. The Israelites were very strong on the "abominations" of those whom they slaughtered and plundered, but the most superstitious idolator could have done no worse than that. Almost any villainy, except worshipping in groves and high places, could be condoned by the examples of the Old Testament heroes—including cruelty to animals which a child hearing the story of Samson and the foxes might well think funny; while the rape of the daughters of Shiloh is on a precise footing with the rape of the Sabine women, which nobody ever suggested had the slightest connection with the Progressive Revelation of the Divine or the Word of God. And yet, as I turned from that mixture of primitive bestiality, history, legend, sweet poetry, rhapsody, aspiration and savage invective, did it never occur to me that within three pages of those last words of Malachi, "lest I come and smite the earth with a curse," I was out in the light of the Sermon on the Mount?

*   *   *   *   *

"Never," I reflected. "Perhaps the music of our version drugged me to it all." Sound is what the Old Testament mostly was to me. I turn the Authorized Version over now looking for those passages which, read as lessons, stirred me most by their imagery and majestic music.* I realize that what they conveyed to me they conveyed by the atmosphere of words and the suggestiveness of sound. I waited always for the return of the last chapter of Ecclesiastes: "Remember thou thy Creator in the days of thy youth." So went on that thing, mightier than elegiac, with more than a resigned Latin *"memento mori,"* but overtones from the spheres in it. "While the sun, or the light, or the moon, or the stars, be not darkened, nor the clouds return after the rain."

"The grinders cease because they are few, and those that looked out of the windows shall be darkened." I have learned since that this is florid Oriental imagery for the failing of teeth and eyes; but when I put no literal meaning to it, it had more in it of our mysterious destiny and "ancestral voices prophesying doom." What meaning did I attach to:

'And he shall rise up at the voice of the bird, and all the daughters of musick shall be brought low.

Also when they are afraid of that which is high, and fears shall be in the way, and the almond tree shall flourish, and the grasshopper shall be a burden, and desire shall fail because man goeth to his long home, and mourners shall go about the streets.

Or ever the silver cord be loosed, or the golden bowl be broken, or the pitcher be broken at the fountain, or the wheel broken at the cistern.'

The poring scholars can explain what "bowl" and "pitcher" were, and why the daughters of musick should be brought low, while "he" should arise with the lark or whatsoever bird.

---

* But these are what matter in poetry, which always has a kinship to wordless music. I distrust most critics of poetry who are not poets; they almost always fasten themselves on what to the genuine poet are incidentals rather than essentials, which is why their judgments on contemporaries and the people they praise are so rapidly superseded. Does anybody suppose that Dante's poetry would have survived on his ideas had he not had a golden voice—or at the opposite extreme of erudition Burns's?

But to me the inexorable progress of the sound, the "Broken
. . . broken . . . broken" led inevitably up to the all too clear
conclusion, "Then shall the dust return to the earth as it was;
and the spirit shall return to God who gave it."

That was great poetry, but not necessarily Christian; some
have even conjectured Greek influence, and they quarrel about
dates; there is kinship to the tragedians if there is no influence.
Granted the poetry, I was content; but I remember—after
being bewildered by all the laboured, well-meant captions over
our Old Testament twistings of prophecies, and even (see
Isaiah 54), sheer wanglings making a prophecy of universal
conquest by the Jews into hope for the Gentiles, and even the
contortion of the Song of Solomon into something suitable to
the Church of England—thinking that I had found (what in
the literature of all ancientry I still sometimes find and am
consoled by) a forethought of Christ in Boaz's instructions
about the wandering young Moabitish widow, Ruth:

> 'And when she was risen up to glean, Boaz commanded
> his young men, saying "Let her glean even among the
> sheaves, and reproach her not: and let fall also some of
> the handfuls on purpose for her, and leave them, that she
> may glean them, and rebuke her not." '

Boaz was one of the first Christian gentlemen of whom we
know. His great-grandson's, King David's, record was patchy;
yet over all the troubled ages rings the cry, "O my son
Absalom, my son, my son Absalom! Would God I had died
for thee, O Absalom, my son, my son!"

*   *   *   *   *

When I grew older, I looked for the music and was proof
against the primitivism. Even in the New Testament the
music sometimes was dominant for me at school. There was
another passage, read in chapel by the Headmaster, which sent
me in search of it, for I must have read it before without
noticing. It came from Jude:

"These are spots in your feasts of charity, when they feast with you, feeding themselves without fear; clouds they are without water, carried about of winds; trees whose fruit withereth, without fruit, twice dead, plucked up by the roots; raging waves of the sea, foaming out their own shame; wandering stars, to whom is reserved the blackness of darkness for ever."

Parts of this, I found, occurred almost *verbatim* in the Second Epistle of Peter; the Epistles also, thought I, were a little Synoptic. But all the while the drama of Bethlehem, and Nazareth and Galilee, the Upper Room, Gethsemane, and Golgotha stood out to me as something apart. The rest was legend and history, commentary and conjecture, fruits of the human mind, body and imagination; this was Revelation, and if it were not we were all in the mist, wandering stars in the blackness whether it were reserved for ever or not. Unconsciously I had come, I think, to the abiding feeling of that Moslem of Basra, quoted at the end of Ronald Storrs' rich and illuminating "Orientations," who cried a thousand years ago: "O my Lord! If I worship Thee from fear of Hell, burn me in Hell; and if I worship Thee from hope of Paradise, exclude me thence; but if I worship Thee for Thine own sake, then withhold not from me Thine Eternal Beauty"—and Christ was the Eternal Beauty made manifest. Like many boys of my time and type, trying to fly from the blackguardism of much of the Old Testament and of Christian history (somebody said that "Christianity must be true because it has survived its professors"),* I tried syncretics. Sale's somewhat in-

* The late Thomas Michael Pope, a very devout Anglo-Catholic, was once lamenting with me over the way in which Christian sects through history, had lived up to the Golden Rule and the injunction to love their neighbours as themselves, and told me a pertinent story. An elementary school-teacher, after trying to ram the story of the Redemption into the head of his class, was examining them to discover what had sunk in. His first general invitation for a reply to the question as to why Our Lord came down from Heaven to save us miserable sinners, produced not one uplifted hand. Singling out one boy he put the question in several different forms. Each time the answer was, "I dunno." In the end, exasperated, he banged the child on the head and shouted, "It was Love, you little bastard!"

adequate Koran I perused; in my last holidays I fished the
sea by day, and at night pored over those vast tomes about
Eastern Religions edited by the late Sir M. Monier-Williams,
and wrote to a school-friend (about the first time I had ever
mentioned religion to anybody, away from the Communion
Rails) that I thought I was a Buddhist; later I toyed with
Comte and all the grim Agnostic publications of the Rationalist
Press Association. But they did not suit me, though they seem
(for in the nineteenth century there were many earnest and
even noble souls who seemed easily to live on a ledge—not now
visible—half-way down the precipice, where the Christian
revelation was lost and the Christian ethic still clung to) to
have been adequate for some. They might have produced
Biblical warrant for their relish of husks. I don't mean the
Prodigal Son who was no testimonial to them at all, and re-
pented him of the evil. I am referring to the first chapter of
Daniel where the rigorous Daniel, Shadrach, Meshach and
Abednego insisted on having pulse and water instead of the
king's tainted meat and wine, "and at the end of ten days their
countenance appeared fairer and fatter in flesh than all the
children which did eat the portion of the king's meat." But,
as Sir John Seeley noted, "there is nothing more dangerous
than a false historical analogy."

*   *   *   *   *

After tea Bliss, who had been driven back from Leamington,
came in and found me dozing. A somewhat fatigued
theological discussion ensued, during which he told me that
he always confused Plymouth Brothers with Yarmouth
Bloaters, though for that matter, for breakfast, he preferred
kippers to either.

We went downstairs, met some men, and played Bar
Billiards—which would be a better game if the local rules
didn't differ so much from place to place.

Then we dined. "I think, Squire," said he, as we sat down,
"that we ought to have a bottle of wine. Don't you think
Burgundy in this weather?"

"Certainly," I said; it came and it was good.

When our excellent dinner was finished I said: "Don't you think we might have another bottle of that Burgundy, Bliss? We can stay by this pleasant fire, and take it at our ease."

"Certainly," he said; so we did. As we raised our glasses, I remembered, "Strong Brother in God and last companion, Wine!"

"Where does that come from?" snapped Bliss, scenting his Faith.

"Belloc."

"I thought I knew his verse."

"This is a recent one and a noble one."

"He is a good poet."

"He is, but the wretches don't know it. Or he can do too many things for them and they don't like it. Or he is too obstinately Christian for them and they can't bear it. Or he is too big for them and they can only see his feet. Or they are afraid he may be right about the prospects of society and it makes them peevish. Or . . ."

"I don't see why that should stop them seeing he writes good verse," grumbled Bliss.

"Perhaps their ears should be sent to Lord Harberton."

*   *   *   *   *

As we sipped and smoked, we regretted the days when good wines were cheaper and our purses not so low. Especially we remembered discoveries we had made in unexpected places. Bliss recalled cellars of his youth, finds in French and Italian inns, though I think not the Chianti I drank near Chianti (a small area), which has made what passes for such impossible for me ever since; I had more recent surprises. I remembered the perfect hock I had got for almost nothing in Edinburgh during the War, at a time when hardly anybody would touch a German wine (as though Prussia ever made wine any more than she made poetry or music), and a woman who dared take a dachshund along Piccadilly was liable to be scowled at. I remembered the original green Chartreuse I found later in a Sussex inn where it had long lingered, rather dusty, on an upper shelf—I paid a few pence for a glass of

L*

what was already fetching about five pounds a bottle, resisted
the temptation to buy the lot from those rustic innocents, and,
later, reflected that very likely next month some rogue had
come along with fewer scruples than I. Then suddenly I remembered something more. "Can you guess, Bliss," I asked,
"where I drank, only a few years ago, the loveliest claret I
ever tasted (barring a few almost inaccessible Lafites), and it
was only five shillings a bottle?"

"How can I guess that?" he retorted, reasonably.

"Blackpool!" I replied.

"What on earth——" he gaped at me, "were either you or
that claret doing in Blackpool?"

"I will tell you," said I.

*   *   *   *   *

"It was nine or ten years ago, Bliss, that I was asked to go,
as it might be in late October, and address the Annual Con-
ference of the British Librarians, as it might be twelve hundred
strong, at Blackpool. They parade from place to place, you
understand, like the British Association, and that year they
were at Blackpool, and my address was to be, as it might be,
on the Thursday afternoon.

"I didn't much relish the notion of going to Blackpool and
facing, by myself, hordes of people with a remote accent, let
alone all those doggedly efficient librarians. Happily, on the
Tuesday afternoon, Alan Pryce-Jones dropped in, and I said
to him: 'Will you come to Blackpool with me to-morrow,
Alan?' and he replied: 'Why, of course,' as though I'd asked
him to go round the corner to the Savoy. 'I'm sure,' he added,
with his customary courtesy, 'that it will be quite delightful.
I've *always* wanted to see Blackpool.'"

"Was it delightful?" asked Bliss, with some scepticism.

"Please wait and listen," I told him.

We thought, since we were going to Blackpool, that we
might as well see the legendary place, so we started the day
before the lecture. We didn't expect to see very much, as the
train rumbled up through the misty Midlands, for it was the

autumnal season when seaside-resorts, especially the 'popular ones,' are completely out of action. The waves wash wistfully on the beaches, unfed by chocolate-wrappers and orange-peel, temporarily deprived of their 'priestlike task of pure ablution round earth's human shores'; the piers have no pierrots; the slot-machines grow rusty in the driven spray; the press photographers have flown to sunnier climes; and the landladies have gone into hibernation, like hedgehogs.

When we got to Blackpool in the dusk the whole place was roaring with life. We said so to the taxi-man; he explained that of late years the ingenious and interested Corporation of Blackpool had realized that they might as well truncate the dead part of the year by having an Autumn Season, as well as a Summer Season—a night-light season as well as a day-light one. When we reached the front it was evident that no half-measures had been taken. Pier after pier, brilliantly lit, stretched out into the dark sea; on the promenade's outer edge festoons of fairy-lamps drooped and rose for miles, into infinity. Trams rattled along, all picked out with arrangements of fairy-lamps which made them look like swans or gondolas against the night; music blared; and multitudes swarmed along the pavements and around the countless booths.

"This is really rather jolly," said Alan; so it was; there was an exhilarating natural vulgarity about it; the common honest Northerner having a go.

For a space we were out of it. We had asked for a quiet and old-fashioned hotel. We got it. The few inmates were already in dinner-jackets and evening frocks, cutting a dash in clothes that seemed rather 'party' for them. After dinner we walked out to see the sights, miles and miles to-and-fro, games, exhibitions and cockshies. Once we found a place which exhibited the sign 'Champagne, sixpence a glass, Oysters, 1½ d. each,' which may be taken as symbolical of Blackpool. It was a noble effort on the part of the proletariat to 'level up' instead of 'levelling down'; we had each our glass and our oyster, and no more.

Late that night, after hours of bathing in that sea of decent, cheerful humanity, we began to walk home. At half-past twelve we were passing a large and brightly-lit tavern from which a loud din was proceeding. "They seem to be keeping it up pretty late," we said, and went in to see what was on.

The place was crowded, in full swing; it was thick with smoke and waiters were active with trays. We found empty seats on a red-plush bench next a burly man who looked, and was, a minor wool-manufacturer from Bradford. It took him no time to get into conversation after he had explained that the authorities in Blackpool were very lenient about licensing hours, as tourists were the town's industry. Before long he was expertly fingering my overcoat. He pursed his lips. "No domn good," he said. Then he leant over and pinched Alan's superior garb. "Quat anoother matter," he remarked, "that's good stoof." Alan gallantly salved my feelings by explaining: "You see my friend has probably paid for his overcoat, whereas I haven't yet for mine."

Late though the hour, when we returned to the hotel lounge for a last cigarette and commentary, our fellow-guests were still at work with the gold-leaved bottles, and loudly applauding a lady of their number who was banging out vile jazz, full of false notes, on a piano right under our ears. When she stopped and rejoined her friends I said: 'Alan, do something in return.' Without hesitation he took the piano-stool and went through one of the deadlier composition of Poulenc. Silence reigned. When he began a second, dismay was writ clear on the faces of the people; they all at once with bowed heads went off to bed. Alan closed the piano and we immediately followed them.

"That's all right," said Bliss, when I had told him all this, "but what about that claret you were telling me about?"

"I'm sorry, I forgot. In point of fact we got it at dinner in our hotel. We called for the wine-list, drew a bow at a venture (the safest venture, as we chose the most expensive of the clarets there, though it was but five shillings a bottle), and were brought Château X of 18—. We had scarcely touched it when we stopped and looked at each other. We lingered long over that dinner, and had a second bottle; we could scarcely hog a third.

" 'Don't you think,' enquired Alan, 'that we could ask them how much they have and buy the lot?'

" 'They'd smell a rat at once,' I said. 'Anyhow, it will always be here, and if we ever want to have some more all we have to do is to come to Blackpool again.'

" 'Yes,' said he, 'I suppose that is so; and, of course, we can make our railway expenses out of the savings on oysters and champagne.' "

"But how," asked Bliss, "could you be so sure about its still being there?"

"For the same reason that it was there at all at that ridiculous price. Consider, Bliss, the clientele of that hotel. If the men are there alone they either drink whisky, or, if they fancy what they call red wine, certainly go for what is generally called Médoc, which is cheap and coarse and of which they have heard. If they are splashing on a holiday with their women, black ties and necklaces, they will certainly order champagne to please the ladies, who will be cheered by the sparkle and expense. Blackpool is a delightful spot in its way, but I cannot suppose that it is haunted by the connoisseurs of vintage wines."

"You may be right," admitted Bliss.

* * * * *

We left the dining-room very contented, went to the door and looked at the weather. The rain had ceased and the skies were clearing, scatters of stars showing between the dark clouds. "Should be all right to-morrow," said Bliss. "I'll meet you in a corner of the lounge in a minute," and went upstairs to his room.

He came down with books and maps. "Now to-morrow morning," he said, "at ten sharp, we start down the Avon, and we ought to get at least as far as Stratford. It's a bit hard that we had that long spring drought and now this spell of bad weather, so that we may have too much water on our backs and too little under our keel. But at any rate there won't be any towing, unless in the wading way, for there is no tow-path, and with any luck we should, now we're turning, have the wind with us."

He showed me, on the map, the course of the Avon—the Stratford Avon: Avons in England are as plentiful as Ouses, or more so, both words being merely Celtic terms, and Avon a very beautiful one, for water. This river, widely known because of a Swan, rises in Naseby Field and is reported to have been canoed from Rugby, which is about ninety miles from its junction with the Severn, but conditions must have been favourable, and the canoeist pertinacious. Bliss says in his hand-book: "It was once a navigation from Tewkesbury to Stratford, these forty-eight miles having been canalized as long ago as 1638 by means of thirteen locks, permitting the passage of vessels of fifty tons burden. It was a flourishing canal till the railways came, but then became neglected, and by 1875, or thereabouts, the locks and weirs were in such bad condition that any sort of barge traffic was no longer possible. When the author first came down it (in 1891) the locks between Stratford and Evesham were mere shells, and their ruins made the channel dangerous. Now you barely see any vestiges of them except in low water, but it is still well to keep a look-out for stumps of timber and sunken masonry when you are passing the site of any of these old locks."

He spoke of the beauty and remoteness of the scenery of that river, below Warwick, the mills, alas desolate, the portages. This was going to be another change, and I looked forward to it immensely.

CHAPTER VIII

Warwick to Stratford

In the morning the wind had changed to south-west, so that we should once more have it in our faces, and very likely rain as well. We got off from the boat-house about ten, Bliss resuming the stern thwart, for we had grown accustomed to our paddling order and thought of change no more. It is only about a hundred and fifty yards to the Weir and the Castle Mill.

At the Castle Bridge there is a chain across the river. To overcome that obstacle one goes to the right arch and gets the bow of the canoe over the chain, which sinks; being held by a suspended weight in the water which is lifted by the weight of the canoe. Immediately afterwards came the first portage of what was going to be a thoroughly exhausting day. We landed on the left bank just above the weir, hauled the canoe some twenty yards and put her in again. The castle rose above us on our right, magnificently sheer; we lingered for a few minutes, then another minute and we were in the heart of the country, on our left a high wooded bank and on our right for a mile and a half that noble Park—so well and variously timbered but so natural. Sunlight broke upon the scene and we glided through a long lovely panorama of green and gold and blue shadow with red cattle grazing placidly here and there, and no sound but bird-song and the plash and ripple of our own motion. We left the Park, passing under a stone bridge of a single span. The country now became very secluded and rural; waterfowl were plentiful, though there were no swans of Avon. Three miles of perfect country and we reached Barford Mill, centuries old if not quite as old as the one of which it was sung:

> She has ground her corn and paid her tax
> Ever since Domesday Book.

A fine old mill-house it is, half-timbered with wooden projecting top storeys, pigeons strutting on the roofs and aspens trembling around. As we stopped to admire it Bliss became mournful. "It was dismantled last year," he said; "I saw the old Mill timbers being taken out. Two-foot-six square oak beams! I wished I'd been a furniture-maker!"

It is sad, and also absurd, that all over England old water-mills are falling out of use and into neglect, much to the loss of the scenery of our rivers. It is said that the reason is the modern fetish of snow-white flour, but it does seem ridiculous that the water-power which drove them should not be used for something.

The river was low and much of the water (since the Mill was not working) going down the weir channel; we had a difficult portage, having to haul her at an uncomfortable height out of the water and carry her over about a hundred yards of rough and bushy ground, and then start off again at a place where it was too shallow. For some time we kept stranding in a wide sweep of weedy shoals and small rapids and runnels, and Bliss got out and waded. It was all very pretty, and the wild yellow irises were out and there were dab-chicks about, but we were glad when we got off. The next landmark was Hampton Lucy Mill, nearly five miles on; by woods and water-meadows we steadily paddled on, as we had lost much time at Barford and wished to lunch at our next stop.

The village of Hampton Lucy lies to the right of Hampton Mill, up a hill; the village of Charlecote on the other bank up another hill. It was in Charlecote Park that Shakespeare is reputed to have been caught stealing Sir Thomas Lucy's deer, and anything more peacefully beautiful than all that stretch of Avon cannot be conceived. We left the canoe above the Mill (which also seemed to be derelict) and walked up the hill, where we got bread and cheese. It was a quiet spot and getting on for two o'clock. There were only two men sitting on a bench against a rough table. One was tall, massive, grey-side-whiskered, apple-cheeked, old and strong; the other was a weather-beaten, fox-faced man of sixty. I passed the time of day while Bliss was getting himself some butter and a tomato, and remarked on the threatening sky. The foxy man said:

> "Between one and two,
> You'll know what the weather'll do."

The old man joined in:

> "Rain before seven,
> Shine before eleven."

It wasn't anything like seven, so the little ploughman repeated: "When I wor a ploughboy o' twelve, ole ploughman 'e said to me, 'e said:

> 'Between one and two,
> You'll know what the weather'll do.' "

I didn't like to suggest that, owing to Daylight Saving, the hours had been upset. But rural lore will always cover the situation and I don't doubt that some time I shall hear from venerable wiseacres:

> "Between two and three,
> You'll know what the weather'll be,"

and

> "Between three and four,
> It sometimes begins to pour,"

and so on through a whole meteorological dodecalogue, in the true traditional strain of Thomas Tusser. . . .

As we approached the village I had remarked on the height and mass of the church and its tower. On closer inspection, after lunch, it turned out to be early nineteenth-century Gothic and, for its date, remarkably interesting, if certainly experimental with its huge rose window at the west end and arches with rather a Moorish touch.

"I can tell, Bliss," I observed, "somewhere about 1820 some Lucy must have spared no expense on this little cathedral." So it proved; underneath the east window was an inscription saying that the Reverend Thomas Lucy had spent *magnam pecuniam* on it.

The air darkened suddenly. As soon as we reached the porch we saw "what the weather would do." The cataracts of heaven were unloosed from a black sky, which thundered and lightened. "I'm going inside until it stops," I said. "And I'm going to make a bolt," said Bliss, "for a doorway where I can smoke my pipe."

I returned to the lofty nave and sat in a pew, content for a time with Il Penseroso's rôle. The fretted ceilings and massy columns were there all right, and if no solemn organ was pealing, I soon heard music, if of a rather unexpected kind, coming from outside in snatches through the storm. At first I only caught phrases, and then I exclaimed: "Well, I'm hanged!" For there I was in a lonely hill village above the Avon, in a large Regency Gothic church with a Moorish tinge, and the school-children without were warbling a German folk-song. "What next," I thought, "will this little cosmopolis produce?"

The resources of Hampton Lucy were not exhausted. Catching sight of some of the usual periodicals on a table I examined them and found one that was like some exotic bird in that sequestered spot. It was called *Bible Lands: Quarterly Paper of the Anglican Bishopric in Jerusalem,* and I took it back to my pew with no more than the intention of perusing it for sidelights on the Near Eastern situation, and passing the time.

One more waft of German folk-song reached my cloistered seclusion when I came across something still more at issue with the Warwickshire countryside. It related to the erection of a Memorial Hall to the late Bishop MacInnes in Jerusalem. There was the customary information about Mission Buildings, School House, ropes, rings, horizontal bars, mats, boxing gloves, etc., and "window-frames which will best match colour-wash on the walls and also be most resistant to school-boys' finger-marks." But the report was distinguished from the usual sort of thing one sees in local and parochial papers by one detail which struck me, in Hampton Lucy Church, as showing a strange adaptability in Mother Church In Partibus. "The roof was finished on Christmas Eve, and, in accordance with Arab custom, sheep were solemnly killed, the blood was allowed to flow over the threshold, and in the evening all those who had been working on the building feasted and danced." Bishops and blood-sacrifices! "This," I thought, "is even broader than Kikuyu!"

The children outside had forsaken their Thuringian Lied for "Come, Lasses and Lads"; I pocketed *Bible Lands,* put into the offertory box what I thought adequate atonement for my theft, and went out to have a look at the weather. The deluge had ceased; there was now merely a downpour, through which Bliss was approaching with the rain dripping off the eaves of his hat. "Look here, Squire," he said, "we've got to go over to Charlecote and get permission to go through the Park; we've got to get to Stratford, you know." We gave it five minutes; the downpour dwindled to a drizzle; and we set off down the hill, which was a muddy stream. We got our permission and the key of Charlecote Church; it was a disappointment. The Lucy tombs were there right enough, but a completely new and heavy little church had been built around them about eighty years ago. No expense, once more, had been spared; but it was sad to see pictures of the old simple village church hanging reproachfully on the wall.

With the key of the barrier from the Estate Office we went back in the soaking rain to the Mill. Bliss got in and, after climbing a fence and sliding down a mud-bank I joined him at the bridge. A man was waiting for us at the formidable barrier just below the bridge; a contraption of posts and cross-bars with a wooden gate in the middle which swung on rudimentary hinges and was fastened by a padlock. I said to the man: "What on earth do they want to put a thing like this across the river for? It isn't like Sir Henry Fairfax-Lucy, who is a very kind man."

"It isn't to stop you, sir," he replied, "it's to stop the deer from swimming away." For if the shade of poaching Shakespeare cared to revisit the glimpses of Charlecote on a shiny night he would still find under its trees and on its wide lawns herds both of red and of fallow deer.

The man wanted to get into our laden canoe with us, and in deep and moving water, to assist in unlocking a rusty padlock. "N.B.G.," muttered Bliss to me; and then, politely, to our friend: "I think we can manage it ourselves." We manœuvred the canoe alongside the barrier. I clung on, while Bliss unlocked the padlock (there was a fast stream running here), let the gate swing open with the current, hoicked her through, pulled the gate back and re-padlocked it. It would not have been difficult, or pleasant, to upset. It was still raining hard.

At the end of that beautiful Park, the man following us along the bank, we came to another barrier. This was a beast, for the padlock was jammed in the links of the chain which held the gate to its post. We clung broadside to the wood-work in the deep swift stream and swore; I heard more than I saw, for my hands were engaged and my spectacles covered with rain and steam. A quarter of an hour's pulling, pushing and coaxing and the padlock was unfastened.

We got through, re-locked the gate, returned the key to the Estate's young man, bade him a suitable farewell, and set off. "Four miles to Stratford," said Bliss, "and one to Alveston Mill, where we shall have to carry for the last time to-day." We went swiftly enough for that mile; the later proceedings were not so rapid.

The mill-stream parted from the river about an eighth of a mile above the Mill. On our right, as we slid down it, high above our heads, rose a steep muddy bank with a jungly fringe of nettles and great fan-like docks; a roar of waters ahead suggested that at any rate this mill was perhaps still working.

"I'm beginning to change my mind," mumbled Bliss, as we approached the Mill. "I used to say when the mills were working that it was always better to go down the mill-leat and carry over by the wheel. But now, especially in a drought year like this, when the mills are derelict, the water is lower, more goes down the weir-stream, there's a steeper lift-out and the neglected mill-gardens and fields are overgrown and awkward."

Experience confirmed this. If anybody who reads this means to go down the Avon I can assure him that rather than go on to Alveston Mill he had better carry by the weir, shoot the weir, or even dive over the weir than undertake that beast of a portage, rain or no rain. Even the hardened Bliss said it was one of the worst portages he had ever known.

It was impossible to get over at the Mill itself, so we struggled back against the stream and picked out the least difficult landing-place, a precipice of mud in which our shoes sank deep. We slithered and scrambled up with our belongings (including that absurd supernumerary keg of cider), Bliss being stung to the withers by nettles, and the rain streaming over our faces; and when, with the most awful efforts, we had hauled the canoe to the top of the peninsula we saw what was in front of us. There was a wide waste between us and the weir-channel. It was mostly knee-deep in weeds, and covered with pits, and every two feet or so there was a tortured osier-stump. It wasn't only the labour; it was that we had to take the greatest pains to avoid getting the canoe stove in by the toothed edges of old wood; and to add to our pleasures some fiend had scattered the place with barbed wire. For seventy yards, scratched and bruised, we dragged her through these stumps and up and down mud-holes, and then when we got to the other side there was a ten-foot drop down a wet and crumbling bank.

At last we loaded and launched her; Bliss said, as I thought: "Meet me below the Mill and we'll go to the inn at Alveston." I thought I should see him again in three minutes; a little later I thought I mightn't see him again that day.

What happened to Bliss, to start with, was that he thought he had told me to meet him at an inn on a road to which I should easily be directed. Wet, stung, angry and thirsty, he paddled round a huge bend of a back-water with high banks over which he could see nothing. After half a mile he looked at the map (which I should have had) and saw no way of getting back to the Mill. He did see that if he went on paddling for a mile the river would take a sweep to the left which would bring him close to the Stratford–Alveston road, and only three-quarters of a mile from the village and the inn. It was not far from six o'clock and he hoped that I had interpreted his arrangements as he had, and would get on without the map, with the help of the people whom he believed to be in the Mill.

For myself, I was, and am, convinced that I had said I would join the canoe farther down the river. My first job was to get to the Mill. It didn't look very far, but that stretch of land was as bad as a jungle of cactuses, with its knots and stumps and spikes, nettles and greasy little ravines on which my rubber shoes would take no hold. Tripping, sliding, knocking ankles and knees, circumnavigating impossible patches—all in rain, rain, rain—I wished I were, or could obtain, a tank. Progress was made, but I was reduced to counting my steps. At last I reached and crossed the little wall at the end and though the building was in excellent state, it was abandoned and locked and there was nobody there to answer my shouts.

The only thing to do was to follow the water's brink and hope to catch up with the canoe. I made the woods resound with the name of Bliss, and got no answer. Then I found that I was marooned; the place was surrounded by a thick new barbed-wire fence, and every gate and hedge lined with the filthy stuff. After a quarter of an hour's search I stripped off my coat and jumper, shoved them on a wire as a lower protection, and forced my way through with some rending of my shirt. Then, after wiping my spectacles with a sodden handkerchief, I looked round; if there had ever been a path leading anywhere it was there no longer. So I began following the water's edge, and after the first few steps had to start swinging myself over the water by overhanging tree-trunks.

Then I got into a field which sloped away to the west. Still trying to keep close to the stream and stick to my contract with Bliss I went through thicket after thicket of gorse and thorn, now and then encountering a greasy gully with barbed wire at the top, and once, forcing my way through wire, having to return to pick up my spectacles, which had been torn off and dropped on the other side. Remorselessly the rain fell; it was very grey and the distance shrouded with mist. So wide was the river's curve that after what seemed miles I could still turn and see that damned mill only two or three fields behind me. I stopped hailing Bliss and began to realize that if I stuck to the Avon I should probably end the night in a ditch. So I decided, after one more fence, to turn left and wallow on until I came to a road.

As I climbed a gate six hunters came trotting up and stood in a semi-circle before me, forelocks dripping and flanks glistening with the wet. Normally I am glad to talk to horses and even give them sugar, but I said: "Go away, you beasts!" They took no notice and, as I turned in my chosen direction, they all followed me. At the end of the field I climbed a barbed-wire fence, and was astonished to see, a quarter of a mile ahead, a church spire peeping over trees; relief at last, where there was a church there must be people and houses. One more hedge, one more inquisitive pony, and I opened somebody's garden gate and crawled into the garden and went round to the front door. I only meant to apologize for the invasion; I was long past entertaining thoughts of loving-kindness or a warm drink. So was the presentable maid who opened the door. She looked suspiciously at my bedraggled hatless locks, my soaked torn clothes, my clay-clotted feet; and when, after my excuses, I asked the way to Stratford, she said: "Turn to the right," and did not close the door until she'd watched me out of the drive.

In the road there was a homing man. "Three miles," he said, "you'd better walk on; the 'bus has just gone." I was standing irresolute when a car suddenly slowed up beside me with a creaking of brakes. A young head popped out: "Hullo!" it said.

The face was familiar but, in my state, I could not place it at once. I looked puzzled. "Puffle of Nuffle," he said; I hadn't seen him for two years. "Jump in," he said.

I jumped in. "But," I asked, "what on earth are you doing here, and how did you spot me?"

"I was looking out for you. I heard you were at Warwick last night and thought you might have got about here by now."

"But I oughtn't to be here; I ought to have been in our canoe."

"Oh, I know those mills; I thought if you got to Alveston about six you'd go to the inn before the last stage. Would your friend be an elderly man who would be there drinking pints of beer with the oldest inhabitants?"

"Almost certainly."

"Well, I'm told he's there. We'll go and look for him."

We had scarcely started when at a cross-roads where we might have missed him we encountered Bliss and stopped. "Bless my soul!" he said, "where have you been?"

I explained; and we differed about the staff-work.

*   *   *   *   *

Bliss had gone on until, by his map, he had judged the river nearest the road. That river, so beautiful in the morning, now seemed to me a circuitous thing meaninglessly meandering past its dank woods and stagnant meadows. Bliss had come to a place of boat-houses and sloping lawns, flowers and private houses, moored his craft and sloshed his way up past rhododendrons and a tennis-court to a house. The owner was charming to him and directed him to his place of refreshment. He had, he said, expected to find me there, and did the journey at a hand gallop.

When he got there there was neither me nor rumour of me. "After all," he reflected, "if he's fallen into the mill-pool it's too late to go back and save him now." After a reasonable delay he thought I must have missed Alveston, and when we met him he was making his way to Tiddington, the next port-of-call on the way to Stratford.

*   *   *   *   *

Puffle drove us there, where I had a warm drink and steamed some of the marshes off myself. Bliss then had to find the canoe. "Bless my soul!" he exclaimed, "I forgot to ask the name of the house where I left it."

The resourceful Puffle suggested asking at every one—there were about a half a mile of them spaced out, with their trees and white gates—until we had found the right one. So we boarded the car again and went from door to door. I stayed in the car, as I was rather done; the other two made the enquiries. After six coverts had been drawn in vain Bliss went alone to a likely-looking house and stayed for ten minutes. When he came out he said: "I met a most agreeable girl in there and wished I'd been able to stay talking to her longer."

"Yes," we said, "but what about the canoe?"

"Oh, she let me come down to the river and look for it, and it's at a landing-stage only two houses off."

He offered to take the canoe down to Stratford, while we drove on and found rooms. The rain had not stopped, but exercise would keep him warm; we parted from him saying we would leave a message at the inn by the boat-houses. In five minutes we were in Stratford. At the first place (kept, oddly, by a Glasgow Irishman) there was no room, but we found accommodation at the "Falcon," and fell to talking in a corner.

"How is Griggs?" asked Puffle. The last time we had met he had driven me a long way to have lunch at Fred Griggs's house in Chipping Campden. "Are you going over to see him on this cruise?" Puffle went on.

"No chance of that," I replied; "a day or two before I started I saw him in a London nursing-home. He was very ill indeed." I did not guess as I spoke that before that canoeing trip was ended, I should casually see Fred Griggs's death announced in a newspaper, and know that I should never hear his rich chuckle again, that he would never again do another etching or another kind deed.

It is odd how little he, one of the best etchers and draughtsmen since Dürer, is known outside the limited circle of critics and collectors. Years ago, just before he became an A.R.A. (and it was not long before he was full R.A.), I was talking about him to one of the most eminent of Academicians (himself an occasional etcher) and he admitted that he had never heard of Griggs. His etchings number only about sixty; he did few prints of each, and destroyed his plates; during the great boom his prints fetched a hundred or two at each auction; then the collectors lost their money and he was little heard of. Not that he minded that, so long as he could do lasting work, keep his family, and have something over for public causes and the entertaining of his friends. But in an age less given to artistic fads and stunts he might have been even more productive and useful and able to concentrate on his finest work.

He was trained as an architect, working with Gimson

(perhaps the greatest of all modern designers of furniture) and his training served his etching. He etched some real places—for instance, that noble tower of Ashwell, the church in which you can see dog-Latin graffiti from the time of the Black Death, as it might be *Johannes est stultus*—and he drew countless old buildings for reproduction. In his finest work he preferred to use his knowledge to represent buildings which were purely imaginary but which, however fantastic, would definitely "stand up" if built. From his etchings could be constructed a mediæval city lovelier than any which exists or, perhaps, ever has existed—the grey Minster on the hill, the houses great and small clustering below it, the long gabled inns, the river with the buttressed chantry bridges, and the Cross over all. He showed them in all weathers, snow and storm and sunshine, and he gave them skies such as etchers, usually safe with white skies or a few scratches, seldom attempt. There is in these works a profoundly Christian spirit and a seeking for those perfections of which the Middle Ages dreamed and sometimes achieved—tower and spire, gable and portal of venerable stone, all imbued with the soul. And the craftsmanship, though his incredible fineness of line and hatching never impairs his mass and proportion, has never been surpassed.

He loved Samuel Palmer and other of the older draughtsmen who had sought the same things in building or landscape; all poets and artists who had his own feeling of the inseparability of the arts from true civilization. And his passion for creation was equalled by his passion for preservation. He had nothing except what he earned, but his overdraft was always at the service of the Cotswolds, and he could always do another etching. If War Memorials were wanted he would design them free to avert the worst. If a Cotswold town had to be saved from red brick he led the agitation. If Dover's Hill, beautiful seat of historical games, had to be saved, his purse and person were in the forefront. If a shop-front in Campden were threatened it was he who saw that necessary changes were properly made. And if one more noble large house should be added to Campden in the old durable golden stone tradition,

with courts and crypt and gateway, it was natural and right
that he, though he never could afford to finish it, should be
the man to design it, build it, and live in it.

Modest, humorous, sociable, enthusiastic, a boon companion,
deeply devout, utterly generous—none but his friends could
know what he was and to them these are but trite descriptive
words. Somebody may collect his letters; they were worthy
of the calligraphy in which they were written. Nothing but
his work can show what he was; and that only to those who
are capable of understanding it.

*　　*　　*　　*　　*

Bliss meanwhile had been paddling to Stratford in the rain.
At the bridge he found no one in the boat-house, so he moored
the canoe, piled the cushions under a dry arch, and staggered
with the bags up to the "Unicorn."

When we went there we found him well away with the Irish
landlord, and what he called saving his life from a two-gallon
jar of rum. There were four men there guessing (for beer)
how many coins in a hand. One always seemed to win; the
one who always lost was superior and I heard him make the
cryptic remark: "She was a Postlethwaite's daughter," but it
wasn't properly followed up. An old man in a corner was
telling another that "a green Christmas means a fat churchyard" and said that he would like to "pop out like a ginger-
beer bottle." Bliss, regaled by the landlord's stories, had forgotten all about his moisture, external. But we drew him away
to a bath, dry clothes, and dinner.

*　　*　　*　　*　　*

Puffle went home and we spent a comfortable hour before
bed in the lounge. There was a bill about Clay-Pigeon Shooting hanging up; I asked him if he had ever shot much. "Used
to a bit," he said; and then, unexpectedly, "when I was at
Stonyhurst I used to shoot pigeons on the chapel roof with a
catapult."

"Did you say the chapel roof?"

"Yes; I once shot one with fourteen acorns in his crop. I

must say I shouldn't find much pleasure in that myself. But God made them, so I suppose they must get something out of it."

"You must have been a young scoundrel, Bliss."

"Yes," he replied, lighting his pipe, "and I daresay you were too, if the truth were known."

But in point of fact I can't remember much rascality in early youth. It can hardly count that I was but nine when I smoked my first clay-pipe (and was very sick but undeterred), encouraged by an older boy, whose fading photograph still adorns my mantelpiece. It was taken just before he went off for the last year of the Boer War, with a Gunner's sash and sword and a spiked helmet under his arm. His other hand rests on a photographer's table of the period. How solemn and dedicated does that young face look, how set the mouth, how soulful the eyes, how curate-like the fringe of fair curly hair! A stranger might think some pious Christian soldier in the straight tradition of Havelock, Lawrence and all those other whiskered saints whose steel-engraved visages still rebuke one so sadly in the studies of one's more elderly military friends. And yet he was a reckless young devil whose candour was flagrant and disarming. I last met him when we played Rugger together just after I came down from the University. In the scrum he pushed like a bull and swore without ceasing. A casual recollection during the War made me look up his name in the Army List. It wasn't there; so I suppose he has gone the darkling way like Lesbia's sparrow—and many staider and less amusing men.

But no, I do remember now. I have just one memory which may compare with the early iniquities of Bliss, or Jean-Jacques Rousseau. I do remember one disgraceful deed.

From the age of nine till the age of twenty-one I was almost continuously in choirs, the last being that at St. John's. I daresay I might be still were not the Church of England so abominably addicted to sermons. My first choir was that at the great old church of St. Andrew's at Plymouth, which is neighboured by an even older monastic building which is now, *more Britannico,* a gin distillery. My mother, who had a fine voice, made me go into it (I mean the choir), and allowed me to give up the piano (I hated the cold keys in the early mornings) as a *quid pro quo*. I think my objection arose from the fact that I had seen, a little earlier, a copy of *The Chorister* by Sir Arthur Sullivan (as sung by Mme. Antoinette Sterling), on the cover of which was a pink mezzotint lunette of a most revolting little chorister with his eyes turned to a Heaven from which he could hardly bear to be parted, even for a moment. However, like Gibbon, I obeyed as a son; and, had she not known me at home, she would have thought, as she saw me march up the aisle with serious face or heard me warbling in antiphony with the Decani on the other side, that I was just like the chorister on the song-cover.

I don't remember much about all those other boys, nor even their names, except those of two who were my friends at home and remained so long after. One, with a very clear virginal treble and a precocious gift for strong language, was the future warrior just mentioned, and the other was a quiet and ingenious wag who is now a retired rubber-planter. I remember that in the summer evenings, after we had coped with our practices of Stainer in A, Barnby in B, Crotch in C, Dykes in D, Samuel Sebastian Wesley in E, *The Heavens are Telling*, or Gounod's *Redemption* and given the Psalms a once-over, they used to play very rough and rowdy games in the Square outside, or, at the season of the year, gnaw green figs from a tree which grew upon dead men's graves.

I don't think I've often been inside that church since I was thirteen and my voice had already wobbled half-way towards a robust baritone, but my memories of it are intensely vivid. The tower is tall, simple and bare, in granite, dark with centuries of rain, as is the rule around the Moor and in South Devon (though on the Dorset and Somerset borders, at places like Ottery and Cullompton—where the stone is red or yellow —decoration runs glorious riot) and it was sweet, above the noise of day and through the quiet dark, to hear the bells chiming out *The Blue Bells of Scotland* or *The Last Rose of Summer*. Closing my eyes I can see at once the three great aisles dim, lights only in the choir, while soft music comes from the Giant's Causeway of an organ. Ghosts steal out of people I haven't thought of for forty years: the little fat-man alto with the bald head and heavy waxed moustache; the good-looking tenor who thrilled me with "Comfort Ye!", and in outside life ran a fine quartette in the evenings and engraved heraldic book-plates (which he once showed me) for the local and more than the local nobility and gentry. And I know that I could find my way to every memorial tablet in the place, and that even in the dark I could grope my way to the pew under the south wall from above which, for hundreds of years, has gazed the vizored helm of a Knight with his coloured coat-of-arms below it.

"Yes," I can hear Bliss say, "but when are you going to come to your crime?"

Well, it was the child who is now a retired rubber-planter who tempted me. As we were putting on our surplices in the vestry he produced two little wooden guns with taut springs on them which fired small lead pellets, and suggested that we should have some shooting practice. The time chosen was the first lesson, when we should be sitting down; we could some-how fumble our reloading, as little of us showed above the stalls, and we could shoot out of our sleeves. Not many shots were fired: it was too risky and too awkward; and aiming was difficult as the trajectory of his guns was something very steep out of the conic sections; one virtually had to fire into the brown. But when we came out this was the conversation:

BERNARD: Did you get anybody?
MYSELF: I can't quite tell. I didn't like to look when I was aiming. But I know I got the colonel in the front row. I saw him rubbing his cheek. Did you have any luck?
BERNARD: I got old X (the fat alto); he stared hard at me and I stopped. Did you try the Archdeacon?
MYSELF: Somehow I didn't like to.
BERNARD: Nor did I.

So the dawn of reverence was there, at all events. Small boys seldom stop to think; it never occurred to us that we might destroy somebody's eye, or what an unholy row we should get into if we were caught. Anyhow we were not quite so bold as the friend of mine, now very devout, who told me that when he was a young acolyte he put percussion caps in the incense.

Rather later, with that same youth, or sometimes another, I used to ride on bicycles to various country towns and fishing villages in South Devon and East Cornwall, where we would make for an inn and refresh ourselves with bad port out of audacity or tankards of beer from taste. There would we sit and listen to the conversation of fishermen, or labourers, or be-gaitered farmers whose cobs or traps stood in yards scattered with wisps of red-and-white clover and hay. The talk of such I always preferred to any, and still do prefer it, and don't get enough of it, being doomed to spend so much time in "the Wen," and seldom seeing the sea or a market-day. That was the pre-Astorian Age; to-day the very Eton boys can't go into their own Tap for a glass of beer because it is undesirable that mothers in Stepney should dope their babies in gin-palaces.

But I cannot (and I can't say that I mind that I cannot) class myself with those who proudly admit that they were devils when young. I never poached—well, except for pheasants' eggs; I never raided girls' schools; I never broke out at night.

*   *   *   *   *

But Bliss had heard none of that, and I had spoken but little of it. We were both dead tired, and had fallen asleep in our warm chairs.

CHAPTER IX

STRATFORD TO TEWKESBURY

"I FEAR I'm developing an incipient cold." I was only half-awake and had not meant to say it aloud to the maid who had brought my tea and was staring at me. "Yes?" she ventured, doubtfully. "I'm afraid I've caught a cold," I translated. She looked sympathetic, and said she was sorry. "So," I went on, "I wonder if you'd mind telling my friend that I shan't be down for an hour. I should like some coffee and a kipper and a paper here in bed."

"Very good, sir."

"And would you mind passing my coat? Thank you." It was *Bible Lands* at which I thought I would take another look. I had not mastered it all in the church at Hampton Lucy.

Rather depressing it was to read a long paper on *Historical Origins of the Present Situation in Palestine.* How politicians are forced to live from hand to mouth! "To Jews and Arabs, therefore, the future of Palestine became unfortunately bound up with the question of documents couched in language which, intentionally or not, was capable of more than one interpretation. In war, men draft documents with less accuracy than in peace. . . ." "Lord Robert Cecil also believed there was room in Palestine for both races. Speaking on the 30th October, 1918, he said: 'I am a great believer in Zionism. I believe it to be one of the noblest movements of the present day. I believe there is room for them all (i.e., Jew, Arab and Christian), that they can all live together, and that it will be the task of the government, whatever it may be that is eventually established in that country, not to favour one sect above another, but to hold the scales of justice with absolute impartiality so that all have an opportunity for self-development and of showing what they are capable of.'" "Room for them all"; "Whatever it may be"; how well-intentioned, and how vague we all were!

I thought of Belloc's book *The Battleground,* that glowing summary of the whole history of that fateful little neck of land between Asia and Africa, the desert and the sea. I thought of the degeneration which had occurred during the three years since I was there, accelerated by foreign complications no doubt, but chiefly due to the fact that there isn't "room for them all." I was only there for a week; you can hardly become an authority in less than a fortnight.

How peaceful in retrospect it all seems! I went there in an aeroplane. It was stormy and for safety's sake we had to land, with a certain amount of bumping, both off the ground and on, in a field near Jaffa and drive the forty miles or so to Jerusalem. The taxi-man was an Arab and lived up to the local traditions of Jehu, but he did not upset us. Those ancient rocky hills were sprinkled with anemones, red and blue; now and then on a hillside—looking like part of the rock—was a village of the immemorial kind; now and then a family in Biblical costume gravely proceeded on donkeys. Everything seemed to be as of old, but as we approached Jerusalem there were eager-looking groups of young Jews, fresh from Europe, mechanics or artisans, and at the approach to Jerusalem there was a whole new town on the usual modern lines.

In the lounge of the vast new King David Hotel, happily outside the walls, sat a huge desert prince, white robes, dagger and all, with Jews at the next table. In the cocktail bar, all chromium and bright leather, were elegant young men, soldiers, policemen, civil servants in club ties with some girls of their kind; they made no mention of impending warfare.

The Berkshires marched to church with the band playing.

At the Wailing Wall—where sad, seedy Jews put their noses to the stones and muttered rather than wailed—an old Arab woman began a disturbance. A young British constable, obviously educated, came up, took her by the elbow and, after the best London models said: "Move on, ma," and she did.

I walked home late from dinner one night; they aren't doing it now.

At Bethlehem it seemed odd that over against the Church of the Nativity there should be a building labelled "Bethlehem Police Station." One thought: "It seems a pity it is necessary even here," but at least it was then a very peaceful spot, and now the building has been blown up by rebels.

Two of us drove in a taxi from Jerusalem to Haifa. All was peace. We stopped at Nablus. On the steps of the little barracks a solitary British soldier was sitting, in shirt-sleeves and shorts, smoking his pipe in the afternoon sun. On the balcony of the hotel was an equally solitary police officer taking his tea. But now the place has been the scene of frequent battles and murders.

M

Farther on, when darkness had fallen, and the moon was up, we stopped again for food. The place was a mixture of inn and village shop, counter and chairs, tinned salmon and bottled beer. The lady in charge was a fat young Jewess. The only other customers were three black bewhiskered ruffians who had come across the desert from Bagdad, in a battered Ford— to post a letter! They were certainly enjoying themselves, and before long, were waving at us, shouting "Good-bye, how do you do?" and then, for our benefit, singing *Tipperary* tunelessly and with incomprehensible words. We bade them a cheerful farewell and went off into the still safe darkness of the Palestinian night; no thought of curfews, or shots from the hill: now uniformed Arab forces range the land and everyone goes in terror of his life. What a pity that so small and beautiful a country should so trouble the world. . . .

Breakfast came and I took it at my leisure. It would have been pleasant to have gone on down the Avon to Tewkesbury and the Severn, but that would have taken more time than we had. So we had decided to send the canoe to Cricklade by rail. Puffle had offered to drive us as far as Evesham; another friend offered to pick us up there, take us to Tewkesbury for the night, and then on to Cricklade next day, which was Sunday.

When I got downstairs, Bliss, who knew the ropes, went off to the station to arrange about carriage; for me, once more I wandered about that pleasant town, at its best when there are few visitors about. On this day there were none conspicuous, though some few of the one hundred thousand or so who visit it each year may have been secreted away in Shakespeare's birthplace, or Anne Hathaway's Cottage. I wondered once more what would happen had that insane theory about Bacon proved true—Stratford would have been ruined and St. Albans made. There cannot be any other town of that size in the world which depends so largely for its existence upon the Fact that one man was born there: Shakespeare is the local industry. I admired once more the brickwork of that stark Memorial Theatre, and entered once more the church to look at that fantastic fat coloured bust. I then went in search of a certain barber's shop, and was disappointed not to find it.

Wouldn't another one have done equally well? In a way it did. But I wanted to see a certain barber's assistant and provoke him to talk, even at the expense of having a hair-cut. For he was a really stout Antinomian.

Two years before I had been in Stratford for the Annual Festival. Before the official junketings began I went to get a shave. A tall young man with a moustache shaved me and made the usual barber's opening about the day's racing. When we had exhausted that theme (naturally, with a razor hovering about, my own contribution was slight) he suddenly (thinking, it seemed, that he had met a kindred soul) said in a puzzled way: "All these foreigners seem to like Shakespeare," and then, leaning over me confidentially, added: "Now, sir, honestly, do *you* like Shakespeare?" "I'm afraid I do," I replied; and he said no more, looking as though I had let him down.

The festivities followed and very odd and charming they were. The streets were hung with the flags of all nations; I daresay that even the Republic of Panama had not been overlooked. Some hundreds of us, officials and guests, were lined up in the street. We were all kinds—I found myself between an affable newspaper peer and a celebrated actress—and we marched under the banners, between crowded pavements, from landmark to landmark. We then proceeded to the Town Hall to eat our fill in honour of the Bard (do they have Dante Dinners in Florence, or merely the speeches?) and luncheon went on a very long time.

I sat, I remember, next to the Soviet Ambassador. We could hardly start cold-bloodedly talking about Oberon or Rosalind, and controversial politics were out of place; the surface had to be stuck to and the only clue I have to our exchanges is that I remember him replying to me gently but firmly: "I do *not* think that Signor Mussolini is a very shy man."

There came a time when faces fell and, between the speeches, conversation flagged. For the speeches were too long, especially one, which was too earnest and scholarly for a post-prandial occasion. It must have been about four before the last speaker was called upon. It was a Mr. Chang, a Chinaman connected with the Drama, and we groaned within us, as we had heard that in the Chinese Theatre time did not matter. We need have had no fears; his speech was dashing, amusing, stimulating, eloquent, and cheered to the echo by an audience "pulled back" in the most extraordinary manner. Tea (of which Shakespeare had never heard) in the Mayor's Parlour followed almost immediately. It was all very simple and provincial in the best sense; this was a locality letting itself go. But I did think that the Lichfield system of having dinner by candlelight in their galleried hall on Johnson's Day was better. There is a mellowness after dinner which there never is after lunch. But then that is a smaller and more private affair. The sort of people who go for that celebration do not want to return to London that night. They are spending an evening with a known and beloved person, not paying tribute to a supreme poetic monument with little more than *nominis umbra* behind it. And it is seldom that the Panamese and Siamese send emissaries thither bearing wreaths of laurel and official greetings.

*   *   *   *   *

Bliss returned. Transport of the canoe to Cricklade had been arranged. "It'll cost pounds, I suppose," I said. "No," he assured me, "only a few shillings." It is, in point of fact, cheaper to send a canoe by train than to travel with it on a canal. But there would hardly be much point in going round the railways of England with a canoe in the guard's van.

Puffle fetched us after lunch and took us to Evesham, where our next pilot picked us up. It was too late for dinner at Tewkesbury, so we supped on the way with certain friends of his, in the parlour of a favourite inn of his. The bacon was good—streaky, unsmoked and crisp—but the mustard had been made the day before and, inadvertently, I said so. They all seemed to think I was complaining about a trifle; but our happiness depends on such trifles. Mustard is really so easy to make; it only takes a minute or so. Nobody likes stale mustard; but we are all so shy in this country that we never make a row about it. Nor, indeed, when we are abroad do we dare to say a thing about what we are given when we ask for English mustard. What they give one—and I have had it from Stockholm to Prague—is a gluey preserved substance out of a bottle. Surely it ought not to be beyond the powers of all the Ritzs Carltons of the world to keep a tin of Colman's mustard!

But large hotels are, I admit, complete mysteries to me. They all seem to think that we have to go there, anyhow, and so must take what they please to give us and pay what they please to ask; but most of them never seem to think: "What can we do to interest visitors in their food?" They all seem to have become standardized. You can still, if you ask for it, get English mustard at any of what they call "the great London caravanserais"; but you have to make something approaching a scene if you want an English cheese. Two or three years ago a Frenchman wrote to *The Times* and complained that whenever he came to England, and at whatever time of year, and asked for Stilton, he was told it was out of season—in other words, either they hadn't got it, or they wouldn't look after it, or they didn't want to serve it. Of course, what happened to him was that wherever he went he was offered all the cheeses he could perfectly well get at home. After I read that I went immediately to lunch at a hotel in the West End and at the end of a simple but pleasant repast asked for Stilton, in that month at its prime. The ensuing conversation was roughly this:

YOUNG WAITER: (*bowing*) Cheese, saire.

S.: A little Stilton, please.

Y. W.: (*with a puzzled frown*) ? ? ?

S.: Stilton. Stilton Cheese. Cheese Ingleesh.

Y. W.: Ve 'ave Camembert——

S.: No, I want Stilton. Steeltong.

Y. W.: Ve 'ave ze Gorgonzola, ze Gruyère.

S.: Will you please bring the Head Waiter?
    (*Brings him.*)

HEAD WAITER: (*twining fingers*) Saire?

S.:   Sorry to trouble you, but I want some Stilton.

H. W.: You vould not vant zat. It ees out of season. Ve have not got.

S.:   Would you mind sending for the Manager?

         (*Brings him, frock-coated, after two minutes' wait.*)

MANAGER: Saire?

S.:   Sorry, but these men don't seem to know what Stilton is. You simply must have some on the premises in a great place like this.

M.:   Certainly, saire, you shall have it, saire; but we are verree seldom asked for it.

S.:   I don't suppose you would be, since you don't put it on the menu.

It came; it was rather hard; but I got it. Usually I am as sheepish as anybody else in these places and loathe making a fuss anywhere; but after that Frenchman's letter I felt that I, or somebody, had a national duty. Yet, what is one amongst so many? It wouldn't have had the slightest effect. If our Government took the slightest interest in the matter things might be different; the Board of Trade prefers to arrange for the import of cheese, and the Board of Agriculture to menace farmers if they dare to send to market any potato weighing more than a pound. Why, in the name of thunder? Cobbett is lucky to be dead; in this age he would have had an apoplectic fit every day.

They are not so silly as that in France. They don't, being extremely insular, and secretly thinking that all their own products (except those of the Tailor Hig-Lif) are better than anybody else's, introduce Cheshire or Double Gloucester to their own population, but they make no mistake about giving the foreign visitor every chance to try every sort of "produce of France." If Wensleydale were made in France we should hear about it, not only in France but in London. They aren't, as a rule, so silly in Italy; though I must admit that, having asked in vain, in Naples and elsewhere, for that stout smoky cheese called Caccio-cavallo, which is made of mare's milk, I never got it until I saw it in an Italian restaurant, far away, on the banks of the rushing Moldau.

But they are certainly as bad in Spain, where, at the end of an excellent Spanish meal, I was told, "No, we have no Spanish cheese, but we have a very nice cheese called Gorgonzola!" (probably that ersatz stuff which the Danes seem to make out of chalk), and I fear, much as I admire the Czechs, they are just as bad in Bohemia.

Imagine yourself arriving for the first time in that noble city of Prague, and dining by yourself, after a long and tiring aeroplane trip, alone, your first evening, in one of the two best hotels of the place—few guests about, and a mass of waiters. Imagine a delightful dinner with a new kind of soup, a new kind of fish from the Danube, an excellent cutlet: and then, once more, the old kind of dialogue.

S.:　　　Now I should like some Czech cheese.

WAITER: Certainly, saire.

　　　　　(Brings a tray with things looking like Gruyère, Camembert, and Gorgonzola.)

S.:　　　But these are . . . do please bring the head-waiter.
　　　　　(Brings him.)

HEAD WAITER: Saire?

S.:　　　I asked for some Czech cheese and he's brought me these.

H. W.: All made in Czechoslovakia, saire. Same as our Worcestershire Sauce. Vairy goot.

S.:　　　But I don't *want* imitations. I want *real* Czech cheese that isn't made anywhere else. There must be some.

H. W.: Yes, saire; but we only keep International Cheeses in this hotel!

S.:　　　But, look here, I'm staying here a fortnight. Go and get me some, there's a good fellow.

He went out, while all his colleagues hung around with napkins and I finished the last of an excellent bottle of white wine (Lobkowitz?) of which I had never previously heard.

After twenty minutes—for I suppose he must have gone out to some Czech Good Pull Up for Carmen, or some such low place where they were really allowed to eat their own country's cheese—he came back with a heaped plateful of a crumbly, creamy cheese the colour of potted shrimps; it was delightful, in flavour unique. "Why on earth," I said, "don't you keep this permanently on your menu, tell foreigners it's the great local delicacy, and charge them all double for it that you charge for all those other things which look as though they were by-products of your Mr. Bata's boot-factory?" He looked at me with a smile bewildered and sad, and I could see his lips framing their old refrain, "We only keep International Cheeses here." Next evening when I asked for it again, there was again a twenty minutes' delay; later they were broken in, and must have got in a stock. But always when I asked for that delicious Czech cheese (Lobkowitz?) they looked at me as a flunkey at the Mansion House might look if one asked him to bring one some pickled onions with one's turtle soup.

*   *   *   *   *

These sort of thoughts were floating through my head as I lay in an arm-chair in a corner under a lithograph of Magersfontein, smoking my pipe and listening with one ear to the conversation of the others. I had dimly observed that Bliss had been in another corner, scrawling on envelopes as is his wont at any odd moment. He came over to me, looked at me intently, and produced a well-turned Ballade with the refrain, "The Beastly Mustard isn't freshly made." I thought he might have sympathized with me more. . . .

"I suppose we ought to be moving on to Tewkesbury," said John.

"Couldn't move to a better place," said Bliss; "that Abbey's one of the noblest things in England."

"The pillars are magnificent," said I, "all like Durham on a small scale, but the roof's lower than it was. They burnt it. They also, in the Wars of the Roses, butchered people there, although it was sanctuary. But it's remarkably unspoilt."

We got into the car. I sat alone with the bags at the back.

I had already developed a temperature, began thinking rather despairingly of what this country would have been had it not been for the rack and ruin of war and iconoclasm, and then began thinking of the evil work of the well-meaning iconoclasm of the nineteenth century. "Restored by" . . . "1865" . . . "at the expense of."

When we got to Tewkesbury I went straight to bed.

*   *   *   *   *

In how many a parish church, even in the most lonely and impoverished places, does not one find these inscriptions triumphing in the murder of old stone and the removal of old wood; some cathedrals have suffered; and even in such places as that glorious church of Wren's, St. Mary-le-Bow, one can find tablets saying that well-meaning but too ubiquitous snail, Sir Gilbert Scott (whose grandson has atoned for him) once crawled over it, and "restored and adorned" it, at the expense of sixty thousand pounds. But what we too seldom remember, as we shudder at our fathers' Philistinism, is that all the architects and all the patrons and all the vicars (who often spent their own money) thought they were, in restoring, showing their reverence for the old work, and, when they removed it, thought they were replacing it by something as good or better and "beautifying" the edifices entrusted to them.

I wonder how often, in that transitional period, before there were Diocesan Committees to control the local people, but after William Morris had started an enlightened campaign for the right care of our architectural inheritance, some devoted parson may not have been made miserable, after spending years of thought and all his money on the "beautification" of his beloved fabric, only to find himself publicly denounced at the end by persons of taste as an ignorant destroyer?

Some old man, in a remote parish, I think of. There would be a story in it. It might begin like this, and be called *Restoration*.

The church of Laverstock is considered to be unique among the churches which fringe the desolation of Dart-

moor. Its size is sufficient to give it the title, contested by
one or two other edifices, of "The Cathedral of the Moor";
any population which that secluded and static hamlet could
ever have had, Dissenters included, would not have half-
filled the nave. But its uniqueness rested not so much on its
size as on the quality of its architecture. Most of the Dartmoor churches, and certainly the neighbours of Laverstock
St. Nicholas on the western skirts of the Moor, are homely
and plain; some of them almost as bare and stern as the
crags above them, crested by blocks of the granite which
forms their walls, their low pointed aisles, and their square,
four-pinnacled towers, all grey-black from the rain and the
mist. They have their beauty, and a kind of beauty which
some lovers of building prefer to any other, but nobody could
call them ornate or magnificent. They are village churches,
and pretend to be no other, provincial and rural as the
thatched cottages and the simple gravestones, boasting only
the least pretentious of carven and heraldic tombs, often
whitewashed within and pleasantly innocent of stained glass.

But Laverstock, of a later date than most, was another
matter. Its true kindred were in East Anglia, those noble
and elaborate churches to which the authors of text-books
are obliged to have such frequent recourse, the most sump-
tuous flowers of the Perpendicular style. Its tower soared
rather than stood, it had a clerestory, fan-vaulting, and
bosses, a little mouldering. And the vicar, the Reverend
William Hawker, loved his church as he loved to hear its
bells pealing over the valleys on a Sunday morning. He
knew all its beauties by heart, he had recovered all he could
about its builders and donors and uneventful history, and he
was never so happy as when some stray visitor came to
Laverstock and gave him a chance of communicating his
local lore, and eagerly squeezing from the stranger the last
drop of admiration for his beloved church. This occurred
all too rarely. Laverstock Church, though of course mentioned in all the county guide-books, was just not exceptional
enough, save in its own locality, to induce students from a
distance to make special journeys to it, and it was too

remote, too far from the railway or any main road, to be
encountered by any man who had not undertaken a con-
fessed pilgrimage to it. Sometimes, from one August to
another, no informed sight-seer would enter the building,
no traveller at all except a few pedestrian tourists with knapsacks making their way across the Moor. It was something
to talk to these, and they were always delighted with the
gentle old vicar. But as a rule they knew little, and had no
terms: spandrils, crockets, triforia, corbels and ogees were
words that merely made them, to his distress, look uncomfortable; the finest points they were often unable to seize.
When one of them appeared the Vicar would talk about
him to his sister throughout the next meal. "You know,
Agnes," he would say, laying down his knife and fork, "that
really was a most intelligent and interesting man who looked
over the church this morning. He quite agreed with me
that Mr. Ruskin ought to have seen our church and would
certainly have written about it. He said he had never seen
a roof so fine as ours, and he was quite sad about the decay
everywhere. What a shame it is that we can do nothing
about it. There is so very much decay, both in the stone and
in the wood. That rood screen is dreadful, and there is
hardly any paint left to see. And if only we could remove
those old pews! You know, Agnes, we have never seen our
dear old church as its builders really meant it to be seen."

"No, William," his sister would answer. She had little
appreciation of architecture and no knowledge of the past;
to her a church was a place where she worshipped and
arranged the flowers. But she loved her brother and was content that he should form her opinions by proxy. Not that he
had many opinions. A less contentious clergyman could
scarcely have been found within the varied fold of Mother
Church. His innocence was so transparent, his benignity so
evident, that the bickerings common in Laverstock as in all
villages were seldom allowed to reach him. He was charitable
beyond his means; and an ugly word or deed not only
wounded but bewildered him; his white head was respected
even by the wicked, and his sermons admirably served the

needs of a simple community, knowing even less than he did of intellectual things, but instinctively responsive to the language of a tender heart. Had there been a local gentry, which there was not, it might privately have referred to him as rather an old fool. Possibly the stranger who had entered his gate and left them may, far away, have sometimes told his tale humorously: "A most beautiful church. The Vicar was hanging about when I went there. Rather a dear old dodderer. I could hardly get away from him." Had a cottager in Laverstock heard such words there would have been black looks or an indignant torrent of rebuke, and the farmers from whom the churchwardens and sidesmen were drawn were capable of defending the old man with their fists.

"Old man": Mr. Hawker was in his seventieth year, and had been at Laverstock half his life. The living had been obtained for him by the influence of a former cricketing colleague, now long since dead; for, in his last year at Cambridge, Bill Hawker had been a quiet and popular, if only moderately successful, member of the University Eleven; no bowler, but a painstaking bat. For some time he had kept touch with his college friends and with some whom he had made when curate in a poor London parish; but in time they all forgot him. It was now twenty years since he had made a journey to Lord's in July, and more since his last effort to make his villagers play cricket had failed. They were too few, too hard-worked; and the difficulties about ground in that hilly country were too great. Change had gradually come; his eyes were as blue as ever, his face as ruddy; but he stooped a little now, and wore white side-whiskers. You could see him in the village street any sunny day, a dingy and friendly little figure, chatting with a gnarled housewife at a cottage door, with Green at the forge, or with Landlord Davey at the door of the "Fox"; talking, always, you might be sure, of the weather or of personal things, childbirth, illnesses, sons and daughters out in the world, the returned prodigal who was seen in church last Sunday, the local chances at the forthcoming flower-show in the nearest small town, the annual choir-treat, the state of the organ. And no day passed but he twice or three times walked round his church, outside and inside, contemplating its beauties, anxiously scrutinizing its condition, dreaming of a repair and a restoration which would bring back its pristine freshness and perfection. Its tower and porch, lace-work in stone, were actually sketched in one of the old rust-spotted books on English Gothic which were far more often opened than the supernatural commentaries and theological lives which filled with them the one bookcase in his small study. He read these works again and again, convinced that his own church could equal in every detail the most splendid structures praised in them; delighted that it had some features which appeared to be precisely paralleled nowhere else. The font, the pulpit, the rood-screen (alas! so mouldering and its paintings so faint), the clerestory, the buttresses, the columns, the capitals, the tracery of the windows: everything at Laverstock he unconsciously regarded as the ideal type to which all things elsewhere should conform. And as year after year went by he was more and more set on the idea of restoration of the whole and reproduction of those parts which had most suffered.

*   *   *   *   *

And how would it go on? I think (and the thing has happened often) he would collect what he could from the parish, add the whole of his own patrimony (his sister perhaps doubting, but never saying him nay), employ a builder from the nearest town to "restore" the stone-work, tear out the old oak pews with their carven ends and substitute pitch-pine, remove the worm-eaten rood-screen and buy a new one from a London firm, put up an East Window in chalky reds and blues, and then have a re-dedication service.

Then some rumour of it would reach the metropolis. A grim-looking man would come down in a car, inspect the church, talk tersely to him, and go away again.

Two days afterwards his sister would try to hide *The Times* from him. But he would see it, and in the Correspondence

find a letter from the Society for the Preservation of Ancient
Buildings referring to "the irreparable depredations of this
reverend vandal," with perhaps a small leading article backing the letter up and demanding preventive measures.

What could the old man, who loved his church and lived
for it, do, after he had believed his eyes? Hardly, perhaps,
burn the church down with himself in it; that would be too
melodramatic. But I think, in a short story, he could shoot
himself in his study; and for this very reason, that I believe it
once happened in real life.

*   *   *   *   *

Yes, I am in bed at Tewkesbury, and asleep, and parted
from the canoe. Where was the canoe, all through that darkness, parted from its companions and away from its natural
element? In some guard's van, I suppose, with hampers,
parcels, trunks, dogs and guinea-pigs. Of its route I cannot
be sure, the connections, physical and moral, of railway companies being so complicated. Looking at the map I should say
that its best route would take it through, or just past, Long
Marston, Church Honeybourne (Cow Honeybourne is quite
near), Willersey, Broadway, Stanway, Stanley Pontlarge,
Gotherington, Cheltenham and Cirencester, Chedworth,
Withington.

I have never, I think, seen Cow Honeybourne, Stanley
Pontlarge, or Gotherington; they sound attractive. Cheltenham we all know. It thinks it is as good as Leamington for
dyspepsia and obesity; it vies with Bedford as to the numbers
of school-children; it thinks that George III liked it as well as
Weymouth; and it is so populous with Anglo-Indians that it
was at one time known as "Asia Minor."

Cirencester should be known by those who don't know it:
the church is superb and the stabling adequate. Broadway is
beautiful, if rather more tidy and self-conscious than its neighbour, Campden; at Stanway there is a lovely house. And at
Chedworth, had I accompanied the canoe thither, and had
Bliss allowed me, I should certainly have got out and seen the
finest Roman villa thus far discovered in England. I say "thus

far" because the soil has hardly yet been scratched in search of that civilization which the Teutonic barbarians swamped. This villa was only found, in 1864, because Lord Eldon had a gamekeeper, and the gamekeeper had a ferret, and the ferret got lost, and, looking for the ferret, the gamekeeper turned up some Roman tesserae and took notice of them.

Such notice would not have been taken by the landlord of a certain village inn near Nailsworth. Some ten years ago I drove about a hundred miles to see that celebrated Roman pavement at Woodchester which they uncover only about once in fifty years. Not knowing precisely where it was, I stopped to enquire at this inn. The landlord, a red pudding-faced man with a heavy moustache, said: "You can't see it. All shut up. Covered it up yesterday."

"But I've driven all the morning to see it."

"Can't be 'elped; all closed," he said.

"Dash!" I said, approximately.

"Don't see why anybody should want to look at that ole rubbish! There's a lot gorn from round 'ere to see it. Working men, too! Paying a bob, too! Gimme a pint of beer if I've got to spend me bobs."

"No accounting for tastes," I platitudinized.

"Wot I say," he insisted, "is this. If you want to see anything wot reely is interestin' look over there!"

There, suspended from the ceiling, like a lump of paper, was a vast hornets' nest. Failing the pavement I examined the nest. It certainly was remarkable.

*   *   *   *   *

But perhaps the canoe didn't go that way at all. It may have wandered round the world under the stars, pausing from time to time at such charming junctional, though not very functional, resorts as Bletchley. Did the guard and the canoe, thus loitering by platform and dim gas-lamp, ever commune together? Might it have been thus?

GUARD: Where do you come from?
CANOE: Stratford.

GUARD: Where are you going to?

CANOE: Oxford, ultimately. Cricklade now, if you care to look at my label.

GUARD: Why don't you go by water?

CANOE: They sent me by train.

GUARD: 'Oo's yer boss?

CANOE: An old boy called Bliss. Says he knew my great-grandfather. Another chap with him: doesn't know so much about it.

GUARD: Been far?

CANOE: A hundred and fifty miles, perhaps.

GUARD: Had a good time?

CANOE: Average. Rather slow as a rule. I must say if I am in the water I like to move.

GUARD: Built for it, as you might say.

CANOE: Yes, and there have been some extremely rough passages on land that rather shivered my timbers.

GUARD: You'd like to be at Oxford, I bet! Smooth water all the time.

CANOE: I won't say that. So long as one doesn't get too badly knocked about, a little shaking and discomfort isn't really a bad thing. Besides, there's the pleasure of getting into easy circumstances afterwards. The contrast appeals to the Epicurean in one.

GUARD: What?

CANOE: Oh, it's a word Mr. Bliss uses a lot; he says he's one. The same thing applies to the night's rest after the day's labours. They left me comfortably moored in several very pleasant places on this trip. One mill-pool I remember in particular. I slept under a willow-tree with the stars looking through.

GUARD: Blimey, I had quite enough of that in the War.

CANOE: Tastes differ. I couldn't possibly get a wink, jolting about in this train of yours.

GUARD: That so? . . . 'Arf a mo' . . . Bletchley.

CHAPTER X

Tewkesbury to Cricklade

It was Sunday again. It seemed more than a week since we had been obstructed by the *Brahmapootra* and the Banbury Town Council and had left the canoe by the Sanitary Inspector's office in the Corporation Yard.

I looked at the Sunday papers. Some sentences of Gibbon's came into my head. I may not remember them properly because I don't know where to look for them, but I think they run roughly: "Before they can conquer they must cease to be barbarians . . . we can therefore acquiesce in the pleasing conclusion that every age of the world has increased, and still increases the real wealth, the happiness, the knowledge, and perhaps the virtue of the human race." It is just as well that he put in at any rate one reservation.

Bliss was out; I had a cold; it was Sunday morning in a provincial hotel, and John Moore was not coming until eleven. I fell into one of those ruminations, so fruitless and so inescapable, about the history of mankind. I had not long before been reading Mr. Eugene Lyons' *Assignment to Utopia,* immeasurably the best book I have seen about post-war Russia, honest and full of power and panoramic scenes. It would make one sick of one's kind were it not that the author himself, having supped on horrors for six years, keeps his faith in justice and kindness and his heart to go on fighting for them.

How relative a term "civilization" is! There is the most violent disagreement about its definition, or, rather, very little attempt to define it. To some it seems to mean only literary and mechanical organization: when Hitler butchers and robs his thousands or Stalin has "a purge" you can hear people saying, "Fancy this happening in a civilized country"—or "in 1938," which is another titan of muddle-headedness and question-begging. Some use it as a term of abuse: Edward Carpenter wrote a book called *Civilization, its Cause and Cure.*

But how get definitions when we aren't even agreed as to whither we want to go? Perhaps we can all agree with cheerful Professor Haldane when he says that "the future will be no primrose path." So long as "tot homines" is true that must be true. In the world as it is—and the Ice Age is ahead—it is well enough to have a Utopia as a standard, not much use to have it as an aim, and still less to find in it a consolation unless we regard it as part and parcel of the consolations of religion.

How circumstances defeat us, and how often does history remind us of the Tower of Siloam! Sodom and Gomorrah may (though very likely not if judged by their own standards, to us peculiar) have deserved what they got; but who knows that Atlantis may not have reached the acme of kindness and justice before the waves came over it? Something always happens to knock mankind off a straight line of movement—irruptions of barbarians, scientists, theories, or what not; apart from all which there is that in us which Chesterton referred to when he said that "if you want to keep a white wall from going black you must keep on painting it white." How, in the light of that, anybody thinks he can transform a whole society in a moment, especially by a bloody revolution, beats me hollow. And I can't understand why most of these revolutionaries should want to, as they are materialists and atheists. . . .

Bliss came in, cheerfully rubbing his hands. "Bliss," I said, "have I quoted to you that remark of the ex-corporal ploughman, 'About this 'ere 'istory, sir, it seems that every x—— thirty years or so some energetic y—— springs up and spoils the 'ole z—— issue'?"

"Several times," said Bliss.

"Well, can you understand why those men should be so energetic about change, or anything but their appetites, when they don't think they're responsible to anything beyond this world? And why should they try to force men to their opinion when they don't claim divine authority for it?"

"Or even diabolic," said Bliss.

"Matthew Arnold spoke of 'a power, not ourselves, making for righteousness.'"

"Others say God," said Bliss; "I think I could get outside a pint of bitter." He rang the bell. "D'you mind chucking over that paper?" he went on. But it wasn't the state of the world or the cricket he was looking for. "I want to see," he remarked, "whether I've won a prize in that competition."

He is always going in for these literary competitions (turning as pretty a verse of the kind as a man could wish) and constantly winning prizes. I sometimes suspect him of having various false names and accommodation addresses so that the literary editors should not guess that he really pouches the lot, if not as W. Bliss then as Ajax, Nemo, Major Road and Edith J. Blenkinsop.

Then John Moore came in, with young fresh face, also brightly rubbing his hands, as people always seem to do when one is feeling a little out of sorts oneself. "Fine bracing morning outside," he said. I shivered. "The Haineses are coming at twelve," he explained, "but if there's anywhere you'd like to go before that, I'll drive you."

"What about Overbury?" I suggested.

"You won't be able to stay long."

"Never mind, I haven't been there for ten years."

"Have you told them you're coming?"

"No, but we can take a chance, and even if there's nobody there it will be pleasant to see that lovely yellow Jacobean front again, and catch a glimpse of Bredon, which is virtually in the garden. I went up it once on a Sunday morning. It was hazy and I did not see many 'coloured counties,' but the church bells trembled through the haze from far and near."

Off we went and soon reached that gracious house. The Holland-Martin family is sufficiently numerous for a plentitude of them to be in church and some still to be at home. So it fell out. We enjoyed all too brief a hospitality, left regards, and fled back to Tewkesbury. The clock was toning twelve as we drew up in front of the fine old "Bell"; from another direction another car drew up simultaneously. "That was well-timed," I thought, and when we were settled down inside I told them about another and stranger meeting at the twelve strokes, long ago.

* * * *

During the years between the War and his death I invariably paid one or more visits annually to Thomas Hardy at Max Gate. There was never anybody else staying. Unless a neighbour called there were only Hardy, his devoted wife (who, until her own death, kept all his friends amongst the young poets and writers, Colonel Lawrence included) and their odd fox-terrier "Wessex." Nothing could have been more varied than the talk of this old man, intensely curious concerning all quaint, strange, beautiful or humorous facts about the past; his melancholy eye and outlook were by no means reflected in his talk; many men, after all, find in writing an outlet for their suffering hearts. Memories crowd in upon me of small things. He was childishly pleased to show the signatures of German prisoners on a shed in his garden. Once he took me out to see his ancestral church at "Mellstock." He showed me the simple tombs of his fathers. I commented on the good lettering of the latest and he said, with his charming simplicity: "If ever you want a good monumental mason, just you drop me a postcard and I'll send you the name of one."

Once as we were leaving the dining-room Wessex leapt up and began to tug at his trouser-leg. "What on earth's up?" I asked. "Oh," said Hardy, "he won't let me leave the room until he's had his few minutes of the wireless." He turned on the machine and we sat down again, while the dog, on his haunches, with his tongue hanging out, delighted in his daily dose of Bach. "Mind you," added Hardy, as we rose again, "he doesn't like the Talks!" The idea of that terrier howling if they gave him "Hints on Poultry" instead of Scriabine always cheers me when I remember it. Once even, when I had a cricket team in Dorset in 1921, Hardy actually offered to umpire in a match.

On this notion Mrs. Hardy's foot was firm. Time came when her foot descended once more. On a night Hardy asked if he might stay up a little after she had gone to bed. "Yes," she replied doubtfully, "provided it is only a little." As soon as she had gone he suggested going back to the dining-room, and produced a bottle of claret.

There we sat until two o'clock, forgetting the time, and talking about the songs and legends of his Dorset youth and the people he had known in London—which included old Mrs. Proctor, who had entertained Lamb and Keats. I'm sure he would have been willing to stay up all night; but it wouldn't do, and at last we crept upstairs and the house was soon dark.

In the morning I was frowned on. Mrs. Hardy—bless her!—treated her wiry old man as though he were the most fragile of porcelain. "Come," she exclaimed, "as usual, but in future you must sleep at a hotel." Her tones admitted of no argument. It would have been no use pointing out, when he came down in the morning, that his eyes were full of sparkle and he was obviously none the worse for wear, in fact all the better for having his tiny fling. She had spoken. I had to be content with the wry consolation that, in me, Hardy, at the age of eighty-four or so, had met, perhaps for the first time in his life, a Demoralizing Influence.

One October evening, after that, I was at a party at a friend's in London. Late, when they had finished giving a concert, John Goss and his quartet came on to assist us to sing. For an hour they performed, in their unequalled way, folk-songs and sea-shanties. I found myself in a corner with John and told him how much I had enjoyed their singing. "I've often wished," I said, "that I could do some small thing for you after all the pleasure you've given me. But I don't suppose there's a thing?"

"Only one," he replied, "and I don't suppose that could be managed."

"Tell me, though."

"I should like, beyond everything," he said, "to meet Thomas Hardy."

"That's all right, I think," I said. "Will you be in England next August?"

"Yes, we're going to America first but shall be back then."

"Where will you be?"

"London."

I was going to be in Cornwall. I thought about dates and then said: "Look here, could you meet me at twelve noon outside the 'Greyhound' at Dorchester on August the 18th, next year?"

"Yes."

"Shall you want a reminder?"

"No."

"Sure?"

"Absolutely."

We left it at that. The ten months passed by; we never once met; we never exchanged even a postcard.

When August 18th came, as I was driving into Dorchester from the west, it suddenly occurred to me how Hardyish the situation would be if it really came off: "One day in mid-August, as the Casterbridge clock slowly boomed out the strokes of noon, two men might have been seen . . ."

But it came off; there were not three strokes between us!

I went inside and telephoned Max Gate and asked if I could bring an extra man to lunch. "Who is it?" asked Mrs. Hardy. I told her. "Well," she said, bringing a little balm to my wound, "if he's a friend of yours I suppose he's all right."

He certainly was. We had not been five minutes at the luncheon table before Hardy and Goss were well away on Dorset folk-songs, and the old church music of fiddle and hautboy and serpent—we were right back in the atmosphere of *Under the Greenwood Tree*. We stayed to tea and we stayed to dinner. The talk they had about the country songs, their keen interest in variants, made me wonder whether our earnest and admirable collectors, who have spent a generation with note-books stirring the memories of toothless and illiterate Methuselahs in tavern and cottage had ever thought of searching the memory of the finest old peasant of them all. From titles they got to tunes, from tunes to singing, from solos by John to duets with Hardy's quaver joining in while his eyes sparkled and his hand beat time. After tea he said: "Florence, my dear, run upstairs and bring down that old music out of that box." The music consisted of songs which had belonged to his first wife, dead long since, and had never been touched since she died.

They were brought. John took the piano-stool; the old man and I stood behind him and we went through the lot, Hardy occasionally, smiling through tears, saying "Dear! Dear!" What they were I can't remember; doubtless some by Thomas Haynes Bayly and certainly a tender duet called "The Cuckoo," redolent of rosebuds and crinolines. . . .

Either that year or next saw the last summer of his life. Six months after one visit I was at that vast funeral in the Abbey, a "little irony" which he might have grimly relished while sighing. He had always wished to be buried in the country churchyard with his sires, and Mrs. Hardy wanted to fulfil his wishes. In one of his last poems he had satirized interment in the Abbey. But Barrie wanted the Abbey; and the widow was overborne. When protests began to be made there was a hurried last-moment dissection, and part of him was buried at Mellstock and part at Westminster.

In a fit of revulsion I wrote a ballad "Hardy in our Abbey," suggesting a further distribution of parts. But it is, I think, for publication a trifle too macabre.

*   *   *   *   *

But we were with the Haineses at Tewkesbury. John Haines, who lives at Gloucester, has for many years been the friend and correspondent of poets. Living ones apart, Edward Thomas and John Freeman were friends of his—two whose gravity, depth and music will be more appreciated if and when circumstances enable men to remove their attention from the daily din and dynamite and the literature inspired by them. But mostly we talked of Ivor Gurney, an intimate of both of us, and a Gloucester man like him, who fought as a private in the Gloucesters in France and never lost the accent of his county.

He died in 1937, having been in a mental home for many years. Had it not been for the War, he would have added great lustre to English music. As little more than a child he was assistant-organist at Gloucester Cathedral. When he went to the Royal College, Stanford told Parry that he had something like a young Schubert as a pupil; when Parry saw him he said: "It *is* Schubert." He had, even then, an astonishing mastery over orchestration and a very great fertility in song-writing; music simply possessed him and when he went to the piano, which he played with great power, he forgot everything around him. With his square face, mop of hair, deep brown eyes, spectacles and firm chin, he certainly looked very like Schubert, but there were times when both his face and his music took a tinge of Beethoven.

He was no shrinker from the War. He wrote a book of war-poems called *Severn and Somme,* in which, with touching simplicity, he said that it was the duty of him and his kind to make "the name of poet terrible in just fight." But he came back shell-shocked and the struggles he had after the War would have been enough to break even a man whose health and nerves had not been injured. He could make no money and he could get but few of his compositions published. He had help from friends, but was usually too proud to take it, and attempted all kinds of unsuitable jobs to keep himself, even spending some days as a meat-porter at Smithfield, for which he was nothing like strong enough.

There came a time when, the cloud coming over him (though his critical talk was still penetrating and his playing superb), he would accept a bed but no food; later, when he would wander in, play, take neither bed nor food, and walk out into the night again. Then he got delusions, was seques-trated, and lost even the desire to play, though he still read. But his heart had broken before his mind; he simply could not understand why powers and energies like his could not earn a man bread and a roof. The last time I looked on him—he had temporarily "escaped" and had all the old passion—I thought, as I thought of what had been wasted and over what years, "There, more than in any graveyard, is the ghastly face of war."

A few scores of songs remain; the Oxford Press are printing the unpublished ones. They are very various, and the inven-tion shown in the accompaniments remarkable. He set the best poets of his time—Bridges, Housman, de la Mare and their juniors. I do not think any Englishman ever wrote a lovelier song than his setting of Edward Thomas's "Lights Out," to mention only one. And his love of his own country was such that none who knew him can ever think of the Severn Valley without thinking of him.

*   *   *   *   *

We parted too soon, and were driven out to John Moore's for Sunday beef. He then drove us the fifty miles or so to Cricklade, through Colesborne and Cirencester. It was an afternoon of sun and shadow and wisps of rain, and that green hilly country was looking very beautiful.

He took his departure, being in a hurry; we booked our rooms, and gave each other Sunday looks in the almost empty hotel. I remembered a friend who lived round the corner, in a pretty little early Victorian house with trellised porch, climbing roses, a well-stocked garden; a drawing-room crowded with the right mahogany and inlay, china, silver, brass, woolwork, chintz, engravings and water-colours; and premises generally infested by dogs, canaries, horses, chickens, geese and bees. Her did I go to call on, and found her busy with her busy bees, apparently talking to them; though she does not go to the length of that other lady who keeps bees in London, puts marks on their backs, and says that she once met, and was recognized by, one of them on Hampstead Heath—though I forget whether the two went home together in a cab. She agreed to come round and dine with us.

We broke up early. I felt shivery and left Bliss talking about fishing to some habitués who had come in with flies in their hats. As soon as I had got into bed I felt quite comfortable again, and settled down to read, for the twentieth time, *The Private Papers of Henry Rycroft,* a copy of which I had picked up in Stratford, feeling that I knew the works of Bliss and Harberton by heart for the time being.

What a charming and touching book that is! Gissing, in his brief Indian summer, surveying the world from retirement, and musing on the contrast between his present country peace and the bitterness of his poverty-stricken life, years of drudgery, of wearing out shoe-leather to save fares, of going without food to buy books. Yet I think Rycroft never once even hints at the chief cause of his miseries—an early and disastrous marriage, the fatality of which it took him years to realize, but which put a millstone round his neck. He took his medicine, and had the two not parted (for she was not the kind of person who would have enjoyed the society of his few friends) nobody might ever have known anything about his tragedy, and he might even have been thought one of those incompetents who are unfit to cope with the practical business of life.

There may have been many such instances. For example, let us try a parable:

I

Light sometimes comes through unexpected chinks, just when we despair of getting any light at all. So it came to James Burgoyne when he was wrestling, despairingly, with the knottiest problem offered him by the life of Wilson Byng. So was Burgoyne assisted to write a standard biography which is never likely to be superseded. And so was he led to a feat of psychological imagination of which the embattled reviewers of two continents observed, with a unanimity which suggested conspiracy or imitation, that it was "masterly," and "a brilliant triumph" and that "Mr. Burgoyne had miraculously succeeded where a host of distinguished critics before him" had failed. It all arose out of his wife's habit of barging in on him in the evenings when he was working—and interrupting him.

For several years Burgoyne had been engaged upon this book. He had first been led to undertake it because of a chivalrous feeling for the dead author. Walter Wilson Byng (1800–1870), unfortunate in life, had been still more unfortunate in death. He had lived long and worked prodigiously, pouring out for fifty years an average of two substantial books a year—essays, histories, travels, poems, plays, political tracts, amateur antiquarianism, and finally memoirs—the memoirs alone, produced when he was an old man, filling three thick volumes. He had edited in youth three Radical newspapers, the outspokenness of each of which had brought him into gaol; and in later and milder days had successfully conducted several magazines of the *Home and Family* type. It might have been thought—especially as he brought a family up respectably—that such a career would have been held up as a model by all the copy-book moralists. On the contrary, for some mysterious reason, he was always spoken of with a compassion akin to contempt: it seemed impossible for his successors to refer to one of his really beautiful sonnets or essays with a bare mention of the author's name. The unhappy name always appeared in company with some derogatory epithet or comparison; it was always "that Micawber Wilson Byng," or "poor feckless Byng," or "that incorrigible borrower, Wilson Byng." These descriptions would seem to suggest that, hard though Byng worked, he was one of the great prodigals; a reckless man of letters, dissipated or at the least extravagant, given to celebrating the end of every job with a champagne supper, if not afflicted with the most expensive taste of all, namely, the taste for an unofficial harem. And yet, there it was, he was always held up as a failure, almost a pitiful warning. His children were forgotten, his wife received the brief compassion due to "a shadowy wife somewhere in the background."

There stood poor hard-working Byng, so temperate, so sunny of humour in face of every misfortune, pointed at by the general finger as the unthrifty grasshopper in a world of careful ants. And why? Simply because, for all he earned, he never had any money? And why had he never any money? That was where the mystery came in; nobody had explained it: they had just easily assumed that it was his own fault and patronized him for it. The only reward of his gallant cheerfulness was that he was regarded as a vagabond who took no thought for the morrow; men with large private incomes admitted that he must have been charming company, but felt obliged to deplore the casual manner in which he took his responsibilities. Yet there was his record, and there, in the old paintings and daguerreotypes, was his face, gentle but not meek, the eyes friendly, the mouth firm and sensitive, the chin not devoid of resolution.

Most of the book was, in a manner, easy to write. A careful study of sources, including Byng's own voluminous works, resulted in several volumes of notes; the rest was a matter of arrangement, illuminating quotation, and straightforward criticism. Burgoyne took some time over it, for he had his literary job on a daily paper, and his private work could only be done in the evening. But he had written most of his chapters, and he was not dissatisfied with them; they were clear and competent; no important facts were omitted; and he had avoided nonsense in his estimates of his subject's writings. The one hurdle still to be cleared was Byng's character. What *did* he do with his money? He felt sure that there was an explanation of the paradox somewhere, but it still baffled him. There was a convincing, rehabilitating defence somewhere within reach; but where precisely?

2

It was after dinner. The only maid was out, and Burgoyne had found a note on the table from his wife saying that she had gone to a cinema and that his food was keeping warm in the oven. This proved true: there was a dish of hot, if hardened, mince and macaroni, and with this, some cream cheese, an apple, and a bottle of beer; he had rapidly satisfied, or destroyed, his appetite. Now he was at his desk in the untidy, flowerless, sitting-room, with shelves all round him, and stacks of books and notes in front of him. For the hundredth evening, staring at the bulb of the green-shaded reading-lamp, he leant his chin on hands, elbow on table, trying to plumb the inner secret of Byng's noted incompetence. Friends who "dropped in" in the evening had grown used to the sight of Burgoyne at his desk, spare, lean, concentrated, abstracted, but never impatient of interruption. His steel-rimmed spectacles were on his wrinkled forehead, his eyes were screwed almost shut, his mouth was tense under his shaggy brown moustache. "I wonder," he said to himself—and how often it had come to this!—if the whole explanation lay in some secret in his private life. But what more was there to be found? There had never been scandal about Byng. There was a gap there, and he simply didn't know how to fill it: yet, if he did not fill it, there would be no convincing vindication, and he might better have been engaged upon some easier and, incidentally, more lucrative compilation.

He rose, and, with bent head, sucking at his pipe, began pacing up and down the room, profitlessly turning over the old, old slag-heap of discarded thoughts. There was a noise at the front door, a shuffle in the passage by the umbrella-stand, and then Maud came in, with her smart hat still on—large, dark, shiny, full-bosomed, deep-eyed, rouged, casual—his wife. "Still at it?" she remarked indifferently. "Pity it doesn't earn more. Been to a flick; I took Clara. Six-and-ninepenny seats; rotten." She slid largely into the big arm-chair, with the same motion (as it seemed) crossing her stout and silken legs and stuffing a chocolate into her red mouth from the cardboard box which she was carrying. "Yes, dear," he replied gently, "did you enjoy yourself?"

"Oh, all right," she said, momentarily ceasing to munch; "seen worse. Vamp not much good. Could have done it better myself."

"Yes, dear," he said. Lying there, in a green dress with a red-figured scarf thrown round her shoulders, she looked like an overblown odalisque. He had for years been able to look at her with scientific detachment, though he effectually concealed the habit. "Yes," thought he, "you've never shown much force or passion in life, but your vanity might produce a very fair imitation of it all if you were posing for the screen." What he said was: "I've always thought you could do anything if you really wanted to."

"Well," she replied, putting another chocolate into her magazine, "I married you instead, and that's that. Reminds me I shall want a tenner in the morning. Woman clamouring about this hat. Get me a whisky?"

Burgoyne obediently left his work, stepped to a corner-cupboard, drew out a bottle, a siphon and one glass, and put them on a small table which he set beside her.

"You on the wagon?" she asked, without interest. He suddenly realized that he might say "No," and take a whisky, or "Yes," and not take one, and it would be all the same thing.

The scales suddenly dropped from his eyes. One problem solved the other. What had happened to him had happened to Wilson Byng. He was a loyal man and had the Shadowy Wife in the Background.

CHAPTER XI

Cricklade to Buscot

In the morning, after breakfast, Bliss spread out the map in front of him. "I," he said, "will fetch the canoe, and will meet you at Buscot this evening." It was disappointing, but I had a marked temperature; it was very cold and I thought I'd better not face the canoe for another day. So, after looking at Cricklade Church,* I set off by car. I stopped at the lovely Norman church of Kempsford, and should have liked to stop at Lechlade, whose spire is so prettily set.

At Buscot House I found the hospitable owner preparing, after lunch, to do a one-night dash by car to make a speech at a by-election. As he was speaking for an Opposition candidate, and the Government candidate was the Duke of Devonshire's son-in-law in what is virtually the Chatsworth Division of Derbyshire, this was a pretty noble effort for one who had an appointment in London next morning. Lunch over, he set out and I retired to bed with aspirin and light fiction, very glad indeed that I had not been laid low at Banbury.

It was a pity about the chill, I thought; with an afternoon to spare there I could easily have walked over to Kelmscott and seen May Morris, whom I used to know well, and had not seen for a long time. It was more of a pity than I knew;

* Dedicated to St. Sampson—is that the strong man?

she died soon afterwards. For many years, when I lived in Chiswick Mall, she had been a neighbour, in her house in Hammersmith Terrace, only a few minutes' riverside walk from Kelmscott House, where her father had revolutionized English printing. I never set eyes on William Morris; I was twelve when he died; but I should liked to have seen the old Manor House by Thames-side in which he found the equivalent of the mellow brick house with water which he describes in one of his earliest poems. So often I had seen Miss Morris's pictures of its exterior, and its rooms full of pictures, tapestries, and painted beds, all deriving from that association of Morris and Burne-Jones, that I almost seem to have been there.

It isn't so long since the last of them went, the youngest of the pre-Raphaelites who were Morris's early associates: Emery Walker and Cobden-Sanderson, who printed with him and carried on the tradition with the Doves Press; J. F. Green and others, who worked with him at the Society for the Preservation of Ancient Buildings; old H. M. Hyndman and (only yesterday) Cunninghame-Graham, who took the platform with that lusty big-bearded poet in his late Socialist days. When one used to ask them about him it usually used to boil down to the story of the Bishop. This bishop went to Queen's Square to order, as it might be, an embroidered altar-cloth or a stained-glass window of Sir Galahad. He was kept downstairs for a long time, probably feeling dimmer and dimmer in an atmosphere of formal tulips, apples, lilies and passion-flowers, figured fabrics, and sketches of wistful knights in plate-mail, pallid princesses with clouds of hair, twisted tree-trunks and castellated walls. He expected to be received by someone who should obviously live up to all that; but in the end he heard a voice roaring from the top of the stairs: "Now, bring up that bloody bishop!" Rossetti was a burly man who wrote broad limericks; Burne-Jones a practical joker who illustrated his letters with comic sketches; and Tennyson, who, on his purest poetic side, was a congener of theirs, was magnificently built, gruff of voice, a tremendous smoker and a mighty consumer of bottles of port. Out of the strong cometh forth sweetness, perhaps;

or they were all getting behind the arras to escape the Industrial Revolution at its foulest and the new Philistines at theirs; or, after the revival of Gothic architecture, the pictures in the missals and the romances of chivalry were bound to return and influence literature.

There was Bliss gently proceeding down that lovely lonely stretch of river, in just the sort of scenery that might have framed the Lady of Shalott. . . .

Fashion had changed with a vengeance. When I was young the sort of youths who now go in for apples by Cézanne, sunflowers by van Gogh, and whitewashed walls by Utrillo, used to adorn their studies with pictures at which their sons and similitudes would raise their eyebrows in pity. On the tables were *Atalanta, Omar, The House of Life* and *Vita Nuova* in limp leather with silk ties. On the walls were brown photogravures of "Beata Beatrix," "The Blessed Damozel," "Cophetua and the Beggar-maid," "The Golden Staircase," and oddments by Millais, Holman Hunt, Ford Madox Brown, with Watts as a flanker.

It was about the end of the vogue. I remember a few years before the War hearing that Burne-Jones's old house—somewhere near that unfindable vagrant thoroughfare, the North End Road—was still to be visited as a museum. So I went there and, after some difficulty, got in. There was his studio full of sketches and (I think I remember) a huge rough draft of *The Death of Arthur*. The place looked as though nobody had been there for months; the result was a not unpleasant feeling of intimacy.

There is, indeed, a peculiar pleasure to be derived from small and specialized museums and galleries. Great collections, National Galleries, Louvres, and Metropolitan Museums, are noble treasuries, but it is a change sometimes to go to Dulwich, or to little Soane Museum in Lincoln's Inn Fields, with its Hogarths and its tremendous sarcophagus of a Pharaoh. I always make it a point, when travelling, to visit the humbler, the unstarred, museums; they so often harbour agreeable surprises. I wonder if the South African museum at Dordrecht still exists?

In nineteen hundred and ten my wife and I toured Holland, on foot and in canal boats. It is a good country for people with knapsacks. The towns are just a convenient distance apart. You can travel in the morning, arrive at lunch-time, and then see the sights. One day, for example, we were arriving at Delft through that "View" (virtually unchanged) which Vermeer painted; next day we were looking at the picture itself in the Mauritshuis at The Hague. We saw many churches and almost all the pictures in the country. But not even the marvellous Hals groups at Haarlem stick in my memory more vividly than something which hardly anyone has ever heard of.

We went, one day, by water to Dordrecht, whose towers are familiar in the pictures of Cuyp and van Goyen, but which, to the extent of a large statue, seems to have been prouder of being the birthplace of that glutinous painter, Ary Scheffer. I noticed in the guide-book a slight reference to a South African Museum, which had been established to commemorate the Boer War (then over for eight years) and stuck, for some unexplained reason, in unvisited Dordrecht. This seemed unusual, so off we went and found a large house in a suburban street, and rang the bell.

The original endowment had obviously been substantial enough to provide for a permanent caretaker; but when he came to the door he did not look as though he expected visitors. As he took us into the main museum-room I thought I had never seen so much dust in my life, and it was lying on a most extraordinary medley of objects—portraits of Cronje, and De Wet and Kruger, articles of bone and wood carved by the Boer prisoners in Saint Helena, great stacks of scurrilous Continental papers full of obscene caricatures of Queen Victoria (relics of an extinct fury) and a litter of objects of daily use and products of the Transvaal and the Free State. For all this the caretaker seemed to care little. The apple of his eye was in the garden: a habitable model of a wooden Boer farmhouse. He took us over it with much eloquence: "Dis is vere de Boer eat 'is food," "Dis is vere de Boer read 'is Bible," and then at last, ushering us on to the real verandah (overlooking not the

N

veldt but a cat-run in Dordrecht): "Dis is de stoep. Dis is vere de Boer smoke 'is pipe." I closed my eyes. The last beams of the sun were striking the elderly Boer, with his wide-awake, his bushy beard and his cartridge-belt, his favourite sjambok lying at his side. He went in. Darkness came with a rush. From far off in the night came that most African of all sounds, the roar of a lion. . . .

Quite recently I found another little-known and visited museum—but this one very rich and new and spotless. It was when I was in Prague. The guide-book at the bottom of its list of local attractions said "The Button Museum." I asked a scholarly young citizen what it was and where; he had never heard of it and, until I showed him the entry, refused to believe in its existence. It could only be supposed that it was what it was stated to be. We got a taxi (the taxi-man had never heard of it either) and rattled out for miles to an industrial suburb full of very modern buildings, of which some appeared to be factories and some churches. There we came on the museum, a large building, adorned with statuary, etc., regardless of cost.

I had said in the cab, with mere facetiousness: "Do you think we shall find rows of trouser-buttons pinned to cards as if they were butterflies, and hung in cases on the wall?" That is what we did find in the first room, and very odd they looked. But the penetralia were a revelation. The opulent button-manufacturer who had made buttons his pleasure as well as his business had collected dress-fasteners comprehensively. There were not only buttons proper of all ages, in bone and metal, pearl, stone and stuff, many of them jewels, but all sorts of pin and brooch and buckle, safety-pins of the Bronze Age, gold buckles of the Greeks, an Aladdin's Cave of precious metals and gems. In a promiscuous national museum one might well have overlooked the lot. As it was, the collection made me permanently "dress-fastener-conscious"; I cannot look at the humblest button now without thinking of its long and august pedigree so crowded with rich relations.

*　　*　　*　　*　　*

The pre-Raphaelites, I was thinking of. But it wasn't only the painting of the century which rushed, in archaistic passion, for something behind the bewigged formality, common sense and classicism of the eighteenth century. Even Wordsworth, for all his theoretical belief in going back to the hodden grey in subject and language, could write of

> Some lady of the lake
> Lone sitting by the shores of old romance.

Keats went back to Spenser and the Greeks: ultimately Milton. The architects rushed in all directions, usually forgetting in their passion for old forms the demands of new functions and the loss of the old craftsmanship. And those of the prose-writers who loved writing best went back to the cadences of former ages, Morris to those of Malory, most of the others to a sonority and richness derived from Tyndale's Bible through the Jacobeans and Carolines, Raleigh, Donne and Browne. How close is the parallel between de Quincey's invocation to opium and Raleigh's to death! How set, involved, and full of artifice seem to this generation those "purple patches" in Ruskin, Pater and their contemporaries which men used to roll over their tongues. The thing became a trick with men stirred by no such power of passion, and no such intense fastidiousness about the sound and colour of words: every pretentious novel came to have its opening resonant passage about sunset and storm; and now all eloquence and music in words are out of fashion, their echoes lingering in the pamphlets of travel-bureaus. The mode and the manner have changed; the baby has gone with the bath; we are now presented, as a rule, by the more intelligent writers, with cool, neat, well-made paragraphs, or else with a series of short, sharp, hard sentences like a succession of bullets from a machine-gun—when it isn't a charge from a sawn-off shot-gun.

Yet I cannot forget the shocks of pleasure I had as a boy from even the most flamboyant of the prose orators. Some time (in the late 'nineties?) a translation of D'Annunzio's *Triumph of Death* was published; afterwards several others

of his. Still under the spell of sound, familiar with mor-
bidity through Baudelaire and the restless opiate dreams of
de Quincey (whom I read, down to the dullest essays on
Kant, in an illimitable green edition), I was carried away by
the great languishing, echoing speeches, which clothed in
glorious organ-music, in one novel or another, the material
of Zola, of Maeterlinck, of the great Venetian painters. I
knew nothing then about Duse; I did not bother then about
that vulgarity in him in the tracing of which Henry James
compared himself to a plumber looking for an escape of gas;
I could not dream that at fifty he would rouse himself from
his opiates and hothouses and become the boldest and bravest
of airmen and adventurers; and I certainly could not guess
that the time would come when I should receive a letter from
him, with a huge, flourishing signature, beginning "Cher
Confrère." Pictures and swelling sound were all I wanted,
and remoteness. To-day, were I to ape anybody's prose, it
would likelier be Addison's, to whom Dr. Johnson suggested
that young authors should devote their nights and days. But
young, new to the tropic jungle of words, bright, wonderful
and varied as orchids, I was likelier to try to constrain them
to make harmonies. Once, at least, some years before that, I
suffered for this. I can have been but thirteen when I had
the worst thrashing of my life: I still remember with what
complacency in the evening I examined my striped flanks and
compared them with the cohorts of Sennacherib which
gleamed with purple and gold.

An impromptu essay on the "The Nile" had been set. We
all scraped away for an hour and, fresh from a first acquaintance with Ruskin and such, I produced, with all the elegiac
pomp I could, great paragraphs full of dead Pharaohs, sphinxes,
pyramids, immemorial shrines, unending sands and unwitting
waters. It didn't do at all. The young form-master—new
from Cambridge, the hound, and still in Crockford to-day—
hauled me up and accused me of cribbing. It was in vain that
I said that I couldn't have known what the subject was to be
and that my paroxysm was (as the pavement artists allege)
"All My Own Work"; I was informed that I must, with

characteristic low cunning and impudence, have found out the subject before, and learnt something by heart out of some book unspecified, by Mr. Ruskin or another. As there wasn't any book I could hardly reveal its identity, which aggravated my offence; so I was sent to higher authority and soundly buffeted. Thereafter I do not remember putting forth my best paces for anybody. Essays I must have written, but the only ones I can recall were done in my nineteenth year for a mathematical specialist who had to show one up each week to prove that he had not lost sight of General Culture in his struggles with the Calculus. He was regularly commended for his style and also for the apt way in which he supported his arguments with quotations from the poets, named or un-named, of the sixteenth, seventeenth, eighteenth and nine-teenth centuries. Masters don't like confessing ignorance; just one inquiry and it would have been discovered (*a*) that Charles hadn't written the essays and (*b*) that all the quotations full of heaven's artillery, russet dawns and sequestered vales, had been faked by me.

     *   *   *   *   *

Tea came. Twilight came. A man came about lights and curtains. Dinner came. Then Bliss came, looking extremely healthy. "I've just had," said he, "a very good dinner and an excellent bottle of burgundy. And what," he went on, "have you been doing with yourself?"

"I read a little," I said, "and then I just let my thoughts wander."

"Where?"

I told him about that juvenile essay. We fell to talking about juvenilia. I said: "It is a pity that everything one writes before he is about twenty can't be automatically destroyed."

"Rossetti," remembered Bliss (had his thoughts been going Kelmscott-wards too?), "wrote the *Blessed Damozel* when he was seventeen."

"I've never believed that," I replied. "Anyhow, it's only one swallow. Think of your friends' first books. Think of the poems at the beginning of collections in chronological order. Think of the things they have dug up of Tennyson's. Think of those awful verses of Shelley's in *Poems by Victor and Cazire*. There may be exceptions, but I'd chance them. You remember what my Uncle Toby said about the work which the learned Lipsius composed when he was three?"

"Yes," Bliss answered, hastily.

"Well?"

"When did you start writing?"

"As far back as I can remember."

"Did you destroy it all?"

"I wish I had. It was all governed by sound. I didn't know the difference between sincerity and insincerity or what accuracy was about thought, sight or feeling."

"How old were you when you published your first book?"

"Twenty-four."

"That's mature enough."

"I wrote them all before I was twenty, mostly at school."

"Did you pay for the publication yourself?"

"Did you ever hear of a young poet who didn't? Flecker and Brooke did, for a start. What was worse, it no sooner appeared (and in stout boards too) than I regretted it. I at once implored the publisher, an enterprising man who soon vanished, to suppress it. He did so on condition that he was allowed to keep the receipts on the two hundred copies sold as well as the cost-price I had paid him. I hated this, but I agreed. He sent me the few bound copies in stock. I still keep them as curiosities, having once (before the justifiable slump in modern first editions) seen one priced in a catalogue at four pounds. One I parted with not long since; a gentleman in Buffalo wrote imploring me for a copy and promising on his honour that if I sent him one he would never so much as open it. But one I *do* wish I had given away. For I was dining the other day, in the Albany (which I cannot bring myself to call 'Albany' any more than I can call H.M.S. *Abominable,* just Abominable, and there I have the sailors in their casual conversation, with me—it's only the Press which is so priggish), with a great friend and he told me that, after long search, and at a great price, he had 'secured' a copy of my first book. 'Good God, X,' said I, 'I'd rather you hadn't seen it at all; but if you must have it I'd much rather have given you one of the copies wrapped and in mint-condition, which are rotting on my own shelves.' As soon as I had said that, I knew that I had made a cruel mistake. . . ."

"Did you say you still had some?" asked Bliss, innocently.

"One or two," I repeated.

"Would you like to spare me one?"

"No, Bliss, most certainly not."

There was a pause. Then I remembered something more.

"Did you ever see, Bliss, George Moore's early attempts at verse called *Pagan Poems?*"

"Heard of it; never seen it."

"Well, don't. It's about the worst there is. Yet, fifteen years ago, a friend of mine picked one up in Belfast and sold it in London for ninety pounds."

"How old was Moore then?"

"I don't know. He never would tell his age; he didn't even lie about it, he just dodged. One Sunday afternoon he and Gosse and I walked up and down by the lake in Regent's Park, and for a solid hour Gosse, who had known him since youth, tried to pump him about his age, out of mere mischief, and to amuse me. He would say, as it were dreamily: 'Let me see, Moore, were you twenty-seven or twenty-eight when those poems of yours came out?'—hoping that Moore would betray himself by indignantly exclaiming: 'Do, odly twedty'—for he spoke in an adenoidal way. But he got no change."

*　　*　　*　　*　　*

Bliss said good night. For a little while I applied my fevered brain to Edgar Wallace's *The Squeaker,* one of the most successful efforts of that master—whose prose, never-theless, was not quite as carefully organized as George Moore's.

Poor old George Moore! Such a devoted artist and so self-centred. The last time I met him was at a bachelor dinner at Evan Charteris's not long before he died. Moore sat opposite Augustine Birrell, who, although far from a egoistic talker, usually could keep a witty monologue going, with just enough interjections from his delighted audience to give him new impetus. That night the other octogenarian reduced him to quiescence with his steady monotone.

Not that Moore wasn't amusing. *Conversations in Ebury Street* represent him very fairly. But his raciness, after a time, wasn't enough to make his vanity tolerable. He had a perfectly childlike jealousy of every living writer of rank, and of those dead who were recent enough to be his rivals. And one could not, when *tête-à-tête,* switch him off, for the subject, in later years, for good as for bad, was his sole theme. One could not have guessed that, as a young man, he had crammed for Sandhurst and been horsy. This is the sort of dialogue I remember with him after dinner, with the celebrated Aubusson on the floor and the Manet on the wall.

M. There are do boderd Edglish dovelists.
S. What about Dickens?
M. He was a cobbod padtry boy.
S. Stevenson?
M. Bad prose, bad prose.
S. Conrad?
M. By dear bad, it's very clever of a Pole to write Edglish at all, but he dever writes a grabbatical sedtedce.
S. Hardy?
M. 'Ardy, he's the worst of theb all. Dever wrote a decedt paragraph.
S. But, I say—have you really read him?
M. Quite edough, quite edough. I've gladced at it!

*   *   *   *   *

Once, when a dinner was being given in honour of an old acquaintance of his, he went. Half-way through the speeches, which were of a suitably fulsome kind, he was found in the next room. "I had to cobe out," he explained, "it was as bad as a Chaddel Crossig." Now whether he really thought that he could reduce everybody's stature and proportionately increase his own by mere assertion I do not feel quite sure. His sarcasms may have begun as Irish puckishness and become a habit; there were moments when he showed glimpses of great charm and courtesy and he certainly loved company. By and large he will be best known, in every sense of the word, by his books of memoirs. The naturalistic books of the *Evelyn Innes* period are strangely outmoded; those later tapestries, to me at least, were always better a page at a time than taken bodily.

* * * * *

However, J. M. Hone wrote a very good book on Moore, and, until the next chapter it must be taken for granted that I am at Buscot, with the light out, fast asleep.

CHAPTER XII

Buscot to Rushey Lock

It was a very beautiful morning and I felt, after breakfast, quite fit enough for a walk. Bliss, when I rose, had already been driven down to the river to do the morning's work for both of us; it wasn't a long stretch and I said I should be quite fit after lunch.

I went down to the lake, where coots, moorhens and ducks abounded and some geese were nuzzling under their wings, across a stone bridge and so, after a mile or so, to the village church, over which (Bliss being absent) I took my time. I noted down an epitaph on the Reverend Robert Reddy, M.A., of whom it is said, with adequate reason, that "His servants to whom he left handsome legacies, found in him a Kind Master." He died in 1791 when they were strong on "lapidary inscriptions" and such things: in an epoch when Louther-

N*

bourg R.A. could be described as having "united a Rational
Enjoyment of the Pleasures of this World with a Confident
Expectation of those of the World to Come," and a dedicator
could say that a noble lord united the Virtues of Dives with
those of Lazarus. Elsewhere (but I had forgotten to put the
name of the church down) I had taken down an epitaph to
a Henry Pye, who was perhaps the appalling Poet Laureate
of that time, but had, apparently, compensating qualities:
"Here lyeth the body of Henry Pye of this place, and afterwards of Knotting in the County of Berkshire, Esquire. He
was descended from an ancient Family, whose Dignity and
Reputation he sustain'd and adorn'd with ye added Meryts
of his own amiable Virtues. He had a Cheerfulness in his
Person, an Affability in his Demeanour, a Courtesy and Politeness in his Manners, with an open Benevolence and Generosity
in his Disposition, which plainly denoted him

The True English Gentleman."

But at Buscot the notable things are the striking modern
stained-glass windows and memorials erected by the present
family in residence. I noticed with especial pleasure that
the artists had made the most of the excellent opportunities
which are offered by armorial bearings, too often nowadays
minimized or neglected except by railway companies and
newly-founded boroughs. I have loved coats-of-arms ever since
I can remember and felt the charm of them at least as far back
as the age of four. In one of my earliest reading books (I was
no such diseased freak as John Evelyn's son who knew—was
it Greek and Hebrew, at five?—but I could read and even
write, at three), there was a picture of the White Ship, which
sank, and King Henry never smiled again. As usual in marine
pictures of those days, whether of Vikings or Normans, the
passengers were extremely crowded. This lot were Normans
and it was no wonder the ship went down. They must have
had just as much simple faith as Norman blood. There
seemed to be no crew. They stood up, with their Norman
helmets, strips of iron over their Norman noses, and chain
mail, packed together in a close queue facing all one way like

Wordsworth's cows, ignoring the Plimsoll line, and liable to rock the best of boats. But they had, each man, their emblazoned shields hung over the gunwhale of the ship. I knew nothing, and could not have known anything about the historical significance of such things; and I don't care even now whether or not I was atavistically harking back to some dark totemic ancestry; but I must have vaguely felt the presence of symbolism, I liked the strength and simplicity of the designs—the saltires, the chevrons and fesses and animals (all hopelessly out of period, no doubt)—and I especially liked the idea that every knight had his own—fore-shadowing of one's now conscious wish for some happy fusion of collectivism and individualism, for they were all otherwise as like as two peas and united in a single expedition.

I still think them beautiful—much more interesting than many of the pedigrees, sometimes genuine, to which they are usually attached. I wish we saw more of them. When I was young people used to lament that the world had gone drab and that colour was dying out; but still the last of the hatchments were displayed and the soldiers had their bright tunics with facings—and, if they really want recruits, the politicians had better restore the uniforms—they damned their policy by implication when they allowed the Guards to retain theirs. The Puritan is still on top of us.

The other day a noble lady said to me about a noble (much more recent) lord: "The man's a damned outsider; he has his coat-of-arms on his car."

I, remembering the maidservant's misfortune in *Midshipman Easy,* asked: "Is it a large coat-of-arms or a little one?"

"Oh, quite small," she replied, "but it oughtn't to be there at all."

"Well, I'm very glad it is there," I said. "We none of us like ostentation, and the days are done when the dukes drove abroad with their Stars and Garters on, but thank goodness for a little colour; what is the good of having a coat-of-arms if you don't show it?"

Don't look at it as a form of boasting but as a contribution to the variety and gaiety of the public scene. I always encourage people to wear buttonholes, not to adorn themselves (though, in many instances, it is a good idea to distract attention from the face to the flower) but in order to cheer up the streets. Though I must admit that even in buttonholes modern middle-class uniformity has crept in. At weddings, evening parties and the Opera it is expected of one to wear a flower: but it must be a carnation, red or white, forced, scentless and too bulbous for the buttonhole—for the flower-breeders are as silly as the dog-breeders (fox-hounds are an exception, for they have to do their work) and go for special "points," forgetting "general utility." This is no new thing; when I was small a man was expected to wear in the evening a red or white geranium with a spray of maidenhair fern.

Imagine the sensation if one turned out with that now! So great is the tyranny of convention that even a modest rosebud attracts undue attention and it is supposed to be meant to do so. However, better carnations than nothing. And even those have their drawbacks. I once donned a red carnation in Rome and an Italian friend advised me to take it off before I went out. "They'll think you're a Red," he said.

"Good God," I reflected, "poor old carnation! Even the flowers of the field, loved by our Lord, are being dragged into our beastly modern politics." However, I threw the fresh thing away; I was in Rome and I did as the Romans did.

*   *   *   *   *

I wandered round the little graveyard and then went to the village inn for a packet of cigarettes. I did not get the ones I asked for, so contented myself with a packet of Player's. On the packet as of old—keeping both lighthouse and ship with an obstinacy unknown to the designers of our coins—was a blue-green, slightly choppy seascape, and, ringed by a corded life-buoy, the old familiar head of a senior non-commissioned sailor with his collar, his cap bearing the inscription "Hero," tout court, and his full beard, of the type once so common amongst warrant-officers, gunners, commanders, captains, and heirs to the throne. The last time I was in one of His Majesty's ships I asked why there wasn't a beard on board, amongst all the six hundred. I was told that beards wouldn't go under gas-masks. It seems rather absurd; it only takes a few seconds to snip off a beard to gas-mask dimensions. They were really thinking, I suppose, not so much about war as about gas-mask drill. But need the Navy be cleared for action quite up to *that* point?

There was a man in the corner. He heard me speaking to the landlord about Test Matches, and butted in. " 'Is Lordship," he said, "is doing very well by this village."

"I'm very glad to hear it," I remarked, seeing no reason to divulge the fact, which my attire would certainly not have suggested, that I had been sleeping the night at 'is Lordship's 'ouse.

"Not only," went on this horsy little man, "does 'e get the grahnd kep' spick and span by 'is gardiners, but 'e supplies free teas for both parties."

"I wish," I agreed, "that everybody in the country who could afford it would do the same thing."

"Yus," he replied (for he was evidently a Cockney sojourner and not a native of Berkshire), "sye wot yer loike abaht 'is polerticks but ter the people 'ere 'e be'ives loike a gentleman."

I murmured that it was just what I should have expected of him.

"Cricketer yerself, I daresye," went on my new friend, scrutinizing the last quarter of an inch in his glass pint mug.

"I still play," I responded, "but I never was any good. I am merely very fond of it."

"Betcher've plyed at the Ouval," he went on—it is always to be noticed that his class, whether Londoners or not, take more notice of the Oval than of Lord's.

"Several times," I admitted, remembering long walks back to the Pavilion, and consoling myself with a few wickets taken, the printing-works issuing their usual bulletins and about six spectators present, in very humble matches.

" 'Ere's yer very best," he went on, "an' I betcher've plyed at Lord's too."

"Once," I said, "and o not out, and I didn't bowl, and I missed a catch."

He simply didn't believe me. I could see that he thought I was some incognito C. B. Fry, hiding my modest head as does the violet, deep in its green and shady dell.

It is rather sad that one should always so pertinaciously plug on at the pastime at which one shines least. The successful, I take it, find out their métier and stick to it. It was never thus with me. I always liked doing what the others did; preferred team games, and liked especially those, making the whole world kin, about which I could talk to all manner of men.

It was always so. People with intellectual interests often say they were solitary and unhappy when young; and the modern school stories are full of young sensitives who shrink from the crudity of common life and retire to corners because a lot of coarse dull cricketers refuse to know anything about Tchekov and Proust. I had my special interests, even loves, even passions, as I have said; but I was happy alone with them when there was none to share. They enriched all one's experience even when one was with others: the mind and the æsthetic faculty, if allowed to be open to impressions, can enjoy private play even when one is doing the most ordinary things with the most ordinary people. But I was generally curious, and had a catholic taste in men, enjoying the company of anybody who wasn't a brute, a boor, or a bore.

But what, in general, did we talk about? Mostly about games or the idiosyncrasies of each other and the masters or the trivial fleeting events of school society.

Even a grown man who reads his *Wisden* will frequently find it easy conversation, though I daresay it might not carry one far at a soirée of the Conchological Society or even (though superficially relevant) at a meeting of the Statistical Society. But a boy, in my time (I do not know what it may be now in a world more sicklied o'er with the pale cast of thought and anxiety), who did not read the cricket-scores and watch the race in the averages was an oddity. So was the boy who was not "keen" on games and the results thereof; though I never came across the worship of the athlete as such, irrespective of his personality: "side," especially, was detested. But there were subjects ready-made, the averages, the county and England Rugger teams, the University matches, the Boat Race and all the rest of it; and in that Zion I was very much at my ease. From infancy I had taken an ardent interest in every form of competition, even including General Elections, of which I did not understand the issues, which involved scores, figures, or times—in those days they were spread over six weeks and the newspapers had daily pictures of little Leading Politicians climbing up the numbered rungs of rival ladders; and every day still adds to the congestion of my memory (if memory can be congested, which I doubt) with figures, and even the initials of total and obscure strangers, which can never profit mind, pocket or soul, though sometimes they lead to amusing surprises in social intercourse.

But I loved playing games too—any game—and still do; being fortified, when I meet the grim, with the reflection that Adam never had to work until he had sinned and been cast out of Paradise. The periods of my life during which I did nothing to which I was disinclined (and if you like doing a thing it can't be called work) have been the happiest. I was short-sighted. It didn't matter at Rugger, either at school or after, except that it compelled me to play, at rather too light a weight, in the scrum. But cricket had to be played in spectacles, and in any event I don't believe I should ever have been able to hit a ball properly; I still play and still can't; perhaps it is because of that that my principal day-dreams for a long time were of hitting sixes at Lord's—I certainly never had a day-dream about becoming Minister of Transport. I was an uncertain catch at the best; and a worse one because when one is fielding, if one happens to be prone to absence of mind, a cricket match, during which one sometimes may not touch the ball for an hour, offers one every temptation: you can't wonder about Bishop Berkeley in a Rugger scrum.

I am not alone in this misfortune. Some years ago I was

bowling (for leg catches, like all my kind) and a man made a huge hit to deep mid-wicket which should have gone into one of the safest pair of hands in the country. As we all turned, thinking "another damned good wicket down, at all events," we noted with dismay that the fieldsman's back was turned. A general yell brought him round; but it was too late; he looked in every direction but the right one and the ball dropped on his head. His explanation afterwards was that he was "admiring a fine old oak"; there was every excuse; it was a glorious private ground, large, in perfect order, surrounded by noble trees, now gone back to park-land because the old owner died and the new one is interested only in foxes. But he has not forgotten it nor has been allowed to forget it; the jokes of cricketers and such ripen like cheese and they prefer the old ones to the new.

But my gross error still stays with me. It was in my last term. I had played no cricket whatever that summer, having a privilege which I exercised. But I was in a study with the Captain of Cricket, who later skippered Balliol at the more important things and played for Oxford at fewer than he should have done, and by a friendly leniency I was allowed to be the last man in the House Team, one of the two best in the School. The game had been going for ten minutes when I received a violent whack in the chest; I was at square leg, my wits were wandering, the ball had been carted violently by the Captain of the other side, and he proceeded to make a hundred.

Twenty years afterwards precisely the same thing happened. I was playing at Lord's for the Authors against the Artists; the two O'Gormans, lusty easy players who had turned out for their county, made a great many runs, and for an age, in that great prairie (which looks so much vaster when spectators are sparsely scattered than when it is crowded with men with top-hats and cornflower buttonholes, women with patterned light dresses—inviting, often with marked success, the rain—or mere enthusiasts with wrinkled brown faces, shapeless hats and one eye on the bars), I had been changing from deep square leg by the "Tavern" entrance to mid-off and back again. Hours passed and the ball never came near me; I moved like a robot, and my movements, in the end, had me hypnotized like the lighthouse-man in Kipling's story who went into a waking swoon because the lines of foam past the base of his building were so regular and relentless—at certain crossings in London one has a similar feeling about the traffic; it just will go on, and one is a helpless fish in a net. (However, this wasn't all quite as regular and ineluctable.) The earlier bats did get themselves out in time, the middle bats made their runs under the soothing August sun, and departed according to their wont to the faintest gusts of clapping from the few friends sprinkled about the vast empty stands; and then, after I had moved, like a mechanical toy, for the fiftieth time, there came another great bang on the chest—I had dropped Gerald du Maurier, who had just come in.

That I don't regret so much; he made a run instead of being caught first ball; he looked extremely elegant at the wicket, and, I am sure, had a shining bag full of the best scarves, blazers and caps—like others I could mention who are not really in the first rank at the game. I didn't know him, and I met him only once again. Near the end of his life, we both made speeches at an *Alice in Wonderland* exhibition at Bumpus's bookshop. The original Alice (Mrs. Hargreaves, then, I think, over eighty, a charming little old Victorian lady, and an almost unbelievable link with the past) was between us; our Wonderland cricket was not mentioned, we chatted, and shook hands; and the other two, the little old famous lady and the fashionable actor who could have equalled his father's reputation in another sphere had he chosen to use his brains to select really memorable plays, went off shortly to die. He had an odd face. He looked as though something (as it might have been a cricket-ball) had smashed it in, and yet he still remained attractive and good-looking.

*   *   *   *   *

Lord Berners sent a car over to fetch me to lunch at Faringdon; the indefatigable Bliss was to be picked up at Radcot Lock and brought there also.

As the car swung up to the house I almost leapt up with astonishment. It is quite usual to find flocks of doves clustering on the steps below Palladian porticoes, and to hear them clattering up against the blue as one approaches. But those doves were always white and these, although they were the right shape, were of every colour in the prism. Some of them had orange backs and wings and chrome-yellow underparts, and some were crimson and scarlet, some ilex-green and sage-green, some ultramarine and sky-blue.

"What on earth!" I exclaimed. "I know I had a slight temperature yesterday, but am I now in delirium?" So astonished was I that as soon as I got inside, almost before I had said good morning to my host, I said: "What in heaven's name has happened to your pigeons?"

"Oh, George is staying here and he has painted them."

"But oil-paint; surely—yes, thank you, a sherry—the poor wretched birds must simply hate it?"

"On the contrary, they love it; didn't you notice how pleased they were looking?"

It did then occur to me that there had been something of easy hauteur about their stride; they had not, as one might have expected, all agreed to mob each other, but were sailing under their false colours as to the manner born. Cosmetics for birds is a new idea, and whoever else may have borrowed plumes, the birds have not. Race-horses are another matter. They have been known to be painted often enough, though seldom for purely æsthetic reasons. For that matter, not only horses. One of the greatest and most secret privileges ever accorded to King Edward VII, when Prince of Wales, came to him when he was taken behind the scenes at a circus and shown the Royal Siamese Elephant in the process of being painted white.

Perhaps if I were writing a manual for grim young canoeists who really want to get on with the work, I should recommend that they should take their lunches always in rude and uncomfortable alehouses, with ancient landlords, watery ale, and Canadian Cheddar (I shouldn't mind it so much if it honestly called itself "Ontario"—which would also induce it to improve) instead of in comfortable country houses, where the temptation always is to stay on for as long as one may be tolerated.

This lunch went on for some time; Bliss and I (every man, on such occasions, feels himself more full of morality and will-power than his companion) may differ as to who made the first move. He would probably say that it must have been he because he wanted to get back to the Thames and "get on"; I that it was I because, owing to my malady, I had not yet been in a canoe on those lonely reaches of our historic river. However, we got off.

After that our proceedings were so complicated that not only can I not sort them out now, but even on that evening we could not sort them out in close and intensive collaboration. "How many cars have we been in to-day?" asked Bliss, late at night, in the lock-keeper's parlour at Rushey Lock, while he pored over maps. I could not tell him. He had brought his luggage to Radcot Lock in the canoe, and come to Faringdon by car. My luggage had to be taken to Radcot Lock by car. But before that—and George dutifully did it for us, bumping over rough pastures, hitherto innocent of wheels—we had to go to Rushey Lock and book our bedrooms for the night. And after that, we had to go to Bampton, on the other side of the river (George again obliging), to see a cousin of Bliss's who lived there, with an old house and a good fishpond, so as to arrange to dine with him. And after that, in the cousin's car, we had to be driven to the canoe again to fetch Bliss's luggage. And after that, in a pleasant evening, we had to drive to Rushey Lock again. And after that the cousin had to fetch us from the cottage, over bumping fields and through gates, take us to his pleasant village for dinner, and then, crashing through the dark, take us back to bed again—to find lock-keeper, wife and dog still awake and welcoming, but the child in bed.

"To-morrow to Oxford," said Bliss; "it will only be twenty-five miles, and seven or eight locks, with keepers to work them; so that even if this wind is still against us (for our enemy had now changed to the east) we ought to be able to get to Oxford quite easily."

"Certainly, Bliss," I said; "now we are going down stream I don't mind forty miles, if necessary."

"You won't be asked to do forty miles," he retorted, with the acidity of a man who had done most of the work in the last day or two.

We went to bed by candle-light. This time the book I took up was called *Three Black Dots,* by a Mr. Otwell Binns. He had apparently written about forty other books. I was ashamed to admit that I had never seen any of them before, though acquainted with the one great sonnet of Blanco White, the one speech of Single-Speech Hamilton, and the uniquely anonymous *Pervigilium Veneris.* This author, who has evidently mugged up Morocco and has a heroic notion of the French Foreign Legion, may not be well known to most of my friends. But the larger public always wants the same sort of thing. If they can't get it from the Stevensons and Haggards, Hopes and Weymans, they will get it from the films or the popular writers. They have no use at all for ingrowing intellectual toe-nails or flaccid adultery over the tea-cups, so they take refuge with those humbler authors who will still give them the Atlas, Klondike, or the North-West Frontier.

In his day they were content with Dickens. So should I have been that evening; only I didn't happen to have a copy with me. Only, still, Lord H—— and Mr. B——, and with these two I now felt united, blood pulsing freely each way, as with stout umbilical cords.

When the hero had got to Fez, in his chase after the heroine captured by bad German traitors and ruthless Mohammeds and Abdullahs, I blew out my light, and listened for a while to the Thames rippling by. To-morrow there would be long, lonely, marshy reaches, equally beautiful under grey or blue skies, with the lines of pollard willows stretching back to the verge of the flats, all the birds in England, and fresh reeds and flowers. The time of the purple loosestrife was not yet come which would glorify those banks, and the red cows might not yet gaze at one knee-deep in the shallows, but there would be loneliness, and water, and weeds flowing with the water, and no sound except the ripple of water and the dip of our paddles, and a wide sky over all.

"I wish," I thought, as I doubled the pillow up and snuggled down, "I wish I were a ferryman in these parts!"

CHAPTER XIII

Rushey Lock to Oxford

WE were actually, when we got up, some three miles from the canoe; even three miles ahead of it. Not yet, however, was I to resume my seat in that canoe, which I had not helped to propel, in fact, since I was lost in rain and thorns near Stratford. For, although, with the help of another stout car, which was willing to face anything which a tank would face, we took our luggage back to Radcot Lock, we were not yet to resume our journey. Bliss had arranged that we should have breakfast with his cousin at Bampton (where they still have mummers) and to Bampton we were brought—to that pleasant house, well-guarded with shrubberies, well-planted with flowers and vegetables, and, inside, full of well-polished furniture, nice prints and china, daguerreotypes, silhouettes and things brought back by judges and commissioners from the East.

We were leisurely over our breakfast; a sound club breakfast, not a snack. After we had been at it for an hour, and I was consuming my first cigarette with my third large cup of coffee Bliss's cousin handed the *Daily Telegraph* over to me and said: "Would you like to have a look at the morning paper?" "Yes," I naturally replied, out of mere politeness, having bothered very little about world-affairs on this excursion; so I picked it up and pretended to study every page with interest. I came, more by luck than by intention, on the Racing Page.

"My goodness!" I said.

"Goodness what?" enquired Bliss's cousin.

"Why, it's Derby Day!"

"Is it?"

"Why of course it is; it's the first Wednesday in June."

"Have you got a horse running?"

"Certainly not, but I should feel wretched if I hadn't my annual bet on the Derby. What time is it?"

"About eleven."

"Is there a telegraph office in this village?"

"Yes."

"Would it be really too much trouble for you to run me along there?"

"Delighted."

So I went in to the telegraph office, looked up the number of a bookmaker I knew, hoped I would be in time, and sent off my modest each-way wager on Bois Roussel.

When I came out Bliss asked me what I had backed, and I told him. "Why?" said he.

"Faute de mieux," I replied, using the horse's native language, "I know nothing whatever against it." Bliss looked as if he were dealing with one of those wild punters who draw cards, have dreams, or blindfold shove pins down upon lists. Perhaps he was; but it worked.

Once more we got into a car and were driven back to Radcot Lock and set out, under a sky of mingled cloud and gleam, indigo and gold, for one of the wildest bits of riverscape in the south of England. After an hour we reached Rushey Lock, and bid our last farewells. In another hour or less we came to a bridge with some boys fishing. "This," Bliss said, "is Tadpole Bridge; we shall now land and go to have our bread and cheese at the 'Tadpole.'" English inns often have strange names; this is one of the oddest that I have encountered.

We re-embarked. For some miles we went past low marshy banks, meeting no craft, seeing no houses; for farm and village were far withdrawn behind the marshes, though now and again the cattle were on the banks or in the water. Flapping herons were more plentiful than ever; and plovers; and twice there were flocks of sandpipers making their phantasmal cries and veering over the water-meadows. Here and there cuttings ran off, devised to assist the river when in flood; passing the surplus to lower on, as it were, and making, on the map, a tangle of blue water-ways. And once, as we were hugging a steep, hollow, moist, muddy, pock-marked left bank, I saw something ahead, stopped paddling, and turned to Bliss with a "Ss-h!" We drifted past; he did not see it, but I did, for it did not scuttle into its burrow until we were almost past it. There was no doubt about it; size, shape, colour and expression, as it were; it was a musk-rat, and possibly the last of its kind in England.

There was a time, a few years ago, when some musk-rats escaped from a farm where they were being bred and cherished for their skins. They multiplied in the usual rodent way, and before long, all over several southern and western counties there were hundreds of thousands of them, and, notably in Shropshire, banks of important rivers and canals were collapsing wholesale because of their sapping and mining. The Board of Agriculture (delighted to get busy on something which didn't involve a Tariff Controversy) took steps at once. A large organization of Musk-rat Wardens (or whatever) was established; tens of thousands of pounds were cheerfully produced; and a campaign of extermination was started.

Myriads of musk-rats were killed. Not long before we started on our canoeing trip it was stated in the Press that the Last Musk-rat had been killed and that the Organization had been Disbanded. And here was one, large and sleek, staring me in the face.

Did I want to shoot it or hit it with a paddle or go to report it at the nearest (miles over the swamps) post-office or fetch spades and terriers, ferrets and nets, from the local big-game hunters? Not a bit of it; my only feelings were of pity and sympathy. "Poor old Robinson Crusoe," I thought, "I do hope you've got a mate, but I don't suppose so. You probably really are the last, living in bachelor chambers away from frequented thoroughfares. Poor old thing, I hope nobody will catch you. . . ."

All this flashed through my mind while I was trying to point Bliss's gaze in the right direction; as usually happens on such occasions, he looked everywhere except in the right one. Just too late he gazed at the very ledge outside the tunnel where the musk-rat had been lying.

"It was a musk-rat," I said.

"Are you sure?"

"Yes."

"Why are they called musk-rats?"

"Why is the skin called musquash? Perhaps they smell of musk."

"Is that so?"

"I can't swear. I've never been near enough to tell. But I've always assumed that of all these creatures—musk-deer and musk-oxen. I suppose you know, Bliss, that the musk-ox, which lives in Greenland and is rather dwindling, isn't an ox at all?"

"If it isn't an ox what is it, then?"

"You'd think, to see its head and horns stuck on the wall, that it was a colossal sort of buffalo. In point of fact it tapers away like anything from the shoulders. Really, it's only a kind of sheep. But tell me, Bliss, you're a botanist—have you got any theory as to why all the musk-plants in the world lost their scent in a single year and it's never come back?"

"No idea whatever. It doesn't seem to make sense at all, but there it is."

"Perhaps the musk was striking against the tendencies of modern horticulture. It may have thought that instead of being allowed to go on pervading greenhouses with the strong scent of its little yellow flower, it would be taken hold of, bred with every object except odour, and finally robbed of its scent, anyhow."

"As good a theory as any other," muttered Bliss.

And so we went on, past Shifford (an ancient ford with an old chapel in the background), through a cutting, then into the old stream again. It must have been at Shifford Lock that I saw a man standing smoking a pipe, bethought me of the Derby, and hazarded that even down here he'd probably know the result of the race from the lock-keeper's wireless. So "What's won?" I called.

"Boys Russell," he said.

"Well, that's all right, Bliss!"

"You ought to have made me do it, too."

"You wouldn't have said that if it had lost."

"There's something in that."

*　　*　　*　　*　　*

All those hours were very pleasant, though the wind was easterly and the sunbeams rare, both the desolate and the inhabited parts having a charm peculiar to the Thames. Bliss has written: "For me all that Cotswold valley of the Thames above Oxford holds a perpetual and abiding charm. There is nothing striking about it. It is just a willowy landscape of meadows and copses and the Thames running through it between beds of reeds and water-flowers. But the sun shines and the wind blows in the willows and turns them to silver; and in the spring the copses are full of primroses, and if you stand up in your canoe as you float down you will see the dikes golden with marsh-marigolds and all the meadows scattered with oases of cowslips; and the mornings are full of larks and the evenings of the chimes of village bells, and cuckoos call all day, and in the weaning time the air is plaintive with the bleating of sheep and lambs in bass and treble—and the whole valley is England *in excelsis.*"

*　　*　　*　　*　　*

We were getting into the "Scholar-Gipsy" country. At New Bridge we got out to stretch our legs and have a cup of coffee at "The Rose Revived."

Bliss went to lean over the old bridge with its cut-waters and watch the rapid waters of the Windrush pouring home. His thoughts, I knew, were with that river which he had known since boyhood and into which he had cast his early flies. "Windrush and Evenlode"—above the Kennet the two main tributaries of the Thames. What lovely names for what

lovely streams, passing through what lovely country! The
Windrush, he followed it up in his mind, past Witney and
Burford, and Bourton-on-the-Water, and then, by its various
arms, through the Swells and the Slaughters, with all the
villages and bridges of the Coln parallel to the west, seemingly endless nooks full of old mellow churches and manor
houses and cottages. For me, I was trying to penetrate, as
through a wind-rumpled veil, now folded thick, now thinning
to clarity, to the phantom of the inn which used to be "The
Rose Revived." But when the picture came clear I could not
be sure that it was the right one, for in youth I had wandered
much in those parts, and talked in the evenings to many old
men, and I was a stranger in that district, and nobody except
someone to whom the place was familiar and even common-
place could tell me whether the picture I thought I recovered
from thirty years ago was a picture of what had once been on
that most efficiently and tastefully redesigned site or something
remembered from some neighbouring village now lost and
unnameable.

I saw—I see—myself coming one evening, not into a Saloon
Bar (for in those days few village inns—what they call
democracy not yet having set in—had such things) but into a
Tap or General Room. It was a low room with low windows;
the floor was of stone; there was a rough table with benches
against the walls; there was a great open fireplace with seats
on both sides, under the chimney-piece, which harboured the
old men, or those newly-come, and cold, from their work; a
place where six or seven gathered at a time, at most; and at
odd hours only a veteran or two who had formed a lifelong
club, before and after retirement.

I can see the place, wherever it was; it may have been in
March, for the logs were burning. After the usual salutations,
in order to get conversation going, I asked them if they had
any badgers thereabouts.

There were three of them. One was very tall, with picturesque
grey hair, bright blue eyes, a trace of side-whiskers, and round
apple-cheeks. He held a stick in both hands and half-leant
upon it. I thought: "A retired farm-bailiff, or a head herds-

man, with a little money laid aside; straight as a die, and his name, I daresay, is Silas."

One was a healthy short-bearded, ruddy, hook-nosed octogenarian, who smiled and said nothing, except that, in intervals of the conversation, he talked about old friends who were ailing, and the funerals which he had recently attended, as though he were playing a friendly cricket-match against all his old friends and hoping to score more runs, or years, than they did.

And one, who did most of the talking, was the youngest; probably a young seventy. He had a lean face, profuse fair eyebrows, a shaggy moustache, tanned cheeks, a stick on which he did not lean, and an affectionate lurcher at his feet.

And he said: "Mister, them badgers is getting scarce; it must be nigh two years since I dug one out."

I could hardly explain to him that I was fond of badgers, preferred them to most men, and thought them falsely accused. There was a time, long ago, in Devonshire, when I asked a farmer (whose fowls were roosting in the gate-house of what used to be a cell of Buckfast Abbey) why he indulged in the cruel sport of badger-digging. His reply was that the badgers ate all the young chickens—which simply wasn't true, for a chicken-eating badger is about as rare as a rogue-elephant. With gusto, he described his latest badger-digging. He said that they had "killed the old 'uns, and let the young 'uns off." I said: "If they're such a pest as all that, why let off the young ones?" He replied: "If us didn't let the young 'uns off us wouldn't 'ave no more badgers to dig."

The badger lives on, a nocturnal, thoughtful creature, who knows nothing about Hitler, Mussolini, Blum, Stalin, Negrín or Franco; a monogamist who avoids the idiotic complications of human life by merely emerging from the woods at night and supping on beetles. The country people (who always like an excuse for their savage sports) still persist in their belief that he raids the hen-roosts. So do they persist in their belief that hedgehogs suck eggs. Miss Frances Pitt, that admirable naturalist and tamer of animals, once had a pet hedgehog.

You can bring a horse to the water but can you make him drink? You can bring a hedgehog to an egg, but can you make him suck? Miss Pitt did her best to make her hedgehog suck eggs; it raised its nostrils and retreated. Even a grandmother would have been more amenable.

While Bliss was dipping into the Windrush and his past I was thinking about the wild life of England. The badgers in their burrows would survive. The pine-marten and the pole-cat were almost gone; the harvest-mouse was barely existing; the wild roe-deer, that flitting shadow in the woods, was up against a new enemy in the Forestry Commissioners; the fox and the red deer were only saved from extinction be-cause they were loved by those who hunted them. "He loved the tall deer as though he were their father," says the chronicle of William the Conqueror, and the paradox still prevails. . . .

We got afloat again and paddled down to Bablockhithe, every wave and tree and cottage now a reminder of Arnold, who rose to such heights in those two great Oxford poems and a few others, and elsewhere could be so dull and even clumsy. Why he should have called the Thames at Bablockhithe "stripling" is more than I can make out; it is already a noble and powerful stream.

As we swung down the strong current the sky ahead of us was grey-black with thunder. Just as we reached Bablock-hithe the first heavy drops splashed on our heads. We tied the canoe up and scuttled for shelter; it thundered and lightened and flung down sheets of water. "Look here, Squire," said Bliss, "what do you think?" "What I think," I replied, "is that we'd better call it a fortnight. Let's ring up Salter's to fetch the canoe and go into Oxford by car."

We did so; went in through Cumnor and stopped at the "Clarendon." Bliss at once resorted to the telephone. "I'm dining out with a man in North Oxford to-night," he said. "I suppose you're going back to London?"

"Yes," I said; but I did not, preferring to spend an evening alone in Oxford, and to visit again Merton and other corners.

How I love that town, even now when it has been infected by roaring industrialism and St. Mary's and Magdalen shake with the tumult of the traffic. Bliss, on this trip, had occasionally remarked to me (in the charming manner of persons with Oxford associations): "It's a most extraordinary thing to me, Squire, that you went to Cambridge, instead of to Oxford." My usual reply was, ungrammatically: "Well, Bliss, somebody has to go to Cambridge, haven't they?"—and I could see in his eye the Frenchman's glinting reply: *"Je n'en vois pas la nécessité."*

We called on Monsignor Knox at the Old Palace, talked to him about his and our canoeing, and then our journey was over.

* * * * *

Well, Bliss, old friend and dedicatee, I didn't go to Oxford, but that evening I walked about in the dark and recovered mingled memories of those two places long ago before the motors had come and the flowers of the forest were a' wede away. And my boyhood too. In Oxford, whither half my friends went, few to survive, I remembered Cambridge.

Home again, I began a book about those first days. As yet it has not got very far. . . .

EPILOGUE

I HAD promised, after my last wandering book, to write a more consecutive set of reminiscences. I found that I simply could not do it, beginning at the Year One, and flogging through elections, dinner parties and important People. I had had my trip in the canoe—it had brought many things and people back to mind, and I could write only about the things which were occupying my thoughts.

I got back to Buckinghamshire, tired and happy.

Well, we were sitting, the two of us, with coffee and cigarettes, on a verandah in the high Chilterns, with a phantom moon scaling the trees to our left and the sun dying

on our right, as for millions of years they have punctually done,
and all "the armies of unalterable law." We were silent for
minutes; the same thoughts were passing through our two
heads and felt in our two hearts as we looked at the hills and
the sky, with dusk coming. The end of day was always the
same as it was always different, and little did it bother about
us and all our self-torment and all our torment of others. Here
was our mood:

> Pale in the east the moon wafts high,
>   By branches carven, black, at ease;
> Southward a greying evening sky
>   Behind a row of poplar trees.

> And in the west a bar of gold,
>   A burning rim that soon must wane,
> While banks of lilac cloud enfold
>   A formless, sinking, ruby stain.

> Still the moon brightens, fades the sun
>   His evening glow of glory spent,
> The birds are silent one by one. . . .
>   That vastness is indifferent

> To us, our longings, hopes and dreams,
>   All fevers in the human breast:
> Nor worth a glance of notice deems
>   Our Ishmael race that cannot rest.

> Above these hills before men came
>   Once washed of old the shifting seas,
> The heavenly pageant was the same,
>   The sun, the moon, the skies were these.

> Yes, all this evening's vivid gold
>   Faded as now to even grey,
> The wide unwitting waters rolled
>   Beneath the unchanging end of day.

And stars gleamed through the darkening air
    Before there was a human heart
To solace, but they did not care
    And will not care when men depart.

And then, as it grew chillier we went within. And there came
a point, after I had been talking about those early days, when
she said: "And what happened after that?" And I tried to
remember. It seemed so far away.